OLD EUROPE, NEW EUROPE A

to Michelle and Amber

Old Europe, New Europe and the US

Renegotiating Transatlantic Security in the Post 9/11 Era

Edited by

TOM LANSFORD
University of Southern Mississippi-Gulf Coast, USA

BLAGOVEST TASHEV
George C. Marshall Association, Bulgaria

ASHGATE

Published by
Ashgate Publishing Limited
Gower House
Croft Road
Aldershot
Hampshire GU11 3HR
England

Ashgate Publishing Company
Suite 420
101 Cherry Street
Burlington, VT 05401-4405
USA

Ashgate website: http://www.ashgate.com

British Library Cataloguing in Publication Data
Old Europe, new Europe and the US : renegotiating
   transatlantic security in the post 9/11 era
   1. National security – Europe – Case studies 2. World
   politics – 1995–2005 3. Europe – Foreign relations – United
   States – Case studies 4. United States – Foreign relations –
   Europe – Case studies 5. Europe – Foreign relations – 1989 –
   – Case studies 6. United States – Foreign relations – 2001 –
   – Case studies
   I. Lansford, Tom II. Tashev, Blagovest
   355'.03304

Library of Congress Cataloging-in-Publication Data
Lansford, Tom.
   Old Europe, new Europe and the US : renegotiating transatlantic security in the post
9/11 era / [edited] by Tom Lansford and Blagovest Tashev.
      p. cm.
   Includes bibliographical references and index.
      ISBN 0-7546-4143-0 (hardback) -- ISBN 0-7546-4144-9 (pbk.)
   1. National security--Europe. 2. National security--United States. 3. World
politics--1995–2005. 4. Europe--Defenses. 5. United States--Defenses. 6. Europe--
Military relations--United States. 7. United States--Military relations--Europe. I.
Tashev, Blagovest, 1964- II. Title.

   UA646.L326 2004
   355'.03304--dc22

                                                                                    2004011993

ISBN 0 7546 4143 0 (Hbk)
ISBN 0 7546 4144 9 (Pbk)

Typeset by Tradespools, Frome, Somerset
Printed and bound in Great Britain by Antony Rowe Ltd, Chippenham, Wilts

Contents

List of Contributors

Scott Brunstetter is currently a Ph.D. candidate at the Graduate Program in International Studies at Old Dominion University. In May 2003, he was selected as a Presidential Management Fellow. From August 2001 to December 2002, he was a Fulbright Scholar at the German Council on Foreign Relations in Berlin, German, where he conducted research on the German Green Party's security policy. He has taught International Peacekeeping at the Joint Forces Staff College in Norfolk, Virginia, History at Old Dominion University and German at West Virginia University. He has published several articles and given numerous talks on various areas of foreign and security policy in both English and German.

Dovile Budryte, Ph.D. is an Assistant Professor in International Studies at Brenau University in Gainesville, Georgia (USA). Her areas of interest include democratization and ethnic politics. She was a 2000–2001 Carnegie Council on Ethics and International Affairs (New York) Fellow and a 1998–1999 Fellow at the College for Advanced Central European Studies at Europa University Viadrina, Frankfurt (Oder), Germany, where she worked on a project dealing with historical memory about deportations. Her articles were published in *Historical Injustice and Democratic Transition in Eastern Asia* and *Northern Europe*, edited by Kenneth Christie and Robert Cribb (Routledge, 2002), *Diasporas and Ethnic Migrants*, edited by Rainer Muenz and Rainer Ohliger (Frank Cass Publishers, 2003), and *Bridges: An Interdisciplinary Journal of Theology, Philosophy, History, and Science* (Fall/Winter 2002). She is currently working on a book about post-Soviet Baltic nationalism.

Chris Davis earned a B.A. from the University of St. Thomas in Houston, Texas. He served as a U.S. Peace Corps Volunteer in Romania from 2000–2002 and subsequently earned an M.A. in Central and East European Studies at the Jagiellonian University in Krakow, Poland. Currently, he is an Adjunct Professor of Humanities at Kingwood College in Houston. In the fall of 2004, he will resume his postgraduate work in East European studies at St. Anthony's College, University of Oxford.

Mira Duric received her Ph.D. in US Foreign Policy from Keele University, England. She has taught at the University of Nottingham and the University of Leicester. Her book *The Strategic Defence Initiative: US Policy and the Soviet Union* was published by Ashgate Publishing Limited in 2003.

Mihail E. Ionescu, Ph.D., is Director of the Institute for Political Studies of Defense and Military History (MOD) and professor at the National School for Political and

Administrative Studies and NATO Studies Center, where he is teaching several graduate and post-graduate courses on international security and world politics. Dr Ionescu has served in the Romanian Armed Forces, and he retired as Major General at the beginning of 2004. Between 1985–1990 he has acted as vice-president of the International Commission of Military History.

Mary Troy Johnston is Associate Professor at Loyola University New Orleans where she teaches courses in European and international politics. She wrote *The European Council* (1994) and continues her specialization in EU decision-making in a recent chapter on the Council of Ministers system for the *Handbook of Public Administration and Policy in the European Union* (forthcoming). She is currently developing an interest in emerging European security values, her first article in this area, "Supranationalism: An Alternative Approach in U.S. and EU Foreign Policy and Security Relations" appears in *Current Politics and Economics of Europe*.

Andrzej Kapiszewski is a Professor of Sociology and Political Science in the faculty of International Studies, Jagiellonian University, Krakow, Poland. From 1990–1997 he served as a Polish Ambassador to the United Arab Emirates and Qatar. He has also been a visiting professor at Stanford University, University of Wisconsin-Milwaukee and Hunter College. He has authored numerous studies devoted to ethnic and national issues, including: *Stereotype of Americans of Polish Descent* (1978), *Assimilation and Conflict* (1984), *Hugh Gibson and a Controversy over Polish-Jewish Relations after World War I* (1991), *Native Arab Population and Foreign Workers in the Gulf States* (1999), *Nationals and Expatriates. Population and Labour Dilemmas of the GCC States* (2001), *Conflict Across the Atlantic. Essays on Polish-Jewish Relations in the United States* (2004).

Tom Lansford, Ph.D., is Associate Professor of Political Science, and Assistant Dean of the College of Arts and Letters, at the University of Southern Mississippi-Gulf Coast. Lansford is a member of the governing board of the National Social Science Association, the editorial board of the journal *White House Studies* and is the book review editor for *Politics and Ethics Review*. He has published articles in journals such as *Defense Analysis*, *The Journal of Conflict Studies*, *European Security*, *International Studies*, *Security Dialogue* and *Strategic Studies*. Lansford is the author and/or coeditor of a number of books, including *The Lords of Foggy Bottom: The American Secretaries of State and the World They Shaped* (2001), *All for One: NATO: Terrorism and the United States* (2002) and *America's War on Terror*, coedited with Patrick Hayden and Robert P. Watson (2003).

Michael Mihalka, Ph.D., is currently a professor at the US Army's Command and General Staff College at Ft Leavenworth, Kansas. From 1997 to 2004, Dr Mihalka was the Professor of East European Studies at the Marshall Center where he lectured on a wide range of topics including security cooperation, transformation and the revolution in military affairs, the democratic transition and the causes of political violence and terrorism. Prior to that he was a senior analyst at the Open Media Research Institute in Prague where he wrote primarily about European security institutions. In the early 1990s Dr Mihalka was a Professor of International Business in Munich. From 1976 to 1990, he was a senior analyst at the RAND Corporation in Santa Monica, California where he oversaw projects on intelligence support for conventional forces, strategic nuclear forces and nonproliferation. Dr Mihalka has written extensively on a wide range of subjects including European security, international relations theory, nonproliferation, peacekeeping, and strategic deception. He has lectured widely throughout Europe and Eurasia. Dr Mihalka received his Ph.D. in political science from the University of Michigan in 1976.

Robert J. Pauly, Jr., Ph.D., is an Adjunct Professor of History and Political Science at Norwich University and Midlands Technical College in Columbia, South Carolina (USA). His research pursuits include US foreign policy, American-European relations, American-Middle Eastern relations and European and Middle Eastern politics and security. He is presently developing a book entitled *U.S. Foreign Policy and the Persian Gulf: Safeguarding American Interests through Selective Multilateralism* for Ashgate Publishing Limited. It is projected to be released in January 2005.

Ivo Samson, Ph.D., graduated with a specialty in the history of Central Eastern Europe from the UJEP University of Brno (former Czechoslovakia) in 1982 and political science from the University of Giessen (Germany) in 1997. He specializes in security policy issues and works as the Head of International Security section at the Research Center of the Slovak Foreign Policy Association (RC SFPA) in Bratislava, Slovakia. He has published in various countries.

Mark Sedgwick is a graduate student in Political Science at the University of Southern Mississippi.

Blagovest Tashev is Director, Security Studies Program at the George C. Marshall Association – Bulgaria, where he works on research and policy projects related to security and defense. He is also an Adjunct Professor teaching undergraduate and graduate level courses on national and international security in the Department of Political Science and the Department of European Studies at the St. Kliment Ohridski Sofia University. His interests include international security, security sector reform, American foreign policy and democratization. Dr Tashev has been a adjunct professor lecturing in world politics and comparative political systems at the Old Dominion University, Norfolk, Virginia and the Christopher Newport University, Newport News, Virginia. Dr Tashev earned his Ph.D. in international studies from the Old Dominion University, Norfolk, Virginia.

László Valki is Professor of International Law and head of NATO Information and Research Center at Eotvos Lorand University, Budapest. Between 1992 and 2001 he was Secretary General of the Hungarian Society of Foreign Affairs. In the 1990s, he was a member of the lawyers' team representing Hungary in the Gabcikovo-Nagymaros case before the International Court of Justice. His major works include *Decision Making in the Common Market* (1977), *The Social Nature of International*

Law (1989). He was editor and co-author of *Changing Threat Perceptions and Military Doctrines* (1992), *Kosovo: An Anatomy of a Crisis* (2000), *War and Peace in Former Yugoslavia* (2003), *The Road to War Against Iraq* (2004).

Petr Vancura is the Director of the BELL – Association for Freedom and Democracy, a non-government public-policy organization concerned primarily with issues of national security and public service. He entered the path of voluntary work after he returned from an assignment with the Czech foreign ministry, as the deputy chief of mission at the Czech Embassy in Washington. Petr Vancura has a degree in mathematics from the Charles University in Prague (1973), and a teacher's degree in Czech language and history from the Philosophical Faculty of the same university (1985). After graduation in 1973, he worked as a cabinet maker and carpenter until 1989. After the fall of Communism he was employed in various positions in the local government in Eastern Bohemia.

Dirk C. van Raemdonck is Assistant Professor of Political Science at Centenary College of Louisiana, where he teaches international relations and comparative politics. He has held prior teaching positions at the University of Georgia and Lafayette College. At the Galen Institute, he has served as Research Fellow. He has published articles in *Journal of Peace Research*, *Global Society*, *Southeastern Political Review*, and *Perspectives on Public Policy* (Goldwater Institute). He would like to thank Josh McFarland for supporting the work of the present article.

Introduction: US Security Policy and the New Europe

Tom Lansford

Beginning with the 1930s, a central component of US security strategy has been the importance of Europe. Successive US administrations have affirmed, or reaffirmed, this strategic imperative which was operationalized through specific policies such as the "Europe First" strategy of Franklin D. Roosevelt or the continuing importance of the North Atlantic Treaty Organization (NATO) in US security doctrine. As with most nations, current US foreign and security policy developed as the result of a range of domestic and international pressures. US diplomacy is also marked by dichotomies which combine stability and evolutionary change. Key to an understanding of contemporary US policy is an examination of the influences which marked the dramatic sea-change in US interaction with global affairs which occurred in the aftermath of World War II.

During the early days of the Cold War, the US developed new foreign and security interests which both complemented and reversed long-standing trends in American diplomacy. These trends, present since the nation's founding, had reinforced American popular preferences which limited US participation in world events. Their reversal was accomplished only through the efforts of American political elites and the recognition of the global threat to American interests posed by the Soviet Union. The core security interests developed at the dawn of the Cold War era continue to guide US leaders and decision-makers and reinforce the importance of Europe to US strategy.

As new threats emerge and old threats gain greater importance, a central question for officials in Washington will be how to balance US national interests in the context of potential divergences with its core allies, the states of Western Europe. Complicating policy choices for US administrations is the fact that US foreign and security policy must be developed in the context of both bilateral and multilateral transatlantic relations.

US Foreign and Security Interests

The national security interests of any individual nationstate are both varied and complex, and they may change over time or quickly in response to developments in the international system. Glenn Hastedt and Ray Knickrehm note that:

> The term *national interest* has a compelling ring. It conveys a sense of urgency, importance, threat and concreteness ... Unfortunately, just as with the concept of power,

the concept of national interest is not easily defined. At the core of the debate over its definition is the question whether the national interest should be treated as an objective, measurable asset or a normative political symbol.[1]

Although interests may be amorphous and may change from era-to-era, for US policymakers, "national interests are expressions of US values projected into the international and domestic arenas."[2]

National interests are best categorized among three levels of priority. First, "vital" or core interests are at the center of national security and involve issues such as protection of the homeland and key allies. When vital interests are threatened, the nation may respond with total mobilization of resources as was the case in World War II.[3] Throughout the Cold War, the containment of the Soviet Union and the security of America's major European allies were considered core national interests. Second, "critical interests" include the range of global issues which "do not directly affect America's survival or pose a threat to the homeland but in the long run have a high propensity for becoming First Order priorities."[4] Regional stability, the promotion and protection of free trade and democracy are examples of broad critical interests. Third, and finally, "serious interests" are those areas which may affect first or second order interests, but are not perceived as either posing a significant threat to the US or requiring the outlay of large-scale resources in order to maintain favorable conditions.[5] Throughout the Cold War era, the pursuit of multilateralism was considered a third level national interest. It was important to policymakers, but would be subjugated to unilateralism if first or second order interests required it.

During the Cold War era, there was a significant recalculation of US security interests. Before World War II, the main core national interest was the protection of the homeland. As the superpower conflict accelerated after 1945, the core national interests of the US expanded. Containment became a core interest since it was perceived that Soviet expansion could erode homeland security. Concurrently, the US expanded the definition of vital interests. By pledging itself to European security through NATO's all-for-one clause,[6] the US made its commitment to European security a national interest (the commitment became the interest).

National interests determine a nation's foreign and security policy by establishing the framework of policy options and priorities. Interests will evolve in response to transformations in the global arena, but there often is a lag between changes and the recalculation of interest. In the post-Cold War era, successive US administrations struggled to revise the national interests. The Cold War provided a ready-enemy, the Soviet Union, and core interests, the containment of communism. As Samuel P. Huntington points out the US may have enacted various specific policies during the bipolar conflict, but "its one overriding national purpose was to contain and defeat communism. When other goals and interests clashed with this purpose, they were usually subordinated to it."[7] Central to the reformulation of interests is the role of foreign and security policy elites. These groups play a disproportionate role in the security calculations that decide interests. A significant feature of US elites is that they remain Euro-centric even as they seek to incorporate longstanding trends in foreign and security policy into the machinations which lead to new policies.

Elites and US Security Policy

American security strategy and foreign policy tends to be dominated by elites. These elites often form the core of the bureaucrats and technocrats that conduct foreign and security policy.[8] The American populace usually abrogates control of foreign policy to elites and instead concentrates on domestic and economic policy. Elites shape the order of national interests by playing a major part in determining first-, second- and third-level priorities. The elites also play a major role in maintaining stability in a political system that could otherwise see dramatic swings in foreign policy every two years based on congressional elections. Gabriel Almond contends that Americans have a tradition of indifference to international affairs, but that this indifference quickly turns to "anger" under the right circumstances (this in turn, leads to "dangerous overreactions" on the part of the American people).[9]

This is not a uniquely American trait, but common to many democracies. Mark Lagon contends that "elites play a surprisingly significant role in democracies, especially in the foreign policy realm, where the mass public consciously or unconsciously cedes influence to experts and self-appointed experts."[10] Richard Herrera explains that this occurs since elites tend to be "more sophisticated politically than the average voter" and possess greater capabilities or craft or shape opinion.[11] Herrera notes that this reflects the findings of V.O. Key who argued that "mass opinion is not self-generating [but] a response to the cues, proposals, and the visions propagated by the political activists."[12] This is not to suggest that public opinion plays no role in foreign and security policy. Indeed elites and "decision makers are also sensitive to the preferences of the electorate," but nonetheless they attempt to shape these preferences through the creation of stable and lasting policy regimes and priorities.[13]

One result of this disproportionate influence is that elites play a significant role in developing and maintaining foreign policy regimes. Elites often develop the norms and principles of foreign policy and only then work to create public support. Elites establish

> linkages that ... between governing institutions and political commitments. These linkages are composed of political norms, public discourses, decision-making procedures, and modes of intervention into socioeconomic relations. The formative element in any given regime is ... not its trademark institutions but the governing cadre that manages them and acts within an intellectual milieu, infusing institutions with meaning, purpose, and direction.[14]

The importance of political elites cannot be underestimated especially in regards to the acceptance and internalization of the new regime. Jeffrey W. Legro asserts that elites can change foreign and security policy through a two-step process: "First, social actors [elites] must somehow concur, explicitly or tacitly, that the old ideational structure is inadequate, thus causing its collapse. Second, actors must consolidate some new replacement set of ideas, lest they return to the old orthodoxy simply as a default mechanism."[15] Elites initiate broad changes in foreign and security and they work to gain acceptance of these changes by domestic interests, including the media, legislature and public. Legro contends that such broad

acceptance occurs under several conditions: "1) when events generate consequences that deviate from social expectations; 2) when the consequences are
undesirable; and 3) when a socially viable replacement idea exists."[16]

One of the most dramatic shifts in US foreign and security policy occurred in the
aftermath of World War II. The cessation of the global conflict did not produce the
expected period of global peace and prosperity, but instead it inaugurated the Cold
War, a new era of international conflict. Elites within the US were able to develop
and maintain a domestic consensus, embraced by both Republicans and Democrats,
that revolved around a renewed American internationalism based on the
containment of the Soviet Union. The new foreign policy regime was based on
the doctrine of containment, however, it also emphasized the promotion of free
trade and greater US involvement on the global stage.[17]

Exceptionalism and Universalism

During the first century of American history, US foreign and security policy was
marked by the drive to settle the interior spaces of the Continental United States.
The historian Frederic Merk summarized the popular American perception of the
eighteenth and nineteenth centuries as the "right of our manifest destiny to
overspread and possess the whole of the continent which Providence has given us
for the great experiment of liberative and federative self-government entrusted to
us."[18] This national inward focus was bolstered by George Washington's
admonishment to "avoid permanent alliances" and the principles of the Monroe
Doctrine which acted as dual constraints on foreign policy outside of the
hemisphere.[19] The result was significant foreign policy constraints in terms of
resources and popular opinion and it led to a policy that has commonly been
referred to as isolationism.[20]

The combination of historical and political antecedents, geography, culture and
the self-reinforcing inward focus of the US during its early years created a
longstanding belief in American exceptionalism – that the United States was unique
among the world's nationstates. Samuel P. Huntington notes that Americans have
always defined "their creedal identity in contrast to an undesirable 'other'."[21]
Joseph Lepgold and Timothy McKeown write that American exceptionalism was
based on the manner in which "Americans depreciate power politics and old-
fashioned diplomacy, mistrust powerful standing armies and entangling peacetime
commitments, make moralistic judgments about other people's domestic systems,
and believe that liberal values transfer readily to foreign affairs."[22] In international
diplomacy, Richard Kerry notes that successive "American presidents have been
addicted to citing the absence of territorial claims as evidence of the high purpose
and moral purity with which the US projects power to far places. This virtue is
believed by Americans to distinguish the US from any other power in the world,
including other democracies."[23] American exceptionalism remains a popular
component of the nation's political culture, however, most scholars, including,
Lepgold and McKeown, point to a disconnect between the rhetoric often employed
by elites and the actual implementation of US foreign and security policy. They
assert that elites use the notion of exceptionalism as a means to develop public
support and justify US policies.[24]

Early internationalist presidents such as Theodore Roosevelt and Woodrow Wilson argued that American exceptionalism carried with it a duty to apply certain "American" traits such as democracy and individualism to the rest of the world. The result was the development of "democratic universalism." This notion was a manifestation of the political ethnocentrism that underlined exceptionalism. Kerry points out that it was the belief that "everyone ought to be like us."[25] At the dawn of the twentieth century, democratic universalism would be used to justify American interventions in the Caribbean and the acquisition of territory outside of the United States. For instance, Wilson would justify military intervention in Nicaragua by claiming that the US actions were designed to "teach them to elect good men."

Democratic universalism also had an economic component centered around the promotion of free trade. Emily Rosenberg in fact rejects the phrase democratic universalism and instead suggests that "liberal developmentalism" is a more apt way to describe US policies aimed at promoting economic and democratic universalism. For Rosenberg, liberal developmentalism was based on five core principles: 1) the idea that all nationstates would be able to copy the economic and political development patterns of the US; 2) the promotion of global free trade and open markets; 3) the championing of domestic free enterprise; 4) support for the free flow of information (including an open and free media); and 5) the extensive use of US policy to protect and promote American business interests.[26] Hence, once the Americanization of the continent was complete through Manifest Destiny, the US would embark on an effort at the Americanization of the rest of the world. The effort at liberal developmentalism became a key component of US foreign policy throughout the remainder of the twentieth century.[27] It also provided an ideological basis to reject charges of imperialism directed at the US in response to efforts to promote American interests.[28]

Post-War US Foreign and Security Priorities

The initial efforts to promote liberal development under Wilson and Franklin D. Roosevelt met only limited success. It would not be until the aftermath of World War II that a series of US administrations codified the universalist strands of American foreign and security policy in effective policy goals. The administration of Harry S. Truman was determined that the lessons of the US retreat following World War I would be converted into interests and commitments. Hence, the US developed a range of programs to provide security and economic support for the states of Western Europe and Japan after 1945. These programs evolved into the institutional framework of the West, marked by organizations such as NATO and regimes such as the Bretton Woods system.

Ultimately, Cold War US foreign and security policy would be based on four main interests. First, and foremost, the US sought to contain the Soviet Union. As aforementioned, containment was a core national interest of the US. To maintain this interest, the US was willing to mobilize significant domestic resources and assume a leadership role among the anti-Soviet allies of the West. Hence, the military and economic aid initiated by the 1947 Truman Doctrine and subsequently reaffirmed by both aid and direct military action by successive administrations.

Second, the US promoted free trade. Free trade was seen as both a means to enhance the domestic economy and to combat communism by improving the standards of living of people around the globe. Third, Washington championed democracy. American exceptionalism was partially based on the notion that free and democratic nations did not seek war and were therefore more likely to be cooperative and peaceful. Both free trade and democracy were seen as critical or second-tier US national interests. Fourth, and finally, America endeavored to establish multilateral frameworks to support its other goals. The institutional framework that became the Transatlantic Alliance was a product of US support for multilateralism.

US post-World War II support for multilateral European security structures was based on its pursuit of core interests, the containment of communism and its commitment to European defense, but European interest in these organizations was multifaceted. For the Europeans "there were three central issues in Western European security: 1) how to counter the Soviet threat; 2) what was the role and place of Germany, even a divided West Germany, in Europe; and 3) how could the West European states best ensure the continued participation of the United States in continental security."[29] Throughout the Cold War and hereafter, these three issues remained central to European policymakers.

NATO demonstrated that it had the capability to satisfy both American and European security concerns. For the Americans, NATO provided a means to ensure military cooperation among its memberstates and to lessen the burden of European defense. For the Europeans, NATO countered the external threat of the Soviets, the internal threat posed by a potentially resurgent Germany and maintained US participation in continental security. All the while, the organization also provided broad leeway for its members to pursue their own national interests. For example, the importance of policy autonomy and the appearance of global stature prompted France to disengage from NATO's integrated military command, yet Paris continued to enjoy all of the benefits of membership with reduced constraints.[30]

Even with the end of the Cold War, NATO continued to serve the national interests of both the US and its European allies. The Alliance proved that it could adapt to counter other external threats besides the defunct Soviet Union. NATO's first shooting wars were in the Balkans and in response to the security concerns raised during the Yugoslav civil wars. NATO has also been tasked to develop a counterproliferation capability and counterterrorism strategies. Concurrently, NATO, along with the European Union and other institutions, remained a means with which to constrain German hegemonic potential and ensure internal European stability by providing behavioral guidelines for aspiring NATO members from Central and Eastern Europe. Finally, of course, NATO continued to serve as a means to maintain Washington's involvement in European security even as there were significant declines in American troop strength in Europe in the aftermath of the Cold War. Between 1991 and 1999, US troop strength in Europe declined from 350,000 to 100,000 and the NATO partners reduced their ground forces by some 500,000. NATO's overall assets were reduced by almost 40 percent.[31]

Multilateralism in a Bilateral Context

The US emphasis on multilateralism in the Cold War era and beyond has always faced both domestic and international constraints. On the domestic level, administrations and foreign policy elites in the United States have had to go to great lengths and expand considerable political capital in order to maintain international commitments in the face of domestic pressure to limit foreign outlays (in both economic and military terms). On an international level, changes in the world system and the balance of power occurred at a dramatic pace, often forcing Washington to develop reactive, instead of proactive, policies. Transatlantic security relations are further complicated by the multiplicity of interests of the major actors. For the US, transatlantic security has to be addressed on a multilateral level through existing institutions such as NATO, the EU and the Organization for Security and Cooperation in Europe (OSCE), and it must be managed on a bilateral basis.

Bilateral relations provide the US with a greater degree of flexibility than do its institutional frameworks. As a result, past presidents have often sought bilateral cooperation on specific interests or missions instead of seeking consensus in multilateral forums. For instance, during the first US-led war against Iraq, NATO resources were used and the WEU deployed forces in support of the UN-sponsored embargo, but the administration of George H.W. Bush deliberately sought to avoid a direct role for NATO. It instead relied on individual memberstates in what became a "coalition of the willing." Coalitions of the willing became formalized within NATO through the creation of the Combined and Joint Task Force (CJTF) system.[32] The CJTF concept allowed NATO to deploy assets outside of the traditional boundaries of the Alliance and without full participation of the allies and to accept contributions to missions by non-NATO members.[33]

ESDI-CFSP

In many ways, the creation of the CJTF concept was a reflection of long-standing trends in the Alliance toward greater European influence and participation. Since the creation of NATO in 1949, the European partners had been under various degrees of pressure to increase their share of burden of European defense (this became known as the burdensharing debate). As Paul Cornish points out, the

> 'burden-sharing' debate – placed NATO's European allies in something of a dilemma. If the Europeans were neither able to organize themselves into amore efficient wing of the alliance nor willing to commit more resources to the common cause, then the very idea of a security partnership could be a stake. If the Europeans could at least organize themselves better, while remaining reluctant to open their wallets, US critics might see the beginnings of a caucus of freeriders intent on unbalancing the partnership and undermining US leadership. But if the European allies could make both an efficient and well-funded contribution to their own defense, what need would there be for US assistance and leadership, and indeed for NATO?[34]

The burdensharing debate never reached crisis point during the Cold War since for the European powers, part of the appeal of NATO was that the US provided the lion's share of the financial and military costs associated with NATO, while such outlays justified American security leadership for policy-makers in Washington. Nonetheless, there were repeated threats of significant reevaluations of American security participation in Europe as a result, reevaluations which were ultimately carried out in the aftermath of the Cold War.

Meanwhile, in the 1980s, the drive for greater autonomy for the European states culminated with calls for a European Security and Defense Identity (ESDI) within NATO. The political goal of ESDI was summarized by the European Council in 1999 which asserted that "the Union must have the capability for autonomous action, backed up by credible military forces, the means to decide to use them, and a readiness to do so, in order to respond to international crises without prejudice to actions by NATO."[35] Those states which sought a strong ESDI, one that could even potentially rival NATO, were generally known as the Europeanist states and led by France. Those states with a strong preference for NATO and continued close cooperation with the US were know collectively as the Atlanticist states and led by the United Kingdom.

As the twentieth century became the twenty first, ESDI became formalized as the Common Foreign and Security Policy (CFSP) of the EU. CFSP is the ongoing effort to coordinate foreign policy among the EU states and to provide the organization with military capabilities. In 1999 Javier Solana, a former Secretary General of NATO, become the first foreign policy "czar" for the EU.

On one level, CFSP seemed to satisfy both sides of the Atlantic. Europeans sought to increase their influence and role in security while the US was able to decrease its commitments. At its 50th anniversary summit in 1999, NATO formally endorsed the concept of a CFSP and stated in the Alliance's *New Strategic Concept* that CFSP "would be compatible with the common security and defense policy established within the framework of the Washington Treaty."[36] The NATO document also declared that the Alliance sought to "develop effective cooperation with other European and Euro-Atlantic organizations as well as the United Nations. Our collective aim is to build a European security architecture in which the Alliance's contribution to the security of and stability of theses and other international organizations are complementary and mutually reinforcing, both in deepening relations among Euro-Atlantic countries and in managing crises."[37]

Missions in the Balkans and other security crises of the 1990s, reinforced the necessity of American military credibility and undermined confidence in the ability of the EU to meet its foreign and security interests without US assistance. This perception was especially strong among US officials. Richard Holbrooke, the US architect of several agreements in the Balkans noted that "Unless the United States is prepared to put its political and military muscle behind the quest for solutions to European instability, nothing really gets done."[38] Former US Secretary of Defense William Cohen, stated that the Balkans were "principally a European problem to be solved. The Europeans did not move. It pointed out that the Europeans do not act in the absence of US leadership."[39]

Most European capitals accepted the utility of US involvement in the crises in the Balkans, but European leaders also articulated perceived problems with US leadership. One issue was American unilateralism. For instance, various European officials complained that Washington "consistently devalued nonmilitary approaches to security."[40] Many European policymakers also deplored Washington's unwillingness to develop a proactive Balkan security strategy through consultations between the US and the European states. Even Great Britain, the staunchest European ally of the US, increased its support for CFSP in response to American policies toward the Balkans.[41] The other major concern among policymakers was the growing disparity between American and European military capabilities. As an article in *The Economist* summarized:

> For the European governments, the spectacle of American power unleashed in their corner of the map was frightening and chastening. They found most of their weaponry humiliatingly obsolete when set against the American arsenal of stealth bombers and precision-guided missiles. Once begun, this [Kosovo] became an American war run from the White House and Pentagon over which the Europeans had little political influence.[42]

11 September 2001 and Afghanistan

The outpouring of public and official support for the United States in the aftermath of the 11 September 2001 attacks proved to be temporary as policies on both sides of the Atlantic continued to reflect the national interests and preferences of individual states. Although the Bush administration endeavored to gain broad diplomatic support for its campaign against the Taliban and Al Qaeda, it also sought a coalition of coalitions that would allow Washington, in the words of Deputy Secretary of State Richard Armitage to "pick and choose among its allies, fashioning the moral authority of an international coalition without having to deal with the problems of the whole alliance."[43] National Security Advisor Condoleezza Rice described the coalition as "a broad coalition in which people are contributing on very different and very many fronts. The key to the broad coalition is to remember that, while everybody understandably wants to focus on military contributions, this is not the Gulf War."[44] Unlike the Gulf War, the Bush administration did not seek substantial troop requests until after the main combat operations in Afghanistan were over. Philip Gordon concluded that:

> The US saw multilateral support as politically useful but not particularly significant militarily. In this case it was reinforced by what many Americans saw as a key 'lesson' of Kosovo. Whereas many in Europe saw the Kosovo air campaign as excessively dominated by the United States and American generals, most Americans – particularly within the military – saw just the opposite: excessive European meddling, with French politicians and European lawyers interfering with efficient targeting and bombing runs, and compromising operational security. This time, the Bush team determined, would be different.[45]

The key difference was that the development of what would be termed the "Afghan Model" which on a tactical level combined the use of precision weaponry with special operations forces and on a strategic level emphasized the use of US forces and assets for direct combat and multilateral troops for the humanitarian and nation-building exercises. Such a division of labor led the Chirac government to object to being forced to "clean-up" after the Americans. Officials in Paris noted that Washington seemed to say "We'll do the cooking and prepare what people are going to eat, then you will wash the dirty dishes."[46]

Cooperative Versus Militant Multilateralism

The US Afghan Model was not based on unilateralism, but it reflected a clear decision to reject many of the constraints inherent in multilateralism, including shared leadership, and it emphasized the use of military force to achieve security interests. In this fashion, the Bush policy was based on militant, rather than cooperative, multilateralism. Militant multilateralism was not a new manifestation of US foreign and security policy, indeed, the phrase could be used to describe US policy for most of the Cold War. The philosophical underpinnings of the Bush policy were based on the notion that, like the Cold War, the US confronted a grave and present danger to its core security interests, including defense of the homeland and defense of key allies, and therefore its range of options were limited.

In his State of the Union address on 29 January 2002, Bush announced that the US would take preemptive military action to counter threats to the US and its core allies. He stated that "I will not wait on events, while dangers gather. I will not stand by, as peril draws closer and closer. The United States of America will not permit the world's most dangerous regimes to threaten us with the world's most destructive weapons."[47] Bush's doctrine of preemption was formalized as a part of US security strategy in the National Security Strategy which stated that "While the United States will constantly strive to enlist the support of the international community, we will not hesitate to act alone, if necessary, to exercise our right of self-defense by acting preemptively against such terrorists, to prevent them from doing harm against our people and our country."[48] The first operational use of the preemption doctrine would be Iraq and the use of the strategy would lead to a deep crisis in transatlantic relations and the "New-Old Europe" debate.

Iraq and the "Old Europe – New Europe" Debate

The 2003 US-led invasion of Iraq created a range of diplomatic and strategic tensions in the transatlantic security alliance and it exacerbated differences in the US over cooperative versus militant multilateralism. Within the administration, Secretary of State Colin Powell emerged as the foremost proponent of cooperation, while Vice President Dick Cheney and Secretary of Defense Donald Rumsfeld led the drive for immediate action, even without strong international support. Powell and the cooperationists initially held sway and during the fall of 2002, the administration worked to develop an international coalition and secure both UN backing and bilateral support from the major European allies.

During this period, domestic anti-war sentiment grew in states such as Germany and France, while domestic US support for the war grew. On 10 October, the US Congress overwhelmingly passed a resolution authorizing the use force against Iraq, even if it meant unilateral and/or preemptive action. Tensions mounted on both sides of the Atlantic. Former US Secretary of State Madeleine Albright summarized the situation as "European unease with American pretensions, coupled with American doubts about European resolve" and contended that the diplomatic conflict "created the potential for a long-term and dangerous rift."[49] A former Assistant Secretary of State, James Rubin, observed that most European leaders perceived that for the US "force had become an object in itself, and that Washington was using diplomacy simply to smooth the way for an invasion."[50] Meanwhile, in Washington, there emerged a perception that the anti-war states, led by France, Germany and Russia, were actively working to undermine the American coalition and using diplomatic pressure to prevent states from supporting the US. There was an especially strong sense that Germany was using its chair position in the Security Council to block support for a UN resolution authorizing the use of force.[51]

European Divisions

Meanwhile, there was a growing awareness that the new and potential new members from East and Central Europe were decided pro-American at the governmental level and backed a coalition of Atlanticist states within the Alliance led by the United Kingdom. Eight NATO members issued an open letter in support of the US on 30 January 2003. The letter declared that:

> We in Europe have a relationship with the US which has stood the test of time. Thanks in large part to American bravery, generosity and farsightedness, Europe was set free from the two forms of tyranny that devastated our continent in the 20th century: Nazism and communism. Thanks, too, to the continued cooperation between Europe and the US we have managed to guarantee peace and freedom on our continent. The trans-Atlantic relationship must not become a casualty of the current Iraqi regime's persistent attempts to threaten world security. In today's world, more than ever before, it is vital that we preserve that unity and cohesion. We know that success in the day-to-day battle against terrorism and the proliferation of weapons of mass destruction demands unwavering determination and firm international cohesion on the part of all countries for whom freedom is precious.[52]

In addition, ten Central and East European states, the Vilnius Ten, issued an open letter in support of the US which declared at one point:

> Our countries understand the dangers posed by tyranny and the special responsibility of democracies to defend our shared values. The trans-Atlantic community, of which we are a part, must stand together to face the threat posed by the nexus of terrorism and dictators with weapons of mass destruction.[53]

At a press conference on 22 January 2003, Rumsfeld made a series of comments which underlined the administration's policy of trying to develop a coalition of willing European states:

> Now, you're thinking of Europe as Germany and France. I don't. I think that's old Europe. If you look at the entire NATO Europe today, the center of gravity is shifting to the east. And there are a lot of new members. And if you just take the list of all the

members of NATO and all of those who have been invited in recently – what is it? Twenty-six, something like that? – you're right. Germany has been a problem, and France has been a problem.[54]

Rumsfeld's comments highlighted the manifestation of the older Atlanticist versus Europeanist debate within the Transatlantic Alliance. A coalition of "Old European" Europeanist states, those that Rumsfeld considered to use "old" thinking, were led by France and Germany.

The divisions among the European states demonstrated the continuation of the Europeanist versus Atlanticist debate in transatlantic security. It also created a backlash against the pro-American states. The most striking example of this involved French President Jacques Chirac publicly berating East European states that supported the US Chirac called the pro-American stance of the East European governments "dangerous" and "reckless" and threatened that their policy positions could "only reinforce an attitude of hostility" in a not-so-subtle threat over future EU membership.[55]

Iraq's Aftermath

In the aftermath of the US-led invasion of Iraq, the US and its supporters and the anti-war coalition have begun to attempt to heal the crisis. The debate over the conflict highlighted the long-standing drive for greater European autonomy on security issues and it exposed the equally long-running divisions within Europe between Atlanticist and Europeanist states. In spite of the rhetoric, governments on both sides of the issue continued to work closely together on a range of security issues, including humanitarian and peacekeeping operations in both the Balkans and Afghanistan and broader counterterrorism initiatives. There was no transatlantic divorce.

Nonetheless, the strains between the transatlantic partners will continue. The inclusion of new members in both NATO and the EU may fundamentally change the balance of power between the Atlanticist and Europeanist states. Conversely, as they are integrated into the institutional framework of the transatlantic region, the former communist states of Eastern Europe may find increasing commonality with the France and Germany, the traditional political and economic leaders of Western Europe. If the United States wishes to rival the natural pull toward "Old" Europe, it must strive to develop complex and multifaceted economic, military and political links with the new memberstates on a bilateral level, all the while maintaining its support for NATO as the cornerstone of European security.

Plan of the Book

While the interests of the United States may best be served through continued close ties between Washington and individual state capitals in Europe, the reverse may or may not be true for those same individual memberstates. The remainder of this work uses a state-centric approach to examine both sides of the old versus new debate over European security. To a large extent, this debate is a reaffirmation of the longstanding divide between the Atlanticists and the Europeanists, but in the wake of the Iraq War, the divide invites new examinations and analyzes in order to frame the debate.

We, the editors, divide the book into two broad sections. The first explores the states of old Europe. Unlike Secretary Rumsfeld, we do not define old or new based on policy preferences, but on length of time as members of the transatlantic community. Hence, within the section on old Europe, we include many of the traditional states of Western Europe, including France, Germany, the Benelux states, Italy and the United Kingdom. We also include Russia, both because of its policy inclinations and because since the end of the Cold War, there has been a concerted effort to include Russia in the security mechanisms and decision-making procedures of the West. The new Europe includes those new memberstates which have recently joined NATO and the EU (or who seek to join the EU within the near future).

The overall goal of the project is to provide some suggestions as to whether the current serious split between Atlanticist and Europeanist states is a short-term aberration or a sign of the long-term transformation of the security system in the Euro-Atlantic space, as perceived, and desired, by various players on the continent. In addition, this project seeks to present national perspectives on the potential divide in the security policies of Old and New Europe. Specifically, each essay revolves around a set of core questions. First, what are the core security priorities of each state? Second, given the recent tensions between the US and some of the major European states, are these interests best served through closer security collaboration with the US or with emerging European structures such as the European Rapid Reaction Force (especially if relations continue to deteriorate in the long run)? Third, what contributions can each nation provide for transatlantic security? Fourth, what role does each state envision for existing security structures such as NATO and the emerging European defense and security structure? Fifth, and finally, what should the role of the US be in transatlantic security?

Each chapter also seeks to answer a set of secondary, policy related-questions in order to address common themes related to the 2003 Iraq War and the future of common European security structures. Among these questions are: what prompted each state to support or oppose the US policy in the most recent war on Iraq? The essays also seek to analyze the impact that the Iraq issue has had on US-European relations from the point of view of each state and to examine the impact of specific initiatives, such as the May 2003 Belgian proposal, on national security policy. For the old states of Europe, the essayists detail the support some East European countries gave the US in the context of whether or not the West European states should change their perceptions of the role and place of both the US and the East European states in the Euro-Atlantic security space. Authors in both sections also examine the security implications of trans-Atlantic tensions for the future of each state. Finally, each essayist seeks to identify the main contributions each state can make toward both transatlantic and European security.

Notes

1 Glenn Hastedt and Kay Knickrehm, eds. (1994), *Toward the Twenty-First Century: A Reader in World Politics*, New York: Prentice-Hall, 142.
2 Sam C. Sarkesian, John Allen Williams and Stephen J. Cimbala (2002), *US National Security: Policymakers, Processes, and Politics*, Boulder: Lynne Rienner, 5.
3 Ibid.
4 Ibid.
5 Ibid., 6.
6 Article 5 of the 1949 Washington Treaty which established NATO states that "an armed attack against one or more of them [NATO members] in Europe or North America shall be considered against them all; and ... each of them ... will assist the Party or Parties so attacked;" *The North Atlantic Treaty* (1949), Washington, D.C., 4 April.
7 Samuel P. Huntington (1997), "The Erosion of American National Interests," *Foreign Affairs*, 76 (5), September/October, 30.
8 Juan D. Lindau argues that the distinction between political elites and technocrats can in fact be blurred to indistinguishability; see Juan D. Lindau (1996), "Technocrats and Mexico's Political Elite," *Political Science Quarterly*, 111 (2), Summer: 295–322.
9 Such "indifference" is ingrained as a result of the vastness of the US and the social tendency for Americans to be self-absorbed about themselves and their country; Gabriel Almond (1960), *The American People and Foreign Policy*, New York: Praeger, 53, 76. Another interpretation of US popular indifference to the world reflects Marxist analyses that assert that the "manipulation" of American popular opinion about foreign policy results from broad efforts by multinational elites to control overseas markets and to constrain cross-border worker movements; see Richard Barnet (1972), *The Roots of War*, New York: Atheneum.
10 Mark P. Logan (2000), "Elite Analysis of Democracies' International Policy," *Perspectives on Political Science*, 29 (1), Winter, 5.
11 Richard Herrera (1997), "Understanding the Language of Politics: A Study of Elites and Masses," *Political Science Quarterly*, 111 (4), Winter, 620.
12 V.O. Key (1961), *Public Opinion and American Democracy*, New York: Alfred Knopf; quoted in ibid.
13 Philip J. Powlick and Andrew Z. Katz (1998), "Defining the American Public Opinion/Foreign Policy Nexus," *Mershon International Studies Review*, 42 (1), May, 30.
14 Karen Orren and Stephen Skowronek (1999), "Regimes and Regime Building in American Government," *Political Science Quarterly*, 113 (4), Winter, 694.
15 Jeffrey W. Legro (2000), "Whence American Internationalism," *International Organizations*, 54 (2), Spring, 254.
16 Ibid.
17 John Gerard Ruggie argues that the transformation in US foreign policy in the post-World War II era marked the country's "third try" at creating a broad, multilateral global order (the first attempt was Woodrow Wilson's post-World War I initiatives, while the second was Franklin Roosevelt's endeavor to bring together the major wartime allies to create a collective security organization: the United Nations); see John Gerard Ruggie (1994), "Third Try at World Order," *Political Science Quarterly*, 109 (4), Fall: 553–70.
18 Quoted in Frederick Merk (1963), *Manifest Destiny and Mission in American History: A Reinterpretation*, New York: Vintage, 31–2.
19 Washington's Farewell Address became a reminder to successive administrations until the twentieth century to reject external political or military ties. The US did enter into a range of bilateral and multilateral economic treaties. Later, the Monroe Doctrine (1824)

pledged American administrations to non-interference in Europe in return for European non-interference in the Western Hemisphere (including no new colonization).

20   Isolationism is a misleading term since the US was very active in hemispheric politics throughout its early history even as it avoided entanglement with Europe. Michael Dunne suggests that "isolationism" should be replaced with the phrase "hemispheric unilateralism" to account for US interventions in the region and efforts to acquire territory or influence the economic and political development of the hemisphere; Michael Dunne (2000), "US Foreign Relations in the Twentieth Century: From World Power to Global Hegemony," *International Affairs*, 76 (1), January, 27.

21   Huntington (1997), 30.

22   Joseph Lepgold and Timothy McKeown (1995), "Is American Foreign Policy Exceptional? An Empirical Analysis," *Political Science Quarterly*, 110 (3), Fall, 369.

23   Richard J. Kerry (1990), *The Star-Spangled Mirror: America's Image of Itself and the World*, Savage, Maryland: Rowman & Littlefield, 3.

24   Lepgold and McKeown, 369.

25   Kerry, 3.

26   For an expansion of these ideas, see Emily S. Rosenberg (1982), *Spreading the American Dream: American Economic and Cultural Expansion, 1890–1945*, New York: Hill and Wang.

27   See Michael H. Hunt (1987), *Ideology and US Foreign Policy*, New Haven: Yale University Press.

28   David M. Pletcher (1998), *The Diplomacy of Trade and Investment: American Economic Expansion in the Hemisphere, 1865–1900*, Columbia: University of Missouri, 1998, 2–3.

29   Tom Lansford (2002), *All for One: Terrorism, NATO and the United States*, Aldershot: Ashgate, 37.

30   For an overview of French security interests and the decision to withdraw from NATO see Simon Serfaty (1968), *France, De Gaulle and Europe: The Policies of the Fourth and Fifth Republics Toward the Continent*, Baltimore: Johns Hopkins; and Michael Harrison and Mark McDonough (1987), *Negotiations on the French Withdrawal From NATO*, Washington, D.C.: Johns Hopkins.

31   Celeste A. Wallander (2000), "Institutional Assets and Adaptability: NATO After the Cold War," *International Organization*, 54 (4), Autumn, 718.

32   The CJTF "is a multinational (combined) and multi-service (joint) task force, task-organized and formed for the full range of the Alliance's military missions requiring multinational and multi-service command and control by a CJTF Headquarters. It may include elements from non-NATO Troop Contributing Nations;" NATO (1999), *NATO Handbook: 50th Anniversary Edition*, Brussels: NATO, Chapter 12.

33   NATO (1996), "NATO's New Force Structures," *NATO Basic Fact Sheet*, 5 Brussels: NATO; Anthony Cragg (1996), "The Combined and Joint Task Force Concept: A Key Component of the Alliance's Adaptation," *NATO Review*, 44 (4), July, 8–9.

34   Paul Cornish (1996), "European Security: The End of Architecture and New NATO," *International Affairs*, 72 (4), October, 754.

35   European Council (1999), Declaration of the European Council on Strengthening the Common European Policy on Security and Defence, NR 122/99, 6 March.

36   NATO (1999), *The Alliance's Strategic Concept*, NAC-S(99)65, 24 April.

37   Ibid.

38   Quoted in William Drozdiak (1996), "Europe's Dallying Amid Crises Scares Its Critics," *International Herald Tribune*, 8 February.

39   Quoted in Barbara Starr (1997), "Cohen Establishing His Doctrine as Clinton and Congress Look On," *Jane's Defense Weekly*, 5 February, 19.

40   Daniel Plesch (1999), "Kosovo: A Symptom of NATO's Strategic Failure," *BASIC*, 7 April, 2.
41   See, for instance, *The Economist* (1999) "The Aging Alliance," 23 October, 6.
42   Ibid.
43   NATO (2001), "Press Availability: US Deputy Secretary of State Armitage and NATO Secretary General Lord Robertson," Brussels, 20 September.
44   Condoleezza Rice (2001), Press Briefing, Washington, D.C., 8 November.
45   Philip H. Gordon (2001), "NATO After 11 September," *Survival*, 43 (4), Winter, 4.
46   Joseph Fitchett (2001), "US Allies Chafe at 'Cleanup' Role," *International Herald Tribune*, 26 November.
47   George W. Bush (2002), "The President's State of the Union Address," Washington, D.C., 29 January.
48   US, National Security Council (2002), *The National Security Strategy of the United States*, 17 September.
49   Madeleine Albright (2003), "Bridges, Bombs, or Bluster?" *Foreign Affairs*, 82 (5), September/October, 7.
50   James P. Rubin (2003), "Stumbling Into War," *Foreign Affairs*, 82 (5), September/October, 49.
51   Melissa Eddy (2003), "Report: Germany Aimed to Block US on War," *Associated Press*, 16 March.
52   The letter also stated that:

     The real bond between the US and Europe is the values we share: democracy, individual freedom, human rights and the rule of law. These values crossed the Atlantic with those who sailed from Europe to help create the United States of America. Today they are under greater threat than ever.

     The attacks of Sept. 11 showed just how far terrorists – the enemies of our common values – are prepared to go to destroy them. Those outrages were an attack on all of us. In standing firm in defense of these principles, the governments and people of the US and Europe have amply demonstrated the strength of their convictions. Today more than ever, the trans-Atlantic bond is a guarantee of our freedom.

     Jose Maria Aznar, Jose-Manuel Durão Barroso, Silvio Berlusconi, Tony Blair, Vaclav Havel, Peter Medgyessy, Leszek Miller and Anders Fogh Rasmussen (2003), "United We Stand," 30 January.

53   Albania, Bulgaria, Estonia, Croatia, Latvia, Lithuania, Macedonia, Romania, Slovakia, and Slovenia (2003), "Statement of the Vilnius Group Countries in Response to the Presentation by the United States Secretary of State to the United Nations Security Council Concerning Iraq," New York, 5 February.
54   Donald Rumsfeld (2003), "News Transcript: Secretary Rumsfeld Briefs at Foreign Press Center," Department of Defense News Transcripts, 22 January.
55   John Vinocur (2003), "Chirac's Outburst Exposes Contradiction Within EU," *International Herald Tribune*, 18 February.

PART ONE
OLD EUROPE

Chapter 1

French Security Agenda in the Post-9/11 World

Robert J. Pauly, Jr.

Introduction

The history of the transatlantic relationship over the past six decades is one that has consistently been defined by episodes of collaboration and discord across a range of economic, military and political issue areas. In that period, the ties between the United States and its European partners have grown perpetually deeper such that anything more than a transitory break in the Atlantic Alliance remains unlikely if not unthinkable. Nonetheless, there remain a variety of serious European-American differences – particularly with respect to security threats and the means through which to mitigate and eventually eliminate those dangers – that divide states on the two sides of the Atlantic generally and pit the United States against France specifically. During the Cold War, French leaders had a tendency to present Paris as a check on (and, to some degree, an alternative to) Washington's transatlantic and global leadership and behave in ways that reflected that perspective. In 1966, for example, France withdrew from the military command structure of the North Atlantic Treaty Organization (NATO). The perpetual growth in the power and influence of the United States since the end of the American-Soviet bipolar confrontation, in turn, has exacerbated past Franco-American disagreements and undermined broader political and strategic linkages across the Atlantic.

The most recent case of a divergence between French and US interests in the European and transatlantic arenas came in the context of the diplomatic maneuvering that preceded, and has since followed, the conduct of the Second Iraq War in March and April 2003. French President Jacques Chirac opposed American President George W. Bush's efforts to confront the regime of Iraqi dictator Saddam Hussein over its weapons of mass destruction (WMD) developmental programs and sponsorship of terrorist organizations throughout the political process that unfolded prior to the US and UK led invasion of Iraq. Ultimately, when the Bush administration indicated it would sponsor a final United Nations (UN) Security Council Resolution to authorize unequivocally the use of force against Saddam's regime (the most recent of 17 previous measures, which was passed unanimously in November 2002, had stressed more ambiguously that Iraqi non-compliance would result in "serious consequences"), Chirac had the following response: "Whatever the circumstances, France will vote no."[1] As a result, the United States chose not to put the resolution forward for a Security Council vote and proceeded, with substantial British support and the cooperation of more than 50 other coalition members, to eliminate Saddam's regime and commence nation-building operations in Iraq.

Chirac's stalwart opposition to the Second Iraq War, a stance also taken by Germany (traditionally among the most dependable of Washington's allies) and Belgium, among others within and outside of Europe, was reflective of two additional fundamental characteristics of the Franco-American relationship that have become increasingly evident since the end of the Cold War in general, and Al Qaeda's attacks on the World Trade Center and Pentagon on 11 September 2001 in particular. First, French leaders are bitter over Paris' lack of global influence relative to that of a United States, a collective of economic, military and political power and cultural outreach of which have been unrivalled since the implosion of the Soviet Union in December 1991. Second, they resent the willingness of the United States (especially the Bush administration) to act with the support of only some, rather than all, of its European allies, let alone the Security Council's imprimatur, to preempt threats to American interests before such threats become imminent. It follows that France chose to obstruct US action against Iraq in the one institution within which Paris and Washington have equal power in the form of a right to veto any measure that comes to a vote – the Security Council.

Above all, the aforementioned divergences and their implications pertaining to the Second Iraq War and its aftermath provide a necessary foundation for a more in-depth discussion of French national interests and the foreign and security policies Chirac and his advisors have formulated and implemented in the pursuit of such interests. The balance of the essay addresses these issues through the presentation of the following six related sections:

- A review of French security priorities at the domestic, European, transatlantic and global levels.
- A discussion of the extent to which French security interests will be better served by collaboration with the United States in the transatlantic context or by orchestrating the development of an autonomous European Security and Defense Policy (EDSP) and managing the use of the nascent European Rapid Reaction Force (RRF).
- An assessment of the ways in which France can contribute most effectively to the enhancement of transatlantic security.
- An examination of the practical implications of divergent American and French security interests during the run-up to the conduct of the Second Iraq War.
- An examination of the French vision for the future of the transatlantic security relationship.
- The articulation of a set of conclusions on the essay's contributions to the ongoing academic and policy debates on emerging post-9/11 transatlantic security dilemmas.

French Security Priorities in the Post-Cold War World

Historically, political leaders have always had a variety of tools at their disposal to employ in the development and implementation of foreign and national security policies. In general terms, the approaches they choose to pursue are typically conditioned by the changing nature and perception of the threats they face and the contemporary domestic and foreign crises to which they must respond. Nonetheless, irrespective of the historical circumstances, three rules have consistently proven indispensable to the effective formulation and implementation of policies designed to safeguard a given state's interests at home and abroad. It is essential first to define one's interests, second to prioritize those interests and third to take policy decisions accordingly. More pointedly, the policies that grow out of such decisions are the product of an admixture of three elements – interests, commitments and capabilities. States develop their interests on the basis of a range of factors, including economics, politics, security, geography, history, individual leadership, culture (most notably ethnicity and religion) and the unpredictability of unfolding events. Consequently, leaders make commitments that are contingent on the state's economic, military and political capabilities at a particular temporal juncture.

The logical point of departure for a discussion of contemporary French security policy is a review of the general characteristics of the strategies it has pursued in the recent past, which, in this case, relate to the Cold War era. In short, France pursued its interests on two fronts – and through two sets of policies that were, at least at times, somewhat contradictory – during the half-century confrontation pitting the Americans against the Soviets. First, with respect to the theoretically existential threat posed to Western Europe by the Soviet Union, France naturally expressed staunch support for the United States, which supplied the vast majority of NATO's military assets and thus provided a necessary insurance policy vis-à-vis Moscow and the Warsaw Pact states it controlled in the East. Second, by contrast, successive French Presidents of both the left and right attempted to cast Paris as a counterweight to Washington in terms of political leadership within the Alliance, the European Community and the developing world over which it had presided before the de-colonization processes of the 1950s and 1960s. In particular, France attempted to enhance its international prestige through the development of an independent nuclear *force de frappe* and withdrawal from NATO's military command structure. Former US Secretary of State Henry Kissinger offers an instructive synopsis of the French approach:

> It is not that France does not understand the United States' role as the ultimate safety net for French (and European) autonomous policy. Nor do French leaders have any illusions about the relative power positions of the two countries. In the major crises of the Cold War – the challenges to Berlin between 1957 and 1962, the Cuban Missile Crisis in 1962, the Gulf War in 1990–1991 – France proved a staunch ally; deployment of medium-range missiles in Germany in 1983 would not have been possible without the eloquent support of French President François Mitterrand. But the Cartesian, ultrarationalist education of French policymakers causes them to believe that the United States will understand their somewhat cynical applications of *raison d'état*, and will always respect the motivations which induce France to define European identity as a challenge to the United States, even while relying on it as a guarantor of France's security.[2]

The closing French assessment to which Kissinger refers has not proven nearly so astute since the end of the Cold War. Transatlantic solidarity was indispensable to the effective containment of the Soviet Union from the 1950s to the 1970s – and, ultimately – to the rollback of its influence by the Ronald Reagan administration during the 1980s and the subsequent orchestration of the conclusion of the bipolar confrontation by the George H.W. Bush administration from 1989–91. However, with the United States advancing toward global hegemony and the lack of a common adversary to confront, divergences in Franco-American interests – and the unwillingness of either side to compromise publicly to the degree they did during the Cold War – have become increasingly more apparent in the 1990s and 2000s. From the French perspective, which is, of course, central to this piece, those divergences are best examined contextually at the domestic, European, transatlantic and global levels.

As is true of any state, France's concerns over security begin at home. Among the most pressing of Chirac's domestic worries, for instance, is the fact that there are presently between five and seven million Muslims residing in France, nearly all of whom have been excluded from the economic, political and social benefits afforded to the majority of the national populace.[3] The potential for unrest emanating from Franco-Islamic communities, ranging from demonstrations and increases in the rate of criminal acts to riots and the commission of terrorist attacks, in turn, is one of the reasons why Chirac has had a tendency to portray the French government as more favorably disposed toward Arab and broader Muslim causes than the United States. Examples include Paris' rejection of the use of force against Iraq by both the William J. Clinton administration in Operation Desert Fox in December 1998 and the Bush administration in the Second Iraq War and a French diplomatic tilt toward the Palestinians in the context of the fleeting Israeli-Palestinian peace process. Put simply, Chirac has used foreign policy to avoid further inflaming already marginalized Muslims that successive French governments have been unable, if not unwilling, to integrate effectively.[4]

At the continental level, French security policy, since the end of the Cold War generally and the events of 9/11 specifically, has been designed to achieve two related objectives. First, as it did during the Cold War, France has attempted with some success to enhance its political prestige by casting itself as the leading proponent of the inter- and intra-European deepening and widening processes. Its end in this endeavor is to increase the economic power and political influence of the European Union (EU) – and, by association, of France itself – relative to that of the United States. Second, it has pressed successfully for the creation of a RRF to afford the EU greater freedom of action to undertake military operations in which the Americans choose not to participate. Notwithstanding the progress the Europeans have made vis-à-vis the RRF, that entity remains largely untested. Nonetheless, the French goal, one Germany shares but the United Kingdom, among others, does not, is that the EU will eventually serve as a reasonably credible counterweight to American military power.

With respect to the transatlantic security community, French policy has proceeded along two relatively straightforward tracks over the past decade. First, France has had a tendency to accept American leadership – and military support – when unable to handle a regional security threat on its own. This was most noticeable in the Balkans, where US-led NATO intervention proved critical in ending the 1992–95 civil war in Bosnia-Herzegovina and preventing Serbian

President Slobodan Milosevic from eliminating the ethnic Albanian minority in Kosovo in 1999. The Europeans, including the French, failed to prevent genocide in Bosnia – and the resultant instability along the periphery of the EU's borders – and recognized that they would be unable to force Milosevic to cease his ethnic cleansing campaign in Kosovo with out American military support.[5] Second, France has understandably refrained from supporting those US initiatives it believes would entail more relative costs than benefits with respect to its interests. The Bush administration's liquidation of Saddam's regime, which Chirac did not deem a direct threat to French interests, is the most significant recent case in point. During the run-up to Operation Iraqi Freedom, for example, Chirac argued that even if Saddam's regime possessed biological and chemical WMD, that would not "in the present situation pose a clear and present danger to the region."[6]

Not surprisingly, the formulation, articulation and implementation of French foreign policies at the global level have been conditioned by assessments of the relative importance of its domestic, European and transatlantic security interests at a given juncture. Its approach to the American-led war on terrorism that grew out of the 9/11 attacks is illustrative of such calculations. Chirac expressed his solidarity with the Bush administration in confronting Al Qaeda and its Taliban hosts in the aftermath of the strikes on the World Trade Center and the Pentagon. French forces played a limited role in Operation Enduring Freedom in Afghanistan from October-December 2001 and Paris' intelligence services and judicial and police institutions continue to cooperate fully with the United States in weakening Al Qaeda's assets within and beyond Europe.[7] That cooperation reflects Chirac's concerns over the potential for Al Qaeda recruitment of individuals from within France's own marginalized Muslim communities. His refusal to back the American-led use of force against Iraq, on the other hand, demonstrated that there are limits to Paris' willingness to provide assistance in the more controversial confrontation of state sponsors of terrorism in the context of the struggle against Al Qaeda leader Osama bin Laden and his ilk. This was especially true in light of the potential for France to use its opposition to the Second Gulf War to present itself as an alternative to US leadership within Europe and at the broader transatlantic and global levels.

To Lead or to Follow

Since the conclusion of the Cold War, France has had myriad opportunities to choose whether to follow the lead of the United States or chart a more independent course with respect to the security challenges faced by the member states of the EU and NATO. The French have responded to those challenges in three general manners: by accepting American leadership in a relatively unambiguous fashion as was the case in Bosnia and Kosovo; by rejecting US initiatives as proved true vis-à-vis the Second Iraq War; or by striking a balance between these two approaches as it has done with respect to the global war on terrorism. Each of those decisions has reflected a more fundamental assessment of whether asserting leadership within Europe is likely to prove more beneficial than playing proverbial second fiddle to the United States in order to maintain cohesion in the Atlantic Alliance at a particular juncture. The balance of this section conducts interest-based analyses of these stances in order to determine the most rational way for Paris to proceed in the future.

NATO's interventions in Bosnia and Kosovo, neither of which would have been effective without America's provision of the political initiative and technologically advanced military capabilities that its European allies lacked, are useful cases studies to employ in identifying the benefits and costs of following Washington's lead, especially from the French perspective. Collectively, such benefits were threefold. First, in each case, NATO's action ensured the restoration and subsequent maintenance of stability in southeastern Europe and thus precluded destabilizing spillover effects on the fringes of the EU's borders. Second, notwithstanding the centrality of American leadership to – and the use of US military assets in – each operation, both could still be characterized as multilateral efforts, which was helpful to the French in rhetorical, if not practical, terms. Third, the Clinton administration used the intervention in Bosnia to launch the enlargement of NATO to the East, which proved a necessary precursor of EU expansion in the same direction under French – and, to a lesser degree – German leadership. As Simon Serfaty, director of the Europe Program at the Center for Strategic and International Studies, explains, NATO operations in Bosnia in 1995 demonstrated "first, that the continued unavailability of European power made American power indispensable and, second, that the persistent centrality of US leadership made NATO central as well, because NATO was the only multilateral conduit to Europe for both US power and US leadership."[8]

The principal costs for the French were twofold. First, the fact that neither France nor any other Western European states – a bloc it had consistently attempted to portray itself as a leader of – proved capable of handling the crisis in Bosnia from 1992–95 on their own belied the image of *grandeur* Paris preferred to project. Second, as a practical matter, the need for the near exclusive use of American airpower in the conduct of NATO's military action against Serbia in 1999 impressed upon Europe's three most powerful states – France, Germany and the United Kingdom – that improvements to their own capabilities would be essential in the future. Subsequently, British Prime Minister Tony Blair was the initial European leader to propose the establishment of an autonomous EU military force, which has since evolved into the RRF. That it was Blair and not Chirac who broached the issue first did not reflect favorably on the French sense of self-importance.

In the end, the concerns Blair expressed in the aftermath of the Kosovo conflict promoted Chirac to play host to a conference in Saint Malo that produced a Franco-British agreement to pursue an autonomous ESDP. The focal point of the ESDP, in turn, was the creation of a 60,000-man RRF with the capacity to deploy to a given geographical context within 60 days.[9] Given the differences in their traditional and contemporary relationships with the United States, France and the United Kingdom characterized the ESDP in alternative manners. The French suggested that the RRF would be a legitimately autonomous force, one likely to afford the EU freedom of action to conduct military operations without direct American support. The British, by contrast, portrayed the RRF as a supplement rather than a rival to NATO, one that would allow the Atlantic Alliance more flexibility in choosing when to deploy military forces outside of the borders of its member states. Not surprisingly,

Washington was supportive of the British, as opposed to the French, spin on the initiative. As Robert Hunter, who served as US Ambassador to NATO from 1993–98, notes, the

> United States … pressed its European allies to maintain defense spending at the highest possible level and to develop capabilities that would promote interoperability and power projection. Thus, the United States accepted, in principal and to a great degree in practice, the EU's development of a European Security and Defense Policy in part because that could provide incentives for European states to take defense seriously for the cause of European integration, even if they would not do so for the cause of NATO's continued effectiveness. At the same time, the United States, supported by some key allies, also argued forcefully for NATO's continued primacy.[10]

The promulgation of the ESDP has been beneficial to France in two ways. First, it afforded Chirac an opportunity to articulate his vision of the EU as a necessary counterweight to the United States in a more comprehensive manner than would otherwise have been possible. The addition of what the French perceive will eventually be a credible military complement to the EU's already substantial economic and political power has the potential to enhance Brussels' – and, by association, Paris' – global influence relative to that emanating from Washington. Second, assuming the RRF continues to build on the successes it enjoyed in limited peace enforcement and peacekeeping deployments to the Democratic Republic of the Congo and Macedonia in 2003, France's consistent commitment to that organization will prove politically useful over the medium and long terms. Should the need arise, for example, for the deployment of a transitory peacekeeping force as part of an eventual settlement of the Israeli-Palestinian conflict, all or part of the RRF could serve in that capacity. That type of endeavor could be used to augment the diplomacy of the Quartet (the United States, Russia, the UN and the EU) to the collective benefit of the Middle East and broader international community.

Yet, despite the RRF's progress to date, it still lacks the capacity to stage the type of operation for which it was designed, particularly with respect to the size of the force to be deployed and the length of its stay in the field. Hypothetically, should a RRF mission face a military challenge to which the EU is unable to respond effectively, it would have no choice but to call upon the United States for assistance. Notwithstanding transatlantic differences over the Second Iraq War and its aftermath, Washington would undoubtedly provide whatever assistance was necessary to bail out the EU. However, such a RRF shortcoming would call into question both the ability of the EU to deal with its own security challenges and French leadership of the ESDP.

Fortunately for France, anything other than an extraordinarily limited deployment of the RRF is unlikely. As Kissinger asserts, "[o]nly a very rash group of European leaders would dare to mobilize the European Force without American logistics and intelligence support or assurances of American goodwill. In practice, the European Force is not so much autonomous as it is designed for such symbolic efforts as peacekeeping or special missions involving few risks."[11] Kissinger's observations help to explain why Chirac's decision to couple leadership in the European context with limited cooperation vis-à-vis American judgments on transatlantic and global security issues – especially since the 9/11 attacks – makes sense. Deferring to Washington would not bolster French influence in Europe or Chirac's own domestic popularity.[12] Refraining from doing so in some instances, such as was the case with respect to the Bush administration's Iraq policy simply had limited costs for France, especially in the short term. Consequently, the course Chirac has pursued, while perhaps not laudable, is certainly understandable.

French Contributions to the Enhancement of Transatlantic Security

As touched on above, Chirac has proven consistently willing to cooperate with, if not always follow to the letter the lead of the United States, when French and American interests coincide within, as well as outside of, the European continent. In light of the existence of such common interests, this section examines past, present and likely future French contributions to the direct and indirect enhancement of transatlantic security. It does so contextually, placing emphases on the European continent, Greater Middle East and broader developing worlds, and the global war on terrorism.

France and European Security

France's greatest present and prospective future contributions to European security grow directly out of its vision for the ESDP, one that, as illustrated in the previous section of the essay, has yet fully come to fruition. Such contributions are twofold. First, by taking the lead in the push for an increase in defense spending by EU members, as French Defense Minister Michelle Alliot-Marie recently suggested would prove to be the case, Paris can help to bolster the capabilities of those states both individually and collectively.[13] Such developments would then help to decrease the burden on the United States in the conducting of ongoing nation-building efforts in the Balkans and in responding to any further disturbances that may erupt either there or within other regions along the EU's growing Eastern border.[14] As Serfaty explains, the "United States will not view the EU as a serious security partner so long as the EU continues to lack in military capabilities, and so long as most of its members (except Britain and, to an extent, France) fail to make the necessary investments to be capable when they are willing, and relevant when they are both willing and capable."[15] Second, so long as France strikes a balance that tilts toward the British perception of the RRF as a partner rather than a rival of NATO, the ESDP should help to deepen security linkages across the Atlantic and between Western and Eastern Europe.

France and Global Security

While France is not now, or ever likely to, possess the requisite economic resources, military capabilities or political influence to respond to global security threats in as regular or robust a manner as the United States, Paris does have the potential to complement rather than complicate Washington's efforts to resolve post-9/11 crises in the developing world before they spiral out of control. France can do so in two ways, each of which will help to ameliorate Franco-American relations without detracting from the image of *grandeur* it is determined to project. One way is by committing itself to intervention – either independently or collaboratively with the United States or its other NATO allies – in regions of the world in which former French colonies are in the process of becoming "failing" or "failed" states. A notable recent example was the cooperative effort between the Bush and Chirac administrations in restoring order in Haiti following the ouster of President Jean-Bertrand Aristide in March 2004 under the auspices of a Security Council approved plan that was first put forward by French Foreign Minister Dominique de Villepin.[16] Second, as touched on previously, small-scale operations designed either to prevent a state from failing or restoring stability after its collapse – assuming the scale of conflict is confined to a limited geographic area – is what the RRF was designed for. The French, for their part, could then claim at least partial credit for the successful use of the RRF in minimizing, if not preventing, a given humanitarian crisis.

France and the War on Terrorism

The first international leader to visit Washington to express his personal condolences and solidarity in the war against terrorism following 9/11 attacks was Chirac. Since then, France has been consistently supportive of the Bush administration's efforts to weaken – and, eventually, eliminate – Al Qaeda's global network and also to capture or kill that organization's leaders, including, of course, bin Laden himself. In addition to playing a limited role in the conduct of Operation Enduring Freedom, France has contributed special operations forces to the continuing hunt for bin Laden and other Al Qaeda and Taliban leaders in Afghanistan's hinterlands, conducted joint operations with the US Navy in targeting terrorist transport networks in the Indian Ocean and Mediterranean and Caribbean Seas, and collaborated in intelligence and domestic judicial and policing capacities in an effort to root out Al Qaeda cells across the globe. By no means should Franco-American differences over Iraq obscure such cooperation in the war on terror.

Franco-American Differences vis-à-vis the Second Iraq War

Notwithstanding the French commitment to the US-led offensive against Al Qaeda, France has been adamant in its opposition to another aspect of the US-led war on terror: Washington's policy toward Iraq. That policy was articulated in the context of Bush's address to the UN General Assembly on 12 September 2002, through which Bush issued a stern warning to Iraq, one demonstrative of a fundamental shift in American foreign and security policy. In that address, Bush made three unambiguous points. First, he demanded that Iraq refrain from the development of nuclear, chemical and biological WMD, a promise Saddam's regime made in the context of its surrender at the conclusion of the 1990–1991 Persian Gulf War and had since broken repeatedly. Second, he challenged the UN to carry out its responsibilities by impressing upon Saddam the need to disarm in an internationally verifiable manner as stipulated in myriad previous Security Council Resolutions. Third, he emphasized the United States would act – multilaterally if possible, but also unilaterally if necessary – to remove the threats posed to American interests by Iraq's development of WMD and support for transnational terrorist groups including but not limited to Al Qaeda.[17]

Five days after Bush's UN address, his administration released its first formal National Security Strategy (NSS), an initiative designed to warn American adversaries generally and Iraq specifically that the United States would no longer tolerate either the development and proliferation of WMD or the state sponsorship of terrorism. Essentially, Bush's NSS represented a shift in strategy from the containment doctrine of the Cold War era and comparably reactive policy-making of the Clinton administration to the use of preemptive means to safeguard US interests at home and abroad. It was a shift necessitated by the changing nature of the severity of the threats posed to American security in the post-11 September world.[18] As National Security Advisor Condoleezza Rice has argued, "some threats are so potentially catastrophic – and can arrive with so little warning, by means that are untraceable – that they cannot be contained. ... So as a matter of common sense, the United States must be prepared to take action, when necessary, before threats have fully materialized."[19]

Put simply, the Bush administration used its policy toward Iraq as a test case for the practical implementation of the NSS. It did so through a three-part strategy that has unfolded between September 2002 and the present. First, Bush attempted to use diplomatic measures to ensure Iraqi disarmament, most notably by securing the return of UN weapons inspectors to Iraq under the auspices of Security Council Resolution 1441, which was passed unanimously on 8 November 2002.[20] Second, when Saddam refused to comply fully with the weapons inspectors, the United States collaborated with the United Kingdom – and, to a lesser degree, allies including Australia and several Eastern and Central European states – to forcibly remove the Iraqi regime from power in orchestrating a campaign that lasted just over one month between mid-March and mid-April 2003. Third, the Americans and British are currently leading a coalition of the willing to build a democratic system in Iraq over the long term.

During the initial stage of the above process, Chirac consistently voiced his unambiguous opposition to the use of military force to disarm Iraq and employed all diplomatic measures at his disposal to block that course of action. For example, although France voted for Resolution 1441, it did so only because that measure did not explicitly sanction the use of force against Iraq. Ultimately, when the United States, the United Kingdom and Spain indicated they would seek a second resolution condoning military action to disarm Saddam's regime, Chirac's response that "whatever the circumstances, France will vote no" ensured that the campaign for any such resolution was stillborn.[21]

Chirac's behavior raises one root question: Why was he so insistent that the United States not remove Saddam from power? In short, there are three reasons, each of which includes both domestic and international components that require more detailed independent explanations. First, France had close public and private economic ties with Saddam's regime, which it was understandably eager to preserve. Second, France plays host to a growing Muslim population, one whose members were unequivocally opposed to US military action against Iraq and by no means averse to expressing their opposition in violent – and thus socially destabilizing – ways. Third, Chirac perceived the Iraq crisis as an opportunity to revitalize flagging French prestige – both within and outside of Europe – in opposition to American predominance in the post-Cold War international system.

Economically, France had much to lose as a result of the liquidation of Saddam's regime. At the governmental level, Baghdad is in debt to Paris to the tune of approximately $8 billion.[22] While the sum itself is not substantial, it suggests the potential existence of linkages between Chirac's administration and the regime in Baghdad that may extend at least peripherally to collusion on the development of WMD. In theory, economic connections between France and Iraq are perhaps even more relevant with respect to the private sector. Most significantly, French oil companies such as TotalFinaElf (TFE) are suspected of negotiating contracts to develop Iraqi oil resources that would enter into force concurrent with the removal of UN economic sanctions against Iraq. While TFE Chairman Thierry Demarest denies signing any such contracts, published reports indicated that the finalization of a deal for TFE to "exploit the huge Majnoon field, with 20 billion barrels of oil, in southern Iraq, as well as the smaller Nahr Umr field nearby" was all but a formality prior to the outbreak of hostilities.[23] Given French opposition to the war, the nascent democratic Iraq is unlikely to treat TFE nearly so favorably as was true of Saddam.

In addition to these economic considerations, Chirac faced equally pressing domestic political concerns over the potentially volatile reaction of Franco-Muslim communities to any governmental support whatsoever for the American-led use of force against Iraq. As a result, Chirac was justifiably concerned over the likelihood, if not certainty, of domestic instability emanating from the urban housing projects in which most Franco-Islamic communities are situated given past acts of Franco-Muslim defiance ranging from public demonstrations to the commission of terrorist attacks. Yet, while Chirac's anti-war strategy mollified France's Muslims in the short term, deeper ethnic and religious divisions are likely to prevail without the development of a more effective governmental strategy to integrate Islamic communities within the societal mainstream over the long term.

Notwithstanding Chirac's domestic economic and political motivations, his opposition to and attempted obstruction of the Bush administration's preemptive strategy toward Iraq was, at its core, a product of the traditional French aversion to the expression of American power in the world. During the Cold War, France consistently sought to create independent roles for itself as a hub of opposition to US leadership within Europe and across the developing world. Manifestations of this trend included President Charles de Gaulle's acquisition of a nuclear *force de frappe* and subsequent withdrawal of France from NATO's military command structure in 1966. It is not unreasonable to characterize Chirac's behavior of late in similar terms to that of de Gaulle. Lacking the economic vitality or military capacity to portray France as a legitimate rival to the United States, Chirac attempted to achieve that objective by using the one body in which Paris possesses power relatively equivalent to that wielded by Washington: the UN Security Council. Regrettably, in the process, he may well have damaged the Franco-American relationship to an extent that will require months – and perhaps – years to repair.

French Vision for the Future of the Transatlantic Security Relationship

Above all, France's vision for the future of the transatlantic security relationship reflects broader European concerns over the predominance of American power in the post-Cold War world and the Bush administration's increasingly proactive expression of its political influence and use of its armed forces since the events of 9/11. Most significantly, two related initiatives – Bush's NSS and the preemptive liquidation of Saddam's regime via the conduct of the Second Iraq War – highlighted a divergence of views between France, Germany and, to a lesser degree the United Kingdom, on one hand and the United States on the other, over the legitimate use of force to safeguard a state's security interests in the contemporary international system. Put simply, the Europeans contend that unless military action is undertaken multilaterally under UN auspices and, more pointedly, with the universal support of one's allies, it will be perceived as illegitimate. The United States, by contrast, has expressed a willingness to act multilaterally when possible and unilaterally when necessary (with or without a UN mandate) to eliminate threats to its security before they become imminent.

As a result, much of the criticism of Bush's foreign policy within and beyond Europe, whether before, during or after the conduct of the Second Iraq War, rests primarily on the premise that he has acted unilaterally more often than not. Responding effectively to that criticism is relatively easy so long as one defines the term unilateralism first. The narrowest definition of the term would suggest that a given state is acting alone – that is, without the support, of any allies whatsoever, let alone the blessing of the UN Security Council or wider international community. A broader definition, by contrast, might indicate a coalition of less than 10 states acting without the authority of a formal Security Council resolution. Yet, neither of these definitions was applicable to US action in the contexts of either Operation Enduring Freedom or Operation Iraqi Freedom. In each case, the United States acted with the direct or indirect military, logistical and political support of no less than 50 states. In addition, the Security Council acceded to the former, albeit not to the latter. As American Secretary of State Colin Powell explains, "Partnership is the watchword of US strategy in this administration. Partnership is not about deferring to others; it is about working with them."[24]

For France and Germany in particular, the most irksome aspect of the Bush administration's selectively multilateral approach to the Second Iraq War was not that the United States failed to earn a Security Council Resolution to use force against Saddam's regime, but that it acted despite their unequivocal opposition. As Robert Kagan, a senior associate at the Carnegie Endowment for International Peace notes, "what Washington's critics really resented was that it would not and could not be constrained, even by its closest friends. From the perspective of Berlin and Paris, the United States was unilateralist because no European power had any real influence over it."[25] Kagan's point is well taken, especially when one considers that the French and Germans had no qualms regarding the lack of a UN imprimatur vis-à-vis NATO's intervention to prevent Milosevic from eliminating the ethnic Albanian minority in Kosovo in 1999. One of the lessons of that operation, according to the man who oversaw it – Supreme Allied Commander-Europe General Wesley Clark – was that, "Nations and alliances should move early to deal with crises while they are still ambiguous and can be dealt with more easily, for delay raises both the costs and risks. Early action is the objective to which statesmen and military leaders should resort."[26]

Chirac would likely agree with Clark's assessment, but only so long as the crisis involved and the resulting decision to take action was – or could be portrayed in some way – to further French interests. In the end, then, the French vision for transatlantic security is one that will hinge on Paris' ability to play a lead role in Europe while acquiescing in the pursuit of US-led transatlantic initiatives that do not entail any serious domestic economic, military or political costs. There are three general means to that end, none of which necessarily entails a sea change in the security policies the French have pursued in the past. First, France must continue to use to its advantage those institutions in which it has equal or greater power than that of the United States, most notably the EU and the UN. Second, France should stay the course in pressing for the development and strengthening of the ESDP but do so in a way that can at least be perceived as complementary to NATO. Lastly, although France should reserve the option to oppose American action the costs of which it truly believes are unsustainable at home, it must make every effort to avoid a break in transatlantic relations comparable to the one associated with the Second Iraq War.

Conclusions

At its core, this essay was designed to examine the continuity and changes in French security policy since the end of the Cold War in general and the events of 9/11 in particular in the context of a five-part discussion. First, it reviewed France's contemporary security priorities at the domestic, European, transatlantic and global levels. Second, it assessed the relative costs and benefits of the expression of French leadership in the EU and Chirac's willingness, or lack thereof, to defer to the United States vis-à-vis its pursuit of American – and broader transatlantic – interests within, and outside of, Europe. Third, it examined past, present and prospective future French contributions to the enhancement of transatlantic security. Fourth, it highlighted those divergences in American and French security interests that manifested themselves most noticeably during the run-up to the conduct of the Second Iraq War. Lastly, it discussed the similarities and differences between French, wider European and US visions of the transatlantic security agenda.

Ultimately, the preceding discussion of these related issues leads to the following conclusions. First, the history of relations between the United States and its European allies generally and Franco-American interactions therein have been characterized by alternate periods of collaboration and discord. Despite short-term European-American disagreements over a variety of economic, military and political issues since the end of World War II – some of which (the 1956 Suez Crisis and stationing of Intermediate Nuclear Forces in Germany in the 1980s, for instance) proved more serious than others – the broader transatlantic relationship has grown deeper with each passing decade. Thus, in one sense, the imbroglio over the 2003 war against Iraq simply represents the latest proverbial broken fencepost for the Americans and Europeans to mend in order to maintain political cohesion across the Atlantic. However, in this instance, the repair work may prove markedly more challenging in this instance than was the case in the past in that it will coincide with the largest widening of the twin pillars of the transatlantic community – NATO and the EU – in either institution's history.

Second, in the process of opposing the use of force to remove Saddam from power, Chirac sparked divisions within both NATO and the EU. Most significantly, Germany elected to join France in obstructing US attempts to forge consensus within NATO on Washington's policy toward Iraq, resulting in a division of the European continent into wings favoring, and opposed to, the Bush administration's doctrine of preemption. These divisions, in turn, had spillover effects in the context of the EU. With respect to transatlantic community broadly defined, France, Germany – and a number of less influential states including Belgium and Luxembourg – entrenched themselves on one side of the debate over Iraq, while the United Kingdom, Spain, Italy, Portugal and the vast majority of prospective EU and NATO members from Eastern and Central Europe aligned themselves with the United States on the other side. Put bluntly, such divisions pose an inopportune – and unnecessary – complication to the scheduled enlargement of NATO and the EU to include several Central and Eastern European states that have staked out positions in opposition to two of the three most politically influential states in Europe.

Third, the United States and France are each at least partially responsible for the predicament in which the transatlantic community finds itself on the eve of the dual enlargement processes slated to move forward in 2004. Bush, for example, could have done a better job accommodating Western European concerns over issues ranging from global warming to the imposition of American steel tariffs in 2001. Chirac, on the other hand, could have been more understanding of US worries over Iraq's development of WMD and sponsorship of terrorist groups, especially in light of the tragic events of 11 September. Yet, irrespective of the share of the blame apportioned to Washington and Paris, the Bush and Chirac administrations now have an opportunity, if not an obligation, to restore cohesion across the Atlantic rather than remain stubbornly aloof and risk a delay – or perhaps a more serious derailment – of the completion of the idea of a Europe whole and free launched in the aftermath of World War II.

Notes

1   Quoted in *The Economist* (2003), "Against America? Moi?," 13 March.
2   Henry Kissinger (2001), *Does America Need a Foreign Policy? Toward a Diplomacy for the 21st Century*, New York: Simon & Schuster, 50–51.
3   Omer Taspinar (2003), "Europe's Muslim Street," *Foreign Policy* 82 (2), March/April: 76–77; *The Economist* (2001), "How Restive Are Europe's Muslims," 18 October; Christopher Caldwell (2000), "The Crescent and the Tricolor," *Atlantic* 287–11: 22.
4   For a detailed discussion of the issue of Islam in France, see Robert J. Pauly, Jr. (2004), *Islam in Europe: Integration or Marginalization*, Aldershot, UK: Ashgate Publishing Limited, 33–64.

5   For detailed examinations of NATO intervention in Bosnia-Herzegovina in 1995 and Kosovo in 1999, see Wesley K. Clark (2001), *Waging Modern War: Bosnia, Kosovo and the Future of Combat*, New York: Public Affairs; Ivo H. Daalder and Michael E. O'Hanlon (2000), *Winning Ugly: NATO's War to Save Kosovo*, Washington, D.C.: Brookings Institution Press; Richard Holbrooke (1998), *To End A War*, New York: Random House.

6   Quoted in *The Economist* (2003), "L'Europe, c'est moi," 20 February.

7   Address by French Defense Minister Michelle Alliot-Marie (2004), "Renewing the Transatlantic Security Partnership," *Center for Strategic and International Studies*, Washington, D.C, 16 January.

8   Simon Serfaty (1999), *Memories of Europe's Future: Farewell to Yesteryear*, Washington, D.C.: Center for Strategic and International Studies, 131.

9   For a more detailed analysis of the European Security and Defense Policy, see Robert E. Hunter (2002), *European Security and Defense Policy: NATO's Companion—or Competitor?*, Washington, D.C.: RAND.

10 Robert E. Hunter (2003), "Europe's Leverage," *The Washington Quarterly*, Winter 2003–04: 98.

11 Kissinger, *Does America Need a Foreign Policy?*, 59.

12 "Against America? Moi?" In a poll taken a week before the US-led invasion of Iraq in March 2003, 69 percent of a sample drawn from the French population indicated they believed France should veto any UN Resolution authorizing the use of force against President Saddam Hussein's regime.

13 Alliot-Marie, "Renewing the Transatlantic Security Partnership."

14 In 2004, 10 new members will formally join the European Union (EU), including eight situated geographically within Central and Eastern Europe and the Baltics.

15 Simon Serfaty (2003), "EU-US Relations Beyond Iraq: Setting the Terms of Complementarity," *Euro-Focus* 11 April, online at www.csis.org/Europe.

16 *The Economist* (2004), "Happiness is Doing Things Together," *Economist*, 6 March.

17 George W. Bush (2002), "President's Remarks at the United Nations General Assembly," New York, White House, Office of the Press Secretary, 12 September.

18 US, White House (2002), *National Security Strategy of the United States*, Washington, D.C., GPO.

19 Condoleezza Rice (2002), "2002 Wriston Lecture at the Manhattan Institute," *White House Office of the Press Secretary*, New York, 1 October.

20 United Nations (UN) Security Council (2002), "UN Security Council Resolution 1441," *UN Press Office*, 8 November.

21 "Against America? Moi?"

22 *The Economist* (2003), "The Cold Calculation of War," *Economist*, 3 April.

23 *The Economist* (2003), "It's Not Easy Being French," *Economist*, 3 April.

24 Colin Powell (2004), "A Strategy of Partnerships," *Foreign Affairs*, 83 (1) January/February, 25–26.

25 Robert Kagan (2004), "America's Crisis of Legitimacy," *Foreign Affairs*, 83 (2) March/April, 83.

26 Clark, *Waging Modern*, 423.

Chapter 2

A Changing View of Responsibility?
German Security Policy in the
Post-9/11 World[1]

Scott Brunstetter

Introduction

In the decade since the end of the Cold War, no other Western European country's security policy has evolved more than Germany's. From Cold War dependence on the US and NATO, German security policy is now reflected more in self-confidence and resilience. Though Germany's security policy nexus incorporated in a number of issues, including proliferation, international crime, and conventional disarmament, the evolution of Germany's stance on the deployment of its armed forces in out of area operations was by far the most reflective of change. Since abstaining from participation in the 1991 Gulf War, Germany has become a regular and important participant in international military operations.

Over the course of this evolution, Germany developed and nurtured its own concept of international responsibility in the context of military operations. Based on its history and the entangling alliances of the West, this idea led to slow, deliberate steps toward greater German participation. Beginning with unarmed personnel in Somalia and then armed peacekeepers in Bosnia, by the time of the Kosovo crisis, Germany actively participated with combat troops and commanded a peacekeeping sector. Today Germany is keenly aware of its strongly developed international responsibility for international crises requiring military action.

Since the 9/11 terrorist attacks against the US, the German approach to international military operations has varied. It contributed a significant number of troops to the war against Al Qaeda and to the peacekeeping mission in Afghanistan. Yet, Germany later chose not to participate in Iraq, with an absolute rejection of military force as a viable alternative. This shift, furthermore, led to considerable consternation in the German-American relationship, as Chancellor Schröder's pledge of 11 September 2001 of "unlimited solidarity" faded into outright criticism by late 2002. As such, it is useful to ask whether Germany's adherence to the idea of international responsibility and coalition partnership has changed since 9/11.

German Security Policy from Unification to 9/11

The ten year progression in the out of area debate from absolute detachment during the 1991 Gulf War to the deployment of over 10,000 troops by 2003 was an *"ad hoc"* improvisation, in large part because of its newness in German postwar history.[2] The move from the euphoria of the end of the Cold War to the acceptance of the harsher realities of the Post Cold War era was a long and "difficult" period for Germany,[3] especially for the young, pacifist leaning Green Party.

An Evolving Stage

No discussion of modern Germany would be complete without evoking the nation's turbulent past. Indeed, since the end of the Cold War, history, or "collective memory," has been one of the key factors in explaining the evolution of modern Germany's security policy. Memories provide a "lens through which the past is viewed" and in many respects are the "foundation stones for contemporary ideologies."[4] Shadows of the past can be both positive and negative, which in turn can have constructive or destructive effects. Indeed, Germany's past continues to "cast a large, inescapable shadow" over German security policy in particular.[5] In general, there is considerable unanimity that Germany's past both constrains and facilitates modern German security policy.[6]

Shortly after the end of the Second World War a distinct historical narrative rejecting the violence of Nazism and turning toward western integration emerged.[7] Germany's destruction that ended the Second World War has long been seen by scholars in connection with the creation of the disdain for war among its leaders and population. The defeat "dealt a lethal blow" to those in German society who favored military practices. Out of the ashes of defeat, a "culture of restraint" developed that acted as an inhibitor on the use of German military forces for anything but self-defense.[8] Within the Left, particularly in the later Green Party, the axiom "never again war" gained prominence. For all political parties, the idea of unilateral military invasion was foresworn based on the memories of Germany's past.[9]

In its place, the concept of multilateralism became the watchword. Construed by many in Germany as the manifestation of the break with the violence of its past, there was a broad political consensus for the adherence to its tenets as a guiding principle of German foreign and security policy.[10] In practice, multilateralism meant that Germany's security policy was intertwined with that of others. Military action was possible only as part of an international institutional, such as in a NATO or UN sanctioned operation.

Germany's defeat in the Second World War also precipitated a sense of malleability that redefined German attitudes about security through new positive experiences.[11] The vacuum of defeat was soon supplanted by over forty years of successful integration into the West and interstate cooperation that would have as profound an effect on Germany as its defeat in the war. Beginning with Konrad Adenauer's early decision to integrate in the West, Germany made conscious efforts to change. Reconciling with erstwhile enemies[12] and integrating within European institutions were active measures designed to create a new view of security for the European continent. Continued German integration in institutions has helped to create a common identity within Europe,[13] providing a foundation for Post Cold War actions[14] based on common approaches and mutual cooperation.

Germany's Developing Responsibility

From the early stages of the debate on German participation in out-of-area military operations and especially as NATO officials openly discussed the worsening situation in the war-torn Balkans, the concept of *Verantwortung* (responsibility) become a prominent feature. In this context, international responsibility referred largely to active participation, most commonly with troops, when such crises emerged.

As Germany's debate evolved, the institutional effects on proper conduct of a state often translated into definitive impacts on policy. International institutions, as some scholars argue, can define what actions are appropriate for member states to take. Constructed rules, shared beliefs, and principles of institutions often provide an understanding of what is important and what the appropriate and legitimate means are to obtain these goals. Institutions help to define the limits of legitimate action and in turn provide a sense of direction for a state.[15] States will accept these rules in order to avoid the costs of being seen as an unreliable partner or a state with a poor reputation.[16] Acting outside of the confines of the institution's goals could bring significant negative consequences.

For Germany, the concept of responsibility was closely linked to one of the defining aspects of its foreign policy – the desire to be seen as a reliable and calculable partner.[17] As the Cold War ended and Germany unified, becoming the largest state in central Europe, latent fears of a powerful and resurgent Germany surfaced amid many of its neighbors. Rejecting an active role in European institutions could actually run counter to German interest, thus endangering its stature in Europe.[18] Remaining intertwined in institutions such as the EU and NATO helped to preserve stability and was thus a vital German interest. Indeed, both Chancellor Kohl and later Chancellor Schröder framed the necessity of becoming involved in international crises as part of Germany's desire to be seen as a reliable partner.[19]

Throughout the evolving debate German leaders often spoke of this developing responsibility. As early as the end of 1990, Chancellor Helmut Kohl (CDU) was already noting the increasing expectations for German responsibility in international security. In a 1991 speech in the German Parliament, Kohl noted that it was "correct" that others awaited a stronger German engagement. As the situation worsened in Bosnia, Kohl continued to call for German responsibility, arguing that Germany could no longer stand idly by as others acted. By 1994, he argued that Germany "wants and must accept responsibility alongside our partners and friends" and called for a reform of the Bundeswehr to permit it to act outside the confines of self-defense.[20] Indeed, the move to a greater German responsibility was one of the main arguments used by the government in presenting its case before the German Constitutional Court in 1994.[21]

As Chancellor Schröder (SPD) assumed power in 1998, the already developed air of German responsibility in international affairs remained, embodied in his notion of continuity and represented by his support for NATO operations in Kosovo. He argued that Germany had "come of age" and was ready to assume responsibilities without hesitation. One month after the 9/11 terrorist attacks, Schröder clarified the new German responsibility, arguing Germany must be prepared to undertake responsibilities outside of Europe.[22] Even amid the Iraqi crisis, Schröder still spoke of a "responsibility for peace," noting Germany's continued deployment of troops in support of the war against international terrorism, while at the same time aiming for a peaceful solution in the Gulf.[23]

The process of developing this German perception of responsibility arose out of a fierce debate among Germany's major political parties.[24] The right-leaning CDU/CSU believed in the need for a more assertive foreign policy, though tempered by the context of multilateral relations and continued cooperation. They argued Germany should participate in the "full range" of military operations that could be authorized by the UN and also recognized the possibility that Germany could participate in military operations authorized by a European organization, such as NATO. The appearance of new challenges to European security, a new German responsibility in the wake of German unification, and a desire for influence in international politics in the name of German interests were given as reasons for this view. In hindsight it is quite clear that the Kohl government was one of the key influences driving the overall evolution in the German stance on out of area operations.

The FDP, like the CDU/CSU, recognized the need for rethinking German foreign policy given the changes since the end of the Cold War and offered similar reasons. Unlike their more powerful partners, the FDP was more hesitant on German participation for both political and legal reasons. They believed that the German Basic Law largely prohibited participation in out of area operations. As such, the FDP was the leading figure in the movement to change German law to permit out of area operations with the approval of the German Parliament.[25]

The left side of the spectrum was rather hostile towards an assertive German security policy. Early on, the SPD championed a much broader perspective of security that primarily encapsulated non-military parameters. Their evolution from a Party that supported only strict UN Chapter VI peacekeeping operations to a broader acceptance of out of area operations, such as in Kosovo and the war against terrorism, has been fraught with sharp debate.[26] Though not as adamant as the Greens or the PDS, the SPD has clearly sought to limit the use of force in international relations and provide security through other means. Indeed, the clear differences between the policies of the Kohl government and those of Schröder provide an excellent illustration of this perspective.

The Greens had by far the fiercest debate on out of area operations. For them, foreign and security policy has always been a "difficult relationship."[27] Since unification the Greens have moved from a party of strict pacifism to one that will accept the use of force in certain situations. The Party was confronted with this debate in earnest when the genocide in Bosnia continued unabated. The two dictums of the Party, pacifism and avoiding genocide, were in essence directly opposed to one another. Shortly after the Srebrenica massacre, party leader Joschka Fischer in a 30 July 1995 letter publicly called for active NATO intervention to quell the violence, which set off a firestorm within the Party.[28]

The evolution of the Party away from absolute pacifism was based on two primary factors – reactions to external shocks and a desire to become a part of the governing coalition with the SPD. The shocks of the war in Bosnia, especially the massacre in Srebrenica, and the genocide in Kosovo forced many in the Party to rethink their views on strict pacifism. That personal reevaluation worked in cooperation with a conscious desire by many, especially Joschka Fischer, to move the Party to a position where it could join the SPD in a governing coalition. In particular that meant moving away from pacifism and accepting international responsibility in military operations, as interviews and internal SPD documents demonstrate.[29] Without such a move, the SPD would never join into a coalition with the Green Party. As such, the Green Party's stance on out of area operations became inexorably linked to its domestic goals, such as environmentalism, education, and women's rights. In order to be in a position to pursue those goals, which required being a partner in the ruling coalition, the Party had to change its pacifist approaches.

The acceptance of German participation in out of area operations within the Green Party is, however, far from unanimous. While many at the federal level are more akin to accept this responsibility, the grass roots of the Party has been much more focused on the founding principle of pacifism.[30] Indeed, at a party day discussion during the Kosovo debate, Joschka Fischer, the party leader and champion of active German participation, was hit in the ear with a projectile by a member of his own party. Later, amid the discussion on the deployment of German troops after the 9/11 attacks, several Green Party Members of Parliament endangered the governing coalition by opposing the deployment of German soldiers.

The public has been largely much more hesitant on accepting the use of force as a method of German security policy. In the early 1990s, there was at most a 25%–33% level of support among the German population for the use of German troops.[31] Peacekeeping operations have received considerable backing, however, since the mid 1990s. Indeed, that measure of support among the population rose from 71% to 93% between 1997 and 1999.[32]

Supporting combat operations, however, has elicited a more differentiated response. At the onset of the Kosovo bombing campaign, there was a clear majority in favor of the bombing, though in part because of a lack of an alternative. Interestingly, by the end of April 1999, 70% of Germans believed that the allied bombing should continue as long as was necessary.[33] Public opinion surrounding the German support on the war against terrorism returned to the trend of hesitancy. A majority of Germans, 57%, opposed German participation in Operation Enduring Freedom just before the Chancellor announced his decision to send German troops,[34] suggesting the population was not as willing as the German leadership.

That tentativeness among the population has remained strong even up to 2002, as a joint Chicago Council on Foreign Relations and German Marshall Fund of the United States survey demonstrated. Only 68% supported the use of troops to uphold international law, while 62% supported using such troops to destroy a terrorist camp. Interestingly, only 58% supported using such troops to "bring peace" to a civil war torn region, such as Kosovo. In all of these cases, German support for such operations was significantly lower that that in other European countries.[35] In general, though support has risen over the course of the last decade, Germans remain much more hesitant to use force than other states.

From Small Steps to Giant Strides

As German leaders celebrated the merger of East and West in October 1990, the newly unified state was confronted by its first security policy challenge – the international community's response to Iraq's invasion of Kuwait. The American led buildup and broad coalition to eject Iraq forced Germany to make a decision on whether to participate militarily. Suspicions of a remilitarization of Germany, a fear of an escalation of the conflict, as well as a desire to preserve the ongoing unification process that came to its fruition during the crisis were some of the reasons for Germany's hesitation. Eventually Chancellor Kohl decided that Germany would instead pay for the coalition and allow for the US to use its bases on German soil, rather than send troops.

Germany's approach to this crisis led to significant consternation with its fellow allies. Within NATO a feeling of doubt about the loyalty of Germany arose, as other states, especially the US, criticized Germany abstinence.[36] This "checkbook diplomacy," as it was termed, became a "point of change" according to Nina Philippi.[37] Germany could no longer so blatantly reject participation in such an international crisis without significant negative consequences for its image as well as its international status, especially in the West. Indeed, Volker Rühe, then Secretary General of the CDU and later Defense Minister, suggested that the Gulf War cast "a bright light on the need to redefine united Germany's international role, particularly insofar as [its] readiness to commit our forces beyond the NATO area is concerned."[38]

Shortly thereafter, Germany began to take on a broader role in international crises. Within two years of the end of the Gulf War, Germany had sent humanitarian peacekeepers with no combat capability to Cambodia and Somalia to assist the international effort. Both of these deployments were first steps in the so-called "salami tactics" of the Kohl government. By undertaking small, low-risk missions, the German government allowed for a gradual acclimation of such missions by the German population while simultaneously giving strong indications to its allies that Germany was interested in taking on a larger international security role.

Yet, it was the collapse of order in the former Yugoslavia that led to significant change in the internal debate. Amid the horrors of the Bosnian war in particular, discussions among political elites on the potential of German participation in out of area operations sharpened dramatically. The Bosnian conflict became a "point of pressure" (*Druckkulisse*) that led to change.[39] As violence in southeastern Europe raged, NATO began to intervene gradually. With the West pursuing intervention, Germany was forced to determine the legality of its possible participation in out of area operations.

Limited by the nebulous nature of the German Basic Law, politicians took the issue to the German Constitutional Court. Its July 1994 judgment recognized the legality of German participation in out of area operations within a collective security system, to include the UN and significantly NATO. It left the decision on the particulars of participation, however, to the German Parliament, whose simple majority was required to approve a deployment. With this verdict the discussion moved from its legal framework to a political debate, as parties displayed their interests and vied for predominance in the domestic sphere.[40]

As events in Bosnia worsened, particularly after the massacres in Srebrenica, the need to become involved, even with military force, became more pronounced. The internal political debate became even sharper, in tune with the heightened posturing from NATO. After the Dayton Peace Accord, German troops participated in the SFOR and later IFOR peacekeeping missions in Bosnia, with German government leaders arguing it was a means to prevent war rather than wage it. Such an argument helped to convince the Left Wing oppositional parties. Indeed, German participation in these peacekeeping missions was supported by a large majority of the Bundestag, including significant numbers in the SPD and Green Party.[41] Both SFOR and IFOR were "key phases" in the "process of normalization" of Germany's security policy. Indeed, their successes over the following three years were "critical" in Germany's development.[42]

Even as Germany remained involved in Bosnia, ethnic conflict brewed in another republic of the shattered remnant of Yugoslavia – Kosovo. Under the prodding of the US Clinton Administration, NATO began to pressure the Serbian government to cease its ethnic cleansing operation in Kosovo, underscored by the threat of attack. With its participation in the bombing of Kosovo in March 1999 Germany took part in an active combat operation for the first time since the Second World War. Agreed to under the Kohl government, it was eventually implemented by Chancellor Schröder's SPD-Green government, an event that was unimaginable even five years earlier. Though lacking a UN mandate, it was still within the multilateral framework of NATO and thus legal under the 1994 Constitutional Court decision. Theories as to why Germany took part range from the pressure exerted by the US to participate as a responsible ally to the moral based need to prevent another genocide.[43] As hostilities ended, Germany took a leading role in the peacekeeping effort, accepting the leadership of one of the zones in Kosovo.

Kosovo was, according to Hanns Maull, an "important step" in the evolution of attitudes toward the use of force, particularly for the SPD and the Greens. Rainer Baumann agrees, suggesting that Kosovo was just "another step" in the evolutionary process that had begun in the early 1990s. Nina Philippi argues, however, that Kosovo made it clear that the idea of rejection of military force has been replaced by the priorities of "solidarity" with NATO and the protection of human rights.[44] With these significant increases in the number of German engagements since the Gulf War, reneging on its international responsibility became increasingly difficult, if not impossible.[45] A little more than two years later, another significant break in Germany's conception of its responsibility would occur, as terrorists stuck at the heart of the transatlantic alliance.

"Unlimited Solidarity" – The German Response to 9/11

The 9/11 terrorist attacks against the United States shocked the world and fundamentally altered the security policy structures of many states. Germany, like most other nations, reacted with strong support for the US and unequivocal condemnation of the terrorists. State Minister Dr. Ludger Volmer (Greens) called it a new "zero hour in foreign policy," that was comparable with the end of the Second World War or the fall of the Wall. Several hours after the attacks, Chancellor Schröder called it a "declaration of war on the entire civilized world" and pledged Germany's "unlimited solidarity with the United States," words that are seldom heard from a German leader.[46]

Even on 11 September, it was clear to the German leadership that a German military deployment might be required. Several days later Germany supported the invocation of the NATO alliance self-defense clause, Article V, which provided that basis for NATO member states' assistance to the US. Moreover, Germany was one of the first nations to call the US and pledge its desire to become involved, even with military forces.[47]

Within days of the attacks, Schröder had begun to publicly allude to the possibility of German involvement. In a speech before the Parliament on 19 September he noted that Germany's involvement in NATO brought forth expectations, including possible active military support.[48] Over the next weeks, Schröder's constant rhetoric on the theme of possible military operations remained the same – they could not be ruled out and Germany had a responsibility to contribute. Other government officials likewise continued to speak of this possibility. Green Foreign Minister Joschka Fischer, for example, often used the rhetoric of responsibility. The prospect of paying, as Germany did during the Gulf War, was decisively ruled out.[49] By October, as the American military began its fight in Afghanistan, German flight crews on NATO AWACS aircraft were already being deployed to the US.[50]

The chance of German soldiers participating in the US led war against Al Qaeda, codenamed Operation Enduring Freedom, brought forth the likelihood of a difficult decision for Germany. Its history of warfare made any decision to take part in a war difficult. Participating in active combat operations outside the context of humanitarian operations, as had been the case with the Kosovo war, would be a new step forward in Germany's use of its military. The CDU/CSU faction leader Friedrich Merz noted in a Bundestag session on 19 September that Germany must now be prepared to go "new and possibly uncomfortable" ways. Joschka Fischer expressed similar sentiments on 26 September, believing the talk of solidarity with the US would lead to some very difficult decisions for Germany.[51] Perhaps in reference to the difficulty of such a decision, Germany also showed some restraint in its rhetoric, claiming that it was ready to undertake risks to fight terrorism, but was not ready to go off on an adventure.[52]

On 6 November 2001, amid some of the hardest fighting in Afghanistan, Germany was confronted with this difficult decision when Chancellor Schröder proposed the deployment of 3900 German troops in support of Enduring Freedom.[53] From the beginning, Schröder suggested that German troops would not take part in active combat. However, 100 of the troops later turned out to be Germany's elite KSK special forces, whose mission necessarily brought them into active combat situations. Schröder argued that Germany was fulfilling the expectations others had of it and doing what was "politically responsible in this situation." The deployment was, moreover, an expression of Germany's growing responsibility in the world." Importantly, Schröder noted that accepting such responsibility was "in Germany's interest."[54]

Within the German Parliament there was widespread support for this deployment. Indeed, both parties of the Opposition, the CDU/CSU and the FDP, supported it. Majorities in both the SPD and the Greens also pledged their backing.[55] Problems arose, however, within a few days, as eight Green Members of Parliament and twenty to thirty members of Schröder's own Party expressed their opposition,[56] enough that he would have had to rely on the Opposition to pass the measure. While normally this might not have been a problem, the Chancellor's inability to gain a majority with his own coalition on the deployment of German troops to Macedonia in August 2001 meant a similar result could endanger his ability to govern. In order to bring the members of his own coalition into line, he linked a Vote of Confidence on his leadership with the vote for German participation. In essence he presented the opponents within his own coalition with a choice – vote for the continuation of the SPD-Green Coalition or force new elections by opposing the deployment of German forces.[57]

In attempting to sway opponents, Fischer warned the Greens not to risk European security, while Schröder spoke of Germany's responsibility to act within the alliance.[58] By the time of the vote, most of the SPD opponents decided to support Schröder, leaving eight Green members opposed to the deployment. In order for the coalition to continue, four had to vote for the resolution.

On the day of the vote, 16 November, both Schröder and Fischer gave speeches urging coalition members to support the resolution. Schröder spoke of the necessity of the military side of the war against terrorism, even suggesting it was an important factor in opening the way for humanitarian assistance in Afghanistan. In framing the reasons for Germany's participation, he reflected often on the international linkage of this decision. It was about the "dependability of [German] policy." With it, Germany "fulfilled" the "expectations of its partners." Significantly, Schröder referred directly to his country's new responsibility: "With this contribution, the unified and sovereign Germany meets its grown responsibility in the world." Germany had become a partner in the international community with new responsibilities.

Joschka Fischer, who had always supported the decision to send German troops, chose instead to speak more about accomplishments of the SPD-Green coalition and the potential of the Green Party. His method of persuasion rested on recalling the merits of the Green Party's domestic agenda. He also evoked the necessity of continuing the efforts to prevent future wars through non-military means, a cornerstone of Green foreign policy philosophy. For Fischer, the vote was a "decision about the future of this country" (Germany).[59]

In the end, four of the eight Greens who had earlier expressed their desire to vote against the German troop participation supported the Chancellor to save to coalition. They knew they could not stop the deployment of the troops, given the level of support within the Opposition. For those on the Left opposed to the deployment, the only thing worse than the deployment of the military was the possibility of a conservative government. Even one of those who dogmatically opposed the German deployment noted that the preservation of the coalition became a central issue for the group of eight. After agreeing as a group to save the coalition the eight published an open letter outlining their rejection of the deployment of the German armed forces.[60]

Making their decision easier was a compromise that limited the deployment of German forces to Afghanistan and the immediate area. For many Greens and SPD members, the possibility that the US would later move against Iraq, which could possibly draw in German forces, became a central concern. An additional factor that likely influenced some of the opponents of the decree was the recent waning of the war in Afghanistan.

Shortly after the approval, German troops were deployed, with approximately 100 KSK special forces troops actively participating in combat operations in Afghanistan. Naval forces were deployed to the Horn of Africa to patrol the shipping lanes; medical transports were readied, and Fox panzers were deployed to Kuwait to help detect chemical, biological, or nuclear attacks in that area. By December, as the war had died down, Germany quickly agreed to contribute peacekeepers, becoming even further involved. Unlike the earlier suspenseful vote, there was little resistance to this deployment. Yet, within a few months of the collapse of the Taliban in Afghanistan and the near collapse of the SPD-Green German coalition, Chancellor Schröder was confronted with another challenge that would place the idea of German responsibility in the international realm in a new context.

Germany and the Iraq War

Even at the early stages of the Schröder government, the situation in Iraq had been problematic. Under his leadership, Germany chose not to participate in the US and British bombing of Iraq in December 1998 for expelling UN inspectors. Just over three years later, Iraq and its defiance of the international community' regarding weapons of mass destruction again came under renewed focus. This time, however, it was under the shadow of the 9/11 attacks, which had fundamentally altered the Bush Administration's perception of international security. President Bush's January 2002 State of the Union address clearly set the stage for a confrontation with Iraq, by including it as one of three nations that made up an "axis of evil."[61] Indeed, over the next 13 months the pressure would escalate, eventually embroiling the transatlantic alliance in its most serious crisis.

In the early months of the crisis, there seemed to be some correlation between the goals of the US and Germany. In a February 2002 speech before the German Parliament, Foreign Minister Joschka Fischer recognized the evils of Saddam Hussein and his attempts to defy UN sanctions. He argued, much like the US at this time, that Iraq must accept the sanctions and permit UN inspectors to return to Iraq.[62] The seeds of disagreement, however, were nonetheless relatively clear even at this point. Whereas the US spoke of war as a possibility, Fischer and other German leaders suggested that inspections, rather than warfare, were the answer.[63]

Though the approaches may have differed, relations between the two states and their leaders remained rather cordial. As Bush visited Berlin in May 2002, Schröder suggested US-German relations were in an "extremely healthy state," noting the common vision of the world situation, while Bush noted how "proud" he was of the US-German relationship.[64] However, the German population was already beginning to express its disdain for the US approach to Iraq. During Bush's visit, entire sections of the capital city were cordoned off and large demonstrations took place, calling for the US not to go to war against Iraq.

Three months later, however, relations soured considerably. By this point, the US had began to increase the pressure on Iraq and the possibility of war was growing. The turning point in US-German relations came primarily with German Chancellor Schröder's position change. In November 2001, Schröder had wanted to discourage the US from attacking Iraq,[65] yet by August 2002 he was actively campaigning against its possibility. Faced with election polls that overwhelmingly predicted his defeat in the September 2002 elections, Schröder gave a speech at an SPD party rally on 5 August proclaiming a "German way" that rejected participation in any "adventures." He promised that Germany would not support a possible war against Iraq with either money or soldiers. Moreover, the Fox panzers stationed in Kuwait under the Enduring Freedom mandate would also be withdraw in case of a war.[66]

In so doing, Schröder reached out to the majority of the German population in an attempt to gain momentum for the upcoming election.[67] Indeed, throughout the crisis Germans overwhelmingly opposed any war against Iraq. In a survey conducted in late September 2002, 95% of the German population expressed their opposition.[68] By early 2003, the German leaders on the Left almost unanimously opposed even the threat of the use of force, while few leaders on the Right even suggested they supported a war in Iraq. There were numerous protests in Germany opposing possible US led military action in Iraq. In the worldwide protests on February 15, 2003 Germans, including some political leaders, took to the streets in large numbers.

The Opposition and some members of the press, however, greeted Schröder's sudden change in August 2002 with criticism. Klaus-Dieter Frankenburger of the influential *Frankfurter Allgemeine Zeitung (FAZ)* suggested that Schröder did Germany "no favors" with his German way. Günter Nonnenmacher, one of the five editors of the *FAZ*, argued that Germany had returned to the "role of a dwarf" with Schröder's Iraq policy.[69] The Opposition rejected this "German way," believing it to be isolationist and harmful to Germany's predictability and reliability, which had driven German security policy. Indeed, in an op-ed article in *The Washington Post*, CDU/CSU leader Angela Merkel argued that Schröder "does not speak for all Germans."[70]

However, the CDU/CSU was also quick to avoid any appearances that they favored war, given the strong opposition among the population. Eventually, the CDU/CSU Chancellor Candidate, Edmund Stoiber, publicly expressed opposition to unilateral US action, even as his position on the participation of Germany soldiers continued to evolve. On 29 August, he made any German participation in a war against Iraq conditional on a UN mandate; two weeks later, however, he ruled out any possibility of German participation.[71]

The US acted quickly to Schröder's change of heart, for US officials were genuinely surprised. The manner of announcing this change, amid a tight political election, led to some consternation. The US Ambassador to Berlin Daniel Coats sent a clear message to Germany – that the US was beginning to doubt its ally, especially in its role in the war on terrorism. He even warned of possible German "isolation" within Europe. Former Clinton advisor Ronald Asmus weighed in with a translated op-ed in the *FAZ*, calling Schröder's policy a "new German irresponsibility."[72]

Relations between the two hit rock bottom just before the 22 September election when the German Justice Minster reportedly compared the politics of George W. Bush with Adolf Hitler at a local meeting. Secretary of State Colin Powell called his counterpart Joschka Fischer to complain, while the German Opposition called for the Minister's resignation. President Bush apparently was quite furious with the comments. This apparent comparison personalized the intense disagreements between the ruling German coalition (SPD-Greens) and the US. After Schröder's victory in the election, in a major diplomatic snub, Bush did not call the reelected Chancellor. Several months later, in January 2003, US Secretary of Defense Donald Rumsfeld made his now infamous reference to Germany and France as "old Europe" that only cemented this negative personalization.

In the end, this spiraling angry personalization made the possibilities of finding a unified approach toward the Iraq crisis between the transatlantic partners in general and the US and Germany in particular all but impossible. As the international community continued to speak of a unified approach to Iraq, Saddam Hussein watched as once solid alliances began to crumble.

Throughout the fall of 2002, pressure continued to build, especially after President Bush's call on the UN in September to confront Iraq. On 8 November the UN Security Council unanimously passed Resolution 1441 giving Iraq one final chance to prove that it was serious about adhering to international accords. It gave Iraq an early test, forcing it to submit a declaration to the UN within thirty days outlining its weapons program. While this resolution suggested international solidarity, in fact it sharpened the debate even more.

By late 2002 two general approaches had emerged. A hard line view that openly included the threat of force, led by the US and Britain together with some European countries, was countered by an approach steeped in diplomatic rhetoric and largely opposed to the use of force, led by France, Germany, and Russia. The personalization endemic of the German-American debate was also reminiscent of other relationships, especially between the US and France. Given these vastly different approaches, the Iraqi reactions to the November UN resolution were necessarily seen through different prisms, thus framing the two sides' views as to whether Iraq was complying.

In early December, Iraq submitted its report to the UN. While the US side saw it as grossly inadequate, leaders of the other camp saw it as a first, positive step. The lines of the debate were now very clear. The primary difference between Germany and the US thus focused on how effective inspectors could be in disarming Iraq. From the US perspective, Iraq had not complied with the inspectors, leading it to believe that continued inspections had little worth, while Germany believed Iraq's agreement to permit the return of international inspectors was a positive step and thus sought to give the inspectors more time.

The debate between the two approaches came to a boil in February 2003, as the UN Security Council met to discuss the earnest situation. Countries sent Foreign Ministers and the US Secretary of State, Colin Powell, laid out the US argument on Iraq's lack of compliance in a one hour presentation. German Foreign Minister

Joschka Fischer suggested in his speech that Iraq still had much to do before being in compliance with UN resolutions. However, he focused on the positive results from the inspectors, suggesting that the threat from Iraq had been "effectively reduced" with their return. Inspectors now had to be strengthened to give them a greater chance of success. For Germany, as well as France and others nations, diplomacy had not reached its end; military methods were not necessary at the moment.[73]

On the very eve of war, German Foreign Minister Fischer argued on 19 March 2003 before the UN Security Council, in a similar vein from his earlier speech, that alternatives remained before military force should be used. Though Iraq had not yet been fully compliant, he asked rhetorically whether that was worth the disastrous results of a possible war. Germany knew of such consequences and wished to avoid them. With little support from the home front, he argued that inspections needed to be continued, rather than resorting to war in March.[74] After the war began on the night of 19 March 2003, Germans took to the streets in planned protests. A peace camps was erected in front of the US Embassy in Berlin, which remained for the duration of the war. As coalition forces went into battle, overwhelming numbers of Germans and their leaders clearly rejected the war.

An Eye to the Future

Born amid the ashes of the Second World War, the US partnership with Germany has seen some monumental events that have led to profound changes. The collapse of the Wall and the dissolution of the Soviet Union altered the security landscape in Europe and brought in new partners from Eastern Europe. Since then Germany evolved, taking on more international responsibility, becoming in essence a normal partner. The events of 9/11 shattered the complacency of the so-called Post Cold War era and placed a new challenge on Germany's international responsibility. Similarly, the Iraq crisis evoked startlingly different challenges and illustrated new thoughts on the limits of German responsibility.

A New German Responsibility

Since the end of the Cold War, the changes in Germany's approach to security policy have been dramatic. From a nation dependant on others for its security in the Cold War, Germany has evolved into a responsible partner in international security. Though difficult, the decade long internal debate on the deployment of German forces outside of the NATO area was successful. External events that shook long held beliefs, internal political decisions, and subtle external pressure all contributed to this evolution. As a result, Germany now has approximately 10,000 troops deployed in the Balkans, Afghanistan, in support of Operation Enduring Freedom, and in other areas.

The most important leitmotif of Germany's evolution and in its debates over the past several years has been its acceptance of the concept of international responsibility. Germany's position within NATO essentially compelled it to act, out of subtle pressure from member states. An internal desire to be seen as dependable and predictable helped push Germany's acceptance of greater responsibility. Similarly, the drive for more influence, which by definition required a greater participation in international actions, fueled this move. Indeed, both Chancellors Kohl and Schröder have evoked this concept to further German participation. In the end, the "rhetoric of responsibility," especially from the CDU/CSU but later also from the SPD and the Greens, was used to pave the way for significant evolutions in the debate on the use of force.[75]

Germany's history, which is never far from any discussion of its security policy, likewise had an impact on the evolution. For example, the decision to participate in the active combat phase of the Kosovo campaign was in part fueled by a desire to prevent genocide, a lingering lesson borne out of the Second World War. Similarly, memories of what the US had done to protect Germany in the Cold War were prominent in the debate on German participation in Operation Enduring Freedom.

With the 9/11 terrorist attacks, the already developed idea of German responsibility stretched to a new limit to encompass the new threat levels that had become clear. Whereas the earlier debate had resulted in out of area deployments limited to Europe, the war on terrorism required German troops half way around the world. Now the rhetoric of responsibility merged with the vivid shocks of the events in New York and Washington. Leaders from all political parties framed the deployment of German military forces in the context of the nation's international responsibility.

Though small groups in the public spoke out against German participation in any war, a clear majority of German leaders in the Parliament, the Vote of Confidence notwithstanding, supported the deployment of German forces. Such backing suggests a strong acceptance for this new step forward in Germany's international responsibility among Germany's leaders. The extension of this deployment's mandate, even amid the acrimonious debate over Iraq, suggests moreover that German leaders are not likely to renounce this new aspect of Germany's international responsibility.

With the deployment of 3900 troops in support of Enduring Freedom, Germany solidified its role as a responsible, global player. Karl Kaiser, the former Director of the German Council on Foreign Relations, argues that the events in the wake of 9/11 led to the third "great reorientation of postwar Germany," leading Germany to assume responsibility in the "context of global strategies." It was "at last stepping out of the shadows of World War II and assuming its role as a functioning democracy with global responsibilities."[76]

The crisis with Iraq, however, evoked a different reaction from German leaders as well as the public. Without a distinct shock to react to, such as genocide or terrorist attacks, the feeling of urgency faded. Germany had never viewed Iraq with a sense of urgency similar to the US. After 9/11 that gap in threat perceptions widened even more. Moreover, while German leaders were able to overcome some minor public disapproval of German deployment in the war against terrorism, the overwhelming public disdain for any war in Iraq, let alone German participation, effectively limited the options of the government.

Germany's decision not to support the war against Iraq in March 2003 was *not* an absolute rejection of its international responsibility, nor was it an indication of a changed conception of responsibility. As the crisis in Iraq became increasingly serious and war clouds loomed on the horizon, Germany did not simply retreat to isolation during the crisis; instead it became an active and confident participant. Speeches from German leaders often recognized the necessity of confronting Iraq, yet hesitated on the question of military force. It supported the unanimous Security Council in November 2002 vote to force Iraq to disarm and open itself to inspections again. At the height of the crisis, Schröder spoke of Germany's "responsibility for peace,"[77] which in German terms meant pushing diplomacy and giving UN inspections more time before entertaining the possibility of invading Iraq.

The intense personalization between the two approaches to the Iraq crisis, especially the deep disdain between US and German leaders essentially severed communications. This absolute division of allies on the approach to confronting Iraq essentially negated any subtle pressures from institutions and their member states that had previously helped to define and enforce the concept of international responsibility. Finally, there was a sharp disdain among Germans for any possibility of a unilateral, aggressive invasion of Iraq. Many Germans believed from the onset of the crisis that the US wanted to undertake such a war irrespective of international wishes.

Though some may suggest that Germany reneged on its international responsibility, in fact, Germany's position on Iraq is perhaps the best representation of its self-confidence and sovereignty in international security issues. History and international realties have coalesced to form a relatively clear policy on German participation that now incorporates military measures when required, but also limits their use when deemed inappropriate by the German government. Germany continues to support operations in the war against terrorism. Yet, there are some clear limits on German participation. Perceptions of aggressive warfare, especially when diplomatic methods remain, create harsh opposition in Germany in large part due to its history. However, when clear mandates requiring military actions exist, such as in response to an attack, German support can be quite swift.

What Now?

More than a year after the difficult squabble over Iraq, it is useful to speculate on the future of German security policy and the US-German relationship. For the foreseeable future, Germany will continue to participate in peacekeeping missions in the Balkans as well as in Afghanistan and in combat operations in the war against terrorism. Yet, economic woes and the limits of the German military suggest that Germany no longer has the capability to participate in any new missions.

A year after the invasion, the US-German relationship is also showing signs of renewal. The sour personalization between the two leaders that had defined the Iraq crisis, has begun to whither. Chancellor Schröder was invited to the White House in February 2004 and had a positive meeting. Indeed, the declaration following that meeting noted the "deep friendship" between the two, their common interests, and similar goals, especially in rebuilding war-torn areas.[78] Yet, it is clear that the future US-German partnership will never be as smooth as in the past. The recent improvements notwithstanding, the challenges faced in the world today, such as terrorism, the proliferation of weapons of mass destruction, and the Palestinian-

Israeli conflict, will bring similar trials to the US-German relationship. Future leaders, irrespective of political affiliation, must strive to maintain an active dialog and cooperate on common interests if this relationship is to be successful.

Notes

1 Significant portions of this chapter are based on or are taken directly from the author's ongoing dissertation at Old Dominion University, "From Green to Olive-Green."

2 Rafael Biermann (2002), "Deutsche Mitwirkung an der Konfliktbewältigung auf dem Balkan–Versuch einer Zwischenbilanz," in *Deutsche Konfliktbewältigung auf dem Balkan: Erfahrungen und Lehren aus dem Einsatz*, Rafael Biermann, ed., Baden Baden, Germany: Nomos Verlagsgesellschaft, 315.

3 Hans-Ulrich Seidt, "Führung in der Krise? Die Balkankriege und das deutsche Konfliktmanagement," in *Deutsche Konfliktbewältigung auf dem Balkan*, 40.

4 Andrei S. Markovits and Simon Reich (1997), *The German Predicament: Memory and Power in the New Europe*, Ithaca: Cornell University Press, xiii.

5 Thomas U. Berger (1996), "Norms, Identity, and National Security in Germany and Japan," in *The Culture of National Security: Norms and Identity in World Politics*, Peter Katzenstein, ed., New York: Columbia House, 355.

6 Arthur Hoffman and Kerry Longhurst (1999), "German Strategic Culture in Action," *Contemporary Security Policy* 20 (2) (August), 31–49; John Duffield (1999), "Political Culture and State Behavior: Why Germany Confounds Neorealism," *International Organization* 53 (4) (Autumn): 801; John Duffield (1998), *World Power Forsaken: Political Culture, International Institutions, and German Security Policy after Unification*, Stanford: Stanford University Press, 6; Markovits and Reich, 2; Thomas Banchoff (1999), *The German Problem Transformed: Institutions, Politics, and Foreign Policy, 1945–1995*, Ann Arbor: The University of Michigan Press.

7 Banchoff, *The German Problem Transformed*, 177. Banchoff is quick to note that this emergence was not without its difficulties as the major political parties in Germany, the CDU and SPD, each approached the interpretation of history from different perspectives. The necessities of domestic political gains required political parties to differentiate themselves from the other.

8 Rainer Baumann and Gunther Hellmann, "Germany and the Use of Military Force: 'Total War', the 'Culture of Restraint' and the Quest for Normalcy," in *New Europe, New Germany, Old Foreign Policy?*, 68. This is not to suggest that Germany became pacifist. Indeed, during the Cold War, Germany's new armed forces played a vital role in the defense of western Europe.

9 Nina Philippi (1997), *Bundeswehr-Auslandseinsätze als Außen- und Sicherheitspolitisches Problem des geeinten Deutschland*, Frankfurt am Main: Peter Lang Verlag, 201.

10 Banchoff, *The German Problem Transformed*, 3, 167.

11 Berger, 330–31.

12 Hans-Dietrich Genscher, Speech at the Deutsche Gesellschaft für Auswärtige Politik, Publication of Hans-Dieter Heumann, *Deutsche Außenpolitik jenseits von Idealismus und Realismus*, 4 October 2001. See also Ann L. Phillips (1998), "The Politics of Reconciliation: Germany in Central-East Europe," *German Politics* 7 (2) (August); Ann L. Phillips (2000), *Power and Influence after the Cold War: Germany in East-Central Europe*, New York: Rowman & Littlefield; Lily Gardner Feldman (1999), "The Principle and Practice of 'Reconciliation' in German Foreign Policy: Relations with France, Israel, Poland, and the Czech Republic," *International Affairs*, 75(2) (April).

13 See for example, Thomas Risse-Kappen (1999), "Collective Identity in a Democratic Community: The Case of NATO," in *The Culture of National Security*, 357–399; Mary N. Hampton, "NATO, Germany, and the United States: Creating Positive Identity in Trans-Atlantia," in *The Origins of National Interests*, 235–69, Glenn Chafetz, Michael Spirtas, and Benjamin Frankel, eds., London: Frank Cass.

14 Thomas Banchoff (1999), "German Identity and European Integration," *European Journal of International Relations*, 5(3), 259–89; Elizabeth Pond (1999), *The Rebirth of Europe*, Washington, D.C.: Brookings Institute.

15 Jeffrey T. Checkel (1997), "International Norms and Domestic Politics: Bridging the Rationalist-Constructivist Divide," *European Journal of International Relations*, 3(4), 477; Martha Finnemore (2001), "International Organizations as Teachers of Norms: The United Nations' Educational, Scientific, and Cultural Organization and Social Policy," in *International Institutions: An* International Organization *Reader*, Lisa L. Martin and Beth A Simmons, eds., Cambridge, MA: MIT Press, 92–3; Martha Finnemore (1996), *National Interests in International Society*, Ithaca: Cornell University Press, 15, 28.

16 Martha Finnemore and Kathryn Sikkink (1998), "International Norm Dynamics and Political Change," *International Organization*, 52(4) (August), 904; Beth A. Simmons, "The Legalization of International Monetary Affairs," in *International Institutions*, 307–36.

17 Duffield, *World Power Forsaken*, 43; Rudolf Scharping (1995), "Deutsche Außenpolitik muss Berechenbar Sein," *Internationale Politik* 8, 38–44; Michael Mertes (2002), "A 'German Way'?" *Internationale Politik, Transatlantic Edition*, 4(3) (Winter), 11–16.

18 Ibid.

19 Helmut Kohl, "Deutschlands Verantwortung in einer Veränderten Welt," speech on 18 April 1994, *Bulletin* 37 (28 April 1994): 330; Baumann and Hellmann, 76.

20 Philippi, *Bundeswehr-Auslandseinsätze als Außen- und Sicherheitspolitisches Problem des geeinten Deutschland*, 19; Helmut Kohl, "Unsere Verantwortung für die Freiheit," speech on 30 January 1991, *Bulletin* 11 (31 January 1991): 61–76; Kohl, "Deutschlands Verantwortung in einer Veränderten Welt," 330; Helmut Kohl, "Vierzig Jahre Bundeswehr–Fünf Jahre Armee der Einheit," speech on 27 October 1995, *Bulletin* 88, 31 October 1995, 854.

21 Duffield, *World Power Forsaken*, 208.

22 Gerhard Schröder, "Regierungserklärung von Bundeskanzler Schröder zur aktuellen Lage nach Beginn der Operation gegen den internationalen Terrorismus in Afghanistan," 11 October 2001, http://www.bundesregierung.de/dokumente/Rede/ix_59425_1499.htm, accessed 12 October 2001.

23 Gerhard Schröder, "'Unsere Verantwortung für den Frieden,' Regierungserklärung von Bundeskanzler Schröder vor dem Deutschen Bundestag zur aktuellen Internationalen Lage am 13. Februar 2003," 13 February 2003, http://www.bundesregierung.de/Reden-Interviews/Regierungserklaerungen-,11638.466959/regierungserklaerung/Unsere-Verantwortung-fuer-den-.htm, 3 June 2003, accessed 31 March 2004.

24 The less influential ultra left wing PDS has almost unanimously rejected any form of German assertion, particularly in military matters. Indeed, as of 2003, they remain Germany's only strictly pacifist party.

25 Philippi, *Bundeswehr-Auslandseinsätze als Außen- und Sicherheitspolitisches Problem des geeinten Deutschland*, 83, 101–02; Duffield, *World Power Forsaken*, 182–84.

26 Duffield, *World Power Forsaken*, 66, 77–78; Philippi, *Bundeswehr-Auslandseinsätze als Außen- und Sicherheitspolitisches Problem des geeinten Deutschland*, 112- 27.

27 Ludger Volmer (1998), *Die Grünen und die Außenpolitik–Ein schwieriges Verhältnis*, Münster: Verlag Westfälisches Dampfboot, 494–95.
28 Joschka Fischer, "Die Katastrophe in Bosnien und die Konsequenzen für unsere Partie Bündnis 90/Die Grünen: Ein Brief an die Bundestagfaktion und an die Partie," 30 July 1995, Bestand A- Winnie Hermann, Akte Nr. 99, AGG; Kerstin Müller, et. al. "Wohin Führt die Forderung nach einer Militärischen Interventionspflicht gegen Volkermord?: Ein offener Brief an die Mitglieder von Bündnis 90/Die Grünen," 31 October 1995, Bestand B.I.10 BuVo / BGST, 1994–1998, AGG.
29 Interview with Karsten Voigt (SPD), Coordinator for German-American Relations, 17 December 2001, Berlin, Germany; Interview with Andreas Körner, Staffer in the Department of Security and Peace Politics, Office of Winfried Nachtwei (Greens), 10 December 2002, Berlin, Germany; Karsten D. Voigt, "Die Friedenspolitik der Grünen: Zwischen Fundamentalismus und Halbem Realismus," September 1989, Y34, Archiv Grünis Gedächtnis (AGG), Berlin, Germany; Wolfgang Bruckmann and Karsten D. Voigt, "Verantwortbar und Regierungsfähig? Eine Kritische Betrachtung der Außen- und Sicherheitspolitischen Vorstellungen von Bündnis 90/Die Grünen," December 1994, Y81, 34, AGG.
30 Interview with Winfried Hermann (Greens), Member of the Bundestag, 20 November 2002, Berlin, Germany.
31 John Duffield, *World Power Forsaken*, 210.
32 Klaus-Peter Schöppner (1999), "So Dachten die Deutschen in April, Weiter so Deutschland," *Umfrage & Analyse*, no. 5/6.
33 Hans W. Maull (2000), "Germany and the Use of Force: Still a 'Civilian Power'?" *Survival*, 42(2) (Summer), 64; Schöppner, 32.
34 *Umfrage & Analyse*, no. 1/2 (2002).
35 The other European countries surveyed were France, Great Britain, Italy, the Netherlands, and Poland. See The German Marshall Fund of the United States, *Worldviews 2002: European Public Opinions and Foreign Policy* (Washington D.C.: 2002), 15.
36 Philippi, *Bundeswehr-Auslandseinsätze als Außen- und Sicherheitspolitisches Problem des geeinten Deutschland*, 75–76; 78.
37 Ibid., 68.
38 Cited in Duffield, *World Power Forsaken*, 181.
39 Christian Schmidt, "Der Bundestag als Feldherr: Die Parlamentarische Beteilung bei Einsätzen der Bundeswehr in der Praxis," in *Deutsche Konfliktbewältigung auf dem Balkan*, 104.
40 Duffield, *World Power Forsaken*, 207–11; Philippi, *Bundeswehr-Auslandseinsätze als Außen- und Sicherheitspolitisches Problem des geeinten Deutschland*, 52–58.
41 Duffield, *World Power Forsaken*, 216; Baumann and Hellmann, 75. By 2003, that support for strict peacekeeping operations has become almost universally solidified among German leaders. Winfried Hermann a self-described pacifist in the Green Party noted that hardly a Green would reject a peacekeeping mission. Interview with Winfried Hermann.
42 Rainer Meyer zum Felde, "Die Deutsche Mitwirkung an den Friedensmission in Bosnien und Herzegowina nach Dayton aus Militärpolitischer Sicht," in *Deutsche Konfliktbewältigung auf dem Balkan*, 58, 61.
43 Baumann and Hellmann, 75; Adrian Hyde-Price, "Germany and the Kosovo War: Still a Civilian Power?" in *New Europe, New Germany, Old Foreign Policy?*, 21–22; Günter Joetze (2001), *Der Letzte Krieg in Europa? Das Kosovo und die Deutsche Politik*, Stuttgart: Deutsche Verlags-Anstalt, 36–39, 59.

44 Maull, 56, 61; Rainer Baumann (2001), "German Security Policy within NATO," in *German Foreign Policy Since Unification: Theories and Case Studies*, ed. Volker Rittberger, New York: Manchester University Press, 174; Philippi, "Civilian Power and War," 65.

45 Ludger Kühnhardt (1995), "Germany's Role in European Security," *SAIS Review* 15, 125; Andrew Denison, "German Foreign Policy and Transatlantic Relations since Unification," in *New Europe, New German, Old Foreign Policy?*, 172.

46 Ludger Volmer, "Grundlinien der neuen deutschen Außenpolitik," speech before the "Politischen Forum Ruhr," 12 November 2001, http://www.auswaertiges-amt.de/www/de/infoservice/download/pdf/reden/2001/r011112a.pdf, accessed 18 March 2002; Gerhard Schröder, "Erklärung des Bundeskanzlers zu den Terroranschlägen in den USA," 11 September 2001, http://www.bundesregierung.de/dokumente/Artikel/ix_55734.htm, accessed 12 December 2001.

47 Bob Woodward (2002), *Bush at War*, New York: Simon and Schuster, 179.

48 Gerhard Schröder, "Regierungserklärung von Bundeskanzler Schröder vor dem deutschen Bundestag zu de Anschlagen in den USA," 19 September 2001, http://www.bundesregierung.de/dokumente/Rede/ix_56381.htm, accessed 21 December 2001.

49 "Der Terror und die Folgen;" "Kujat: Einätze gegen Terror möglich," *FAZ*, 8 October 2001, p. 4; Hans-Jürgen Leersch, "Berlin bereitet sich auf Teilnahme an internationaler Militäraktion vor," *Die Welt*, 5 October 2001; "Kämpfen statt Zahlen ist diesmal die Deutsche Devise," *Die Welt*, 2 October 2001, 2.

50 The deployment of German flight crews on NATO AWACS aircraft so quickly is quite significant, for the possibility of such a deployment to Bosnia in 1994 was what led to the court case before the German Constitutional Court. That they could be deployed with relative ease this time is yet another indication of the strong evolution Germany has undergone since 1990.

51 "Abmarsch in die Realität," *Der Spiegel* 46, 12 November 2001, 25; Joschka Fischer, "Rede von Bundesaußenminister Fischer vor dem Deutschen Bundestag am 27.09.2001 zu den international Konsequenzen der terrorischen Angriffen in den USA und ihren Auswirkungen auf die Außenpolitik der Bundesrepublik Deutschland," 26 September 2001, http://www.ausaertiges-amt.de, accessed 23 November 2001.

52 "Der Terror und die Folgen: Rot-grüne Regierung und Opposition sind sich einig in der Unterstützung der USA," *SZ*, 20 September 2001,13; "Konsequenzen aus den Abschlägen für Deutschland," 18 September 2001, http://www.bundesregierung.de/Dokumente/Artikel/ix_56164.htm, accessed 12 December 2001; Gerhard Schröder, "Regierungserklärung von Bundeskanzler Schröder vor dem deutschen Bundestag zu de Anschlagen in den USA," 19 September 2001, http://www.bundesregierung.de/dokumente/Rede/ix_56381.htm, accessed 21 December 2001.

53 Schröder suggested that the deployment arose out of US requests. However, some questions remain as to whether that was in fact a way to gain more public support. Responding to a US request could be framed more solidly in the context of responsibility and would limit any perceptions, particularly among the Left of Schröder's coalition, that Germany was becoming more militaristic.

54 Gerhard Schröder, "Regierungserklärung von Bundeskanzler Gerhard Schröder vor dem Deutschen Bundestag zur Beteulung Bewaffneter Deutscher Streitkräfte an die Bekämpfung des Internationalen Terrorismus," 6 November 2001, www.bundesregier-ung.de/dokumente/Rede/ix_62094_1499.htm, accessed 7 November 2001. Karsten Voigt, an influential SPD leader offered a partial explanation as to why it was in Germany's interest, arguing that only "military relevant" partners would have influence. See Gerold Büchner, "Nur Militärisch Relevante Partner haben Einfluss,"

Berliner Zeitung, 9 November 2001, www.berlinonline.de, accessed 10 November 2003.

55 "Union unterstützt deutschen Beitrag," *Frankfurther Allgemeine Zeitung (FAZ)*, 7 November 2001, 2; "Gerhardt fordert regelmäßige Konsultationen," *FAZ*, 7 November 2001.

56 Interview with Winfried Hermann.

57 Though the CDU and the FDP supported the deployment of German soldiers, they would vote no on a vote of confidence. Thus, in order to keep governing, Schröder had to attain a majority within his own coalition between the SPD and the Greens.

58 "Teil der Grünen nehmen Bruch der Koalition in Kauf," *Süddeutsche Zeitung (SZ)*, 9 November 2001.

59 Deutscher Bundestag, Plenarprotokoll 14/202, 202. Sitzung, 16 November 2001.

60 Peter Carstens, "Nein, aber Ja," *FAZ*, 21 November 2001; Interview with Winfried Hermann.

61 Of the three states mentioned, Iraq by far received the most attention with five sentences as opposed to one each for North Korean and Iran. See George W. Bush, "The State of the Union," 29 January 2002, http://www.whitehouse.gov/news/releases/2002/01/20020129–11.html, accessed 20 March 2004.

62 The inspectors had left in December 1998 after disagreements with the Iraqi government. In response, the US and Great Britain launched air strikes in an operation codenamed Desert Fox.

63 Joschka Fischer, "Rede von Außenminister Fischer zur USA-Irak Problematik vor dem Deutschen Bundestag, 22.02.2002," 22 February 2002, www.auswaertiges.amt.de/www/de/aussenpolitik/friedenspolitik, accessed 8 May 2002.

64 "President Bush Meets with German Chancellor Schroeder: Remarks by President Bush and Chancellor Schroeder of Germany," 23 May 2002, http://www.whitehouse.gov/news/releases/2002/05/20020523–1.html, accessed 20 May 2004.

65 "Schröder Discourages US From Launching Attack on Iraq," *FAZ (English Version)*, 29 Nov 2001, http://www.faz.com/IN/INtemplates/eFAZ/docinfocus.asp?rub={B1312000-FBFB-11D2-B228–00105A9CAF88}&sub={C09564E2–2C4D-463B-B607–3D580697DFC1}&doc={A7FD66E9–691D-4BF2-ADCD-7F80CD0C560C}, accessed 4 September 2002.

66 Gerhard Schröder, "Rede von Bundeskanzler Schröder zum Wahlkampfauftakt," 5 August 2002, http://www.spd.de/servlet/PB/show/1019519/Schröder%20Rede%20WahlkampfauftaktHannover.pdf, accessed 10 August 2002.

67 At the time, the discussion of the possibility of war was at best rather hypothetical since the international community had yet to act decisively against Iraq. Schröder, however, argued that Germany needed to make its stance this early because the day after the elections NATO would hold a summit that would "decide" the policy in Iraq. This argument was rebuffed both by the US as well as German military officers in the Defense Ministry. See "Militärs erbost über Schröder: Offiziere widersprechen beim Irak-Einsatz," 11 August 2002, *Frankfurter Allgemeine Sonntagszeitung*, www.faz.de, accessed 11 August 2002.

68 "Einigkeit in der Kriegs-Frage," *Die Welt*, 2 October 2002, http://www.welt.de/daten/2002/12/02/1002de360014.htx, accessed 2 October 2002.

69 Klaus-Dieter Frankenberger, "Kein Ersatz für Politik," 21 August 2002, *FAZ*, p. 12; Klaus-Dieter Frankenberger, "Deutscher Irrweg," 11 August 2002, *FAZ*, www.faz.de, accessed 11 August 2002; "Rückfall in die Zwergenrolle," *FAZ*, 14 September 2002, 1.

70 Angela Merkel, "Schroeder Doesn't Speak for All Germans," *The Washington Post*, 20 February 2003, A39.

71 "Auch die Union ist Gegen einen Amerikaischen Alleingang," *FAZ*, 29 August 2002, p. 1–2; "Kein Deutsches Engagement im Irak," *FAZ*, 13 September 2002, 2.

72 "Graben zwischen Deutschland und Amerika," *Die Welt* (online news ticker), 4 September 2002, http://www.diewelt.de/service/newsticker/ticker.htx?ressort = pol&special = &koop = 0&id = 4642969, accessed 4 September 2002; "US-Botschafter warnt vor deutscher Isolation," 4 September 2002, *SZ*, http://www. sueddeutsche.de/index.php?url =/deutschland/bundestagswahl/51717&datei = index.php, accessed 4 September 2002; Ronald Asmus, "Die neue Deutsche Unverantwortlichkeit," *FAZ*, 17 September 2002, 2.

73 Joschka Fischer, "Rede von Bundesaußenminister Fischer im Sicherheitsrat der Vereinten Nationen in New York am 14. Februar 2003 zur Lage in Irak/Kuwait,"14 February 2003, http://www.auswaertiges-amt.de/www/de/ausgabe_archiv?archiv_id = 4074, accessed 30 March 2004.

74 Joschka Fischer, "Rede von Bundesaußenminister Fischer vor dem Sicherheitsrat der Vereinten Nationen, New York, 19.03.2003," 19 February 2003, http://www. auswaertiges-amt.de/www/de/ausgabe_archiv?archiv_id = 4223, accessed 30 March 2004.

75 Baumann and Hellmann, 72.

76 Karl Kaiser, "German Perspectives on the New Strategic Landscape after September 11," 2002, http://www.aicgs.org/publications/PDF/Kaiser.pdf, accessed 4 June 2002, 4.

77 Gerhard Schröder, "'Unsere Verantwortung für den Frieden,' Regierungserklärung von Bundeskanzler Schröder vor dem Deutschen Bundestag zur aktuellen internationalen Lage am 13. Februar 2003," 13 February 2003, http://www.bundesregierung.de/Reden-Interviews/Regierungserklaerungen-,11638.466959/regierungserklaerung/Unsere-Ver-antwortung-fuer-den-.htm, accessed 3 June 2003.

78 "Das deutsch-amerikanische Bündnis für das 21. Jahrhundert: Gemeinsame Erklärung von Präsident George W. Bush und Bundeskanzler Gerhard Schröder am 27. Februar 2004," http://www.bundesregierung.de/artikel,-613898/Das-deutsch-amerikanische-Buen.htm, accessed 20 March 2004.

Chapter 3

Britain and Transatlantic Security: Negotiating Two Bridges Far Apart

Mary Troy Johnston

Introduction

In an age where global issues threaten the very survival of states, as a country with an enormous scope of contacts and a vast network of influence, Britain is better placed than most countries to confront threats that emanate from anywhere in the world. The legacy of Britain's past as a powerful country with connections to countries of equal and greater status serves it well; the irony is that connections to the increasingly distressed lot of 'failed states,' desperately poor and suffering states, some of them having become 'rogue countries,' in far-flung places, have become more important. Therefore, the traditional role of the United Kingdom, that of building bridges, is more necessary and potentially more "profitable" in geopolitical terms than at any time in the post-WWII era.

This chapter focuses on a particular pair of bridges that consist of the privileged relations Britain maintains with continental Europe and the 'special relationship' the country values with the United States. The Euro bridge is built on proximity, shared history, the EU legal regime that incorporates economic, political and, recently, security cooperation, and developing relations with the new democracies of Central and Eastern European Countries (CEEC). The Atlantic bridge is also built on shared history and spans all of the same areas of cooperation without the binding socio-economic policies common to EU member countries. Rather, it is characterized by an informal, even intimate underpinning and highly developed security cooperation. The most important security link between the two bridges has been NATO up to now.

Heretofore, Britain has been able to manage the transatlantic relationship to its benefit, serving as balancer. British leaders have even been able to trade off one relationship to enhance their influence in the other relationship, and the strategy has worked in both directions. The British are quick to admit, "This country's status as a leading member of the European Union adds to rather than detracts from its role as the premier ally of the United States." Britain has earned credit with the United States as a sponsor for US interests in Europe and around the world. After September 11, Blair logged incredible mileage in support of the War on Terror and in making approaches to countries, Pakistan, for example, with whom the UK could boast more historical knowledge than the United States. By the same token, successive prime ministers and politicians have served as interpreters of European perspectives to their counterparts in the United States. Partly owing to Britain's ability to play the various relationships while maximizing influence in world events, British diplomats are credited with superior skills. Even an observer as critical as former US Secretary of State Henry Kissinger prized Britain's abilities. She was, he claimed, an example of a country which, through the exercise of outstanding diplomatic skills, enjoyed more influence than her physical power strictly warranted.[1]

A tumult of events since the end of the Cold War has unsettled the balance Britain has worked for over half a century to maintain in transatlantic relations. This essay examines Britain's dilemma in trying to negotiate and reconcile two bridges far apart, the Atlantic and Euro bridges. What are Britain's security objectives in its relations with the United States and Europe? To what extent does each relationship contribute or conflict with Britain's security priorities? To what extent are the relationships mutually beneficial or mutually exclusive? Can NATO continue to play the role of unifying transatlantic security communities? Specifically, how is the balance of these relationships affected by a series of events that add fluidity to the security environment? What is the impact on Britain's position of the rethinking of security in Europe, including the inclusion of the CEEC in transatlantic security cooperation? How has Britain responded to new security threats, from genocide in the Balkans to the emergence of global terrorism as a major threat, in defining its central security relationships?

In answering these questions, this chapter examines the national security objectives of Britain and how they are served by the 'special relationship' and participation in the EU and NATO. What does the transatlantic crisis over going to war in Iraq suggest for the future of these relationships? In the final analysis, do the old bridges continue to have utility for Britain's security strategy in a dramatically changed security environment?

Changing Security Priorities

In an already radically changed security environment, Britain conducted its Strategic Defense Review (SDR) in 1998.[2] One of the main objectives at the time was to enable Britain to operate in a mobile, forward fashion, "to go to the crisis, rather than have the crisis come to us."[3] The difficulty of being able to pin down future threats had already become apparent. The previous decade had seen two major crises emerge without prediction, Saddam Hussein's invasion of Kuwait in 1991 and the crisis of the former Yugoslavia that continued throughout the decade. For that matter, the collapse of the Soviet Union in the previous decade had not been predicted. Therefore, the SDR was cognizant that it needed to place priorities in the context of "a changing world."

Despite the onrush of unanticipated events, many of the lessons learned reinforced familiar tendencies and confidence in existing structures. The tone of certainty can be found in the SDR's first statement of 'interests and goals,' "Our security is indivisible from that of our European partners [a reference to NATO's partner for peace] and allies. We therefore have a fundamental interest in the security and stability of the continent as a whole and in the effectiveness of NATO as a collective political and military instrument to underpin these interests. This in turn depends on the transatlantic relationship and the continued engagement in Europe of the United States."[4]

The report had a decidedly European emphasis, logical, considering insecurity in the Balkans, inherited concerns continuing around the former Soviet Union and the pending enlargement of NATO. Indeed, the SDR recognized a window "to maintain and reinforce the present favourable external security situation." The text continued, "We must consolidate the changes that have taken place in Eastern Europe," stating this as a "first requirement of our foreign and defence policy."[5]

The end of the century can be seen as the height of 'architectural planning' in European regional security as European leaders, eurocrats and national officials erected new security structures, merged and reformed old ones, and decided the fate of Cold War relics. Despite the fact that Britain had participated in the Gulf War in 1991, little was known at the time how much 'regional' security would come to represent outmoded thinking, along with many of the concepts, including deterrence and large defensive ground forces, that had served stability in Europe throughout the post-WWII period. Even the idea of architecture that represented stability to decision-makers at the time has since appeared a staid and stodgy approach, especially to military modernizers in the United States.

Whereas Europe was central to British security, it was Europe with the United States. The revitalization of NATO had succeeded despite the failure of the transatlantic relationship to find an early solution to the crisis of the Balkans and intervene to stop genocide. Before the ink was dry on the SDR, NATO would decide on its first military adventure and the first collective forceful humanitarian intervention in history in Kosovo where Europeans lined up behind US leadership, despite grumbling, and the United States tolerated their input.

The SDR reflected certainty that Britain's interests were worth defending in another region, "We have particularly important national interests and close friendships in the Gulf."[6] Of course, Britain's policy in the Gulf had a decade in which to unfold since the first War against Iraq in 1991, not to mention the UK had not withdrawn entirely from Iraq but patrolled no-fly zones in the North and the South alongside the United States. As for North Africa, Britain maintained an 'indirect' interest in the region.

1998 turned out to be a watershed year for British security, the result of a meeting Prime Minister Tony Blair had at St. Malo with French President Jacques Chirac. This marked the occasion when Britain decided to cooperate with EU plans to develop a security dimension. After having blocked this development, Britain sided with the efforts to give Europe an autonomous military capacity and the advent of Europe's Rapid Reaction Force. St. Malo redefined Britain's bridge to Europe, the weight of which had mainly been carried by NATO in military terms. The politics of this groundbreaking initiative were as important as the content and will be discussed later.

NATO's endorsement of the Defense Capabilities Initiative (D.C.I) in 1999 has also had an impact on military planning in Britain. According to Sloan, an experienced NATO observer, "The DCI, adopted at the Washington Summit, was designed to stimulate European defense efforts to help them catch up with the US Revolution in Military Affairs."[7] NATO's military intervention in Kosovo in 1999 had exposed the severe capabilities gap between the United States and its allies.

Britain became resolute in closing the gap and in leading NATO members to do the same, to convince the United States of the continuing military value and relevance of the alliance. Sloan reports, all of NATO did not share the same enthusiasm for the DCI which "had not been taken seriously by most European governments."[8]

In 2002, the British added a New Chapter to the SDR to incorporate lessons learned in the intervening military actions in Kosovo, Sierra Leone, and Afghanistan.[9] Of course, Afghanistan figured most prominently in new considerations. Although the SDR had put defense planning on the right track, especially in terms of thinking on the increased role for expeditionary forces and the need for greater spending, terrorism posed specific challenges. So did military cooperation with the United States, which the report refers to as Britain's "most important ally." The forward thrust of UK security, leaving behind a geo-specific emphasis, was again underlined, as well as the need for 'rapid reaction,' having learned "opportunities to engage terrorist groups may only be fleeting."

The New Chapter confirms the British remain intent on exploiting their comparative advantage, military capabilities that enable them to share the same battlefield with US troops, as few countries in the world are able to do. The combination of rapidly and dramatically changing technologies and the US willingness to make the financial commitment, so far, insure that only a handful of countries, if that many, will be able to qualify for war-fighting alongside the United States. Britain is making the investment in cutting-edge technologies that collect, process and disseminate intelligence in split seconds. New equipment is being integrated into command structures to shorten reaction time, such as that employed by both countries in 'strike and find' missions in Afghanistan to hunt down, target and eliminate elusive terrorists. Enlarging and effecting the so-called 'network centric capability' require the acquisition of a range of new items, including some 'big ticket' items, in order for the UK to hold its own beside the United States. The shopping list for the electronic battlefield ranges from unmanned aerial vehicles that collect intelligence, to information systems that, in turn, crunch information and communicate it to battlefield commanders, who, then order what has increasingly become, the 'precision strike,' all of this occurring in near-coincidence with the suspect activity on the ground.

A century's divide radically separates the prosecution of war, Kosovo-style, and combat against terrorists. As for the former, targeting was the subject of intense debate in NATO, a more centralized command structure prevailed, and the application of international law was the focus of lengthy multilateral discussions. At present, for the United States, intent on eradicating terrorism while it has the military advantage, all of this adds up to dangerous delay. The United States has found in Britain the same recognition of sea changes in the nature of military threats and the need to transform military approaches. Britain is modeling the United States' Revolution in Military Affairs (RMA), a neo-conservative blueprint that, although heatedly debated in the United States, bears the conviction of the Pentagon. Partly as the result of shared perceptions of security needs in a world changed, at once and forever, Britain has become the most willing member of the Bush administration's favored operational format, US-led 'coalitions of the willing,' which effectively seem to have left behind NATO combat operations.

The Renewed Atlantic Bridge

Britain's 'special relationship' is special because no other European country, or for our purposes, any European country, has a relationship with the United States that delivers the same benefits. When a new US president signals he is going to extend the benefits usually reserved to Britain to another country, the 'special relationship' is seen to be in decline by skeptics in the UK, the same ones who have long warned against depending on the United States.

Interestingly, the same fears were raised at the outset of the Bush presidency. UK politicians were quick to notice the new administration's interest in upgrading relations within the hemisphere, as the Commons Foreign Affairs committee deliberately noted in 2000,

> The President's earliest foreign visits were to Mexico and to Ottawa, while his first visit outside the Americas was to Madrid. As recently as 5 September, President Bush spoke of the United States as having "no more important relationship in the world than the one we have with Mexico."[10]

To the extent the relationship has waxed and wane according to the rapport US and British political leaders have been able to muster and maintain, the relationship is one vulnerable to politics, especially presidential electoral politics in the United States. This fact, to a certain extent, recognizes the power of the US president either to endow the relationship with the essence that makes it 'special' or to permit other countries to bask in the attention of the world's preeminent leader.

Besides the transitory element of the exchange of political favor between British and US leaders, the relationship has durable content in security terms. The relationship has also waxed and waned in response to dangers in the world, or rather, perceptions of danger in the world. In fact, as the contemporary security relationship was forged during WWII, maintaining itself through NATO during the Cold War, common perceptions of danger in the world renews the primal *raison d'être*. However, this is not to say that the two countries' perceptions always agree. For example, Britain did not join the United States' anti-communist fight in Vietnam. As for the present threat of global terrorism, both countries leaders, US President Bush and UK Prime Minister Blair, personally, share the conviction terrorism is the greatest challenge history has presented to them.

The current ideology of the 'special relationship,' that of good confronting evil and the sense of historical mission being understood by only a few, hark back to the Great War between democracy and fascism. The rhetoric both leaders utilize in relation to the terror threat has a definite Churchillian flourish. Oddly enough, memorializing wartime cooperation between the closest of allies, Blair presented a bust of Churchill, Bush's hero, on his first visit to the new American president. Blair embodies, by Bush's own estimation, so many of the qualities the president lauds. Loyalty, morality, and political realism, all exhibited by Blair, are in sync with the tone of Washington. That the British prime minister had to brave a course in face of so much dissent in Europe (read betrayal in Washington) to support the United States in Iraq moved the relationship beyond 'special' and renewed its exceptionalism.

For the usually pragmatic British, the security relationship has yielded numerous, measurable, advantages, but not without costs. In terms of individual self-defence, Britain has benefited from intelligence cooperation, the closest that the United States has had with any country. Indeed, since September 11 and US-UK military cooperation in Afghanistan and Iraq, the countries' intelligence communities have developed even closer means for cooperation.[11] The Commons Foreign Affairs Select Committee confirms "long-established mechanisms" that have been useful in the Afghanistan campaign, for example, "the placing of eighty British intelligence personnel in the United States Central Command headquarters in Tampa, FL."[12] This level of cooperation is no small gain in the war against terror as much as it depends on intelligence networks that span the globe. Furthermore, as long as the United States has superior technologies and has acquired capabilities in the collection of intelligence, partnership with the United States is critical if Britain wants to maintain an edge.

If Britain had to choose between cooperation with the EU and cooperation with the United States, EU advanced intelligence technologies compare unfavorably, although human intelligence compares favorably. The Kosovo bombing campaign shed light on this high-tech disparity, leading observers to recommend the EU bridge the gap. "The United States conducted over 90 percent of advanced intelligence and reconnaissance missions during the Kosovo campaign. Given the other demands on US intelligence capabilities, the EU would be wise to reduce this dependence, focusing its spending on tactical assets, such as unmanned aerial vehicles and AWACs aircraft."[13]

Britain is also well-advised to maintain independent capabilities lest the United States overstretches its resources in areas not of direct interest to the UK However, it is clear a delicate balance must be found, as a more efficient means to becoming independent may include drawing from US superior technologies.

Britain's first strivings for an independent nuclear deterrent have been explained in terms of getting the attention of the United States, "To be heard, she [Britain] had to be able to make a big bang too."[14] Determined to maintain the deterrent, which otherwise speaks to the limits of the 'special relationship,' the UK depends on the United States as a supplier of technologies and equipment, not to mention for a good price. This, too, may be a double-edged sword. Historically, the Macmillan and Eisenhower era marked a "restoration of Anglo-American nuclear cooperation, which had been abruptly terminated at the end of the war."[15] Successive British Prime Ministers have faced the same quandary former British Prime Minister Margaret Thatcher reportedly faced, "She had to keep the deterrent, but she could not afford to pay too much for it."[16]

The renewed nuclear threat from so-called 'rogue countries' seems to continue to justify nuclear-based defense. However, at the end of the Cold War with the nuclear threat in decline, it seemed that Britain could lessen its reliance on nuclear technologies. Removal of the nuclear threat has led to the removal of an important rationale for Britain's choosing the United States over other allies. By the same token, multiply the nuclear threat and, perhaps, overwhelm Britain's ability to cope individually and in exclusive partnership with the United States. The UK's commitment to multilateral arms control, one that is not shared at present by the United States, is a reflection of a more European approach to nuclear issues.

Enduring questions attach themselves stubbornly to the UK decision to remain a nuclear power. Can the country continue to pay for these technologies without cutting in too much to domestic spending, especially as costs of conventional warfare increase? Can Britain keep pace with rapidly changing technologies, especially in the new phase of National Missile Defence (NMD)? If the investment does not sufficiently reduce risks, British politicians will have difficulty convincing the public on nuclear spending. Indeed, the nuclear threat is more elusive and threatening than ever considering alternative delivery strategies, for instance, the nuclear device in the suitcase, and the potential inadequacy of nuclear defense technologies amidst proliferation. So far, it is the 'special relationship' that has helped sustain the strategy of deterrence. As nuclear powers move beyond deterrence, a host of difficult issues must be resolved. Deterrence had the advantage of equalizing the playing field by spreading out vulnerabilities, a situation that tends to promote consensus. To the contrary, the strategy of NMD, initially, is a strategy of individual self-defense although the benefits should eventually be shared. However, that the United States has, unilaterally and determinedly, in the face of opposition in Europe, made its own national preparations and put those ahead of allied nuclear defense planning is problematic. The scenario that easily comes to mind is one where the United States is enough defended that one of its enemies decides as an alternative to launch a nuclear attack against one of its, relatively, 'undefended' closest allies.

Theoretically, the asymmetry in power between the United States and Britain goes to the heart of whether the relationship is sustainable as one that is mutually beneficial. At what point do power relations become so unequal that Britain cannot conduct an independent security policy? At what point does the imbalance affect US interest in the relationship? These are questions that continental observers bring up often in light of their own experiences, especially in relation to NATO. Nonetheless, the asymmetry of the relationship so far has motivated Britain to try to close the gap through continuous military cooperation with the United States over the last decade beginning with the Gulf War. Indeed, when one considers the decision of the UK to stand by the side of the United States in Iraq in the context of over a decade of military cooperation, one can see the policy as an extension of previous policy, not to mention in accordance with the SDR's identification of the Gulf region as a strategic priority. Stated in theoretical terms, British and American elites had an identity of interests in Iraq even though their publics may have needed to be brought up to speed.

It must be remembered that the United States and Britain had been exchanging fire with Iraq since the first no-fly zone was created in Iraq in the North in 1991, initially with French participation; the French later withdrew and refused to join the zone added in the South. Ironically, Britain had used its 'special relationship' with the United States to convince the first Bush administration, intent on making a clean and quick exit from Iraq, to do something about Saddam Hussein's air assault on Kurds and Shi'ites who, at the end of the war and on the urging of Americans, had rebelled to overthrow the ruler. Thus, on the initiative of former British Prime Minister John Major, the first safe zone was established in the name of humanitarian intervention.

In political terms, the lines had already been drawn in the UN Security Council, responsible for maintaining the post-war sanction regime against Iraq. Throughout the second-half of the 1990s, the UN Security Council remained split between the British and US, in one camp, bent as they were on enforcing the sanction regime, and the French and the Russians, in the other. The deadlock concerned when and under what circumstances economic sanctions should be lifted against Iraq. In addition to political pressure, Britain and the United States had maintained military pressure on Iraq. Consequently, when the time for the second war approached, British and American militaries had developed enmity in clashes with Iraqis.[17] They had also secured advantages from their patrol of the no-fly zones. After the second war, Rear Admiral Snelson reported to the Commons Defense Select Committee, "Of course, right up to outbreak of conflict the coalition [principally, Britain and the United States] dominated that airspace because of Operation Southern Watch under UNSCR regime."[18]

After September 11, the British and Americans had also expanded their joint presence in the region. With the United States, the Royal Navy had set up a headquarters in Bahrain to support the military operation in the first phase of the war in Afghanistan. By the account of the same Rear Admiral, "The decision to establish this headquarters was a significant factor in the success of the UK maritime contribution to the Iraq operation."[19]

Indeed, Afghanistan proved to be a good training opportunity for Iraq. Brigadier Dutton makes the point to the Commons committee as to 'equipment performance' in Iraq, "most of this equipment was not unfamiliar because it had been acquired for the operation in Afghanistan the previous year."[20] Anticipating Iraq, Britain had been the preferred partner in Afghanistan. An informed journalist recounted, "Though some 80 countries had made offers to help [in Afghanistan], only the British would participate in the first wave of strikes."[21] Clearly, the temptation existed to continue with a winning strategy, to build in Iraq on the successes achieved in the war in Afghanistan, while much seemed to be in place. At least the success of the military campaign in Iraq reinforces the 'special coalition' prosecuting the next war together.

Clearly, the terror threat compels Britain to continue with its power ambitions whereas the Soviet threat, especially the nuclear dimension, justified the global thrust of its military policy in the past. However, if terrorism does not prove vulnerable to military defeat and if other security crises and threats assert themselves to create insecurity, Britain has alternative strategies to choose from and insurance in other relationships.

The Shaken European Bridge

Whereas the relationship with the United States symbolizes the power aspirations of Britain, the relationship with Europe symbolizes that Britain's security depends on collective defense. As early as the Defense White Paper of 1957, Britain had come to the reality that most of its military action would be "collective," "except the most 'bushfire' of operations."[22] Hence, the Atlantic bridge cannot be understood in isolation but as part of a strategy of building bridges to cover a more expansive network of security interests. In a wider context, the 'special relationship' serves Britain's primary interest of keeping the United States in Europe.

In the past, the chronic concern of Europeans, even the French, was that the United States would draw down its forces in Europe and focus its attention on other regions of the world. Frequently, politics in the US Congress reinforced this insecurity. For instance, during the worst moments of the burden-sharing debates in NATO, Senator Michael Mansfield presented legislation more than once to reduce US troops in Europe until Europeans did more in their own defense. These threats have not only been resurrected post-Iraq, they look as if they may finally come true. In the wake of disunity in NATO in face of Iraq and new security challenges, the Pentagon seems bent on restructuring forces in Europe, by as much as one-third.[23] Dempsey quotes a NATO official, "If anything, the troops taken out of Europe will be sent home." He adds, "From there, they will be sent on exercises or training missions to small bases established on a temporary basis in Poland, Romania or Bulgaria."[24] Although solid geopolitical and security reasons exist for moving troops forward to the CEEC and shifting to a lighter presence as large bases present an invitation to terror attacks, the underlying message is pronounced: 'Old Europe' can and must take care of itself.

The enlargement of NATO risked diluting the military dimension of the organization, as countries joined that were poorly equipped militarily. Donald Rumsfeld's delimitation of "Old Europe and New Europe" was insightful, but, perhaps, not in the way the Defense Secretary intended. Enlargement clearly changed the political balance in NATO and presented new opportunities for political and military coalitions. The CEEC countries that joined added an Atlanticist tilt which the United States was keen to exploit. However, NATO as a consensus-based organization, is paralyzed by division, even if one side of the divide has heightened Atlanticist loyalties. Whereas Rumsfeld correctly denominated the politics of NATO, he may not have carried through on his own logic, of what good is a dysfunctional alliance to the United States, or to Great Britain, for that matter. To borrow from EU conceptual vocabulary, if enlargement succeeded in 'widening' to the sacrifice of 'deepening,' the result is a detrimental one.

One way of correcting for the requirement of consensus in NATO has been to permit 'coalitions of the willing' to carry out actions as long as those member countries who do not want to join do not block the effort. In decision-making terms, their silence is not interpreted as a negative vote, which in NATO would, otherwise, be a veto. In this way, NATO was able to wage the bombing campaign in Kosovo, allowing for members of the Alliance for whom this was politically sensitive to opt out through silence. On one level, such coalitions enhance the functional level of NATO and correspond to the requirements military planners emphasize so much in the present security environment, those of flexibility and speed in reaction time. However, to the extent these formations are utilized not so much for reasons of military efficacy but to circumvent serious political opposition, they may be more of a fudge than a practical instrument, and they fail to provide the desired political legitimacy. This occurs when 'coalitions of the willing' cannot be mustered in NATO, and the United States has to resort to the so-called 'international coalition,' as it did in the war against Iraq. During the first Gulf War, NATO could not officially participate since it could not 'go out-of-area' at the time, a situation later remedied. However, NATO demonstrated the political will to participate and played an important 'unofficial role,' as the United States was able to avail itself of NATO assets. Therefore, the international coalition had as its core, NATO, unlike the recent coalition that prosecuted the second war against Iraq, a difference with a meaning, in that legitimacy problems have plagued the more recent US effort. Britain seems to have adjusted expectations as to the future course of coalitions. The public discussion of the New Chapter of the SDR took note that "Different military deployments with different roles will have different, and changing compositions." In addition, "We recognize the need to build and sustain military relationships on both a deeper and wider basis." The new reality also adjusts for the possibility of European-led coalitions, given the active role Britain has taken in the development of the ESDP.

In Afghanistan, the question of NATO participation was not one of political will, as NATO members fully supported the US self-defense action there; it was a question of whether the United States wanted to include NATO: "Although Washington eventually associated with its military efforts small numbers of cherry-picked European forces, and although NATO's contribution in terms of logistics and infrastructure was not insignificant, the Afghan War was anything but a NATO operation."[25]

As indicative of the new strategy of Washington, the Pentagon made it clear that command for Afghanistan would be centralized in that department, not in the White House. Even the United States' most trusted ally, the British Prime Minister, had to bow to the Pentagon, "more than once embarrassing Blair by delaying the deployment of British forces in the combat theater."[26] Afghanistan can be seen as a special case, as America's war. However, in the wider War on Terror, one would expect the effort to be more NATO-centric. Nonetheless, Rumsfeld again departed from previous norms "when he declared that the mission to defeat terrorism should determine the coalition rather than the coalition the mission."[27]

Whereas many Europeans believed that the 1990s had provided some useful architecture for collective defense, and the Kosovo experience, mistakes included, would yield lessons for future military cooperation, US decision-makers took away the lesson that 'unilateralism' better served its purposes. Indeed, US disappointment in the conduct of a 'negotiated war,' as Kosovo turned out to be, and the European contribution to it came home to roost in the Bush administration. The mismatch between US and European capabilities was eye-opening for both sides. The superior capabilities of the United States in conducting pinpoint strikes with accuracy also made the United States less tentative about the use of force. Kagan sums up well the differences in capabilities and attitudes Kosovo exposed:

> The effect of this technological gap, which opened wide over the course of the 1990s, when the US military made remarkable advances in precision-guided munitions, joint-strike operations, and communications and intelligence gathering, only made Americans even more willing to go to war than Europeans, who lacked the ability to launch devastating attacks from safer distances and therefore had to pay a bigger price for launching any attack at all.[28]

It seems the United States had already decided on a military strategy of 'shock and awe.' That is precisely the effect it had on Europeans; awed by the demonstration of new technologies, they were equally shocked by the insistence of the United States to escalate bombing while the allies suggested 'bombing pauses,' and by the seeming wrecklessness of the United States to rule out publicly the use of ground troops in the initial stages of the conflict.

After Kosovo, the prevailing wisdom, especially from the British perspective, was that NATO would be of no use to the United States if it did not bridge the capabilities gap. Scholars delivered serious warnings, "In one way the greatest threat to NATO is that the military forces of the United States and Europe will be unable to work together."[29] Despite all of the attempts to rescue NATO in the 1990s, it still suffers from being a dinosaur, from the US perspective. Staid and unshifting alliances based on complicated political consensus-building in respect of a legal framework – qualities of NATO that used to be valued for the stability they provided – do not seem to mesh with US security approaches. If the War on Terror is fought at the expense of NATO, Britain, even though its bilateral relationship with the United States may be shored-up, will have a hard time making the case that the transatlantic relationship counts as much for European security.

The US has more convincingly universalized the terror threat than other countries. In its framing of the war, the United States is fighting the war for all freedom-loving countries. British Prime Minister Tony Blair agrees that international interests are at stake, "This is not a battle between the US and terrorism, but between the free democratic world and terrorism."[30] It is arguable whether other European countries feel they are targets to the same degree as the United States. Kagan maintains,

> Europeans have never really believed they are next. They could be secondary targets- because they are allied with the United States- but they are not the primary target, because they no longer play the imperial role in the Middle East that might have engendered the same antagonism against them as is aimed at the United States.[31]

Besides, Europeans have their own security concerns that rival terrorism in terms of the scale of potential human destruction and economic disruption. It must be remembered that the genocide in the former Yugoslavia was Europe's 11 September, where the death toll mounted to the hundreds of thousands and the refugee crisis posed a direct threat to all of Europe, with a quarter of a million people streaming over borders. Whereas the United States peripheralized the crisis as a problem in the European 'backyard,' the British could not deny responsibility, nor could other EU members. A commitment to a security policy based on humanitarian objectives had already established itself across party lines in Britain. Elites in Europe convinced themselves that intervention was required "to stop the killing" along with prevention of the spread of a wider conflict, considering the history of the Balkan tinderbox. The crisis exposed the ill preparation of the international community and its primary collective security organizations, the UN and NATO. It also dealt a severe blow to transatlantic relations. The United States refused to join Europeans in a UN peacekeeping effort on the ground in Bosnia, Europeans refused to cooperate with the US desire to lift the UN arms embargo against Croatia, seeing as they were on the ground in the region. The arguments continued to mount. Finally, NATO took to the air to conduct punitive strikes against Serb positions and, effectively, along with a Croatian offensive, forced the Serbs to the negotiating table. How to respond to crises in the future figured large in security thinking throughout Europe, just as countering terrorism has for the United States.

Britain's change of mind on security cooperation in the EU can be understood in several contexts. Crisis management had raised to the top of the global security agenda in the previous decade. Certainly, the context of the revival of nationalist grievances with the collapse of the former Soviet Union held sway. Former Soviet leader Gorbachev, himself, had embraced the idea of giving the UN a rapid reaction force and, coincidentally, France and Britain earmarked troops to serve this purpose for the UN. The transatlantic friction on this issue stemmed from the United States aversion throughout the Balkan crisis to committing ground troops, either in a peacekeeping capacity in Bosnia or a combat capacity in Kosovo. Thus, British Prime Minister Tony Blair could defend his position that EU security plans were not meant to compete with NATO, as he was convinced the United States was not at all interested in policing the world. When Bush campaigned against nation-building while suggestions floated that a Bush presidency might draw down US stabilization troops in Bosnia, the message was very clear. Britain was as clear about its intention to intervene in the world, as the SDR puts it, "to do good." The British expeditionary force that went to Sierra Leone in May 2000 reflected that spirit, especially since the initiative was strictly British and brought no political advantage. Blair was the only one to respond to the call for help from UN Secretary General Kofi Annan for an intervention force to protect UN representatives and stop a rebel onslaught, which the British succeeded in doing.[32] The recent decision to pair with France in creating a joint rapid reaction force designated for crises in Africa shows how serious Britain is in finding ways to implement humanitarian and stabilization missions.

For most of the 1990s strengthening the European pillar of NATO had been the politically correct reason for EU security initiatives, and it was unquestionably the reason that predominated in British defense circles. By the end of the decade, the EU had its own reasons, without reference to NATO, which enticed Britain to closer defense cooperation. According to Boniface, "NATO is no longer the unique power multiplier for Great Britain. Europe is now perceived as a second one."[33] Observers may succeed in being derisory about Europe's military might, however, the enlarged EU of twenty-five will have muscle in a variety of fora and regions, owing to its numerical strength in international organizations and its ability to commit or deny financial resources in connection with its emerging foreign policy. Post-Iraq, the EU has flexed its muscles by being less than generous with financial assistance. As the United States has reconstruction contracts in Iraq to award, and has so far denied them to EU member governments who opposed the war, the EU has bargaining tools of its own.

Seeing as the EU succeeded in its goal of EMU, Britain does not have as much reason to dismiss plans for ESDP. As the United States left no doubt it was going ahead with NMD, the same can be said for Belgium, Luxembourg, France and Germany. An understanding has come about in Britain "that European progress is unavoidable, and the only choice consists of trying to have a leading role or being left standing on the platform as the train pulls out." Evidently, British leaders employed that reasoning in supporting the development of a planning cell for ESDP, the infant military "headquarters" the United States had clearly opposed as a duplication of NATO structures.

As important, Britain has foreign policy goals it has negotiated in common with other EU member countries, goals that to be credible need to be linked to a security policy. EU foreign policy is still subject to unanimous agreement, and that agreement has been more in evidence in the Middle East than elsewhere. The EU has committed itself to working for the Middle East peace process in a series of 'joint actions' that have entailed election monitoring and assistance and training to Palestinian police forces. Of the different means available to the Common Foreign and Security Policy (CFSP), joint actions are considered to be the 'strongest instruments.'[34] Once initial agreement is achieved at the level of EU heads of government for a joint action, it is up to the EU presidency to implement the 'bindin' policy. Britain can be seen working within an EU framework developed since the early 1980s and fulfilling its EU obligations when it stresses with the US president the priority that should be given to the Middle East peace process. Britain was fully on board when EU heads of government committed themselves to a Declaration on the Middle East at their meeting in June 2002. The following statement suggests the future EU policy stance in that region: "The European Union stands ready to contribute fully to peace-building, as well as to the reconstruction of the Palestinian economy as an integral part of regional development."[35]

This general statement, translated into concrete policy terms, suggests a range of instruments the EU may be willing to apply, including some type of physical intervention, ideally, to implement a political solution. In a carefully balanced approach, Britain twins its participation in US-led military policy in the region with support for a broader EU policy. The latter comprehends a variety of needs and the complexity of social, economic and political breakdown in the Middle East.

In fact, Europeans see themselves as being more sympathetic to the 'failed state' thesis of dangers in the world, after the disintegration of Yugoslavia, as opposed to the conviction that drives US policy, that the 'terror threat' poses the overriding danger. Middle East policy in the EU seeks to promote stability by building the institutions of state, society and economy from the ground up. EU support for the Palestinian Authority (PA), seen by many Europeans as the only game in town with a chance of governing and stemming chaos, can best be understood in these terms. Single efforts on the part of the EU in the context of a multi-faceted 'peace-building' strategy do not always appear as linked segments in a coordinated strategy crafted over more than three decades, if they even appear to be serious efforts at all. By the same token, British initiatives in the Middle East do not always reveal themselves as joint cooperation with the EU policy, as indication of a shared consensus. Progressively, the EU and the United States have been cooperating within a Quartet of parties interested in the region and have more closely aligned their positions as they endorsed the so-called international Road Map to peace. In March 2004, the British proposed to give economic assistance to the PA for a unified command, to bring under control security forces whose rivalry has been a source of violence and potential civil strife.[36] The proposal does not reflect the seriousness it deserves unless seen in light of meeting a requirement of the Road Map and implementing EU style state-building.

This example suggests the promise of transatlantic cooperation in the region; regrettably, disunity on Iraq crosscuts other areas of significant agreement. Transatlantic progress has been made in a number of issue areas related to security, including the combat of terror financing and arresting terrorists, in which the EU has made remarkable strides, despite the constraints of sovereignty. Such was the case with the common arrest warrant EU countries decided in the immediate wake of 11 September in a gesture of reassurance to the United States, not to mention a substantial act of security cooperation. Cooperation in the Balkans had put Europeans and US troops in the field together and had improved relations, interestingly, with the French who have a reputation for being tough in the field. Members of the US military recognize the advantages of sharing dangerous battle conditions with French soldiers.[37] This experience in the Balkans had succeeded in reinforcing military respect. Nonetheless, transatlantic relations have been in disarray with serious implications for NATO, which provides another reason for Britain to firm up ties and use its influence in Europe.

The UK Ministry of Defense saw in the St. Malo initiative an avenue for increasing military capabilities in Europe, realizing NATO would continue to decline in importance to the United States as it refused to invest the resources needed to modernize. Indeed, the DCI had determined the plan for modernization, and the United States viewed this as a measuring stick of European intent. Europeans, for their part, were not convinced they could get public support for increased spending at the level the DCI required unless it was done in a European security framework, evidence that transatlantic issues were not a mere problem for political elites to negotiate, but that they were imbedded in EU public attitudes that diverged from those of the US constituency. Following this logic, it is not surprising the United States has seen in the plans to increase capabilities in the context of ESDP a duplication of NATO's DCI. The wedge that existed in transatlantic relations was opened wide with the disputes over Iraq. In strictly technical terms, the capabilities issue stands to be exacerbated by the absence of key NATO members in the combat phase in Afghanistan and Iraq, reinforcing the war-fighting partnership of Britain and the United States. Politicians in Britain are mining the lessons learned in these theaters to inform weapons and technology acquisitions. Actual shortages, failures, and lack of equipment that, in reality, imperiled soldiers make a convincing case to the public to increase investment.

While Britain is intent on acquiring new tools to be able to wage war with the United States and fulfill its NATO responsibilities, other Europeans, especially in the countries of 'Old Europe' are not so sure. NATO's critics dismiss the alliance as a 'tool bin,' airing frustration over the capabilities issue and minimizing what holds the alliance together. From the US view, it is the tools that divide; another view, more popular on the continent, maintains the cause is the erosion of common values, among other important differences, about when and how to use force in the world and for what purposes. In this light, Britain's moving even closer to the EU on defense issues must be seen as an effort to keep key European countries engaged in NATO.

For a country 'that can go it alone,' the splintering of the alliance does not have the same implications it has for countries who can neither afford 'to go it alone' nor choose to do so as sound policy. Indeed, the Bush administration tends to see the present situation in NATO as the reshaping of an enlarged alliance, a 'New Europe' with increased opportunities for coalition-building. Temporary coalitions, changing according to the outcome of political bargains and the kind of low politics seen in the run-up to Iraq, are no substitute for a strong alliance that serves as the foundation of Britain's strategy of building bridges in the pursuit of collective security.

Notes

1   Christopher John Bartlett (1977), *A History of Postwar Britain, 1945–1974*, White Plains, NY: Longman, 1977, 127.
2   UK, Ministry of Defence (1998), *The Strategic Defence Review, 1998*, London: HMSO, online at http://www.mod.uk/issues/sdr.
3   Ibid.
4   Ibid.
5   Ibid.
6   Ibid.
7   Stanley R. Sloan (2003), *Nato, the European Union and the Atlantic Community*, Lanham, MD: Rowman & Littlefield, 174.
8   Ibid., 188.
9   UK, Ministry of Defence (2002) *The Strategic Defence Review New Chapter*, July, online at http://www.mod.uk/issues/sdr/newchapter.htm.
10 UK, Foreign Affairs Select Committee (2001), *Second Report on British-US Relations*, 18 December, online at http://www.publications,parliament.uk/cgi-bin/ukparl_hl?DB = ukparl&STEMMER = en&W.
11 An unusual and, perhaps, unhelpful example of intelligence cooperation is the United States using Britain by proxy to spy on the UN Security Council members and the General Secretary during the failed negotiations to get a second UNSCR authorizing use of force in Iraq.
12 UK, Foreign Affairs Select Committee (2001).
13 Kori Schake (2003), "The US, ESDP and Constructive Duplication," in Jolyon Howorth and John T. S. Keeler, eds., *Defending Europe: The EU, NATO, and the Quest for European Autonomy*, New York: Palgrave Macmillan, 23.
14 H.G. Nicholas (1963), *Britain and the United States*, London: Chatto & Windus, 129.
15 Geoffrey Smith (1990), *Reagan and Thatcher*, London: Bodley Head LTD, 33.
16 Ibid.
17 As a part of building morale in the US military for action against Iraq, it is reported that Secretary of Defense Rumsfeld "staged a show at the Pentagon featuring gun-camera footage of Iraqi anti-aircraft artillery firing at Britain and American warplanes patrolling the 'no-fly zones' of northern and southern Iraq;" see Chalmers Johnson (2004), *The Sorrows of Empire: Militarism, Secrecy and the End of the Republic*, New York: Metropolitan Books, 232.
18 UK, Select Committee on Defence (2003), Minutes of Evidence, 3 December, online at http://www.parliament.the-stationery-office.co.uk/pa/cm200304/cmselect/cmdefence/57/31.
19 Ibid.

20 Ibid.
21 Bob Woodward (2002), *Bush at War*, New York: Simon and Schuster, 203.
22 Nichols, 127.
23 See Judy Dempsey (2004), "US Plans to Cut Troops in Europe By a Third," *Financial Times*, 3 February, online at http://ft.com. She reports, "The US has 119,000 troops in Europe, 80,000 of which are stationed in Germany. At the height of the Cold War, Washington had more than 300,000 troops in western Europe."
24 Ibid.
25 Jolyon Howorth and John T.S. Keeler (2003), "The EU, NATO and the Quest for European Autonomy," in Howorth and Keeler, eds., *Defending Europe*, 14.
26 Philip Stephens (2004), *Tony Blair, A Biography*, New York: Viking Press, 205–206.
27 Stephens, 205.
28 Robert Kagan (2003), *Of Paradise and Power: America and Europe in the New World Order*, New York: Alfred A. Knopf, 23.
29 James Fergusson (2003), "The Coupling Paradox: Nuclear Weapons, Ballistic Missile Defense, and the Future of the Transatlantic Relationship," in Alexander Moens, Leonard Cohen and Allen G. Sens, eds., *NATO and European Security: Alliance Politics from the End of the Cold War to the Age of Terrorism*, Westport, CT: Praeger, 165.
30 Stephens, 197.
31 Kagan, 39.
32 William Shawcross (2004), *Allies: The US, Britain, Europe and the War in Iraq*, New York: PublicAffairs, 48–49.
33 Pascal Boniface, "European Security and Transatlanticism in the Twenty-first Century," Moens, Cohen and Sens, 58.
34 Carol Cosgrove Sacks (2001), "The EU as an International Actor," Cosgrove-Sacks, ed., *Europe, Diplomacy and Development: New Issues in EU Relations with Developing Countries*, Houndmills, UK: Palgrave, 24.
35 EU (2002), Presidency Conclusions, Seville European Council, 21 and 22 June, *Declaration on the Middle East*, online at http://europa.eu.int/comm/external_relations/euromed/publication.htm.
36 See Harvey Morris (2004), "Britain Ready to Fund Palestinian Security Force," *Financial Times*, 3 March, online at http://www.ft.com.
37 Based on comments by NATO officials at SHAPE, Summer 2001.

Chapter 4

Russia and the 'Old' Europe versus 'New' Europe Debate: US Foreign Policy and the Iraq War 2003

Mira Duric

Introduction

The Iraq War of 2003 caused a split in the European security system. The Secretary of Defense in the George W. Bush administration, Donald Rumsfeld, termed the Atlanticist states – those nations that were part of the Western European system after the Second World War – 'Old' Europe. They tended to disagree with US policy towards Iraq. In contrast, the Eastern and central European states – that were once part of the Communist bloc – were defined as the 'New' Europe and tended to support US policy.[1] Is this 'Atlanticist' – 'Europeanist' split a short-term aberration or is it the beginning of a long-term transformation of the European–Atlantic security system? This chapter aims to address this issue vis-à-vis the Russian national perspective on the 'potential' Old–New Europe divide.

The Core Security Priorities of Russia

Chechnya and Terrorism

Russia's security priorities encompass both domestic and foreign policy concerns. In 2003, the key security interest of Russia was to maintain its internal security. Engaged in a war against the rebel Muslims in Chechnya, Russian President Vladimir Putin arguably has exhibited political–military signs of his desire for an 'imperial' Russia: a territorial aggrandizement of Russia similar to its USSR predecessor. For instance, in 2002, there were negotiations regarding Russian reunification with Byelorussia and the Ukraine. In addition, Russia seeks closer overt and tacit ties with a range of countries which made-up the former USSR.

The price of Putin's policy in regards to Chechnya has been a protracted insurrection marked by a range of suicide bombings and other terrorist attacks in Chechnya and in Russia. In one of the most publicized acts, on 23 October 2002, armed separatists occupied a theatre in Moscow threatening to kill the audience if Russia did not withdraw its troops from Chechnya. During the siege, 129 hostage civilians and 40 separatists were killed.[2] On 5 December 2003, outside Yessentuki, close to the Chechen region, a suicide bomb on a commuter train in southern Russia killed 40 people. The conflict in Chechnya highlights Russia's continuing ethnic strife. There also exists potential for both further 'intra' and 'inter' state conflicts. In addition, Russia has a problem with organized crime which has now transformed into transnational crime. Russia's Interior Minister, Boris Gryzlov, identified "terrorism, illegal migration and economic crimes," among Russia's key concerns.[3]

Military Reform and Innovation

One of Russia's core security priorities is to reform its military. The military is currently short of modern equipment.[4] Its present equipment has also been seriously degraded. While this affects all of the branches of the military, Russia's Navy is "probably the worst hit by the degradation in the military."[5] For example, there is the potential problem of Russian submarines leaking radioactive materials.[6] Unlike European governments, the Putin government is not overly concerned with "environmental matters such as pollution as well as humanitarian issues such as migration and refugee movements."[7]

Linked to military reform and innovation is control over security technologies and weaponry. This includes the spread of information concerning the development of weapons of mass destruction (WMD). Similarly, the actual proliferation of ballistic/nuclear missiles remains a concern for Russian policy-makers. Security experts around the globe are concerned that political instability in Russia could allow WMDs to be acquired by non-state terrorist actors. Radioactive materials went missing in Russia in 1997. Russian General Alexander Lebed "claimed that the Russian Government had lost 134 suitcase bombs." Interestingly, there were reports that the Chechen guerrillas had sold 20 of these to al-Qaida.[8] Furthermore "accidental launches of missiles also threaten the US,"[9] Russia, and global security. As a result, Russia seeks the "preservation and strengthening of non-proliferation regimes providing both global and regional stability and security."[10]

The Historical Legacy

The historical paradigm remains important in Russian security calculations. For centuries, Russia has feared invasion of the 'motherland' by its neighbors. This was the reason for the satellite nations after the Second World War. They were to be a buffer against potential German aggrandizement. Such a view continues to be a factor influencing Russian security priorities. Russia's decline as a superpower also exerts pressure on Moscow. Russia perceives itself as an important actor in the international arena. It desires an 'equal partnership' with NATO and Moscow is keen to play an important role in European security. Russia advocates a 'multipolar world' and 'global cooperation'. Russia desires international institutions to solve global crises in compliance with international law as a means to preserve Russian power. Does Russia consider itself a superpower? The answer is unequivocally 'yes.'

Closer Security Collaboration with the US or Europe?

It is desirable for Russia to maintain collaboration with the US and with emerging European security structures, namely the European Rapid Reaction Force. Collaboration with America could theoretically provide Russia with humanitarian and economic assistance, as well as increased security for Russia's eastern border (the two nations, logistically, are separated only by the Bearing Strait and the US will likely be the dominant power in the Pacific for the near term). Russo-American cooperation also offers Moscow the means with which to influence future US policy. However, in the wake of the Iraq war, the current prospects for close security cooperation between the two former Cold War enemies seems remote. America is the world's only superpower, yet it has transcended this even further; America today is a 'hyperpower.'[11] In addition, the Bush administration has demonstrated a willingness to proceed with or without Russian assent on a range of security issues.

The largest threat to world security today is terrorism, the power of which was demonstrated by the 11 September attacks. Russian alignment with the US in its War on Terror could dramatically increase the threat of attack by indigenous cells, mainly, religious separatist terrorists. Osama bin Laden pledged in November 2003 to attack those nations that supported US policy towards Iraq. These countries included England, Spain, Italy, Turkey and Japan. In November 2003, Turkey suffered four terrorist attacks by al-Qaida and in March 2004 Spain suffered an attack which cost the pro-American government the subsequent elections.

Russo-European Interests

Geographically and fundamentally, Russia is closer to Europe than the US. Europe has experienced the carnage of wars above and beyond the US experience, most notably the world wars where the US initially showed little interest in entering. Furthermore, the US does not have a fundamental priority interest in Europe in the way that individual European states do. Regardless of potential benefits from cooperation with the US, Russia should seek closer collaboration with existing and emerging European structures.

As part of this effort, Russia should engage in greater bilateral ties with Europe. Germany is the strongest economic–political power in Europe. Bilateral German–Russian relations should be extended into the security realm.

Since the end of the Cold War, Russia and France have increasingly cooperated on a range of issues, most notably in opposition to a US bent upon exerting hegemonic force over concerns such as Iraq and the Balkans. Putin should endeavor to expand relations with Paris.

The area with the greatest potential lies in increased collaboration with the UK and the Scandinavian states. As the Baltics are set to enter both NATO and the EU, this could counter any lingering anti-Russian sentiment among those states.

The key to European security will remain NATO in the near future. However, NATO has recently experienced internal controversy as parochialism and regional interests proliferate. For instance, during the NATO bombing of Serbia in March 1999, Greece (Serbia's Orthodox ally) was against the bombing, much to the dismay of other NATO members. Meanwhile, the security priorities in North Europe are clearly different to those of central and Eastern Europe, the latter of which have suffered brutal ethnic wars.

An American role in the European alliance is desirable mainly to prevent domination by any one entity in Europe. The American role also has been a stabilizing influence in European security. Nonetheless, the political maneuvering of the 2003 Iraq crisis has shown that certain actors in the continent, namely France and Germany, desire a politically diminished role for the US in the European security system. Even within the framework of increased Russian ties to the West, the continuing presence of the US in European security is necessary, even if only to allay fears of Russia by the states of Central and Eastern Europe. As new euro-centric institutions or strategies are developed, Russia should not work to alienate or undermine the US role in transatlantic security.

A dual track approach for Russia is therefore desirable: 1) to maintain and expand its security relationship with America; and 2) to do the same with the emerging European structures. However, in return, the transatlantic security actors (America and NATO) should try to incorporate Russia into their framework as soon as possible. The Euro–Atlantic community needs Russia as a key player to help meet the challenges that Europe will face.

The transatlantic community must treat Russia as an essential actor on the international stage. Russia still has enormous military capabilities (including nuclear war-fighting capabilities), and it continues to be in a state of transitional uncertainty which could cause instability in the international system. The actors need to exert a stabilizing influence on Russia. An unstable Russia within the NATO alliance is preferable to an uncertain Russia outside the European security structure. Russia can act as a restraint/intermediary between both the Atlanticist powers that seek to diminish American influence in the continent, and on America itself.

Russia's Contribution to Transatlantic Security

Russia's current contribution to transatlantic security is substantial and could be dramatically increased. Russia could provide intelligence, resources (including troops, transport and ammunition) for both NATO and the European Rapid Reaction Force. On a broader economic level, Russia can provide oil and gas to Europe and America and thereby lessen dependence on the Middle East. Such a role is to a great extent dependent upon Washington recognizing that it should be prepared to trade with Russia on a much larger scale and, more significantly, encouraging its allies to freely trade with Russia.[12] Secretary of the Russian Security Council, Vladimir Rushailo, stated that Moscow desires to cooperate with the European Union (EU) on a variety of fronts, including "in the fight against the drug threat and in the formation of a common European law enforcement space" and that Russia can contribute "transport aviation for the needs of the European Rapid Reaction Force."[13]

Russia has (inadvertently, if not politically) assisted America with the "war on terrorism." For instance, Russia has apprehended many terrorists that America has sought. This might be the state's most tangible, short-term contribution to transatlantic security. When the USSR federation was in existence, the Soviet Union had three and a half million soldiers. Russia's current smaller army, albeit plagued by problems of degradation, could contribute in a large part to the fight against terrorism. This could be its greatest long-term contribution. If NATO were to expand globally (as it intends),[14] Russia's membership would be invaluable to the alliance. It would provide NATO with increased security on its eastern border. It would also give NATO parameter influence on a country with nuclear weapons.

Russia's membership in NATO, and involvement in the European Rapid Reaction Force, would heighten its prestige and international standing. Any attack on Russia would be met with assistance from NATO due to Article 5 of its charter. Notwithstanding, Russia has already demonstrated its contribution to international security. In the prelude to the Iraq war, Russia offered the UN weapons inspectors "planes and drones" (intelligence gathering aircraft).[15] Russia has also participated in a range of humanitarian missions, including those in the Balkans and Russia provided intelligence and military assistance to both the United States and the Northern Alliance during the invasion of Afghanistan.

Russia's Vision for Existing and Emerging Security Structures

Russia envisions an 'equal partnership' with NATO. It also envisions eventual membership in the alliance with the aim of increasing Russian and NATO security; hence a mutually beneficial relationship. Whilst fundamentally this would be desirable, in practice it is probably unlikely as long as America (and NATO) continues to perceive Russia as a potential threat. Interestingly, Russia now appears to be closer to the Europeanist states of France and Germany, because of their opposition to America's 2003 Iraq policy. Significantly, Russia's equal partnership with NATO, therefore, could be likely, or inevitable, if Germany supports Russian membership. It would be inevitable if the US role in the transatlantic relation were downgraded. Russia further envisions membership in the European Rapid Reaction Force. Unquestionably, Russia would feel less strategically threatened if it were a partner (or even a member of NATO and the ERRF).

So what are the current security threats to NATO? Potential threats to NATO and the emerging European security structures are generally also threats to the US and the global community. These include threat of weapons of mass destruction, biological and chemical weapons, (both proliferation and attack) AIDS, poverty, refugees, immigration and environmental dangers.[16] However, state and non-state terrorism appears to be the most fundamental threat to NATO today. Terrorism combined with an anti-American fundamentalism from both Islamic and non-Islamic sources constitutes the greatest threat to America and, consequently, its allies.

The threat to NATO would be significantly reduced if it were not allied so closely with America. As long as America dominates Europe, NATO will be a target for these terrorist cells. The threat of terrorism is transnational and difficult to detect. Countries in NATO themselves have indigenous terrorist cells operating within their boundaries, although these have been relatively dormant as certain

NATO members opposed the US policy towards Afghanistan in 2001, and Iraq in 2003.

Following the 9/11 attacks, the world entered a new epoch in its history. America declared war on terror. Initially, the world grieved with the US over its Twin Towers tragedy. However, America's unrestrained foreign policy has been met with criticism from those states – both Islamic and non-Islamic – which sympathized with America's great loss. In defining terror, one needs to be precise. Terror does not just encompass Islamic terrorist cells. Terror constitutes any action deemed hostile and any unilateral attack against another entity. It is made more dangerous by the fact that terrorist groups operate independent of their respective countries. Many now question the US foreign policy as that of an aggressor nation.

It can be argued – albeit from a European perspective – that as long as America maintains its unwavering support for Israel, the Middle Eastern crisis will continue; and as long as America continues its role as a military enforcer of peace, terrorist attacks are likely to continue and intensify. Ironically, Islamic terrorism is in part a phenomenon of the Cold War legacy. It is in large part the product of the followers of Islam who have reacted with disenchantment against the legacy of American and Russian exploitation of their countries for resources and political gain. Now they have unleashed their Jihad against American imperialism. In Chechnya, Islamic militants are fighting for their independence against Russia.

Russia–NATO/EU Relations

In 1997, the NATO–Russia Founding Act on Mutual Relations, Cooperation and Security was established to "develop a strong, stable and enduring partnership." The NATO–Russia Permanent Joint Council (PJC) was created to provide a "mechanism for consultations and to the maximum extent possible ... for joint decisions and joint action."[17]

Russia's attitude towards European Security Defense policy (ESDP) and the rapid reaction capabilities are driven by political considerations.[18] These two actors furthered Russia's aim of a multi-polar world. Russia–EU (ESDP) interaction help assert Russia's place in Europe. A Russian–EU (ESDP) partnership would also help to increase Russia's role in Europe.[19]

Under President Vladimir Putin, the EU–Russia strategic partnership became the "definitive priority in Russian foreign policy." Russia advocates a mutual partnership with the EU, and has always advocated "dialogue on international policy and security as well as practical cooperation" in its relations with the EU.[20] President Putin expressed his interest in "forming EU security and defense policy" in the Joint Statement of the Russia–EU Summit in May 2000.[21] Russia desires to increase the EU's political standing, which is consistent with Russia's concept of a multi-polar world. This would increase the potential for a two-sided strategic partnership which would be imperative towards integrating Russia into Greater Europe. The consequence of this would be to strengthen Russia's "security aims ... and its own voice in Europe."[22]

Furthermore, Russia wishes to influence EU crisis management capabilities. This cooperation would be based on principles of equality and common decision-making. Russia aims to cooperate with the EU's rapid reaction capability (ERRC) in order to increase Russia's ability to influence the RRC. Moscow seeks tri-lateral NATO–EU–Russia cooperation in crisis management.[23] Consequently, strengthening EU–Russian relations would help to strengthen Russia–NATO relations. In April 2003, Russian Foreign Ministry official representative Alexander Yakovenko revealed that Moscow favored "parallel development of co-operation" with the EU and NATO.[24]

At the NATO summit in Prague in 2002, NATO invited seven former Communist countries to join the alliance, including Estonia, Latvia and Lithuania, states that were once part of the Soviet Union.[25] Russian Foreign Minister Igor Ivanov stated that Russia would work with NATO as long as the alliance focused on "opposing new threats and challenges of this contemporary world." According to him, both Russia and NATO were determined to promote a new post-Cold War "architecture of security."[26]

Ivanov stated that Russia continues to oppose the 'mechanical expansion' of NATO. This view is prevalent among Russia's military and foreign affairs establishment, which still urge Moscow to adopt policies to return Russia to superpower status.[27] Nonetheless, Russia has reconciled itself as unable to stop NATO's expansion. It consequently has sought a 'NATO plus one' policy representing a closer political link with the alliance with a recognition that currently Russia's influence "over NATO's decision making process is limited."[28] In Russia, only a minority of the public believe that Russia will join the alliance.[29]

At the Prague Summit, NATO members decided to create a rapid response force to deal with crisis situations around the globe. This included reacting in WMD environments "where they [NATO forces] may be faced with nuclear, biological and chemical weapons."[30] In 2001, Russia, Belarus, Kazakhstan, Kyrgyzstan, Tajikistan and Armenia (the Commonwealth of Independent States Collective Security Council) met to discuss its own rapid reaction force to fight international terrorism, primarily the threat of Islamic extremism in Central Asia.[31] The rapid reaction force for Central Asia, of Russia, Kazakhstan, Kirghizia and Tajikistan, started functioning on August 1, 2001.[32] Interestingly, the NATO Rapid Reaction Force was aimed to check the European Union's (EU) intention of setting up ERRF[33] (now manifested in the form of the European Defense Union, proposed by Germany and France.) Washington and Atlanticist states believe that this can lead to a "withdrawal of European countries from NATO."[34]

The US Role in Transatlantic Security

America will continue to play an interventionist role in Europe. First, Economic diplomacy and historical legitimacy will ensure this. The Europeanist states may try to diminish the role of America in their security infrastructure, but there is no denying that America will continue to exert an influence that befits a global power. Second, America's close relationship with Great Britain, which is a crucial element of western European security, will ensure that America's interests will be defended as Britain will continue to be a bridge between the US and the EU. Third, America will exert an influence on European security because of the support that it has from the Atlanticist states of the eastern periphery of Europe, which are being integrated with varying speed and degrees into the NATO alliance/EU.[35]

What should the role of the US be in Europe? Who knows what Europe would be like without US influence? With American influence in Europe, armed, interstate conflict has been essentially eliminated within the NATO/EU states. It can be asserted that American influence has helped keep the peace in a continent where wars have historically raged. If America was to withdraw from the alliance, the same imperial rivalries of the European nations that once contributed to the First and Second World War could possibly flare up again. The whole security structure could destabilize and, perhaps, disintegrate. Yet, this structure might disintegrate anyway as a result of French and German opposition to America's foreign policy.

It is prudent for France, Germany, Belgium and Luxembourg to propose a European Defense Union. Yet what would happen if Germany attempted to dominate this new forum, as one might expect it too? The argument that NATO would be in a better position without America's role in its alliance – to determine its own agendas, pursue its own interests and actions – does not stand up to historical scrutiny. An American-free European continent would be desirable if the states of Western Europe had the necessary strength, resolve and diplomacy to pursue policies which would prevent regional hegemony and preserve the rights of the smallest states. This would be difficult to achieve and yet such an alliance unquestionably requires Russian involvement.

America's continuing role in Europe is to a large extent dependent – and should be dependent – upon its willingness and ability to moderate its policies globally, a course the Bush administration does not appear willing to take. Instead, America supercedes international institutions and sets its own law. American foreign policy continues to be the preeminent force that shapes global affairs. Inevitably, its impact on transatlantic security will be significant. America should have an proportionate role in Europe – as an ally of Europe – but one where European interests are given greater consideration. This role should also ensure that the Europeans (including Russia) are dominant within their own security structures, such as NATO and the ERRF.

Transatlantic relations should continue to be the basis for regional security in much the same manner as they were before the Iraq war in 2003, but with a greater European role and increased influence for the EU. Hopefully events following the Iraq crisis will not split the alliance further. Transatlantic relations must be a mutually dependent relationship based on equality, although the stabilizing force of the US, as the guarantor of peace on the continent for more than 50 years, should be recognized. America should not use Europe as a stepping-stone towards world domination, but perceive it as a partner in transatlantic relations and the effort for global peace and stability.

Russian Opposition to US Policy Towards Iraq

In early 2003, America began developing a coalition to attack Iraq due to allegations of WMDs and alleged Iraqi support for terrorism. The coalition efforts were in spite of a lack of concrete evidence of WMDs.[36] They were also in spite of

French, German and Russian reservations about the US actions (France led the opposition at the United Nations[37]). Tangibly the three countries did not provide forces for the US led coalition, although later other nations that supported the US position sent troops to Iraq.[38] France, Germany, Russia, China and Syria all opposed the second US-led UN resolution authorizing the use of military force in Iraq. On 10 March 2003, Igor Ivanov stated that "Russia believes that no further resolutions of the UN Security Council are necessary."[39] Russian officials argued that additional time was needed to assess whether there was a WMD threat from Iraq. Above all, Russia advocated a UN settlement for the Iraqi conflict.

Opposition to US policy was not based solely on diplomatic concerns. France, Germany and Russia were all documented to have had a stake in Iraqi oil agreements. In 2003, Russia signed an agreement with Iraq valued at £40 billion for economic trade and oil. Iraq originally appeared to renege on the agreement and then later confirmed it. To put it succinctly, most of the strongest nations of the European security system (the Europeanist states) opposed the US policy on Iraq, whilst the weaker emerging nations of Eastern Europe supported it. 'Old' Europe and America were in a serious political dispute, which threatened the foundations of the transatlantic alliance. There were anti-Americanist feelings in Europe and anti-Europeanist feelings in the US.[40] British Prime Minister Tony Blair "pleaded with Europe and the United States to heal their diplomatic rift over Iraq." This was to "prevent the replacement of their historic friendly partnership with a bipolar rivalry which would be disastrous for world stability."[41]

Russia's reaction to the war was significant although Moscow sent mixed signals to Washington regarding the war. For instance, there were "threats from hard-liners like Igor Ivanov, the foreign minister, that Russia would veto any vote in the UN Security Council for war." However, there were also "assurances from moderates that it would not."[42] For his part, Putin called the Iraq war a "big political mistake".[43]

Gradually, the Russian position hardened. On 17 March 2003, Moscow termed the US military action in Iraq "illegal." After weeks of silence, Putin warned that war "would be fraught with the gravest consequences, will result in casualties and destabilize the international situation in general."[44] He added that Russia wanted to resolve the situation through peaceful means. In reaction to the criticism of mixed Russian statements regarding opposition to the war (as well as his own avoidance of the crisis), Putin asserted that Russia's position had always been "clear ... and unwavering."[45]

Lilia Shevtsova contends that Putin was concerned that the Iraq issue would "destabilize the region close to Russia's borders."[46] It has also been asserted by Sergei Karaganov that despite Europe's significance to Putin, he was more similar to Bush in policy terms.[47] Recognizing the potential for a rapprochement, US National Security Adviser Condoleezza Rice stated that America should "punish France, ignore Germany, forgive Russia."[48]

In Russia, there was political opposition to the US unilateralism. Following the war, Russia rejected a US offer to coordinate postwar issues, including humanitarian aid.[49] Meanwhile, Gennady Seleznyov, Russia's parliamentary speaker, declared that the attack on Iraq would cause the world to perceive that "the US is a terrorist state that can only be dealt with in the Hague tribunal."[50]

Why did Russia oppose America's Iraq policy? Was it because of Russian oil or business agreements with Iraq? Was it for humanitarian reasons? Was it to diminish US global primacy? By siding with the French, Russia appeared to play into the hands of the nationalists who were angry at the US and NATO for their humiliation of Russia on various foreign policy issues. *The Economist* identifies these issues as being "the humiliation of Russian forces in Kosovo in 1999, the expansion of NATO to include former Soviet satellites" and "America's withdrawal from the Anti-Ballistic Missile Treaty."[51] Were these humiliations the reason for Russia's opposition to war, or was it that Moscow perceived a chance to assert its political hand, as an important actor in the international arena, by contesting US policy? Did Russia oppose US policy towards Iraq because of the impact on Arab world opinion, and the destabilizing effect that it would have on "stability and security in the Middle East?"[52]

On 1 June 2003, Bush and Putin met in St Petersburg. The US delegation insisted, "the two nations have overcome their Iraq differences more quickly because of the good personal relations between the two presidents."[53] *The Guardian* newspaper commented, "Though they managed to paper over the cracks in their relationship, there were signs of edginess during their meeting."[54] On 23 July 2003, Bush declared that the death of Saddam Hussein's sons Uday and Qusay marked the end of the regime in Iraq.[55] Fighting between the Iraqis and the Americans, however, continued. Violence also continued in Iraq, after the capture of Saddam Hussein (by US soldiers, on 14 December 2003). Most Russian officials believed that the capture of Saddam Hussein would only increase Arab nationalism and Islamic fundamentalism.

For Moscow, Iraq destabilized the Euro–Atlantic security infrastructure, and ironically, brought Russia closer to both the US and the Europeanist states. Simultaneously, it has intensified the divisions between Russia and the Eastern European states – the 'new' Europe where hostility toward Russia has been endemic. Russia has found itself politically closer to France and Germany because of their common Iraq policy. Nevertheless, a US rapprochement has been made with Moscow. From the point of view of Russia, the Euro–Atlantic divisions have opened the possibility for Russia to become a key player in international events. Russia's credibility has been strengthened. Its population, however, has not been overly concerned with the issue, as they are concerned with Russian domestic factors, including internal terrorism and the ongoing conflict in Chechnya.

Russia and the European Defense Union

In Egmont Palace, Brussels, on 29 April 2003, Germany, France, Luxembourg and Belgium announced a new agreement on European defense: the creation of a European Security and Defense Union (ESDU). The nations did recognize the continuing importance of the transatlantic relationship in the meeting. They declared that Europe and the US shared values and ideals. Furthermore, the Europeanist states declared that "The transatlantic partnership remains an essential strategic priority for Europe."[56] The nations announced that their commitments to the Atlantic Alliance and the European Union – namely NATO and the EU – were "complementary."[57] Nonetheless, they called for the development of a "European rapid reaction capability" to help achieve the "goals of the European Union and strengthen the European contribution to developing a NATO Reaction Force" and declared that any new security structure would be under the "auspices of the United Nations."[58]

On 30 April 2003, Javier Solana, the European Union's High Representative for Common Foreign and Security Policy met in Moscow with Igor Ivanov, Russia's Foreign Minister. Solana stressed that the initiative of France, Germany, Belgium and Luxembourg would "become an important step towards improving the effectiveness of the EU in politics and defense."[59] According to Solana, the effects of the European Union to enhance its military performance "should be welcomed."[60] He stated that the European Union intended to "cooperate with partners, including Russia."[61] For his part, Ivanov stated that Moscow considered the European defense initiative "a start of the process within the EU and will follow attentively its progress."[62] According to him, "Russia would develop full-fledged cooperation with the European Union in all spheres, including security and defense."[63] The potential development of this new institution could serve to meet a variety of Russian goals. It could enhance Russia's influence in European security issues while diminishing that of the US and it could restore Russian international prestige.

Reassessments of Transatlantic Security?

Most East European countries officially supported the US policy towards Iraq. However, it must be stressed that, initially, the only East European country that contributed to the US efforts towards Iraq, by providing troops, was Poland. Other East European nations did support US policy but did not provide troops until after the initial phase of the war. Poland, and the other East European nations that supported the US, are not big powers, but ones that are swayed by dollar diplomacy.[64] They seek to attain American political, security and economic assistance, and consequently, acted in favor of the Bush administration's tactics even though it may have created fissures between East and West, Old and New Europe.

The ominous warnings of an Atlanticist – Europeanist split in the alliance can be construed as an over-exaggeration of the current situation. The states of Eastern Europe do not have significant individual power and influence in the international arena. However, they have a direct impact on Euro–American relations. These nations are likely to act as subsidiary powers for the US. They will most likely vote in the favor of US actions and policies. Furthermore, they will join with the Atlanticist states, led by the UK to create a potential geographical – symmetrical 'Three way split' in Europe with the UK and 'new' Europe supporting the US, whilst France and Germany and the 'old' Europe (including Russia) opposing the US policy.

It is in the interests of the Western European states to acknowledge that the Eastern European states will inevitably support American policy in the short term. In this respect, the Western European nations need to reassess the role that the Eastern states will play in the alliance, and, consequently, recognize the biases of these nations. The Western European states can try to exercise leverage on the

Eastern state. For instance, they could exert their own 'euro diplomacy' on the Eastern states to try to influence their policies by providing them with incentives to support Eurocentric policies.

While the Western states could attempt to reassess and revoke the US influence in transatlantic security, this risky strategy carries significant geo–political–military consequences and should be avoided. The most plausible policy for the Europeanist states is, therefore, to press for a mutually beneficial US–European partnership in transatlantic security. In order to accomplish this, parameters for US policy must be set so that Washington does not dominate European affairs and so that the US does not conduct an unrestrictive foreign policy. Meanwhile, it remains important to keep the US involved in European security in order to prevent potential German or Russian domination.

'Old' Europe versus 'New' Europe: Round Two: the EU Constitution

In early 2003, Poland, the Czech Republic and Hungary pledged not to block the policies of Germany in regards to the future of the EU. It was noted at the time that "[n]either are these countries much bothered by the threat of a Franco–German hegemony in the enlarged Union."[65] Instead, it was recognized that "[o]nce they learn the ropes, the smaller nations will use weight of numbers to contain the old founder-nations" and that "France and Germany will eventually have to settle for less influence in a bigger, livelier Union."[66] However, ten months later, in December 2003, Poland was "already flexing its muscle" regarding the EU constitution.[67] The Brussels summit collapsed due to the failure to reach an agreement on voting rights in the new EU constitution. Berlin believed that is was "intolerable" that Poland, a "poor undeveloped nation," with a smaller population than Germany, would become "one of the largest beneficiaries" of the EU budget, (to which Germany contributes 25%) and have almost as many votes as Germany in the "EU decision-making process."[68] Poland's "disproportionate number of votes" would mean it could "punch well above their weight" and Berlin wanted to "get a deal that reflects its size and clout as the EU's paymaster."[69] Germany and France required Spain and Poland to "have fewer votes at the EU's Council of Ministers." Countries spoke of a "two-tier Europe",[70] with Germany, France, Belgium and Luxembourg constituting the "fast track" alliance.[71] These diplomatic wranglings seem to reinforce perceptions of the dominance of Germany and France in regards to the small states.

Britain played a "peacemaking role between France and Germany on one side and Poland and Spain on the other."[72] On 15 December 2003, Tony Blair revealed that Britain had "joined forces with France and Germany to demand cuts in the EU's budget that will effectively punish Poland and Spain for blocking agreement" on the draft EU constitution.[73] The influence of the new Europe appears to be marginalized, and ironically, by the UK, one of the staunchest Atlanticist states.

The Security Implications of Transatlantic Tensions for Russia

The only nation that transatlantic tensions could benefit is Russia. However, Moscow has been preoccupied with its internal policies and parliamentary and presidential elections and has taken a back seat in the international relations sphere. Consequently, Britain has played the role of mediator in post-Iraq issues between the US and 'old' Europe. However, there exists the potential for further US–Europe crises. When they happen, Russia – if it chooses to be a diplomatic player – can be a stronger unbiased mediator than Britain.

That transatlantic tensions could benefit Russia is ironic considering that historically the transatlantic alliance was directed against Russia. Russia is in the unique position of being able to facilitate discussions between – and help reconcile – America and 'old' Europe. This can heighten Russia's international standing and prestige and enhance Putin's domestic standing. The security implications of transatlantic tensions for Russia are dependent on the nature of such strains. Russia can mediate between these two poles regardless of the US role in Europe. Hence, Russia could bridge the transatlantic security gap all the while maintaining the US security presence in Europe. Russia could essentially take over the role currently played by Britain.

Russia should pursue a proportionate relationship with both NATO and America by adopting a conciliatory policy towards both, but not focusing exclusively on one or the other. Ultimately, transatlantic tensions could be the gateway for Russian entry into the NATO alliance. Within NATO, Russia could offer a counter to both the Atlanticist states and the Europeanist states. Unlike these two groupings, Russia could be a neutral force in the transatlantic union.

Diplomatically, transatlantic tensions could also offer Russia the opportunity to reassert itself as an important player on the international scene. This could be vital for future crises where the Europeanist states oppose the US and the Atlanticist states support the US. Russia could act as an intermediary, but would Moscow ultimately support the Atlanticist states or the Europeanist states? Russia is clearly linked to the states of 'old' Europe more so than the 'new' states which were for so long under Soviet rule during the Cold War. In addition, the states of 'old' Europe are more powerful and exert a stronger international influence than the 'new' states. Consequently, Russia would most likely align itself politically with the Atlanticist states and therefore undermine its role as a mediator.

For instance, regarding Iraq, Russia stood by its convictions – or its economic interests – and was against US policy. Whether Russia would support the US in the future will to an extent be dependent upon domestic factors. Transatlantic tensions could empower Moscow internationally; however, these strains could also strengthen reactionary forces within Russia, and could provide an impetus to hard-line nationalists who wish to exploit US–European tensions for their own domestic benefits.

Implications of the Atlanticist–Europeanist Split

It can be argued that the Europeanist states that opposed US policy towards Iraq did not do so because they desired a transformation of the transatlantic security system. They opposed US policy because they had stakes in Iraq. The Eastern states did not sign any agreements with Saddam Hussein, and so it was beneficial for them to support US policy since they hoped to benefit from their pro-American stance (in terms of both aid and involvement in the postwar reconstruction of Iraq).

Certain players on the continent do desire a change in the transatlantic system, with America playing a smaller role in European affairs. Despite protestations by Germany, France, Belgium and Luxembourg, to the contrary, the proposal of a European Defense Union appears to legitimate this contention. The reality is that the EDU could result in a permanent change in the Euro–Atlantic security space. The European Defense Union of France, Germany, Belgium and Luxembourg will eventually marginalize the influence of NATO, and thereby, the US in European affairs (even if it is carried out under the auspices of NATO, US marginalization could be inevitable).

The future of European security could be the development of two alliance systems, as was the case during the Cold War. There could be a restructured, possibly renamed, American- led NATO alliance, consisting of certain Atlanticist states and the 'new' European countries of Eastern Europe. This system would spread its peacekeeping and rapid reaction force military operations globally (including operations in the Asian continent). The alternative alliance could be the European Defense Union (led by Germany) – consisting of the 'old' European nations which would contain their operations to the defense of Western Europe and those interests on the periphery (such as Northern Africa).

Where would Russia stand in a potentially divided transatlantic alliance system? During the 2003 Iraq war, Russia supported the Europeanist states. The expansion of America's influence in the East – on Russia's Western border – could add additional impetus for Russia to align itself to the European Defense Union, especially if the nationalists gain domestic political power or influence, and if Moscow perceives itself capable of reasserting itself as a world power. If Russia is in the hands of the moderates, it is likely that Russia will support the US alliance and US policy.

It is possible that the European Defense Union could supercede the NATO alliance altogether. However, this possibility is unlikely as long as the 'new' Europe is in NATO, as the Eastern countries would defend American interests. The alliance would remain, with the center of its gravity "shifting to the east," much as Donald Rumsfeld predicted. With the potential of being outnumbered, the old European nations could consequently leave NATO. However, Rumsfeld's January 2003 statement is an over-exaggeration of the Atlanticist–Europeanist split, as it attributes a greater importance and power to the Eastern nations than they possess. In terms of American interests and perceptions, Rumsfeld's statement is an accurate interpretation. America currently seeks to build bases in the strategically important area of Eastern Europe as a means to move its military assets closer to the Middle East and Central Asia. This year America even threatened to move NATO Headquarters when Belgium contested American opposition to the creation of an International Criminal Court. Belgium withdrew its opposition to the US and NATO remains in Brussels.

The Bush administration brands states that do not cooperate with US policy as either pariah states or in the case of its European allies, 'old' Europe. Nonetheless, states still seek ties with Washington. After a decade of conflict with the US, in July 2003 Serbia and Montenegro's Prime Minister Zoran Zivkovic went to Washington to offer the Americans 1,000 Serbian troops for Iraq.[74] This was despite American military strikes against Belgrade in 1999, and Serbian trade ties to the Saddam regime. Nations compromise ideals and pride in order to receive aid and support from Washington. Eastern Europe's support for the US in Iraq is an example of this. Russia has made such compromises before and it is also possible that Moscow will do so again in the future. Even after the differences with America over Iraq policy, following the capture of Saddam Hussein, France and Germany sent "effusive congratulations" to President George W. Bush, although Russia and China reacted in "muted terms".[75] Ultimately, all nations conceded to the US. On 20 December 2003, longtime American foe, Libyan Colonel Gaddafi, promised to end his WMD program.

In history, there has never been an international power quite like the United States. America has learned from the failures of previous empires and it will likely remain a superpower because of its economic, military and soft power. In terrorism, however, the US has met its match. Its military preponderance and technology is incapable of defeating international terrorism or preventing future terrorist attacks. One result is that the US increasingly recognizes the need to ally itself with other states to defeat terrorism. For instance, the NATO alliance that America developed to defend the transatlantic region against the Soviet Union during the Cold War is allied with Russia. The former Russian satellite nations are also now resolutely in the US orbit. Recent trends in international relations have shown that even the 'old' European states of France and Germany will align their policies with the US now that interest in the Iraq crisis has subsided. US and UK (especially the latter's) efforts at the political reconstruction of France and Germany into the US sphere has begun. In late September 2003, Gerhard Schröder had talks with President Bush after the Iraq row. Meanwhile, Jacques Chirac and Tony Blair met on November 24, 2003.

The Reconstruction of 'Old' Europe: European Security Defense

Due to Britain's intermediary role on behalf of American interests, French and German plans for European Defense have been modified. The scope of the intended European Union defense force has been widened though its role has been limited. Hence, it is promised that the force will not "dislodge the role of NATO."[76] This reflects American interests. Furthermore, the EU agreed that "NATO can have a permanent liaison office at EU military HQ in Brussels" as a "further concession to the US."[77] French and German plans to reassert dominance in the transatlantic security sphere through their European Defense force have now been modified to suit American policies and interests.

Initially, Britain opposed the Franco-German military plan for the EU, which called for a "new EU military HQ at Tervuren, near Brussels."[78] Later, Britain drew-up plans with France and Germany to "create an independent military arm of the EU," which would "enable the EU to conduct military operations using NATO resources."[79] This would tie the new organization to NATO's existing capabilities. Blair stated that the military plan would not rival NATO.[80] He also insisted that the plan would not "infuriate" Bush or future American administrations.[81] The British, French and German agreement would instead "create an autonomous EU military headquarters in the Brussels suburbs" and the "EU planning and operational capacity" would be used in a crisis if NATO were not involved, although NATO would have "first refusal" over involvement.[82] If NATO chose not to be involved in a specific operation, then the EU countries, through their defense initiative, "may run an operation using NATO facilities."[83] The US has accepted the British-brokered plans for European security. Prompted by Britain, the French and Germans have consequently "bent over backwards to assuage US concerns."[84]

US Versus Europe: Rounds 2 and 3: Iran and Iraq

Differences over global security between the US and the Europeanist states were not limited to Iraq. On 18 November 2003, America and Europe clashed over the "nuclear threat posed by Iran."[85] On 20 November, America launched a "bitter attack" on the EU and the UN's nuclear watchdog over "their reluctance to declare Iran in breach of its nuclear obligations."[86] Meanwhile, at the EU summit in Brussels, on 12 December 2003, Iraq again caused a split between the EU and America. The US decided to "bar countries that opposed the war from bidding on contracts to rebuild the country."[87] At the same time the US tried to "drum up support from France, Germany and Russia for writing off the Saddam regime's $125bn (£72bn) debt."[88] This angered Russia, France and Germany. The US essentially stated that the "countries cannot participate in tenders," whilst simultaneously "asking those same countries to cooperate on debt."[89] Compromises were developed, but the bitterness remained.

Conclusion

Britain's alignment with France and Germany ('old' Europe) over the issue of EU voting rights (instead of 'new' Europe's, Poland), and the French and German modification of their European Security Defense Union to accommodate US concerns, has reaffirmed the status quo in US–European relations at their pre-Iraq war 2003. Whether this status quo will be maintained remains to be seen. There should be little doubt that it will be challenged – past US–European clashes over Iran and postwar Iraq attest to this. Whether Russia will take over Britain's role as mediator for 'old' versus 'new' Europe also remains an open question. The implications of Moscow's posture towards the Iraq war would lead one to believe that Russia would be in the ideal position to assume this intermediary role. However, inevitably Russia will be superceded by Britain's diplomacy: the diplomacy of America in Europe.

Is the Atlanticist–Europeanist split over Iraq a short-term aberration or a sign of the long-term transformation of the transatlantic security system? In the long-term, it was undoubtedly a short-term aberration. Historical precedent and the preponderance of American power in the world ensures that the Euro–Atlantic split was, and will only be, a short-term aberration in transatlantic relations. Nevertheless, it has the potential to be the beginning of a long-range transformation of the Euro–Atlantic security space. Such a transformation would more reflect the preferences of France and Germany instead of the US and the UK (and indeed, Eastern Europe). Even before the US–European clash over policy on Iraq, US and EU priorities had diverged over issues "such as climate change and Palestine."[90] Inevitably, however, transatlantic policies tend to converge for political reasons. This convergence between the policies of old and new Europe is manifested in general support the US.

As an inadvertent legacy of America's war on terror, the real significance of the Atlanticist–Europeanist ('new' versus 'old' Europe) may accelerate a transformation of the transatlantic alliance.[91] This will be inevitable if America continues to supercede the very rules and international norms that it promoted and that it expects other nations to abide by. The transformation will be inevitable as Germany accrues more power and endeavors to assert its will within the EU. However, this many only reinforce the preference for an American presence in Europe by a range of states, including Russia. Hence, it is difficult to avoid the conclusion that "Europe and America need each other and to split these two great centers of democracy apart does no service to either side of the Atlantic."[92] Poignantly, Blair asserted, "Europe should be the friend and partner of America, not its rival."[93] This position seems to be the choice of Russia even as it enters the old-new Europe debate.

Notes

1 "You are thinking of Europe as Germany and France. I don't. I think that's old Europe ... The centre of Gravity is shifting to the east;"cited in *The Guardian* (2003), "The Iraqi Crisis: The Path to War: 12 Page Special," 16 March, 12.

2 Nick Paton Walsh (2003), "Families Claim Death Toll From Gas in Moscow Siege Kept Secret," *The Guardian*, 18 October, 19; Nick Paton Walsh (2003), "Ready to Die for Allah in Battle for Chechnya," *The Guardian*, 2 October, 19.

3 *Pravda* (2003), "The Interior Minister Satisfied With Cooperation Between Russia and Georgia," 29 April, online at http://newsfromrussia.com/main/2003/04/29/46511.html.

4 Steven Ecke (2002), "Russia's Rocky Relationship with NATO," *BBC World Edition*, 22 November, online at http://news.bbc.co.uk/2/hi/europe/2503893.stm.

5 "The exercise in which the *Kursk* sank was part of the navy's attempt to reassert itself as a bulwark against NATO, soon after a Russia–NATO showdown over Kosovo;" *The Economist* (2003), "Russia's Navy: Low, Inglorious Death," 6 September, 42.

6 Rees, G. Wyn (1998), "Conclusion," William Park and G. Wyn Rees, eds., *Rethinking Security in Post-Cold War Europe*, London, Longman, 175.

7 Ibid., 174–175.

8 Mira Duric (2003), *The Strategic Defence Initiative: US Policy and the Soviet Union*, Aldershot: Ashgate Publishing Limited, 2003, 154–155; Julian Borger and Ewen MacAskill (2001), "Black Market Means Bin Laden May Already Have a 'Dirty' Nuclear Bomb," *The Guardian*, 7 November, 3.

9 Duric, 155.

10 *Pravda* (2003), "Moscow Stresses Necessity to Prevent Proliferation of Nuclear Weapons," 29 April, online at http://newsfromrussia.com/main/2003/04/29/46533.html.

11 Ash, Timothy Garton (2003), "Why Are the US and Europe At Loggerheads?" *The Daily Telegraph*, 6 February, 20.

12   'Energy' is the new issue in American–Russian relations: "At a Kremlin summit in May 2002, Presidents George W. Bush and Vladimir Putin pledged to work together to reduce volatility in global energy markets and promote investment in Russia's oil industry;" David G. Victor and Nadejda M. Victor (2003), "Axis of Oil?" *Foreign Affairs*, **82** (2) March/April, 47.

13   *Pravda* (2003), "Javier Solana Meets With Secretary of Russian Security Council," 30 April, online at http://newsfromrussia.com/main/2003/04/30/46553.html.

14   On 15 October 2003 NATO launched its elite rapid reaction force which it aimed to deploy anywhere in the world.

15   Editorial (2003), "No Grounds For War: Mr Blix Makes the Case for More Time," *The Guardian*, 15 February, 23; See also Julian Borger and Ewen MacAskill (2003), "A Case For War? Yes, Says US and Britain. No, Say the Majority," *The Guardian*, 15 February, 1.

16   Duric, 153.

17   Willem Matser (2001), "Towards a New Strategic Partnership," *NATO Review*, Winter, 19–21, online at http://www.nato.int/docu/review/2001/0104–05.htm.

18   Francois Heisbourg (2001), "IISS/CEPS European Security Forum: Chairman's Summing Up," http://www.iiss.org/eusec/heisbourg19.htm.

19   Ibid.

20   Dmitry Danilov (2001), "The EU's Rapid Reaction Capabilities: A Russian Perspective," IISS/CEPS European Security Forum, 10 September, online at http://www.iiss.org/eusec/danilov.htm.

21   Ibid.

22   Ibid.

23   Ibid.

24   'Moscow Favours Parallel Development of Co-operation With EU and NATO', Pravda (14:25), April 29 2003, http://newsfromrussia.com/main/2003/04/29/46507.html.

25   *BBC* (2002), "Bush to Reassure Russia on NATO," 22 November, online at http://news.bbc.co.uk/2/hi/europe/2501389.stm.

26   Ibid.

27   Steven Ecke (2002), "Russia's Rocky Relationship with NATO," *BBC*, 22 November, online at http://news.bbc.co.uk/2/hi/europe/2503893.stm.

28   Ibid.

29   Ibid.

30   *BBC* "NATO Creates a Rapid Response Force," 21 November, online at http://news.bbc.co.uk/2/hi/europe/2499455.stm.

31   Sophie Lambroschini (2001), "Central Asia: CIS Plans Rapid Reaction Force to Fight Terrorism," Radio Free Europe/Radio Liberty, 22 May, online at http://www.rferl.org/nca/features/2001/05/22052001112028.asp.

32   *Pravda* (2001), "Collective Rapid Reaction Force Starts Functioning in Central Asia," 1 August, online at http://english.pravda.ru/world/2001/08/01/11523.html.

33   The Voice of Russia (2002), "What's the Aim of NATO Rapid Reaction Force?" online at http://www.vor.rul/Exclusive/excl_next3616_eng.html.

34   Ibid.

35   Polish newspaper editor Adam Michnik stated, regarding the US and Europe, "we do support a long-lasting Euro–Atlantic alliance because the US presence in Europe serves Europe well and we won't support any actions that try to eliminate the US from Europe;" Ian Traynor (2003), "New Boy Poland Flexes its Muscles," *The Guardian*, 10 December, 17.

36   "In the course of these inspections, we have not found any smoking gun;" quote by UN chief weapons inspector Hans Blix after briefing the UN Security Council, 23 January 2003; cited in "The Iraqi Crisis: The Path to War," *The Guardian*, 12.

37   Did these nations not support the US policy towards Iraq because of the potential threat of Islamic fundamentalism? These nations have large Muslim populations: "French and Russian officials repeatedly assured Saddam in late 2002 and early this year that their governments would be able to block an invasion with vetoes and delaying tactics at the security council;" Julian Borger (2003), "France and Russia 'Convinced Saddam He Could Survive War'," *The Guardian*, 4 November, 14.

38   Britain, Poland, the Netherlands, Denmark and Spain have troops in Iraq; *The Economist* (2003), "Charlemagne: Europe and Uncle Sam: Will Europeans Try to Help the Americans in Iraq – or Gloat Over Their Discomfiture?", 6 September, 44. Bulgaria, Estonia and Italy also have troops in Iraq.

39   Nick Paton Walsh and Brian Whitaker (2003), "Russia and France Promise to Use Veto," *The Guardian*, 11 March, 4.

40   For an interesting discussion on why this Europe–US dispute occurred, see Ash, 20–21. Timothy Garton Ash argues that Europe is now not the centre of America's war on terrorism as it was during the Cold War, the heart of the dispute between the US and Russia; ibid., 20.

41   Michael White (2003), "Blair Pleads For US and Europe to End Rift Over Iraq," *The Guardian*, 26 March, 2.; see also Patrick Wintour (2003), "Blair Acts to Reassure Europe on US Plans," *The Guardian*, 1 April, 10.

42   *The Economist* (2003), "Which Way Really?: Sidelined by the War on Iraq, Russia Could Still Win the Crucial Role it Seeks," 5 April, 44.

43   Ibid.

44   Nick Paton Walsh and Jon Henley (2003), "Moscow and Paris Issue Dire Warnings: Putin Warns of Gravest Consequences as French Reject Blame for Diplomatic Failure," *The Guardian*, 18 March, 2.

45   Ibid.; Vladimir Putin stated that "The United Nations charter has nothing that would allow the UN Security Council to take decisions on changing the political regime in this or that country, whether or not we like that regime." He also stated "Russia shares the position of our American partners which is that we must do everything to ensure full Iraqi cooperation with UN inspectors. The difference of approach lies in this: we believe the problem can and must be solved by peaceful political and diplomatic means." For Vladimir Putin's ambiguous statement, where he supported everyone at once, see Yelena Suponina, Pyotr Rozvalin and Yuri Shpakov, "Old Europe V. New Europe: Russia: Putin Supports Everyone, But For How Long?", *The Guardian*, 11 February, 17.

46   "Which Way Really?: Sidelined by the War on Iraq, Russia Could Still Win the Crucial Role it Seeks," 44.

47   Ibid.

48   "Charlemagne: Europe and Uncle Sam," 44.

49   Walsh and Henley, "Moscow and Paris Issue Dire Warnings," 2.

50   Ibid.

51   "Which Way Really?" 44. This Russian anger stems over their marginalisation of influence in the western anti-Serbian Bosnia and Kosovo policy, which Russia opposed. Russian anger also encompasses NATO's expansion in the former USSR's satellite nations, incorporating Estonia, Latvia and Lithuania; a closing frontier on Russia's western border. Does Russia fear an invasion of its territory as it has done so on many occasions previously? On the issue of strategic defence, the US withdrew from the 1972

ABM Treaty in July 2002 and decided to proceed with their National Missile Defense (NMD) system, which Russia opposed.

52 *Pravda* (2003), "Russia in consultations with US, EU, Arab Countries on Iraq Problem Settlement," 30 April, online at http://newsfromrussia.com/main/2003/04/46574.html.

53 Nick Paton Walsh (2003), "Putin and Bush Heal Rift on Iraq in Midst of Festivities," *The Guardian*, 2 June, 4.

54 Ibid.

55 Julian Borger, "Bush Hails End of Regime," *The Guardian*, 24 July, 1.

56 EU (2003), "European Defence Meeting: Conclusions (Egmont Palace, Brussels)," *Meeting of the Heads of State and Government of Germany, France, Luxemburg and Belgium on European Defence, Brussels, April 29, 2003*, online at http://europa.eu.int/futurum/documents/other/oth290403_en.pdf.

57 Ibid.

58 Ibid.

59 *Pravda* (2003), "Javier Solana on Initiative of 4 European Countries to Set Up Defence Union," 30 April 30, online at http://newsfromrussia.com/world/2003/04/30/46573.html.

60 Javier Solana quoted in ibid.

61 Ibid.

62 Igor Ivanov quoted in ibid.

63 Ibid.

64 For the price that America will pay for the war, see Lola Okolosie (2003), "The Price America Will Pay For War," *The Observer*, 23 February, 4.

65 Neal Ascherson (2003), "Brawling Europe Must Pull Together," *The Observer*, 16 March, 19.

66 Ibid.

67 Ian Traynor (2002), "Polish Threat to Block EU Vote on Constitution," *The Guardian*, 4 December, 19.

68 Editorial (2003), "The European Union: Back to The Future," *The Guardian*, 15 December, 17.

69 Gabby Hinsliff and Ian Traynor (2003), "Europe's Grand Folly," *The Observer*, 14 December, 16.

70 Gabby Hinsliff and Kamal Ahmed (2003), "Europe Summit Ends in Chaos on Constitution," *The Observer*, 14 December, 1.

71 Hinsliff and Traynor, 16.

72 Ian Black and Michael White (2003), "Disarray in the EU Gives Blair a Respite," *The Guardian*, December 15 2003, 13.

73 Michael White and Ian Black (2003), "Blair Backs Move to Punish Spain and Poland," *The Guardian*, 16 December, 2.

74 This was due to political reasons; 'to get Kosovo back', despite it actually being a province of Serbia; *The Economist* (2003), "Cuddling Up to the Americans: Forgetting Old Quarrels, the Serbians Look for New Political Gains," 23 August, 31.

75 Hugh Muir (2003), "Germany and France Send Effusive Congratulations," *The Guardian*, 15 December, 7.

76 Patrick Wintour and Ewen MacAskill (2003), "Blair and Chirac Mend Some Fences," *The Guardian*, 25 November, 1.

77 Ian Black and Michael White (2003), "Washington Accepts EU's Independent Military Plan," *The Guardian*, 12 December, 1.

78 Ian Black and Patrick Wintour (2003), "Straw Sets Limits to EU Military Plan," *The Guardian*, 21 October, 18.

79 Sophie Arie (2003), "EU Military Force Won't Harm Nato, Says Straw," *The Observer*, 30 November, 21.
80 Ibid.
81 Ian Black (2003) and Michael White, "Britain Agrees European Defence HQ," *The Guardian*, 29 November, 3.
82 Ibid.
83 *The Guardian* (2003), "The EU Considers its Defence Options," 8 December, 20.
84 Ian Black and Michael White (2003), "Washington Accepts EU's Independent Military Plan," 1.
85 Ian Black and Ian Traynor (2003), "US and Europe Clash Over Iran," *The Guardian*, 19 November, 14.
86 Ian Traynor (2003), "Americans Attack EU Leniency on Iran," *The Guardian*, 22 November, 19.
87 Ian Black (2003), "Iraq Splits EU Summit as Blair Backs US," *The Guardian*, 13 December, 18.
88 Ibid.
89 Ibid.
90 Editorial (2003), "The Widening Atlantic: Iraq Splits Point to Far Deeper Divisions," *The Guardian*, 11 February, 19.
91 The attacks of 9/11 gave moral legitimacy to the US in its crusade against terrorism. The US foreign policy towards Iraq demonstrated the failure of Russia and 'old' Europe to influence American foreign. It demonstrated the failure of global mass protests to impact either US and British foreign policy. Public opinion now appears to have little sympathy for a nation which it mourned with over 9/11. By bombing Afghanistan into submission in 2001, and Iraq in 2003, America's actions appeared to have strengthened terrorist cells in these nations further. Despite the capture of Saddam Hussein, no weapons of mass destruction – America's reason for war – were found in Iraq.
92 Denis MacShane (2003), "Europe Must Now Be United: A New Surge of Anti-Americanism Will Only Damage the EU's Standing in the World," *The Observer*, 23 March, 19.
93 Ian Black and Anne Perkins (2003), "Blair Tries to End European Rift," *The Guardian*, 22 March, 11.

Chapter 5

Benelux Security Policy

Dirk C. van Raemdonck

The European Context for the Security Policies of Belgium, the Netherlands, and Luxembourg

In February 2004, the United Kingdom and France, the only two European nations with a substantive capability and will to project military power, agreed to create detailed plans to permit the training and deployment of rapid reaction joint battlegroups. These are intended to be deployable to most anywhere in the world within two weeks on the initiative of the two countries or the European Union and in cooperation with NATO and the United Nations. Other EU countries are to have the opportunity also to contribute forces in the future. The missions envisaged are short-term and will include interventions in failing and failed states.[1]

Like the Franco-German brigade and the Franco-German-Spanish-Belgian-Luxembourg Eurocorps, the battlegroups initiative is one of a series of initiatives on the part of France and Germany over the last decade and a half to create an integrated and interoperable multinational European force that can function inside and outside of the context of NATO. Following the end of the Cold War and the disappearance of a direct and immediate security threat, Western European countries significantly reduced their defense commitments. Consequently, these plans for multinational European forces have not moved far beyond forces of symbolic value. Budgetary issues, especially on the part of the smaller participants, have caused implementation delays and reductions in projected force levels.

Since the late 1980s, the European Union has made great strides in deepening economic and political integration to the point where the first steps have been made towards an EU-wide foreign and security policy. European integration raised the hope and expectation of ambitious members such as France that the EU could play a global great power role. Concurrently, the absence of a Soviet threat caused many to question the political justification for the compromises and concessions to US leadership that are at the basis NATO.

For the small countries in the cockpit of Europe; Belgium, the Netherlands, and Luxembourg (collectively referred to as the Benelux), all this major power activity around them presents serious challenges to their security policy. Their dilemma is simple: They both need and fear the great powers. Surrounded as they are, how can they ensure survival *and* freedom of action? The former requires some form of cooperation with a much larger partner and the latter demands that they keep the great friend at a distance so as not to be dominated.

The security needs of small countries are inevitably regional or, at most, continental in nature. Their national interests and potential enemies are dangerous only at the regional or continental level. The major powers' interests extend to bordering continents or even the whole world. Joining in alliances is therefore a double-edged sword for the minor power. The major provides security through greater common strength and thus greater deterrent capability. It may even allow the junior partner(s) to reduce their own financial commitment to security. However, the alliance can become the mechanism that drags the small state into international adventures and war in the wake of the major. How then does one constrain the great power without making it lose interest in protecting the small countries?

The major European powers have the converse dilemma. They do not need the smaller powers for protection but, at least in the European Union institutional decision making context, they need their agreement. From a strategic point of view, the majors need to prevent smaller powers from becoming Trojan horses or launching pads for enemies. If the goal is to make a global power, the medium-sized powers that are Britain, France, and Germany need the smaller nation-states to join them in a large compact for there to be enough critical (military) mass to countervail the United States or China in the 21st century.

Two international organizations give an answer to the security needs of smaller European nations: NATO and the EU. The latter's security-related tasks are mere pretensions at the present time, given the lack of institutional substance and policy coherence behind the so-called Common Foreign and Security Policy (CFSP). The deep split in the European Union between those who supported the United States in its Iraq war policy and those who sought to block US military intervention to destroy the Saddam Hussein regime in 2003 showed the illusory nature of a common EU foreign policy. The creation of joint forces is a suggestive measure but, in the absence of agreement between European states over basic interests and how to pursue them, it is an agreement of aspiration rather than implementation.

Nevertheless, even in its present state as an economic giant and security dwarf, the EU provides a security blanket that cannot be ignored. Of the ten states that will join the EU in 2005, six (Estonia, Latvia, Lithuania, Poland, Hungary, and Slovakia) have very strong reasons to fear for the long term security of their borders. Their fear is so strong that, only a few years after regaining independence or control for themselves, they are willing to cede substantial sovereignty in return for security.

While the EU treaties do not include the explicit collective security guarantees of NATO's Article 5, it would be nearly impossible to imagine that the EU would allow one or more of its members to be invaded or annexed without resistance. If anything, the political logic that follows from the kind of economic and monetary integration which the EU practices would make even the prospect of an invasion disastrously disruptive. In the face of a clear and present threat, it would force member states to assist each other in putting up a credible military deterrent regardless of the absence of a specific security arrangement or institution.

From the perspective of smaller states in Europe, the EU and NATO are both necessary. NATO is needed to counterbalance the influence of the Franco-German axis with American power and influence. An American-led NATO is a partial guarantee against any intra-European disunity on security policy and against French, British, and/or German willingness to sacrifice smaller states in order to buy security for themselves. The experience of Czechoslovakia, Poland, Norway, or Finland in 1938–1939 is a case in point. The Cold War passivity of Western Europe in the face of Soviet domination, annexation, and brutal repression of popular will in Eastern Europe does not inspire great confidence in the all too often cynical great power politics of the European majors. France's frequent decisions to go it alone and ignore NATO allies and EU partners, such as in the 1966 decision to leave the integrated NATO military command, can only generate distrust. Equally troubling is Germany's public refusal in 2003 to contemplate any intervention or assistance at all under any circumstances, whatever the verdict of the United Nations Security Council on a war over Iraq and weapons of mass destruction.

The EU in turn is an insurance policy guarding against the potentiality of US withdrawal from Europe or the weakening of its resolve to commit to Europe's security. It has not escaped the leaders of the small powers that France attempts to use the EU and its CFSP as a stepladder to a French global leadership position equal to the US and, in the future, China. Seen within that context, it becomes clear that there is more than meets the eye to the strong opposition from, among others, Poland and Spain to France's attempt to create an anti-US bloc and to the recent Franco-German attempt to dominate the highest councils of the EU by changing voting procedures. The smaller EU members are seeking to preserve an internal balance of the majors and the minors in order not to become mere objects or tools of great power ambition and adventure.

The foregoing provides the broad conceptual framework for the security policies of the Benelux countries. Their security policy has been dominated by three successive different threat environments. The first set of circumstances lasted from the countries' appearance on the European stage early in the 19th century until the outbreak of World War II and was characterized by a local threat to the Benelux in the form of spillover from the feud between their French and German next-door neighbors. During the Cold war, the threat environment was clearly continental in scope and determined by the fear of an aggressive Soviet Union. From the point of view of the Benelux, the post-Cold War environment is characterized by the absence of any definable, organized direct local or continental threat.

How the three countries respond to the small country security challenge in the post-Cold War world has varied significantly at the political level, despite the very close cooperation between the militaries of all three countries. The reasons for this are to be found in the historical, institutional, and socio-cultural differences between the largest of the three countries. For the present to be understood, one must first analyze the peculiar historical circumstances of these countries at the crossroads of Europe and in the way of the armies of the great powers.

Maneuvering between Rampaging Elephants: Benelux Security Policy until World War II

The contemporary Netherlands, Belgium and Luxembourg are the product of the aftermath of the Napoleonic wars. The Congress of Vienna, the peace conference where the great powers sought to establish a stable post-Napoleonic European order, created a Kingdom of the Netherlands, comprising most of the strategically important present-day territory of Belgium, Netherlands and Luxembourg. The point was to force a retreat of France to it pre-1792 borders and to create neutral buffer states that would inhibit the major continental powers from threatening each other or Britain.[2]

In 1830, a rebellion in the south of the kingdom, driven mostly by francophone middle class and elites, resulted in a breakup into a Kingdom of Belgium in the south and the Kingdom of the Netherlands in the north. The Grand Duchy of Luxembourg did not emerge as an independent state until some years later in 1839. The London Conference of that same year reiterated the obligation of a neutrality policy for Belgium and the Netherlands and the British guarantee of this neutrality.

The Netherlands

Though all three countries committed to a policy of neutrality in international disputes, they did interpret the requirement in very different ways. The Dutch continued their traditional focus on their overseas colonies and on trade with anyone who could pay. While maintaining a tradition-rich navy in the interest of the defense of those far flung colonial and commercial interests, the army received little attention and even fewer funds as it lacked any meaningful political support.[3] Elevating neutrality to absolutist dogma, the Netherlands adopted a security posture that relied on an informal maritime ally (Britain), international law (the Hague conventions, including the Permanent Court of International Arbitration), a sense of ethical superiority, and denied itself the option of aggression even in defense of the national territory.

Even the idea of closer political or military ties with Belgium was not an acceptable topic for discussion, despite the logic and non-threatening nature of such small state cooperation. The assumption was that any ties to Belgium, which was perceived as the immediate victim of any Franco-German conflict, would only drag the Netherlands into war. Any alliance would restrict Dutch political freedom of movement.[4] The reasoning behind the absolutist neutrality policy also assumed that the absence of an offensive military capability would make the country a negligible threat to its powerful neighbors. The absence of threat would result in the absence of fear in the mind of a potential European adversary, who would then decline to attack. Defense budgets were minimal despite a significant manpower expansion of the land army after 1901. Annual defense expenditures for the period 1900–1913 averaged about 2.2 percent of Net Domestic Product.[5]

The Netherlands escaped the scourge of World War One, not due to neutrality, but because the German General Staff calculated that a flanking attack on France could be carried out solely through Belgium and thus avoiding the encumbrance of also violating Dutch neutral territory.[6] The lesson drawn by Dutch political leaders was that a nearly unarmed defense posture was indeed the proper policy. The presence of a strong moralistic streak of partially Calvinist origin encouraged the continuation of the neutrality dogma. Thus, it continued to seek security by promoting international law. The pacifism of the political left, which achieved substantial representation in parliament in 1913 but refused to participate in government until 25 years later, encouraged the maintenance of a rather passive neutrality policy. Furthermore, a conflict was perceived between a policy of avoiding posturing moves that might upset any other power, on the one hand, and, on the other hand, the League of Nations' collective security *conditio sine qua non* of preventive or punitive joint action (whether armed or otherwise) against those that threaten the peace. The result was that the Netherlands opted out of any requirement for collective action and thus, ironically, contributed to the impotence of League of Nations.[7] Until 1937, when a new general staff study of the Netherlands' strategic situation in case of a new Franco-German war shattered some of the neutrality illusions, post-World War I annual defense expenditures remained very low at an average of 1.68 percent of the Net National Product.[8] On the eve of war in May 1940, the Dutch managed to mobilize an army of 250,000 mostly ill-trained conscripts out of a population of 9 million.[9]

Belgium

The London Treaty of 1839 not only formalized the acceptance by the Netherlands of the new Belgium, but also confirmed a British guarantee of Belgian neutrality. The King, Leopold I, as constitutional Commander-in-Chief of the armed forces in name and in practice, continually emphasized that the country's geographic proximity to France and Germany required a policy of well-armed neutrality. Unlike the case of the Netherlands or Luxembourg, his international and domestic stature and influence was such that he dominated the Belgian foreign policy making process at the expense of parliament's prerogatives. His successors, albeit to a much lesser degree after World War II, all managed to strongly influence foreign policy as well.[10]

Consequently, though there was only limited political and public support, even following the scare caused by the Franco-Prussian war of 1870–1871, successive Belgian monarchs still managed to convince the government to maintain armed forces and fortifications of greater size and quality than those of the Netherlands. Despite opposition in parliament and government, the fundamental policy of armed neutrality and the active defense of the national territory were never seriously in doubt.

Scarred by German occupation and the horrors of WWI trench warfare, successive postwar Belgian governments and parliaments were much more receptive to royal arguments about strong armed forces. The Versailles Treaty allowed Belgium freedom in its foreign policy by relieving it of the strict neutrality requirement of the 1839 London Treaty. Belgium pursued a double-track policy of engaging itself deeply in collective security agreements such as the League or Nations and the Briand-Kellogg pact and also, more controversially, entering into a largely secret defensive military alliance with France. This alliance did much to sour Dutch-Belgian relations and prevent military cooperation useful for their common interests. The threat of renewed Franco-German war caused Belgian leaders to fear that Belgium would be used by France as a shield to keep the war outside France. The alliance was dissolved in 1936 and Belgium returned to armed neutrality and eschewed alliances. The outcome of this policy shift was that Britain and France agreed in 1937 to guarantee the inviolability of Belgian neutrality and both countries extended a promise of military assistance in case of attack.[11]

The adventure of the interbellum period exemplifies the security dilemma experienced by small powers like Belgium or the Netherlands. The alliance with France might have deterred an aggressive Germany, but at the consequence of being dragged into a French foreign policy debacle such as the 1923 occupation of the German Ruhr area. The resulting costs involved international (especially British) disapproval, a further alienated Germany, and a suspicious Netherlands. The latter would mistrust Belgian intentions and fear a Franco-Belgian military intervention onto Dutch territory in order to cover against or outflank German units in case of a war between France and Germany. French military planning and the location of its Maginot defensive line indicated that the only feasible approach into France for a warring Germany would be through Belgium and the Netherlands. Clearly then, an alliance with France meant that a Franco-German war would be fought with certainty in Belgium. Survival would then depend entirely on French goodwill. On the other hand, independent neutrality made Belgium dependent on German goodwill. Only with the Netherlands did national interests really coincide, but the gap between the two over the content of a neutrality policy and basic trust was too wide to allow any joint front.

During those inter-war years, long-growing fissures began to open in the Belgian social, political, and cultural fabric. The domination of the life of the country by francophone elites was in slow decline and the struggle for power and control between Belgium's linguistic communities achieved an intensity that, by the 1980s, resulted in the transformation of a unitary and very centralized political system into a highly decentralized federal state. The antagonistic relationship between the Dutch-speaking Flemish and the francophone Walloons continue to this day to play a significant role in the formulation of Belgian foreign policy. Before World War II, these internal divisions affected foreign policy in that it encumbered security cooperation with the Netherlands. The secrecy involving the alliance with France limited public debate on that topic.

Flemish public opinion (especially those who espoused Flemish nationalist sentiments) showed itself very suspicious of French entanglements and sensitive to the pacifism not only of socialists, but also of Flemish war veterans who harbored a strong resentment to what they saw as prejudicial treatment by the francophone officer class. Still, the dominance of the executive (King and Cabinet) largely shielded security policy from party politics and parliament supported large military budgets, especially after tensions began to increase in the 1930s. Attacked in May of 1940, Belgium managed to mobilize an impressive but still under equipped force of 650,000 out of a population of 8.4 million. A further 250,000 men of military age were ordered to France for training.[12]

Luxembourg

By far the smallest of the Benelux nations (population 283,000 in 1945; 420,000 at present), Luxembourg's limited resources made armed neutrality unfeasible as a security policy. Instead, it relied on others to provide the military muscle to deter potential aggressors. After independence in 1839, it joined the German Confederation, a collective security system aimed at preventing Prussian dominance in Germany. The demise of the confederation in 1866 led to the departure of Confederation troops and Luxembourg choosing a permanent demilitarized neutrality which lasted until 1940, when, as in 1914, the country was overrun by German troops.[13]

Post-WWII Security: A Regional Alliance Framework with Transatlantic Counterweight

An Alliance, But Which One?

The rapid military defeats and surrender of The Netherlands and Belgium after, respectively, four and eighteen days of battle in May of 1940 put the neutrality policy into receivership. The British and French 'guarantee' proved to be a woefully ineffective deterrent to the Nazi aggressor. The defeat of France also cast doubt on what, at least to the Belgians, had seemed to be the one alternative to neutrality: A bilateral alliance with France, for Britain historically eschewed formal alliances.

The governments of the Benelux countries fled into a long London exile and drew the conclusions of their defeat: The policy of avoiding commitments had been unsuccessful and likely even contributed to war. Divided, they had been easy prey. Any post-war security would have to be built on a multilateral basis with firm commitments and many powerful partners. Equally clear was that the small powers needed to cooperate closely in order to have their voices heard and their interests served. Asymmetrical bilateral alliances like the Franco-Belgian agreement of 1920 were the wrong tool.

Within weeks, the first foundations were laid for a new post-war security architecture by the initiation of a continual process of close consultation, cooperation and planning between Belgium and the Netherlands in security and economic matters. This led to the 1944 Benelux Economic Union agreement (patterned on the 1921 Belgian-Luxembourg Economic Union), which came to be the model for European economic integration. Already in the fall of 1940, the two governments also agreed on a common defense goal: A regional and European collective security system linked to a great extra-continental power.

What also surfaced were the different national interpretations of how to put the security goal into practice. The inclusion of the greatest number of European nations was to act as the means of countering German or (in the future) Soviet power. However, the Dutch thought it imperative to attach the United States and Canada to this new security system as the ultimate guarantee in case the European system could not muster sufficient will or strength to stop the two largest continental powers. On the other hand, the Belgian analysis saw such a system as replacing the domination of Europe by one great power with the domination of an extra-continental power. The Belgian government's more modest plan would avoid collecting too many nations of too many differing interests and views and focus on a regional (west) European arrangement with the United Kingdom as the great power anchor. The decline of British and French power and status due to the world war made this scheme impracticable and the Dutch analysis dominated until the end of the Cold War.

Economic factors play a role as well in the security thinking of the Benelux. Though all three countries are among the most globalized, as their limited home markets require them to seek export markets, there are nevertheless real differences in their historic trade patterns and international outlook. The Dutch, who built a global trading empire in the 16th and 17th centuries, have to this day nurtured a global outlook with the British as their reference point. Their fear, born of the experience of the Napoleonic wars, World War I, and World War II, was for a French or German protectionist trade regime that would cut off the Netherlands from its global markets. The Belgians' economic focus has always been continental, in large part due to foreign occupation, denial of access to the seas by the Dutch, and their late arrival as an unenthusiastic colonial power in 1909. Furthermore, for a long time, Belgian elites, for cultural and linguistic reasons, used France as their reference point.

A fundamental belief common to all three countries was that the wartime coalition of nations from across Europe should be retained as a means to promote the relaxation of tensions and preventing Europe from dividing and repeating history.[14] This theme continues to this day to underpin the foreign and security approaches of the Benelux countries.

Following the end of the war in Europe, security thinking was dominated initially by fears of an eventual German resurgence, but, quite rapidly, it became clear that the USSR would not demobilize, sought to exert increasing control over the eastern European states, and was using the western European communist parties as some form of fifth column. The Benelux countries lost faith in the United Nations as a collective security mechanism. Major power vetoes in the Security Council indicated that it could not guarantee security in Europe.

The Benelux approach threw off its first fruits in response to a 1947 Franco-British defense alliance aimed against Germany. When individual offers for participation were made to each of the Benelux countries, the three pursued a collective approach and jointly proposed to the UK and France the formation of a European multilateral organization with responsibility for collective defense, economic, social, and cultural matters. A supranational body was to be charged with security planning and consultation on other issues. The UK and France countered that such a supranational body would cause the US to disengage from Europe. The Benelux demurred, arguing that the Truman Doctrine and the Marshall Plan suggested otherwise. (Later events proved the Benelux analysis correct.) France and the UK relented and the Brussels Treaty was signed in 1948.[15]

Thus, the Benelux had achieved their collective goal of creating a regional security system that permanently tied the UK to the continent *and* included a structure that would give the small powers a means of controlling, or at least restraining, the major powers *and* that would allow their interests to be respected at the decision making table. As we will see later, the search by the Benelux countries for a viable security system during this period reveals much of their underlying motivation and is of considerable use in understanding the behavior of the Benelux governments in the face of more recent events, such as the 2003 Iraq war. The Brussels Treaty signatories proceeded to set up the Western Union Defense Organization with a military command and staff structure and appointments were made. However, the founding of NATO the following year caused the military functions to be moved to NATO. What remained was renamed Western European Union in 1955 in connection with the accession of the Federal Republic of Germany and Italy. Though members continued to meet, the organization did not return to an active role until the late 1980s, when it conducted a small minesweeping operation in the Persian Gulf.

When the question of German rearmament was raised by the US in 1950, the French response was to seek the creation of a European Defense Community (EDC) as a means of integrating German military units into a unified European army designed to prevent the emergence of independent German military capabilities. Belgium supported it because it fitted in well with the Belgian vision of European integration and would pacify anti-German feelings that were still strong so shortly after the war. It also was a way of strengthening European resistance capabilities with German resources but without arousing too much Soviet anger.

The Netherlands saw US participation in NATO and European security as an absolute necessity and was therefore very wary of the EDC proposal, fearing that an independent European army would drive a wedge into the transatlantic relationship, undermine American leadership, diminish NATO effectiveness, and thus endanger Dutch security. From the Dutch perspective, an exclusively continental alliance would be too dominated by purely French interests, too unreliable (France had been defeated in the war), too weak, too likely to drive Germany into neutrality or into Soviet hands. Only after initial American and UK coolness had been overcome would the Dutch participate in the EDC negotiations. Eventually, however, the issue of a European army became moot as the UK pulled out and France scuppered its own project.

During all of this diplomatic maneuvering towards a security architecture for Western Europe, the Luxembourgers were nearly invisible. Security policy was coordinated with Belgium as the two countries' security interests are largely similar and are viewed in the same way. Other than membership and moral/diplomatic support, Luxembourg's size made it impossible to contribute much more than a token force of 4500 men drawn from conscripts and a territorial militia. Since it was the most enthusiastic supporter of European integration and since its interests focused on the bordering countries, Luxembourg would have agreed to any regional security alliance that involved, tied, and pacified all those countries in one organization. In that sense, US participation was secondary for Luxembourg as it has no choice but to embrace and support whatever friendly alliance is available.

The Benelux countries' main concerns during the Cold War were to maintain a viable alliance and safeguard their right to be consulted as equal alliance members. When France withdrew from the military side of the alliance in 1965 and forced the removal of NATO institutions from French soil, Benelux states worked together to put forward a common position on the issue and a common plan for the transfer of NATO facilities to sites in their countries. It was a coup, as it raised their profile in the alliance and gave them a better platform from which to promote their interests, including the equal right to full consultation and an equal, full role as members of the alliance.

This right repeatedly came under direct and indirect attack. The major NATO powers on several occasions attempted to centralize some or all political and military decision making in a body made up exclusively of major powers. The alliance's formal consultation and decision making processes in the North Atlantic Council (NAC) can be time-consuming, require unanimous consent, and thus consensus building that limits the freedom of action major powers tend to favor. At each juncture, the Benelux nations strongly opposed any move away from the existing system of deliberations in NAC, where each member had an equal voice and where the right of small-country consultation would be assured. For example, in 1965, US Secretary of Defense McNamara proposed that the five largest NATO members form a group to handle nuclear planning for all of NATO. The Netherlands and Belgium stonewalled and, in the end, all NATO members could be on the Nuclear Defense Affairs Committee and Belgium and the Netherlands would rotate a seat on the more select Nuclear Planning Group.[16]

Post-Cold War Security: Atlanticist Netherlands, Europeanist Belgium

The Netherlands: Consensus Lost, Consensus Regained

Dutch foreign and security policy from 1945 to 1990 was characterized by a continuity unaffected by the party composition of the coalition governments and based on three principles: First, the Atlantic security relationship is the only durable security option; second, the European economic integration must be deepened and broadened; and, third, using democratic supra-national institutions and regulations, it was necessary to limit or prevent the domination of European decision making by the large countries. So, where France might have seen a European Union as a means of pacifying Germany, the Netherlands and other small powers saw the Union in some measure as a security straitjacket with which to restrain the antagonistic and hegemonic tendencies of the great European powers.[17]

In the long run, these principles could not coexist forever. The first assumption can last only so long as the United States is committed to defending Europe. The second assumption breaks down under its own integrationist logic: Eventually, economic integration creates pressures for integration in other areas. Freedom of movement of goods, services, people, and money within the European Union soon enough begs for joint regulation of borders, internal security, and, eventually, external security. The third assumption fails when decision making and pooling of resources is supranationalized, as with the Common Agricultural Policy and monetary policy, it becomes increasingly difficult to avoid the notion of efficient pooling of military resources and making security decisions at the supranational level.

The unification of Germany, the collapse of the Soviet Union, and the democratization of Eastern Europe challenged the underpinnings of both the EU and NATO. The asymmetry in power between Germany and the other large European powers created fears of German dominance. A free Eastern Europe would come knocking on the EU door, threatening all existing institutional and decision making structures and thus the tenuous balance between large and small. The absence of a real threat led very quickly to a significant reduction in US forces in Europe and the process of rethinking US foreign policy priorities.

Early on in the 1990s and in concert with many other small European states, Dutch foreign policy began to emphasize more strongly the use of large multilateral organizations as tools for peace and security in the unstable Eastern Europe. The disappearance of East-West antagonism unblocked the UN Security Council and allowed for increasing consensus in the OSCE, raising hopes that the United Nations and the Organization for Security and Cooperation in Europe (OSCE) could now begin to play the pacification role for which they had been designed.

The wars of the dissolution of Yugoslavia proved that path to be a dead end. In the violence that engulfed the new post-Yugoslav republics, the EU sent monitors in order to dissuade the violence. They were ignored and some were killed. The EU withdrew. The UN and the OSCE sent peacekeeping forces to provide and protect humanitarian assistance and safeguard populations at risk. The Dutch participated enthusiastically at first. The 1995 mass-murder of Muslim civilians at the Bosnian town of Srebrenica supposedly under the protection a Dutch battalion of UN blue helmets gave stark evidence of the lack of international and Dutch institutional and individual resolve to act in the face of a determined opponent. Such lack of resolve only encouraged the authors of ethnic cleansing and empire building.[18]

The UN and OSCE could not make peace, because they could not make war. Violence in the Balkans was stopped only when the United States and NATO forced the local aggressors into negotiations through aerial bombing in Bosnia in 1995 and in Kosovo in 1999. These events taught once more the lesson that those determined to use violence can only be deterred by those who have the capability and the will to answer with equal or superior violence.

The conclusion drawn in the Netherlands was that Dutch and European security was still best guaranteed by NATO and a United States committed to Europe and the Atlantic partnership. Government and parliament welcomed initiatives such as NATO's Partnership for Peace Program and NATO membership for the Central and Eastern European countries. The Atlantic relationship reacquired its primacy among Dutch foreign and security policy values.

The 1992 Maastricht treaty, signed in the euphoria of the end of the Cold War, committed the members of the European Union to the principle of a common foreign and security policy (CFSP). The practical application of this principle is quite watery. The treaty and subsequent modifications are very vague as to the goals (such as "preserve peace and strengthen international security" and "promote international cooperation"). While a small "policy planning and early warning unit" has been added, the implementation of policy is still the responsibility of the individual states and the decisions, should they be forthcoming, are still the preserve of that most intergovernmental of EU institutional creatures: The Council of Ministers.

This is the point where the Dutch practice of separating foreign/security policy from economic integration collided with the consequences of integration. During the first half of the 1990s, when the Netherlands moved in the OSCE-UN direction, the CFSP may not have seemed a problem, but when the consensus shifted back towards Atlanticism, it found itself in a difficult position.

The Netherlands has long been a strong proponent of supranationalism and thus the use of common decision making as a means for small countries to prevent domination by the large players. Now that security policy has become potentially subject to an EU vote, we see a move on the part of the Dutch and others back towards intergovernmentalism and a member country's right of self-exemption from the consequences of EU decisions.[19] The suspicion is that, especially after the expansion of the EU to 25 members, the desire for institutional effectiveness and coherence will generate a move towards a 'directorium' or exclusive group of mostly major countries that will come to dominate agenda setting and decision making. This fear has been fanned by increasingly frequent get-togethers of some combination of British, French, and German heads of government before or during major EU summits.

The Netherlands Army

Since the collapse in 1954 of the effort to build a European Defense Community, only the dormant Western European Union (WEU) has represented the idea of a purely European force.[20] After coordinating a small operation in the Persian Gulf in the 1980s, it was to form the umbrella for some European forces in the 1990–1991 Gulf conflict, but that clearly exceeded its limited organizational capabilities.

In the so-called Petersberg Declaration of 1992, member states agreed that the WEU can be used to run humanitarian, rescue, peacekeeping and other crisis management tasks. Since then, it has taken part in various smallish operations in southeastern Europe in conjunction with NATO, the UN, and the OSCE. There is much division among EU members as to the true purpose of the WEU. Some see it as the nascent military arm of the CFSP while others see it as the European pillar of NATO. The Achilles heel of the WEU is that it has no troops of its own. It must ask members to provide the troops and their equipment. After the Petersberg Declaration, several small multinational units were created or reassigned and could be perceived as the testing ground for a European force that might operate outside of the NATO command structure.

Like other NATO members, the Netherlands reduced the size of its armed forces after the collapse of the Soviet Union. Personnel strength has decline by 43 percent from about 132,000 in 1990 to circa 75,000 at present. Notable is that nearly a quarter of the effectives are civilian employees. Conscription was abolished in 1996. Reserves allow for an additional 55,000 to be called up, but only one tenth of these forces can be considered active reserve with recent training. Adjusted for inflation, the Netherlands spends about 20 percent less on defense than it did in the last years of the Cold War.

The mission of the Royal Netherlands Army (RNLA), Royal Netherlands Navy (RNLN), Royal Netherlands Air Force (RNLAF), and Royal Netherlands Marechaussee (RNLM – a constabulary police force with both civilian and military tasks) has come to be described in increasingly broad terms. In the past, the mission was focused on deterring and fighting a (Soviet) threat to the national sovereignty of the country and its allies. In the present, the threat environment has been defined in the broadest fashion, including the political, social, economic, humanitarian, and ecological spheres. The mission is therefore not only to protect the territorial integrity of the Netherlands and its NATO allies, but also carry out global crisis management operations of a humanitarian, peace-building, peace-making, and peace-enforcing nature.[21]

A small country in a large alliance and faced with the centrifugal budget pressures of a typical democracy seeks cooperation for both symbolic and economic reasons. Pooling of resources and specialization generates needed savings. A significant part of the Navy's Marines are integrated into a brigade-sized United Kingdom/Netherlands Amphibious Force and most of the Army is integrated into a joint German-Netherlands army corps structure headquartered in Germany. Since 1996, the Dutch and Belgian Navies have operated under a joint command headed by the 'Admiral Benelux' at the Den Helder naval base and logistics and training have been integrated. One notes here that Luxembourg maintains a small funding participation in the Belgian Navy. In the air, cooperation has taken the form of Belgium providing airlift for both countries and the RNLAF providing aerial refueling services. The Netherlands, Belgium, and Germany cooperate in ensuring national airspace protection. Luxembourg participates in that it will fund one of the new A400M military cargo aircraft on order for the Belgian Air Force.

One notes that all this cooperation occurs in a NATO context. When France and Britain announced in 1998 their intent to create European armed forces with the capability to operate both within and outside the NATO organization, The Netherlands' government was quite taken aback and reacted very coolly to the idea, fearing that this would dilute or directly harm NATO. However, the integrationist logic is now catching up on the Netherlands and it cannot really unilaterally withdraw or isolate itself from the trend towards some kind of European force. With much trepidation and despite its opposition to Eurocorps, the government agreed to participate and contribute to the expenses, while it seeks to restrain such a force from operating outside the NATO umbrella.[22]

Belgium: Political and Budgetary Chaos

In Belgium, the NATO commitment was never underpinned by the regular parliamentary re-affirmations of support one could find in the Netherlands. Foreign policy decision making in the Belgian political system is the prerogative of the executive. Parliament is largely limited to using parliamentary debates and questions after the fact to try and exert some influence over future policy. Furthermore, the evolution of the practices of governance and the political culture in Belgium have gradually reduced parliament to a virtual rubberstamp. Policy decisions are the product of a negotiated consensus within and between the Cabinet and the leadership of the parties in the governing coalition. Parliament is then presented with a take-it-or-leave-it deal. Party discipline almost always prevails among the members of parliament of the governing parties.

During the last 50 years, Belgium has increasingly suffered from severe disputes between the two main ethno-linguistic groups: The Dutch-speaking Flemish of Flanders and the Francophone inhabitants of Wallonia and Brussels. Paranoia and mistrust of each other's intentions marks every move in Belgian politics. The political response to the forces that threatened to split Belgium down the middle was the self-transformation of the Belgian state between the late 1960s and the late 1990s from a highly centralized system of government into a highly decentralized federal monarchy. This process and its results and consequences are significant for understanding contemporary Belgian foreign and security policy. It set in train or magnified a number of new and pre-existing trends that shattered the superficial consensus underpinning Belgium's support for NATO and the Atlantic Alliance.

The traditional political parties split exist along linguistic lines and the spectrum is made broader by the presence of regional nationalist or separatist parties. Governing coalitions number anywhere between 4 and 7 parties. Decision making processes have slowed down and policy is made up of compromises that are tenuously complex affairs of interlocking bargains made to satisfy all participants, be they political parties, organized interests, government institutions at federal and state levels, and linguistic communities. Not surprisingly, newspaper columns frequently complain that the country has become ungovernable. The secrecy of the political bargaining process, necessary to prevent the inflaming of intercommunal tensions, has only increased the existing lack of transparency in the making of foreign and security policy.

The rise of the environmental movement and quality of life concerns in the broader population from the mid-1970s on has produced the appearance of so-called 'green' political parties. These parties, at least in Belgium and the Netherlands, combine previously politically inactive young people, environmentalists, anti-nuclear groups, anti-globalization activists, pacifists, and communists who sought a home after their party ceased to attract voters, as well as other members of the political left who did not feel at home in the traditional socialist parties that supported collective defense and industrial development. In the 1990s, the green parties achieved the electoral success that allowed them to influence policymaking through their entry in the government coalition in Belgium. At the same time, Flemish separatists made strong electoral gains as well, bringing into parliament another group that took a dim view of Belgian armed forces and the Atlantic alliance.

The Belgian political landscape is thus characterized by strong political movements against war no longer held in check by a fear of the Soviet Union and by suspicious communities that require a governmental decision making process that requires a very high degree of pacification and compromise. In this climate, it is easy to understand that, in combination with the economic and budgetary difficulties, the political climate is not conducive to defense spending, NATO, and an alliance with the one remaining superpower.

More so than most Western European states and unlike the Netherlands, Belgium has suffered from severe structural budgetary and economic problems since the oil shocks of the 1970s. This is largely caused by a lack of political will and maneuvering room to make more than minimal, gradual reforms in rigid labor markets, high direct and indirect taxation, health care, pensions, and other components of the overly costly welfare state.[23]

In addition, Belgium faced serious difficulties in reaching the goal of joining Europe's single currency, the Euro, in 1999. Belgium violated two of the major norms set for entrants: Annual budget deficits of no more than 3% of GDP and a net public debt of less than 60% of Gross Domestic Product (GDP). The reality of the 1980s and early 1990s was a national debt to GDP ratio that was the largest in the EU, peaking at 134% in 1993, and a persistent government deficit that hovered often far above 6 percent of GDP during the 1980s and into the early 1990s.[24] The combined result of the aforementioned structural factors was to create tremendous pressure on the Belgian government to cut discretionary spending for a long time into the future in order to meet the Maastricht targets and concurrently finance the welfare state.

On the political front, the Post-Cold War environment contained nothing to restrain massive cuts in the defense budget. As in the Netherlands, defense spending in Belgium does not have the kind of constituency enjoyed in say Britain or France or the US. There are few, if any defense contractors of note. Total defense industry employment is at about 7000 jobs, concentrated in Wallonia.[25] There is a small aerospace industry, but it is oriented towards Airbus, the giant pan-European commercial airline manufacturer. It occasionally picks up subcontracts. Only small arms are manufactured indigenously by the FN Herstal company in the francophone part of Belgium. Peculiarly, the military is unionized, but the small numbers do not create political weight and the same can be said for veterans. Belgium has no historical military tradition, unlike for example the Royal Netherlands Navy.

Based on the party election programs, no political parties can be counted on as being particularly supportive of sizeable armed forces. The green and socialist parties are either outright pacifist in their outlook or contain large pacifist wings. If industrial jobs in the francophone region of Belgium are on the line, the francophone socialist party may be counted on to support a company like FN. Flemish nationalists distrust the armed forces, which they tend to see as a bastion of francophone power. The other parties of the political center and right, though not pacifist, do not see defense as a priority, especially as there is no discernible direct threat for the short-medium term.

There is little public discussion of defense in Belgium. For example, the armed forces are not to be found on the agenda of recent conventions of the francophone socialist party. ("De uitdaging. Andre Flahaut") This party, which dominates Wallonia, is the party of Andre Flahaut, who has served as Minister of Defense since 1999. He is not known as a major national political figure, unlike defense ministers who served during the Cold War. Clearly then, the ministry has lost much political clout. Even more significant is that the coalition agreement and government policy declaration (always given when a new Prime Minister and cabinet take office) of the 1999–2003 cabinet of Prime Minister Verhofstadt did not even mention defense.[26]

Even should there be a direct threat, one would still have to contend with what economists call the free-rider problem. Small, post-colonial states like the Benelux countries, surrounded by much larger allies with sizable armed forces and even nuclear weapons, have little incentive to invest in armed forces themselves unless they are forced to do so by others. This is even true for medium-sized countries such as Italy. Ever since joining NATO, defense budgets in the Benelux and Italy have declined significantly from 5% or more of GDP in 1950 to between 1 and 2% of GDP. An additional indicator of this problem is that the budgetary share of investment in equipment declines and the share of personnel cost increases. In 2001, the latter percentage was 67.6% for Belgium and 40% for the United Kingdom.[27]

The Belgian Armed Forces after the Cold War: A Case of Political Neglect

The Post-Cold War evolution of Belgian defense spending should thus come as no surprise. In early 1989, even before the cold war was over and in a climate of relaxed tensions due to Soviet President Mikhail Gorbachev's cautious internal reforms, budgetary pressure on the Ministry of Defense forced Chief of Staff Lieutenant-General Charlier to formulate a plan for deep cuts to operating expenses. The end of the Cold War increased the pressure and Charlier offered a revised plan ('Charlier-bis'). This new plan called for a near 50% reduction in the number of the land army's operational battalions from 41 to 22. The air force had to consolidate bases, lost 20 planes, and was required to reduce the operational readiness of the remaining fighter units. The Navy also would have to reduce operational readiness and would suffer the non-replacement of 14 ageing minesweepers. Lastly, the plan envisaged the withdrawal of most of the troops of the mechanized division (undersized with two weak brigades) that had been stationed in Germany since the 1950s. The plan received bitter criticism from within the military. As usual, it became the subject in 1991 of communal political tensions between Flemings and Walloons over the intended locations for resettlement of the troops returning from Germany and the closure and consolidation of military bases.[28]

In quick succession, responding to budgetary pressures and the changes in the external threat environment, new plans for further reductions followed during the 1990s. In 1993, the multi-year Delcroix plan, named after then Minister of Defense, ended conscription and reduced manpower further to about 42,500 military personnel from the 1990 level of about 95,000. Major armaments programs were canceled. All services closed bases and released for sale up to 30% of their major materiel. A reserve of 30,000 was promised, drawn from retired military and retired short-term (max service term of 5 years) volunteers.[29] In 1996, the spending freeze was unfrozen for a further reduction and then re-frozen and extended.

Political, budgetary, and electoral considerations fueled the chaotic haste with which these decisions were made and carried out. As a consequence, Belgium has ended up with poorly motivated, dysfunctional armed forces running on insufficient and outdated materiel. Particularly troublesome are the fundamental imbalances in the structure of the forces, such as a 20% excess of NCOs and an age average for the military that is 10 years higher than found in the US and the UK. Quite aside from the obvious lack of fighting capability, the budgetary outcome of these structural problems is to further weaken the Belgian armed forces. The personnel budget eats up 68% of defense spending, as it must pay for a top-heavy and (relatively) aged armed force at the high end of the pay scales. The problem of severe underinvestment in equipment and operations is thus further amplified.[30]

The poor shape of the armed forces has led to the development of the first meaningful long-term strategic plan in more than two generations: Vision 2015. According to this plan, the purpose of the armed forces is to contribute to the defense of the territory of NATO allies and to participate in crisis-response and non-combatant evacuation operations (NEO). It further assumes that all operations, save for NEO, will be conducted in an international framework.

These tasks are to be accomplished with a small, mobile, modular, well-equipped, quick intervention force. Force levels will be reduced to 35,000 uniformed personnel under a unified armed forces staff and command. Rejuvenation of personnel will be used to reduce personnel costs and fund increased investment, because the defense budget is to remain frozen in real terms for the foreseeable future (and this after a long freeze of the nominal defense budget has significantly eroded its current value). Investments will focus on improving air and sealift capabilities and acquiring such other materiel as light armored vehicles in order to improve mobility. Operational units are to be strengthened and administrative units trimmed.[31]

Where the Dutch cooperated inside the NATO context through integration in the GE/NL corps, Belgian policy has been to seek further integration in a European context. In a 2003 interview, Defense Minister Flahaut stated that Belgium would emphasize the development of the European defense capabilities and international cooperation. As for NATO, he stated that "the development of the European defense pillar is not aimed against NATO, but we cannot allow Europe to be subservient to NATO."[32]

The foreign and security policy declaration of the current government in Belgium is titled "A Strong Europe" and speaks of creating a renewed and reformulated Atlantic Alliance based on two strong pillars: A European and a North American pillar. Also projected are a review of existing NATO agreements, an evolution of NATO towards an organization that protects world peace under UN mandate, and a joint availability of NATO military assets to the EU and vice versa.[33] The main military vehicle for this policy appears to be the Franco-German so-called Eurocorps, to which Belgium in 1993 offered virtually its entire land army. We should emphasize here that such units would be 'double-hatted,' meaning that they concurrently fulfill a NATO and Eurocorps role and should be callable by each. For immediate response to crisis situations, Belgium has offered a brigade of 3000 plus air and sea assets for the European fast intervention force that is currently being created.[34]

The Iraq Crisis and the Future of Benelux Security

For small countries, an EU foreign and security policy represents a collective security umbrella that they need. This matters especially for the Eastern European aspirant members who still cast a weary eye on Russia and the Balkans. Even though the EU is not a military alliance, the level of integration in the EU makes it unlikely that an attack on one member could be left unanswered by the other members without causing the collapse of the whole edifice.

Present weighted voting procedures in the European Council, the top decision making body of the EU, allow the small countries to block the large countries. From the perspective of the small powers, this is a necessity as small country interests are regional or continental, while Britain and France define their interests in global terms. Inevitably, this leads to clashes with the EU over the CFSP. While Britain prefers to see the EU in shape of an economic club and an intergovernmental cooperative mechanism, France sees the EU as an opportunity.

Both countries still nurture a self-image as global power broker, even though they themselves know this power is a hollow perception. If France can dominate it, the EU becomes the hydraulic platform for French ambition to return to true global power status. Thus, France's ambitions stand diametrically opposed to those of the small powers, whose national interest is to prevent the great powers from dragging them into extra-European adventures. Everybody wants a CFSP, but for mutually exclusive purposes. Therefore, CSFP is doomed to remain a goal.

The European reactions to US and British military operations in Afghanistan and especially Iraq in 2001–2003 gave all too clear evidence of the mirage that is CSFP. The EU had no voice as members split into different camps speaking harsh words. Countries of the western and southern peripheries of Europe, with their maritime outlooks across the ocean and those living on the eastern periphery, uncomfortably near the Russian Federation, were more supportive of the US.

The Eastern European members-to-be, their eyes firmly fixed on their eastern border and their newly acquired membership of NATO, pursued their interest in nurturing a security relationship with the US and supported its war in Iraq and Afghanistan. French leaders spoke bitter words implying Eastern European betrayal of the EU and punishment after entry into the EU, an attitude that must have looked quite ironic to the victims of French and British pre-World War II appeasement. The Eastern European countries' policy reflected a desire to prove their commitment to their US ally in the hope of promoting in return a long term US commitment to their security. While the EU serves a purpose as a back up to NATO security guarantees, its value for now lies more with market access, assistance, and economic growth. The continentally oriented nations of Europe, safely in the middle, such as Belgium and Luxembourg, joined the French and German chorus of opposition and criticism to the United States' Iraq policy.

The four reasons at the basis of this behavior were domestic politics, personal egotism, enthusiasm for a European defense and foreign policy, and fear of American unilateralism.

The Belgian government faced an election in June of 2003. The six party coalition of right of center liberals, socialists, and greens had shown serious signs of instability during its time in office. Frequent rows erupted between the greens and their coalition partners. Adopting a course even mildly or verbally supportive to the US would have caused the pacifist greens and possibly even Flemish socialists to bolt from the coalition. A collapse of the government within weeks of a general election was a scenario no incumbent government or candidate wished to face, let alone the fact that public opinion was strongly opposed to US policy and the idea of deploying troops outside Europe. Peace activists had on several occasions attempted to stop the transport of US military materiel passing through Belgium on it way to the Middle East.

Electoral and domestic political calculation often encourages Belgium's voluble Foreign Minister Michel into raising his public profile on a regular basis when domestic capital can be made of foreign affairs. Michel and his right of center Liberal Reform party are locked in a struggle for political primacy in Wallonia. The same can be said for its Flemish Liberal Democratic sister party in Flanders. Both parties' election manifestoes have migrated increasingly towards the political center and left in order to capture larger numbers of voters. Expressing skepticism of US intentions and stressing international law and international organizations (the UN and the EU) as cornerstones of foreign policy works well with those center-left voters Michel is seeking to woo.

Politicians in the francophone parts of Belgium (that is Wallonia and Brussels) often take cues and inspiration from France. The Flemish tends to be more inward looking and do not share the Atlantic orientation of the Netherlands. For example, at the time of NATO's deliberations over the modernization of tactical and intermediate-range nuclear weapons in the early 1980s, the Walloon political parties originally opposed the modernization, only to reverse course after the French Socialist government under President François Mitterrand announced its support for modernization. In addition, both France and Belgium are experiencing difficulties integrating large legal and illegal immigrants from the Mediterranean and Africa. Conservative and other right of center parties experience strong competition from parties of the far right who have raised immigration and especially Muslim immigrants as an electoral issue. At the same time, one is fearful of antagonizing Muslim immigrants. From the left comes a multicultural message of tolerance that attracts votes from that community. Therefore, given shared problems and interests, one should not be surprised at the Belgian orientation towards the French position.

As emphasized repeatedly, the lesser powers use multilateral organizations to restrain the greater powers. One recalls the previously mentioned interview with Belgian Defense Minister Flahaut, in which he implied that Europe and the United States should act as equal partners. The NATO institutions, while giving voice and veto to all members nevertheless also affirm American primacy and, to some, act as a limitation on European integration. Equality in relationship may give Europe the ability to balance the power of the US at some point in the future.

Shorter term, the fear is that a unilateralist United States as sole surviving superpower may drag European countries via NATO or some other way into conflicts that these countries do not wish to contemplate. The US vision of a global war on terror strikes fear in the hearts of many Europeans. Their own historical experiences with terrorism suggests that, while one might be able to subdue a single group, such a war would be endless in time and treasure. Other than Britain and France, none of the European nations define their interests as global. A global project is therefore anathema.

Occasional US rhetoric of crusades against evil play poorly with many a European public. Small nations have small horizons. That is how they survive. Generations of successful resolution of political problems with pacification and consensus politics makes it difficult to accept that there are circumstances when violence may have to be used. The political cultures of the Benelux instinctively turn against such unilateralist interventionist US policy and seek some means of limiting its freedom of action. Hence, one sees the appeals to international law, a requirement for UN Security Council imprimatur, and a EU Common Foreign and Security Policy. This is the way of Belgium and Luxembourg. The Dutch, preferring to stake their security more on a proven NATO than an unproven EU, like the British, see more success in efforts to restrain the United States by assisting it and thus gaining a voice as coalition partner.

Where is Belgian security policy going? On the face of it, the turmoil and neglect of the 1990s seems to have abated. The Vision 2015 plan suggests a more carefully considered policy with reasonable long-term objectives and the assignment of roughly equal weight to NATO and EU as implementers of security. The plans for the Belgian military component in this security system are well defined and, given the tasks set, they are broadly reasonable.

Unfortunately, there are strong indications that the Belgian security policy may amount to an unfunded or unaffordable mandate. The text of the 2003 government declaration on security policy is very vague on how it will be funded. Disturbing is the language on the re-equipment of the armed forces after more than a decade of neglect: To become both mobile and modern, heavy investments will be necessary. This will occur 'gradually,' the document states. There is no timetable. The experience of the last fifteen years is one of frequent cancellations of new equipment purchases. The financing method specified relies entirely on wringing fat out of an army that keeps getting smaller and smaller. This does not bode well.

The graying of Belgian demographics will not stop during the foreseeable future. The budget pressure from social spending on pensions and health care will only increase. European Union rules on budget deficits and public debt have not gone away, at least not for the smaller member states. If a political choice has to be made towards equipping for peacekeeping operations, the temptation will be large and the political cost of free riding in the NATO and EU security alliances, respectively dominated by the US-UK and France-Germany, will be negligible. The US may leave the continent, but France and Germany cannot.

Lastly, contemporary currents in Belgian politics will conspire against the fulfillment of Vision 2015. Political competition in Belgium has for some years now focused on a rivalry between a leftist socialist-green combination on the one hand and a right of center Liberal movement on the other hand. In the struggle for votes and influence in a post-industrial, perhaps even somewhat post-materialist society, there has emerged a tendency on the part of both sides to tell voters that government policy and programs do not have to cost money. For example, the seductive solution touted for traffic and pollution problems in Belgium is free public transport. This already has been partially implemented in certain towns and for retired persons. The example is but one illustration of a dangerous trend of fiscal irresponsibility in Belgian public policy and public discourse that will put further pressure on public finances.

The case of the Netherlands is a simpler one on which to conclude and point towards the future. The Dutch have managed the post-cold war transformation of their armed forces in a much more orderly manner than the Belgians, but then their political system lacks the chaos so endemic to Belgium and their budgetary resources are more flexible than those of Belgium. Still, Dutch security policy and, more broadly, its European policy are adrift because there is no clear Dutch European strategy or goal. As noted by van der Harst, the Netherlands is experiencing insecurity, because, in an expanding EU, it loses more and more the ability to be assertive of its own policy preferences.[35] Integration thus collides with national interest and the old certainties about the goodness of integration evaporate.

At the outset, I indicated that small countries have a difficult path to steer between doing what is necessary to find security in partnership with great powers, while hanging on to enough independence of action to retain control over their lives. In an international system that is still in transition from the Cold War order to whatever comes next, we find the Benelux countries uncertain whether to throw their lot in with the old, changing alliance or with the new, still embryonic European security architecture.

Belgium is in a position where it seems to have made a choice for a slow transition towards a European Union security system, but it is drifting towards a Luxembourg-like membership with little input and little influence over the future. The projected inability to fund even a very small armed force will deprive it of a voice at the table where security concerns are discussed and military plans are made.

The Netherlands seems to have the will and the state finances to take command of its security future in Europe and play a meaningful role in the creation of a European Union security arm. The logic of economic integration leads directly to the need for a common capability to safeguard the whole of the EU. That requires integrating security policy and the means to implement such policy. However, aloofness is keeping the Netherlands from playing the founding role in which it can influence together with others security integration in such a way that it does not clash with the goal of preserving the Atlantic alliance. In this, it should join in and follow the example of the United Kingdom, which has recognized that joining in the construction of a future European defense force is the best guarantee for the survival of the Atlantic alliance.

The long-term security challenges for a European Union will be global in nature and that suggests close coordination with the United States and Canada. European and North American interests are not mutually exclusive: Freedom of trade and investment and a peaceful international system. To retain the long-term global influence necessary to achieve these goals, the Atlantic alliance of North America and a cohesive European Union is an enduring necessity.

Notes

1   Judy Dempsey and James Blitz (2004), "Britain and France Join Forces to Create Rapid-Reaction Military Units," *Financial Times*, 10 February, 1.
2   De "nederlanden" ("low lands"), from which the English "Netherlands" originates historically referred to an area roughly comprising the territories of present-day Belgium and The Netherlands. They have experienced many foreign occupations. The most important event in their history was the permanent split caused by the Reformation into a Protestant United Netherlands in the north and the Catholic Spanish Netherlands in the south. That historical process plays a key role in the differences in outlook between Belgium/Luxembourg and the Netherlands.
3   George J. Stein (1990), *Benelux Security Cooperation: A New European Defense Community*, Boulder, CO: Westview Press, 2.
4   W. Klinkert and G. Teitler (2003), "Nederland van neutraliteit naar Bondgenootschap," Bob de Graaff, Duco Hellema and Bert van der Zwan, eds., *De Nederlandse buitenlandse politiek in de twintigste eeuw*, Zoetermeer, Netherlands: Boom, 9–13.
5   Calculated from Historical Tables, Netherlands Central Bureau of Statistics.

6	William Jannen, Jr. (1996), *The Lions of July: Prelude to War, 1914*, Novato, CA: Presidio Press, 159.

7	Stein, 4–5; Klinkert and Teitler, 18.

8	Netherlands Central Bureau of Statistics.

9	E. De Bruyne, G.B.J. Hiltermann, and H.R. Hoetink (1952), *Winkler Prins Encyclopedie Deel 14*, Amsterdam: Elsevier, 366.

10	Els Witte, Jan Craeybeckx and Alain Meynen (1997), *Politieke Geschiedenis Van Belgie: Van 1830 tot Heden*, Antwerpen: Standaard Uitgeverij NV, 45; also see Chapter 2 of Mark van den Wijngaert, Lieve Beullens, and Dana Brants (2000), *Belgie en zijn koningen: Monarchie en macht*. Antwerpen: Houtekiet.

11	Witte, Craeybeckx and Meynen, 186–190 and 217–225.

12	Roger Keyes, (1984), *Outrageous Fortune: The Tragedy of Leopold III of the Belgians 1901–1941*, London: Martin Secker & Warburg, 104; Wally Struys (2002), "Country Survey XV: Defence Policy and Spending in Belgium," *Defence and Peace Economics*, 13 (1), 33.

13	Stein, 2–5.

14	Ibid., 5–6.

15	Ibid., 8.

16	Ibid., 16–17.

17	Jan van der Harst (2003), "De verdwenen voorspelbaarheid: Het Nederlandse Europabeleid tijdens en na de Koude Oorlog; een vergelijking," Bob de Graaff, Duco Hellema and Bert van der Zwan, eds., *De Nederlandse buitenlandse politiek in de twintigste eeuw*, Zoetermeer, Netherlands: Boom, 132.

18	Details on the Srebrenica drama can be found in Jan Willem Honig and Norbert Both (1997), *Srebrenica: Record of a War Crime*, New York: Penguin Books; and Frank Westerman and Bart Rijs (1997), *Srebrenica: Het Zwartste Scenario*, Antwerp: Uitgeverij Atlas.

19	Van der Harst, 141.

20	Current membership of the WEU includes: (full members) – Belgium, France, Germany, Greece, Italy, Luxembourg, the Netherlands, Portugal, Spain, and the UK; (observers) – Austria, Denmark, Finland, Ireland, and Sweden; (associate members) – Iceland, Norway, Turkey, Czech, Hungary, and Poland; and (associate partners) Bulgaria, Estonia, Latvia, Lithuania, Romania, Slovakia, and Slovenia.

21	Jan van der Meulen, Axel Rosendahl Huber, and Joseph L. Soeters (2000), "The Netherlands' Armed Forces: An Organization Preparing for the Next Century," Jürgen Kuhlmann and Jean Callaghan, eds., *Military and Society in 21st Century Europe: A Comparative Analysis*, New Brunswick, NJ: Transaction Publishers, 285–286.

22	Van der Harst, 137–138.

23	André Leysen (1993), *De Naakte Staat*, Tielt, Belgium: Uitgeverij Lannoo nv.

24	Ibid., 88–96; Belgostat.

25	Struys, 45.

26	Bart Dobbelaere (2003), "Flahaut vraagt vriendelijk om meer geld voor defensie," *De Standaard*, 27 February, online at http://www.standaard.be/Misc/print.asp?articleID=DST27022003_012.

27	Giancarlo Graziola, Carlo D'Adda, Lorenzo Belfiori and Stefania Tomasini (1996), "Size, Determinants and Effects of Italian Military Spending," Nils P. Gleditsch, Olav Bjerkholt, Ådne Cappelen, Ron P. Smith, and J. Paul Dunne, eds., *The Peace Dividend*, Amsterdam: Elsevier, 173.

28	Mark Deweerdt and Rolf Falter (1992), "Overzicht van het Belgische Politiek Gebeuren in 1991," *Res Publica-Belgian Journal of Political Science*, 34 (3–4), 334–335.

29 Mark Deweerdt and Rolf Falter (1993), "Overzicht van het Belgische Politiek Gebeuren in 1992," *Res Publica-Belgian Journal of Political Science*, 35 (3–4), 320–322.

30 Mark Deweerdt (1995), "Overzicht van het Belgische Politiek Gebeuren in 1994," *Res Publica-Belgian Journal of Political Science*, **37** (3–4): 303–304; Mark Deweerdt (1999), "Overzicht Belgisch Politiek Gebeuren in 1998," *Res Publica-Belgian Journal of Political Science*, 41 (2–3), 226; Philip Shishkin (2003), "Growing Soft: How the Armies Of Europe Let Their Guard Down – Guaranteed Jobs for Soldiers Leave Little Room to Buy Equipment or Even Train – Battle of the Belgian Bands," *Wall Street Journal*, 13 February, A1; Struys, 32.

31 Struys, pp. 32–33; Mark Deweerdt (2001), "Overzicht van het Belgische Politiek Gebeuren in 2000," *Res Publica-Belgian Journal of Political Science*, 43 (2–3), 302–303; André Flahaut (2003), "De uitdaging. André Flahaut," *De Standaard*, 27 September online at http://www.standaard.be/Misc/print.asp?articleID=DST27092003_034.

32 Cited in Bart Dobbelaere (2003), "Flahaut vraagt vriendelijk om meer geld voor defensie," *De Standaard*, 27 February, online at http://www.standaard.be/Misc/print.asp?articleID=DST27022003_012.

33 "HET REGEERAKKOORD. Een hecht Europa" (2003), *De Standaard*, 10 July, online at http://www.standaard.be/Misc/print.asp?articleID=DEXA10072003_012.

34 Deweerdt (2001), 304.

35 Jan van der Harst (2003), "De verdwenen voorspelbaarheid: Het Nederlandse Europabeleid tijdens en na de Koude Oorlog; een vergelijking," Bob de Graaff, Duco Hellema and Bert van der Zwan, eds., *De Nederlandse buitenlandse politiek in de twintigste eeuw*, Zoetermeer, Netherlands: Boom, 145.

Chapter 6

Italian Security in the Berlusconi Era: Business As Usual

Mark Sedgwick

Introduction

As a nation which traditionally champions the role of the United States and the North Atlantic Alliance in providing security both to itself and to Europe at large, Italy has been especially sensitive to the strains in transatlantic relations which were exacerbated by the recent British-US military action in Iraq. The coming of the second Gulf War, however, was merely a catalyst which brought to the surface a number of issues spawned by the end of the Cold War[1] and shaped by the advent of a new brand of terrorism – terrorism with a global reach and no discernable desire to negotiate within the confines of the current international system.[2] Italy, like most nations of the world, has been forced to reassess the threats it faces, evaluate the means by which it counters such threats, question the nature of its traditional security strategy, and decide how best to attain its own national security interests given the existing nature of Western alliances and defense regimes.[3]

This essay attempts to reveal the way in which Italy has reacted, and continues to react, to changes in the international security realm. It tracks the historical forces which have shaped the nation's strategy for defense, including an examination of Italy's relationship with the United States, NATO, and the EU, and also reveals a new threat which seem to necessitate formulation of new structures and/or new strategies. As NATO attempts to conform to a changing international environment, so does the European Union in its struggle to define both a defense identity and a practical defense plan. Italy, as a member and supporter of NATO and the EU, maintains its allegiance to both institutions even while it seeks to exercise national preferences via bilateral relations with individual states. Where do Italy's loyalties lay, and what conditions them? Has the transatlantic rift caused a sea change in Italy's security outlook, or has it been characterized by relative continuity? If any shift in allegiances or preferences is apparent, is systemic change the reason, or are individual relationships responsible? How can Italy best contribute to transatlantic security, and what sacrifices or compromises must be made to ensure a meaningful contribution? What hard- or soft-power capabilities does Italy offer to the service of either the international community or its allies?

In order to answer these and other parallel questions, one needs to examine the history of Italy's foreign and security policy since the end of World War II up through the end of the Cold War. In addition, one must look at NATO's role in Europe, especially from an Italian perspective. Likewise, one must seek to understand the desire for a European defense capability such as that envisioned by the European Security and Defense Plan. Both NATO and ESDP are the central pillars in Italy's official security strategy, although recent events, such as the Brussels "mini-defense summit" in April 2003,[4] dramatize the potential for paradox as Italy continues to support both institutions simultaneously. This essay also examines the actions taken by Italy in response to operation Enduring Freedom, as well as military action and post-war operations in Iraq. Ultimately, the focus of such an inquiry must take into account what Philipo Andreatta and Christopher Hill have posited to be Italy's central dilemma: how does a weak nation fulfill its most crucial function, the provision of security and defense?[5]

When assessing Italy's behavior in security matters, one is best served by using a realist framework.[6] Realist theory helps explain how the drive for state survival, the goal of any rational security strategy, is the primary agent animating policies concerned with defense. Within the context of defense and security alliances, recent scholarship hypothesizing the emergence of "security networks" that supercede traditional alliances has entered into the literature. This essay takes such new scholarship into account in order to render a well-balanced examination.

Transatlantic Divide and the Unipolar Moment

Since the efforts of Kagan and others have focused attention on the nature of transatlantic relationships, it is fitting that this chapter focuses attention on current scholarship discussing the "rift" between Europe and the United States.[7] At the outset, awareness dawns on the least initiated reader that when one talks about Europe, one has no single entity which to address. Though the integration of Europe is substantive and demonstrable, one could still agree with Kissinger that phoning Europe might necessitate many appeals to directory assistance, especially when attempting to reach Europe's security division.[8] As it was in Kissinger's era, Europe is still a collection of states that hold and attempt to exercise specific national preferences. It that were not so, no state would have sought negotiations over the Maastrict Treaty, every state would participate fully in the eurozone, and with enthusiasm and outstretched hands Turkey would be invited into the fold of EU membership. In Europe, the state still matters.[9]

Though states matter, alliances have had a significant effect upon Europe's economic, political, and defensive development. NATO, WEU, and the on-going integrationist project that is the EU, have conspired with the help of a bipolar system and copious defense expenditures by the United States to ensure European peace and prosperity for over fifty years. Some allies in the bipolar system were subservient to Washington,[10] others bound themselves to the concept of a unified Europe in order to live down past aggressive tendencies,[11] and still others imagined themselves 'leaders of Europe' capable of exercising power which no longer existed.[12] All benefited through their "consumption" of security provided by the West's largest security "producer," (the United States) and to lesser or greater degrees all were free to concentrate upon economic development and political unification. The end of the Cold War saw the demise of a threat which had drawn both sides of the Atlantic close together, though many commonalities, not the least of which were shared political and material cultures, transcended the struggle against communism.

With the fall of the iron curtain, European leadership was faced with an opportunity to pursue national interests on a scale not deemed possible since before the end of WWII. Mainly comfortable with the status quo, however, Europe maintained faith in NATO, and strode more forcefully toward integration. The crisis in Bosnia, followed by that in Kosovo, unfortunately illustrated that Europe could not command the political will necessary to implement military solutions for problems requiring the exercise of power.[13] Capital, political and military, was in short supply on the Continent.

The transatlantic "drift" of which analysts speak today seems to pivot around differing perceptions of threat, as well as differing notions about how to respond to threats. Osvaldo Croci notes that Europeans and Americans may identify the same threats, though interpretation of those threats may vary widely.[14] Interpretation has a direct bearing on the level of intensity generated by the threat; in turn, level of intensity appears driven by national interests. For instance, Americans are conditioned to think in terms of *global* threats, owing to their equation of universal free trade with peace.[15] Al Qaida-brand terrorism has been identified as a global threat carrying the potential for violence anywhere; thus, it has the potential to disrupt world trade. Still, it was America that received the major damage from this threat, not Europe.

Europeans tend to think in terms of *regional* threats, with the Balkans being highly illustrative of this point. To many in Europe, Saddam Hussein was a distant threat at most, while to others, especially those dependent on imported energy sources, his regime was not much of a threat at all. Even if all parties astride the Atlantic are in full agreement on the saliency and nature of a threat, each camp has its preferred methods of action. Both Millen and Pargeter note that Europeans generally favor conflict resolution that addresses the perceived root causes of objectionable behavior (for example, poverty, human rights deficits, ethnic strife, religious friction, and so on[16]). Thus, their emphasis is on diplomacy and other soft-power techniques like trade and aid. Croci notes that although the United States employs a range of soft power weapons, its capabilities and preferences incline it toward military intervention.[17] Currently, US strategy is based on the concept of eliminating potential threats, with the full force of the military if need be, before they bloom.[18]

Despite this difference in perception and means, latent idealism still exists in American policy just as Europeans still practice Realpolitik.[19] National interests shape policy in European capitals much the same as they do in Washington, and the United States often talks of its desire to spread democracy and prosperity. Its relative power position, however, allows America to act transparently when identifying it interests; Europeans are more constrained in such matters, and may couch interests in the idealistic pursuit of *alliance* or *integration*. Of special merit is Croci's assertion that Europe's lesser powers (Italy would fall in this group, as would the newly ascending states) have tended to side with the US during recent transatlantic tensions, a signal that they believe America's 'unipolar moment' has not yet passed.[20]

Whither Italy? The 'Special Relationship' and European Alliances

Given this brief overview of the current state of transatlantic affairs, one must ask where Italy fits into the picture. Though considered a lesser military power on the world stage,[21] Italy sent troops and military assets to Bosnia, Kosovo, and Albania in the 1990s to stabilize those regions on behalf of NATO and the UN.[22] Since 11 September Italian troops have taken part in combat and peacekeeping operations in Afghanistan,[23] as well as peacekeeping and humanitarian relief efforts in Iraq.[24] Its soldiers and Carabinieri have been shot at and truck-bombed.[25] Italy has been bloodied in conflicts that were directed neither by NATO nor by the EU (in the form of the paper tiger European Rapid Reaction Force); rather, its casualties have come while serving new combinations of allies – some old and some new. How did this staunch supporter of the Atlantic Alliance and the European Security Defense Plan (the military embodiment of the EU's Common Security and Foreign Policy) end up part of an *ad hoc* "coalition of the willing"? In part, the answer relies on investigation of Italy's foreign and security policy since the end of WWII.

As Italy emerged from the shadow of Mussolini's fascist state in 1943, its aspirations to play power politics were eviscerated. For the first half of the twentieth century Italy's military ambitions outpaced its capabilities. Douglas Forsyth notes that modern Italy has always relied on a foreign sponsor to compensate for relative weakness, either economic or military.[26] Using Forsyth's framework, Nazi Germany "sponsored" Mussolini, a fact that allowed Italy to attempt a projection of power it was unable to consummate. Even before the war was over, Washington began the processes responsible for the rebuilding of Italy's social and political institutions. Italy was readmitted to the family of nations thanks in large part to its inclusion in Europe's emerging multilateral institutions such as NATO and the European Coal and Steel Community.

Leopoldo Nuti writes that the single most enduring characteristic of Italian security and foreign policy, continuity in its support for the US, NATO, and the various stages of European Union, had its genesis in Washington's strong presence in post-War Rome.[27] The United States helped prop up the Christian Democrat regime (in order to quash aspiring leftists), provided Italy with security, and defended Italian re-integration in the face of often hostile allies. Nuti believes that Rome could have played the Moscow card, but the Christian Democrats stood to lose ground to the socialists on the domestic front. While in general Italy accepted giving up its sovereignty for a measure of security,[28] the relationship of Rome to Washington may be incorrectly labeled as subservient. Italy used its 'special relationship' with America to pursue its own interests, such as its ties to Arab states (for example, Libya). From a realist standpoint one can certainly understand Italy's desire to seek diplomacy with Libya, given Libya's undercapitalized energy resources and the North African nation's potential to destabilize the Mediterranean region.

Though Italy exercised limited sovereignty vis-à-vis the United States and on occasion demonstrably came to odds with its indispensable ally,[29] many instances covering the breadth of the relationship between Rome and Washington show how far Italy was willing to go to *strengthen* the bond. Nuti reveals that when the US advocated European deployment of ICBMs in the late 1950s, the Farfani government accepted them on Italian soil – something that no other European state cared to do at the time. The plum for Italy was gaining, by proxy, nuclear status without having to develop its own nuclear arsenal. In the late 1970s, when the Socialist Craxi led the government, again Italy accepted tactical weapon deployment that the rest of its allies had rejected.[30] By virtue of this acceptance, Italy became a vital pivot-point in NATO security policy. In a yet another example of the Italian propensity to honor its allied duties, Cremasco illuminates the choices made by the D'Alema government leading up to and during the NATO campaign in Kosovo. D'Alema himself was a former communist party member, the first Italian prime minister to hail from that ideological camp. In the US and among NATO allies, questions arose as to how Italy would respond to its Alliance commitments. Despite domestic backlash, D'Alema stayed true to NATO, giving high-profile support by allowing air basing at Vincenza and offering Italian aircraft to the air campaign.[31] Moreover, those times when Italy was forced to take a stand between the preferences of Paris, Bonn, or Brussels and those interests espoused by Washington, Italy tended to lean toward the latter.[32]

Croci notes that weak states tend to seek out multilateral arrangements in their dealings with stronger states because of the voice it provides them,[33] while Lansford states that alliances "permit states that have a power or territorial inequality to compensate for that deficiency through cooperation."[34] Applied to the Italian case, these observations ring true. The two pillars upon which Italian security policy has rested, and continues to rest, are its special relationship with the US and dedication to European institutions, both NATO and the EU.[35] To this day, both official rhetoric and observable action demonstrate Italy's continuing commitment to these pillars. Nuti points out that Washington also supported EU defense plans as a way for Europeans to share the burden of security costs.[36] With America's backing, Italy finds it easy to reconcile its support for ESDP. Besides, Rome's lack of defensive capabilities condition its support for collective defense.[37] Pargeter notes that up until the end of the Cold War, the potential for bilateral relationships was limited,[38] although other scholars might argue that Italy experienced a vigorous bilateral relationship with the US *throughout* the second half of the twentieth century.[39]

As for Europe, Italy has repeatedly stressed its preference – which it shares with the United States – for NATO primacy in the Continent's security realm. At the same time, Italy has shown energetic support for ESDP and its organization of a rapid reaction force of 60,000 soldiers which could be used in 'out-of-area' operations for up to one year.[40] Italy also insists that the EU stay true to its original vision for ESDP, which placed it within the NATO framework of operations. The Atlantic Alliance provides for Italy one of the three original *raison d'etre* of the North Atlantic treaty – to keep the US engaged with Europe.[41]

What began as the vague notion '*European Security and Defense Identity*' came into clearer focus during the Maastrict process which created the European Union out of the European Community. With the Cold War ostensibly won and no new security threats easily targeted, NATO looked a bit anachronistic. Integrationists in Europe desired a shared foreign and security policy to complement their single market. ESDI dovetailed with a newly formalized *Common Foreign and Security Policy*, and in turn CFSP was ensconced as one of the three pillars providing the foundation for the EU. Italy supported ESDI, CFSP, and its military progeny ESDP – again, just as long as NATO was neither duplicated nor superceded.[42]

Pargeter points out that Italy aggressively sought to shape ESDP by making its preferences known, not an easy task since a core group composed of France, Germany, and Belgium seemed to be constructing Europe's hypothetical defensive capability to its own specifications. Fear of being excluded from the ESDP formulation process animated Italian policy makers and statesmen in the early 1990s; they had seen their aspiring European voice quelled when, after contributing to a naval blockade in the Balkans, Italy was not invited to participate in the diplomacy efforts of the Contact Group.[43] Pargeter believes that the fear of being marginalized prompted Italy's bilateral action with France, Operation Alba,[44] which swung into action after Albania imploded in 1997 and triggered massive migratory outflows across the Adriatic.

Current Threats, Common Goals

All of the facts presented up until this point are historical in nature, and lead to a discussion of the current climate and a glimpse into a hypothetical future. In 1997, Andreatta & Hill stated that Italy could not continue to "free-ride" in a security regime that had its roots in the Cold War. They advocated extensive retooling of Italian military structures, as well as aggressive funding for new defensive equipment and technology. They reasoned that Italy's enthusiastic support of both NATO and ESDP necessitated fiscal commitment to defense, not just lip service.[45] By looking at current evidence, can one discern a change in Italy's defensive posture or a new orientation within the international system?

At the beginning of this chapter, the proposition was put forth that an historical examination of Italy's relationships with the United States, NATO, and the EU would help explain its current behavior in the international security realm. However, history reveals only part of the picture. Exogenous events – such as the advent of coordinated, global terrorist acts, the ensuing war against the Taliban and al Queda in Afghanistan, and the second Gulf War centered on Iraq – have caused Italy to re-evaluate its threats and scrutinize its military capabilities. Italy also closely watches the continuing evolution of ESDP and notes the strains placed on time-honored alliances as bilateralism finds both greater use and tacit acceptance. Thus, this examination turns toward a discussion of Italy's reaction to its current threat matrix; changes in NATO's roles; the evolution of ESDP; war in Afghanistan and Iraq; and Italy's own military capabilities.

The single biggest change in Italy's threat analysis is caused by the emergence of 'new terrorism,' a variant of terror activities characterized by mass casualties (often aimed at civilians), a high degree of organization (though not necessarily centralized), and – as in the case of al Qaeda – no discernable desire to win concessions or force negotiations.[46] Italy has passed laws, fortified its counter-terrorism measures in law enforcement, initiated investigations of groups tied to known terrorist organizations, and cooperated with both EU, G-8, and NATO anti-terrorism efforts.[47]

In addition to the heightened threat posed by terrorism, Italian security strategy is still predicated upon regional geopolitical threats. At the top of this list is concern over the Balkans. Italian policy makers also focus their attention on the broader Mediterranean Basin as the nexus of future potential conflict.[48] Speaking to a NATO conference attended by members of the Mediterranean Dialogue initiative in 2002, Speaker of the Italian Chamber of Deputies, Ferdinando Casini, noted that "no one can ignore the reality" that the specter of new terrorism – such as 11 September – "has one of its nerve centers ... in the Mediterranean Basin." Casini stated his belief that "the peace of the whole world depends on efforts to stabilize that region.[49] Related to the relative stability of these two regions are a series of concomitant threats: mass immigration, religious fundamentalism, ethnic strife, proliferation of WMDs, and the spread of organized crime. Italian security strategists must also be concerned about any potential threats to the procurement of energy sources.[50]

NATO and ESDP

Evidence shows that Italy has relied on the United States to provide its security indirectly through the Atlantic Alliance. At the same time, Washington has encouraged NATO members to reinforce Europe's defenses and thereby assume a greater share of the cost burden.[51] Italy has not wavered in its support of NATO primacy in the European security picture, though it also champions ESDP evolution – up to a point. That point is where Italy's interests and 'Europe's' interests appear to differ in character or intensity. Even during the left-of-center D'Alema government, Foreign Affairs Undersecretary Umberto Ranieri did not hide the fact that NATO served Italy's national interests. He characterized Italy's support for the NATO campaign as "the pursuit of national interest, as other normal countries would do."[52]

Three salient features condition Italy's current relationship with NATO. First is the enlargement process, second is Italy's attempt to focus NATO policy on the Mediterranean region, and third is NATO's position relative to ESDP development. Ratti notes that the end of the Cold War allowed for an expression of Italy's regional preferences vis-à-vis the US and its leadership position within The Atlantic Alliance. On example of Italy's more aggressive, self-interested policy has arisen out of the NATO enlargement debate. Italy pushed hard for the candidacy of both Slovenia and Romania, primarily because of geostrategic considerations.[53] Thus, Italian policy makers voiced their preference: they would like to see NATO's center shift to the south and the east. Though both states ultimately lost out to central and northeastern European countries, Ratti speculates that Italian disappointment in this outcome will not cause Rome to wander too far away from Washington's preferences.[54] Italy will still manage to find an appropriate arena in which to champion its regional interests.

Since 1994, when NATO formed the Mediterranean Dialogue,[55] Italy has readily pursued an active role in that diplomatic forum. As one might expect, the Dialogue is a relationship-building initiative, and is restricted to multilateral discussions. Soft power instruments such as diplomacy and trade and aid provisions fall comfortably within Italy's competency. Efforts to foster and mediate north-south relationships in the Mediterranean Basin may be Italy's greatest potential contribution to the provision of both international security and transatlantic harmony. Croci notes that Italy already plays a mediating role within NATO, smoothing out divisions caused by differing threat perceptions and the appropriate means by which to counter those threats. He believes that such mediation is focused upon improving the Atlantic-European connection, something that Italian Defense Minister Martino has stated publicly.[56]

NATO's relationship with the EU is also a subject of interest in Italian security circles. As previously noted, Italy advocates ESDP within a NATO framework. For some time, it has looked as though practical interpretation of the previous notion would forever escape European understanding. As EU states established official positions either supporting or rejecting the idea of armed intervention against Saddam Hussein in 2002–2003, the evolution of ESDP proceeded, if somewhat haltingly, unabated. Some analysts point out that ESDP presents many obstacles of its own making which reduce its capacity for effectiveness. Shepherd points out that the earmarking of troops by each EU member state for ESDP's European Rapid Reaction Force represents force capability only; it does not represent a standing army. These disaggregated forces which some day might be constituted into an RRF, are kept under the control of their respective national governments. Shepherd also notes that EU defense spending is at "an all time low,"[57] a fact which does not bode well for the construction of new force capacity, regardless of how many troops and assets EU member states pledge to provide.[58]

Neil Winn points out that ESDP relies on unanimous decisions to determine when, where, and with whom its forces are allowed to engage. In light of the current ideological fissures in Europe, it appears that finding consensus may be particularly difficult in the near future.[59] NATO also requires unanimity before taking action, but as Mansoor reminds the reader, the Alliance – not ESDP – contains the one ingredient that can alter disparity of opinion: the power of the Unites States.[60] Almost in the same breathe, however, Mansoor speculates that as the United States comes to rely on bilateral relationships with countries like Italy to create 'coalitions of the willing,' American policy makers may make the decision to reduce its troop strength in Europe – allowing ESDP to take up the slack by default.[61]

Recently, Italian President Ciampi stated to an American audience that the US should not fear Europe's autonomous defense initiatives. "For years you have been urging us to share the burden in this [defensive] field." He went on to say that ESDP will gain credibility if it is constructed as "fully complementary [with] the Atlantic framework."[62] However, one might argue that a reduction of US troop strength would not *bolster* NATO capacity, but instead would have the opposite effect. It is hard to imagine that Italy would welcome such an occurrence. However, from a realist perspective, one can understand Italy's desire to establish a voice within ESDP to hedge its bets against the potential diminishment of the Atlantic Alliance's influence in 'core Europe.'

In the past, ESDP has been considered a paper tiger because all of its assets must be loaned from NATO common stock. In March 2003, the EU and NATO agreed to the "Berlin-Plus" arrangement whereby NATO members may make assets available to the EU on an as-needed basis.[63] The EU quickly made use of this arrangement as European forces assumed peacekeeping duties in the Congo and in Macedonia – the latter dubbed 'Operation Concordia.' Recent indications are that NATO may turn over peacekeeping operations in Bosnia (SFOR) to the EU force, though the US is reportedly opposed to the idea.[64] It appears, then, that despite both obstacles inherent to EU structures and interest-based divisions in the transatlantic world, ESDP is experiencing some limited success. One must note, however, that these peacekeeping missions are not the type of actions that would draw much protest from any particular corner of Europe. The real test for ESDP will come if, or when, it is called to duties that appear to serve some national interests more than others. It is important to note Croci's recent, and starkly realist, analysis that "the EU remains a strident mosaic of national interests ready to diverge on issues of importance. Without a security culture, the EU is incapable of giving its own answer" to European security questions, let alone questions affecting the world at large.[65]

Afghanistan and Iraq

Intuitively, Italy and the rest of its neighbors in Europe recognized that America's initial response to the terrorist attacks of 11 September provided an opportunity to prove their worth as allies. Even states that traditionally placed greatest rhetorical emphasis on humanitarian grounds for military intervention dropped such platitudes in favor of pragmatic US goals.[66] Like many other European alliance members, Italy offered its military assistance to America. The problem was that despite invocation of the North Atlantic Treaty's Article V, the United States planned to execute Operation Enduring Freedom using NATO members in *ad hoc* fashion, thus by-passing NATO command structures altogether. Though this went against the Cold War script which most allies had prepared to act out when contemplating Article V, the United States employed an accepted interpretation of the Treaty in order to forge bilateral agreements granting it access to common NATO assets.[67] Thus was formed the first post-11 September "coalition of the willing."[68]

After initially providing several naval assets to the US, Italy eventually sent approximately 2,700 troops to Afghanistan during the course of Enduring Freedom.[69] (This was before NATO took control of the UN-sponsored International Security Assistance Force in August, 2003). Operation Nibbio, deployed from March to September of that year, comprised a self-sufficient contingent of 1,000 soldiers who provided target acquisition, tracking, and engagement.[70] The Alpini paratrooper battalion L'Aquila became part of Italian military history when it became the first ever Italian unit to practice combat air assault. This action was also Italy's first combat mission since WWII.[71] Aliboni points out that through its tactical support, Italy acquired a voice in contemporary crisis management on the international level. He believes this marked a distinct change from past Italian contributions to global security dilemmas. From Aliboni's institutionalist perspective, he sees Italian power – which had been employed for humanitarian reasons throughout the 1990s – now bent toward Western defense and interest protection.[72]

Though ostensibly the Atlantic allies supported America's goals and actions in Afghanistan, the next phase of the Bush administration's War on Terror (WOT) did not inculcate a similar level of international consensus. From the mouths' of Italian leaders, at least those in the Farnesina, Italy staked out a position sympathetic to the US. Margherita Boniver, Undersecretary for Foreign Affairs, noted that America and Italy faced a common threat, one upon which words had little effect. To Boniver, it was illusory to think that the 'new terrorism' plaguing the world could "be defeated through economic development and [attention to] human rights." She stated that in order to prevent future al Qaedas, "We must forcibly deal with what [sources of terror] we are confronting today."[73] However, other voices in the Farnesina had previously sent a slightly different message, at least in terms of EU-US relations. Undersecretary of State for Foreign Affairs Alfredo Mantica stated in August 2002 that "We are America's allies, and this needs to be restated. But an alliance is based on loyalty, not fealty."[74] One speculates that either Mantica represents dissenting opinion in the Farnesina under Berlusconi's watch, or he was merely appeasing a domestic audience.[75]

However, as talk of war turned to action, rather than commit all its political capital to an intractable position Italy choose to play a mediating role between European voices opposed to war and the position signaled by Washington. Minister of Foreign Affairs Franco Frattini outlined Italy's three-way mediation mission as occurring between EU members, between the EU and the US, and between Italy and the Arab world. One may surmise that not only did mediation play to an Italian strength – diplomacy – but it also provided Italy a prominent place on the world stage. Frattini did reveal Italy's preferences, however, noting that his nation could not provide military assistance[76] without a UN mandate, he advised his European neighbors that "[a] Europe which counts is not a Europe which opposes the United States."[77] Even after combat actions began, Italy continued to show rhetorical support for Washington. Frattini reflected upon America's contribution to Italy during WWII, noting that "there [were] thousands of boys who gave their lives to free [Italians] from Nazism."[78]

Once the initial British-US campaign to liberate Baghdad was completed in April 2003, Italy provided troops and other military assets based on bilateral agreement between Rome and Washington. Operation Old Babylon sent approximately 2,400 military personnel and Carabinieri to Iraq for peacekeeping and humanitarian missions.[79] One such mission was to provide airbase perimeter security, and was handled in conjunction with a Dutch contingent. Italians manned checkpoints and offered a rapid-reaction capability. NATO procedures guided inter-force operations.[80]

NATO Challenged?

Though Italy, Spain, and many of the Central European states anticipating entry into either NATO or the EU gave aid or showed support for the British-US joint prosecution of the Iraq war, France, Germany and other states in Western Europe appeared poised to set out on a new course for European collective security.[81] The so-called 'Gang of Four' Brussels mini-summit held in late April, 2003 was attended by the leaders of France, Germany, Belgium, and Luxembourg, although a previous mini-summit in Ghent (2001) between Blair, Schröder, and Chirac may have set the precedent.[82] The Brussels conveners issued a communiqué stating their desire "to pursue the adaptation of the Atlantic Alliance."[83] Discussion surrounded the establishment of a command headquarters for EU military operations in Belgium, a move which appeared to duplicate or even compete with NATO. Early deliberations also called for an EU mutual defense clause along the lines of the North Atlantic Treaty's Article V, though later this idea was dropped. The impression in the minds of uninvited EU/NATO members was that the anti-Iraq camp was attempting to fashion a military leadership 'core' for Europe.

Speaking from a British perspective, Paul Robinson surmised that the summit's agenda indicated that both CFSP and ESDP were not based on sound defense policy goals, but instead on wayward integrationist idealism.[84] Foreign Minister Frattini stated his concern about the emergence of a "micro-territory" within the EU attempting to assume leadership outside of regular channels. He also affirmed his belief that a European military alliance which did not include the UK was unimaginable, and that if the Brussels *ad hoc* group felt comfortable taking it upon themselves to establish a "mini-military alliance," then Italy, the UK, and Spain might be compelled to do likewise.[85] By the fall of 2003, emotions had cooled and both France and Germany took pains to distance itself from the summit's backlash. The importance of the UK to European security had been affirmed by voices *outside* of London, Madrid, and Rome. Still, the greater powers seem determined to establish some type of core European security identity.[86]

The Italian Military: Ready or Not?

As one can see, future security arrangements in Europe are as still indeterminate, since this time period is marked by a certain fluidity and flux. However, as many observers agree, America's interests in Europe are not destined for radical change. The same can be said for Italy: it will continue to rely on Washington even as it angles for influence among its closer neighbors. Power distributions are still roughly equivalent to the immediate post-Cold War era, though for a time alliances may become less important than bilateral relationships. Anticipating these realities, and casting an eye toward Italy's future place within the international security regime, one must assess Italian military capabilities.

If Italy seeks to project power in either the multilateral or bilateral realms, it must direct resources to its military. Potential bilateral partners, most notably the United States, will also be looking closely at Italian capabilities. Croci notes that despite Italy's new found enthusiasm for high profile peacekeeping missions (Bosnia, Kosovo, Guatemala, Lebanon, Albania, Afghanistan, and now Iraq), its desires outstrip its military capacity. Its air and sea transport inadequacies are especially apparent when it attempts to place peacekeepers far from home. Once there, they usually are not self-sustaining, relying instead on hosts or allies for their provisions.

Croci also believes that Italy lacks a credible defense culture capable of concentrating political willpower.[87]

Andreatta and Hill point out that when compared to Europe's other major powers, Italy's troop size is comparable to that of France, Germany and the UK, but its quality falls below the mean. They also note that talk of force revision in the mid-1980s failed to translate into action, though in the mid-1990s Italian strategists seized on the need to streamline forces, to turn them into efficient units that actually could be used to fight.[88] Efficiency and capability will be important considerations given the mandates specified by Minister of Defense Antonio Martino in 2002. Martino feels the geographic scope of Italy's responsibilities are unlimited. In order to live up to the "legacy of the Atlantic Alliance," the defense minister stresses the necessity of initiating "a far larger increase in military and security expenditure than anyone could possibly have foreseen."[89] Italy must help strengthen NATO and ESDP competencies, Martino has stated, because in his estimation *ad hoc* coalitions are not preferable to alliances.

Former Defense Minister Sergio Mattarella has stated his opinion that Italy must become a security 'producer' rather than merely a 'consumer.' To accomplish this goal, he stresses the need for bipartisan development of "a culture of security and defence."[90] The former minister notes that Italian forces are working toward interoperability in compliance with NATO's Defense Capabilities Initiative of 1999, a step which he feels simultaneously improves both transatlantic and inter-EU relationships. Fiorenza reports that Italy has improved its airlift capabilities, though this observation came before Italy withdrew from the A400 program.[91] He also notes that Italy is prepared to offer NATO headquartering for an additional RRF unit which would be similar to the current ARRC (Allied Command Europe Rapid Reaction Corps).[92]

The "New Defense Model" envisioned by Italian military strategists, wherein the old corps structure has given way to ten brigades capable of rapid deployment, has proceeded admirably. The new structure is designed for out-of-area implementation in which interoperability with allied forces is imperative. A more thorough overhaul of the military will be necessary to meet basic security responsibilities.[93] Dottori and Gasparini reveal a litany of items which Italy must address: the Italian navy faces simultaneous obsolescence of major platforms, the army has been lax in replacing materiel, current spending on new technologies is among Europe's lowest, the army needs to professionalize its ranks, conscripts are lacking both in number and quality, and the anticipated changeover to a volunteer force may be hampered by low pay.[94] One may glean encouragement, however, from the news that the Italian Air Force plans to expand its capabilities by adding a hundred-aircraft combat wing to its system by 2007. The unit would be deployable abroad, and capable of sustaining its staff of 2,000 men. In order to implement the project, command structure must change and the country must purchase or lease several new aircraft.[95] Considering spending as a whole, analysts lament the fact that Italy spends over 46 percent of its defense budget on personnel costs alone. As mentioned previously, the government will have to make increases in defense expenditures a priority. Otherwise the hundred-wing force will remain a few wings short of its goal.

Clearly, Italy's heads of state have their work cut out for them if, indeed, they intend to leverage their political capital for the fight. The need to adapt to the changing security environment, however, may be overpowered by domestic concerns about aging populations, growing pension costs, and the need to stay under the EU's stringent fiscal guidelines. However, it is important to shift focus back to those who cultivate – but do not necessarily wish to inhabit – the security culture: diplomats and politicians.

The Berlusconi Effect

As prior evidence has revealed, many scholars are in agreement that Italy's foreign and security policy has shown remarkable continuity over the past 50 years, especially when one considers the end of the Cold War afforded Italy the opportunity to make significant changes to its policies. Despite former communists manning the helm for a time, it did not do so. Still, the question lingers: has the resurrection of Silvio Berlusconi to the office of prime minister in some way altered or shaped Italian foreign and security policy? Can one man matter?

Aliboni thinks one man *can* matter. To him, Berlusconi represents a departure from Italy's traditional foreign and security policy stance. He sees a pattern of "national assertion" beginning to occur in connection with the Berlusconi government's apparent willingness to engage in bilateral relationships, while simultaneously downplaying multilateral engagement. Aliboni thinks that Berlusconi has pulled Italy away from Europe, as evident in the decision to retire from the Airbus A400 program and initial rejection the EU arrest warrant legislation. "With an eye to preserving rather than going beyond national sovereignty," Berlusconi, writes Aliboni, takes Italy away from helping to develop "a European aggregation that can in some way ... maintain a multipolar structure on the planet, ... promote sustainable development and ... avoid destabilizing disequilibria."[96] One must pause and ponder this critique: it seems that Aliboni is not admitting the truth that other European states also advocate preference, but they may do so in a multilateral setting. Treacher notes that France has merged its identity – a vision of grandeur lost – into the EU identity. French power is thereby magnified by the very institution which requests the tithe of sovereignty in return.[97] In a way, by championing a multilateral EU, France is pursuing its national interest, though in an opaque manner. Aliboni seems to find fault with the *transparency* of Berlusconi's pursuit of interests.

Nuti notes that Berlusconi has been criticized for being less than enthusiastic about some aspects of integration, but notes that if this is true, one might explain such behavior by the cool reception which the new P.M. received from other heads of state just after the election in 2001.[98] If his counterparts have pushed him away, this might also explain why Berlusconi has established a close friendship with George W. Bush. Some believe that Berlusconi has much more in common with Bush – a man of commerce like himself – than Chirac – a man trained to be a civil servant in the Elysee style.[99]

According to Nuti, substantive issues may also call into question Berlusconi's 'enthusiasm' for the increased integration. The author reveals that even before 11

September, Berlusconi displayed an Atlanticist leaning by showing a willingness to listen to Washington's plans for anti-missile defense. Since then, Berlusconi has openly supported the US on Afghanistan and – as much as it could – on Iraq. One might also be convinced of Berlusconi's affinity for Italy's special ally, as well as justifiably confused, by a statement from the prime minister which Ratti relays. Berlusconi stressed that a bilateral relationship with America was the "central pillar" of Italian security policy, though no mention was made about that *other* pillar which places prominence on Italy's relationship to Europe and the Alliance.[100]

Countering the voice of Aliboni, Croci believes that if Berlusconi's government represents a true departure from the nature of previous Italian governments, it is merely a shift in style. The Berlusconi government is simply more outspoken in its relations with the rest of Europe. Croci also states that the charge of euroscepticism leveled at Berlusconi is a misinformed opinion; close examination reveals that Italy's perceived turn from Europe is exaggerated. Croci does not see how voting against (along with Germany and the UK) a United Nations Human Rights document which condoned the use of terrorism in order to win Palestinians their freedom is a turn against Europe – even though France, Belgium, Portugal, Spain, Sweden, and Austria all voted yes.[101] Noting that although Berlusconi may have displayed a little more distance from the Palestinians than his immediate predecessors, Croci points out that the current Italian government has since put forth the bold (if somewhat fanciful) "Marshall Plan for Palestine." In summation, Croci opines that "there is no doubt that the [current] government is as pro-Europe as its predecessor. The problem is that [the government's] view of what 'Europe' should be is more British than Italian ... "[102]

A Realist Summation

Upon review, it appears that Italy's loyalties in the defensive and international security spheres remain today where they have been for the past fifty years: Italy holds steadfast to 1) its bilateral relationship with the United States; 2) its commitment to NATO primacy on the Continent; and 3) its support for EU defense and security initiatives as long as those initiatives do not imperil items one and two. Italy's behavior has been conditioned via the shared history of Italian and American governments since the days of De Gasperi and Truman, by common security interests, first allied against Soviet Moscow, and now united against global terrorism and regional instability, and as a result of Italy's relative weakness within the international system.

Continuity, not change, most accurately characterizes the tenor of Italy's foreign and security policy in face of the transatlantic world's state of flux. A slight divergence from tradition may be detected in Rome's willingness to enter into bilateral arrangements *outside* of NATO – arrangements which have been integrated into 'coalitions of the willing.' Italy's pursuit of national interests did not begin at the Cold War's end, but since the demise of the Soviet threat Italy has been more aggressive in at least *voicing* its own preferences to an international audience. Thus, deviation from what may be considered Italy's security policy 'mean' has been primarily influenced by the change from a bipolar system to one which more closely resembles a unipolar system. The effect of Berlusconi and his government on Italy's slight jog toward the Atlanticist pole of its attitudinal continuum may be conditioned by his status apart from the political elites of "Old Europe," his affinity for George W. Bush as a businessman not unlike himself, or a pragmatic recognition that the current state of the international system demands bilateral cooperation on a scale which strategists in 1990 might have thought quite unlikely. As for the "partisan rage" which has recently fanned the flames of conflict on both sides of the Atlantic, Croci believes this behavior is best explained not by the appearance of seismic ideological shifts, but stem from "symbolic differences in language and style."[103]

So what does the future hold for Italian security vis-à-vis the United States and it various European partners? Chantal de Jonge Oudraat has speculated that the alliance system which held together throughout the Cold War is now being superceded by what she refers to as "security networks."[104] According to Oudraat, the characteristics of a security network are as follows: 1) a fluidity which allows for *ad hoc* network formation guided by issue-specific dictates emanating from rapidly evolving events; 2) network actors are states, and these states rely primarily on bilateral relationships; 3) network cores are "supplemented" by existing institutions (for example, NATO, EU, G-8). The great powers use institutions on an as-needed basis; 4) security networks are "relatively autonomous," that is, economic regimes do not seem to overlap or conflict with security networks; and 5) network activities are fairly secretive and may lack oversight by democratic institutions. Oudraat believes that NATO's mission may no longer be appropriate to counter current and future threats. Likewise, she characterizes ESDP (pre-Berlin Plus) as little more than a Potemkin village. Her thesis states that while the last half of the 20th century was epitomized by the military alliance, the 21st century appears head toward the establishment of fluid collective defense coalitions.

Are current events in Europe confirming Oudraat's thesis? Analysts may have to rely on the tincture of time to supply a satisfactory answer. Other scholars have committed themselves to limited predictions about Italy's future behavior in the European security environment. Ratti believes that Italy will continue to support ESDP because it allows the country to avoid subjugation both to the United States and to other, more powerful EU members.[105] If power projection is not an option, and for Italy this is the dominant case, a state must use whatever instruments it has at its disposal to extend its reach on the world stage. For Italy, this means both diplomacy and power magnification using either bilateral or multilateral alliances. Italy would treasure the flexibility to choose which type of relationship it should employ to achieve its national interests as changes dictate, but that freedom of choice belongs only to the strongest of states in the system.

Hall Gardner believes that the transatlantic relationship will endure, possibly in new combinations and at varying levels of intensity.[106] In this opinion he unwittingly may be supporting Oudraat's argument. Regardless, Italy will undoubtedly keep its options open and support both NATO *and* ESDP until one eclipses the other, or both fade in importance and give way to a new regime. Croci notes that if the United States continues aggressive military prosecution of the War on Terror, a geographically-diffuse undertaking, it will need to withdraw manpower from Europe and start relocating it to other areas of the world. At that point, European states will get what they have been asking for – the responsibility to defend themselves. One wonders what will happen when they finally get it.

Notes

1   Yury Fedorov, Roberto Menotti, and Dana H. Allin (2003), "European Security Strategy: Is It For Real?" European Security Forum Working Paper No. 14. Discussing the current transatlantic state of affairs, Federov states that "many believe that the Iraqi war was not the basic cause of these divisions but has accelerated and fuelled the decline of Western defence and security unity – including the identity crisis in European security – which began after the end of the Cold War. In this light, the formation of a set of bilateral security relations between the US and the member states of Europe is often seen as more important than the presumptive disintegration of multilateral institutions .... In this light, the principal question arises as to whether the current crisis in Euro-Atlantic relations is a tactical, short-term phenomenon or whether the community of democratic nations is fundamentally dividing with respect to primary international security issues;" ibid., 7–8. Osvaldo Croci (2002), "The Second Berlusconi Government and Italian Foreign Policy," *The International Spectator*, 37 (2), April-June, notes that the purely passive mode of Italian foreign policy which characterized the post-WWII period did not survive the Cold War's end. Still built on US, NATO, and EU relationships, the new policy is marked by a pragmatic pursuit of national interests – even if those interests are best attained by becoming the world's preeminent peacekeepers. See especially page 91.

2   Marie Cristina Paciello, ed. (2003), "After September 11, Governing Stability Across the Mediterranean Sea: A Transatlantic Perspective Conference Report," Rome: International Affairs Institute, 21–23. Paciello summarizes the comments of Ian Lesser regarding 'new terrorism.' Lesser points out that the perpetrators of new terrorism do not seek negotiation. Rather, their goal is to impose Islamic order across the globe.

3   Luca Ratti (2003), "Continuity and Consensus in Italian Foreign Policy," Draft paper from 52nd Political Studies Association conference, Aberdeen, Scotland, 5–7 April. Ratti states that Italy's geostrategic interests trump all other security and foreign policy concerns.

4   See *The Economist* (2003), "Will a Quartet of Euro-Enthusiasts Undermine NATO?", 3 May.

5   Filippo Andreatta and Christopher Hill (1997), "Italy," Jolyon Howorth and Anand Menon, eds., *The European Union and National Defence Policy*, London: Routledge.

6   Ratti compares five interpretive 'lenses' – realism, liberal-institutionalism, bureaucratic theory, legitimization-seeking theory, and political-ideological theory – to explain the consistency of Italian foreign policy during the tenure of both center-right and center-left governments. He determines that realism has the greatest explanatory and predictive power; Ratti.

7   In *Of Paradise and Power*, Kagan states that Europe and the United States think in diametrically-opposed ways, one inhabiting the orbit of Venus, the other of Mars. Europe is institutionalist and Kantian in outlook, while the US is realist and Hobbsean. The two are thus traveling in separate cars, on separate tracks, and heading in separate directions: divorce is inevitable; Robert Kagan (2003), *Of Paradise and Power: America and Europe in the New World Order*, New York: Knopf.

8   See Antonio Missiroli (2003), "Building a European Security and Defence Policy: What Are the Priorities?" Cicero Foundation Lecture Series, 12 June. Missoroli might

dispute this statement, for he feels the EU's Javier Solana can not only be reached by phone, but that he also has the auspices to put Europe's muscle wherever it may be needed to quell conflict. However, Missoroli may be dismissing too easily the fact that placing the call and getting prompt action are two very different things depending on who calls and whose interests are being served. The need to reach consensus on concerted European action – and this is especially salient for emergent situations – may be just as problematic for ESDP practitioners as it was for Europe's heads of state during the Yugoslav crises of the 1990s. National interests will still be in play.

9   See Raymond Millen (2003), "Strategic Effects of the Conflict with Iraq: Europe," Carlyle Barracks: Strategic Studies Institute.

10 See Leopoldi Nuti (2003), Leopoldo. "The Role of the US in Italy's Foreign Policy." *The International Spectator*, 38 (1), January-March, 92–93.

11 See Adrian Treacher (2001), "Europe as a Power Multiplier for French Security Policy: Strategic Consistency, Tactical Adaptation." *European Security*, 10 (1), Spring: 22–44, especially page 26, wherein the author discusses Germany's acquiescence to France's desire to act as Europe's leader during the Cold War.

12 In Treacher, the author's thesis revolves around the fact that France acted like a great power in its external relations in a way which belied its true status in the international system. A unified Europe became France's power surrogate, the Union an instrument by which faded Gaullist glory could be magnified; ibid.

13 See Millen, especially pages 7–8, for one point of view on Europe's "deeply rooted fear" of using force to end conflict. In Millen's opinion, European fear of destabilizing conflict emanating from the Middle East can only be allayed through action (meaning force). One notes that Millen's hardcore neo-realist assessment also predicted that Iraq would not experience a "firestorm of terrorist retribution" after major operations concluded there, because peacekeepers and reformed Iraqi law enforcement would "hamstring terrorist activities." To him, the post-war Iraqi scenario would not be as threatening as that which "Israelis must combat daily", Millen, 7–8.

14 Osvaldo Croci (2003), "A Closer Look at the Changing Transatlantic Relationship," *European Foreign Affairs Review*, 8, 473.

15 Of course, this is not to say that peace – nor free trade – are the only reasons motivating American policy makers. Obviously, America has it own interests in the Middle East, with access to oil being but one.

16 See both Millen; and Alison Pargeter (2001), "Italy and the Western Mediterranean," *Working paper 26/01* from the ESRC "One Europe Or Several?" Programme, Sussex European Institute, for discussion of Italian soft-power approaches to threat reduction.

17 Croci, "A Closer Look." Many analysts make the same claim, including Millen.

18 Croci, "A Closer Look."

19 Ibid.

20 Ibid.

21 This is an issue of perception, since Italy was the eighth-leading defense spender in 2002 among all nations, and has been in the top ten for some time. Within NATO, Italy only trails three European allies in defense spending: the UK, France, and Germany. All data comes from the Stockholm International Peace Research Institute.

22 Osvaldo Croci (2003), "Italian Security Policy in the 1990s," draft paper from 52nd Political Studies Association conference, Aberdeen, Scotland, 5–7 April. The author reports that Italy is the third largest contributor of military assets and manpower for UN peacekeeping missions. In addition, it is the fifth largest contributor to the overall UN operating budget. During the latter half of the 1990s, Italy's peacekeeping forces averaged above 9,000. See pages 5–6 for greater detail.

23 In US, Department of Defense (2003), "Nibbio Task Force Target Acquisition Detachment," *Freedom Watch* 26 April, US Centcom reporters describe one aspect of 'TF Nibbio' in Afghanistan, forward target acquisition. Christine Bhatti (2003) reveals in "Italians, US, Afghans Come Together in Historic Mission." *Coalition Bulletin No. 5*. Public Awareness Working Group of the Operation Enduring Freedom, May, the Alpini battalion D'Aquila made history by taking part in Italy's first combat mission since WWII.

24 BBC (2003), "Italy's Iraq Deployment," 12 November, reports that Italian forces in Iraq numbered 2,400, 400 of which were Carabinieri.

25 Frank Bruni (2003), "Italian Forces Will Stay in Iraq, Berlusconi Says," *New York Times*, 12 November.

26 Douglas J. Forsyth (1998), "The Peculiarities of Italo-American Relations in Historical Perspective," *Journal of Modern Italian Studies*, 3 (1), Spring, at http://www.brown.edu/Research/Journal_Modern_Italian_Studies/3.1/.

27 Nuti.

28 Croci, "Italian Security."

29 In "Continuity and Consensus," Ratti gives the example of the Achille Lauro incident in 1985 which caused a tense stand-off between US special forces and Italian military personnel. The author notes that this incident was the by-product of Italy's longstanding attempts to protect its interests vis-à-vis the Arab world. He infers that though a left-of-center government was manning the Italian ship of state, Italian actions were consistent with the policies favored by previous right-of-center governments; Ratti.

30 The weapons were Cruise missiles and Pershing II missiles.

31 Maurizio Cremasco (2000), "Italy and the Management of International Crises," Pierre Martin and Mark W. Brawley, eds., *Alliance Politics, Kosovo, and NATO's War*, New York: Palgrave.

32 Italy's position over the Suez crisis is a prime example. See Nuti, 94.

33 Croci, "A Closer Look."

34 Tom Lansford (2000), *Evolution and Devolution: The Dynamics of Sovereignty and Security in Post-Cold War Europe*, Aldershot: Ashgate, 49.

35 Italy "About Italy: Foreign Policy." Italian Presidency of the Council of the European Union website. Also, see the discussion in Andreatta and Hill – the authors note that NATO support has remained a predictable constant in Italian foreign policy.

36 Nuti.

37 Andreatta and Hill.

38 Pargeter, 2.

39 See Nuti, "The Role of the US" as well as Croci, "Italian Security Policy," Cremasco, "Italy and the Management of International Crises," and Ratti, "Continuity and Consensus."

40 Italy, Ministero della Difesa (2003), "Italy's Contribution to the European Defence," Ministero della Difesa website, 1 June. The Italian Defense Ministry has earmarked 12,500–14,500 troops for the EU/ERRF, nineteen naval units, 18 aircraft, and one Multinational Specialized Unit from the Carabinieri.

41 As defined by Lord Ismay, the other two reasons for NATO's existence – to keep Germany down and the Russians out of Europe – have become anachronistic.

42 Nuti. As another piece of evidence that US influence over Italy has remained virtually unaltered from WWII to this day, Nuti points to Italy's continual and forceful insistence – primarily to France – that EDSI not challenge, alter, or duplicate NATO's traditional roles.

43 See Pargeter. Osvaldo Croci makes a similar observation in "Italian Security Policy in the 1990s." He points out Italian concerns about being kept out of ESDP policymaking if Italy does not take assertive action to carve out its own role in Brussels.

44 For an institutionalist explanation of Italian thought driving this operation, see Paolo Tripodi (2002), "Operation Alba: A Necessary and Successful Preventive Deployment," *International Peacekeeping*, 9 (4), 89–104.

45 Andreatta and Hill.

46 This description of new terrorism comes, in part, from the mind of Ian Lesser, whose contributions to an Institute of International Affairs (*Instituto Affari Internazionali*) conference in Rome, 2002, are mentioned in footnote number two above.

47 See Italy, Ministry of Foreign Affairs (2002), "Anti-Terrorism Measures," Rome: Ministry of Foreign Affairs.

48 Balkan and Mediterranean stability are the top two concerns according to Italian Minister of Defense Antonio Martino. See Antonio Martino, "Europe Must Make a More Balanced Contribution," *European Affairs*, 3 (2), Spring.

49 Pier Ferdinando Casini (2002), Address of Welcome by the Rt. Hon. Pier Ferdinando Casini, Speaker of the Italian Chamber of Deputies," Rome, Italian Parliament, 30 September.

50 See Ratti.

51 See Martino, in which the Italian minister of defense advocates "a fairer sharing of the relationships and costs" among NATO members. Of course, this message has multiple meanings. The minister infers that his government should increase defense spending, while admonishing other member states to do the same. He also infers that for the amount of financial and political support Italy gives to the Alliance, it deserves more say in NATO decisions.

52 Croci, "A Closer Look," 11.

53 Peter Mansoor (2003), "US Army Europe 2010: Harnessing the Potential of NATO Enlargement," William Murray, ed., *National Security Challenges for the 21st Century*, Carlisle Barracks: Strategic Studies Institute. The author notes that southeastern NATO enlargement (for example, Slovenia, Romania, or Bulgaria) would allow for troop transport by rail to the borders of the Middle East. One wonders, given the tragic case of Madrid on March 11th, whether European rail lines represent a secure method of troop transport.

54 See Luca Ratti (2001), "Italian Diplomacy in the NATO Enlargement Process," *Mediterranean Politics*, 6 (1), 57–58. Croci, "*Italian Security Policy in the 1990s*," echoes Ratti's assessment. See pages 8–12.

55 Alberto Din (2002), "NATO's Mediterranean Dialogue: A Post-Prague Perspective," *Mediterranean Politics*, 7 (2), Summer, provides a brief overview of the Mediterranean Dialogue – its formation, operation, and goals. Din reports that one of the main factors motivating the Dialogue concerns perceptions (perhaps faulty) within the minds of non-Alliance states regarding NATO's strategic interests in the region. NATO does not wish, says Din, to appear like it is drawing a 'red line' along the Mediterranean's northern shore, with "us" operating north of the line and "them" below it. The Dialogue partner countries are Egypt, Israel, Mauritania, Morocco, Jordan, Algeria, and Tunisia.

56 Croci, in "A Closer Look," writes about Italian mediating skills and proclivities. See also Antonio Martino's remarks in "Europe Must Make a More Balanced Contribution." Martino believes that facing the common threat of terrorism should bring the two sides of the Atlantic closer, not farther apart. One also must note that one of the primary goals of the Italian Presidency of the EU in the last half of 2003 was "rebuilding a climate of trust and complete cooperation between the two sides of the

Atlantic." The latter quote is found in Italy (2003), "About Italy: Foreign Policy," Italian Presidency of the Council of the European Union website, 1 June.

57   Alistair J.K. Shepherd (2003), "The European Union's Security and Defence Policy: A Policy Without Substance?" *European Security*, 12 (1) Spring, 49. The author points out that All EU states *combined* spent less than half the US total in 2001, and that Europeans spent a much lower percentage than the US on 'R & D.'

58   In Julian Lindley-French (2003), "Are Reinforcing the ESDP and Improving Transatlantic Relation Compatible Objectives?" Cicero Foundation Lecture Series, 10 June, Lindley-French somewhat sarcastically notes that states that have called the loudest for ESDP implementation possess the least adequate military capabilities. Although this is meant as criticism, a realist perspective provides ample room for understanding: those with underdeveloped security capabilities will naturally seek a 'free-ride' in the collective setting.

59   Neil Winn (2003), "CFSP, ESDP, and the Future of European Security: Whither NATO?", *The Brown Journal of International Affairs*, 9 (2), Winter, online at http://www.watsoninstitute.org/bjwa/archive.cfm?targetpage = 9.2. Winn goes on to say, however, that the European Commission recognizes the stumbling block that unanimous voting presents to emergent reaction in times of crisis. The EC has recommended that a supermajority vote be incorporated in ESDP protocol. While this may take away an impediment to 'rapid reaction,' less influential states such as Italy may grumble about its intent. As the EU expands, even finding a supermajority on some proposed actions may be difficult. Inevitably, the question comes down to weighting in the EU system. Does Germany's vote equal Estonia's? Does France's vote count the same as Slovakia's?

60   Mansoor.

61   Croci, in "A Closer Look," makes the same prediction. These predictions take on more gravity with the recent US decision to reduce American troop strength in Europe by 30 percent.

62   Carlo Ciampi (2003), "Prepared Remarks by Carlo Azeglio Ciampi, President of the Republic of Italy," 17 November.

63   See Paul De Witte (2003), "Taking EU-NATO Relations Forward," *NATO Review*, Fall, online at http://www.nato.int/docu/review/2003/issue2/english/main.htm, for a further discussion of the Berlin-Plus agreement.

64   EU (2004), "EU Peacemakers to Take Over in Bosnia." *EUObserver.com*, 2 January, online at http://www.euobserver.com/.

65   Croci, "A Closer Look," 489.

66   See Deniz Altinbas Akgul (2002), "The European Union Response to September 11: Relations with the US and the Failure to Maintain CFSP," *The Review of International Affairs* **1** (4), Fall, who also quotes the Spanish Defense Minister, "Because no other state can protect Europe better than the US, the best alternative for [smaller countries] is to remain dependent on the US in security and military areas," 15.

67   See Brian Collins (2002), "Operation Enduring Freedom and the Future of NATO," *Georgetown Journal of International Affairs*, 3 (2) online at http://journal.georgetown.edu/.

68   In fact, many more were willing than the US had need for. Some sources speak of Italy having to convince the US to accept its help, not unlike the suitor who has to press his affections upon an unresponsive paramour. The fact was that very few forces matched up well with the US teams. Even if integration and interoperability had not been major stumbling blocks, the technological gap – as Kosovo had shown two years earlier – was formidable.

69 See *GlobalSecurity.org* (2003), "Operation Enduring Freedom Deployments," *GlobalSecurity.org*, 6 August, online at http://globalsecurity.org/.

70 *Freedom Watch* (2003), "Nibbio Task Force Target Acquisition Detachment," 26 April.

71 Christina Bhatti (2003), Christina "Italians, US, Afghans Come Together in Historic Mission," *Coalition Bulletin No. 5*, Public Awareness Working Group of the Operation Enduring Freedom, May.

72 Roberto Aliboni (2003), "Neo-Nationalism and Neo-Atlanticism in Italian Foreign Policy," *The International Spectator*, 38 (1), January-March.

73 Margherita Bonvier (2002), "Italy's New Foreign Policy After September 11th: Facing Threats to Security, Promoting Stability and Development," Speech by Margherita Boniver, Italian Deputy Secretary for Foreign Affairs, New York, University, 5 November.

74 Italy (2003), "Interview with Alfredo Mantica, Italian Undersecretary of State for Foreign Affairs," Rome: Ministry of Foreign Affairs, 8 April.

75 See especially Alfredo Mantica (2003), "No More Hypocrisy, Military Force Is the Key to Be Resolved." Secolo D'Italia, 9 May. In this op. ed. piece Mantica presents nothing less than a realist manifesto from an Italian point of view. One might speculate that Mantica's intent may have been to elicit public support for increased military spending.

76 Not including NATO commitments, such as the use of Italian AWACS pilots already then in theater.

77 Italy (2003), "Forum with Franco Frattini, Italian Minister of Foreign Affairs," Rome: Ministry of Foreign Affairs, 1 March.

78 Italy (2003), "Briefing with Franco Frattini, Italian Minister of Foreign Affairs," Rome: Ministry of Foreign Affairs, 31 March.

79 See *BBC* (2003), "Italy's Iraq Deployment," 12 November.

80 See US, Department of Defense (2003), "Italians, Dutch Provide Air Base Security," American Forces Information Services, 8 August.

81 Oddly, Mantica may have presaged a European split over the direction of ESDP vis-à-vis NATO when in early April, 2003, he addressed the subject of European unity in light of the fall of Baghdad. Mantica stated that, "No country that takes part in determining the EU's policy can consider supporting a position antagonistic to the United States." See Italy (2003), "Interview with Alfredo Mantica, Italian Under-secretary of State for Foreign Affairs," Rome: Italian Ministry of Foreign Affairs, 8 April.

82 In Akgul, the author points out this summit produced backlash among the lesser powers of Europe since it appeared the 'big three' were firmly in control of directing EU policy. The author speculates that this display of a disjointed Europe may have affected Washington's proclivity for bilateral ventures, but one suspects US strategists knew not to count on European unity, and had thoroughly planned on using individual countries on an *ad hoc* basis.

83 See the entire communiqué, Germany, France, Luxembourg and Belgium (2003), "Meeting of the Heads of State and Government of Germany, France, Luxembourg and Belgium on European Defence," Brussels, 29 April.

84 Paul Robinson (2003), "Back to Basics for EU Defence Plans," *EUObserver.com*, 30 April, online at http://www.euobserver.com/.

85 See Sharon Spiteri (2003), "Mini-Defence Summit Leaves EU Divided," *EUObserver.com*, 29 April, online at http://www.euobserver.com/, and *BBC* (2003), "Italy Attacks EU Defence Summit," 28 April.

86   See Charles Grant (2003), "Reviving European Defence Cooperation," *NATO Review*, Winter, online at http://www.nato.int/docu/review/2003/issue2/english/main.htm. A more cynical, though perhaps telling, assessment of the summit's *raison d'etre* come from a Radio Netherlands report, Radio Netherlands (2003), "EU Cracks Harden In Brussels," 29 April. The report quotes an analyst who asserts that the summit was cooked up by Belgium Prime Minister Guy Verhofstadt to support his re-election campaign.

87   Croci, "Italian Security."

88   Andreatta and Hill.

89   Antonio Martino (2002), "Europe Must Make a More Balanced Contribution," *European Affairs*, 3 (2), Spring, 4. See also Fiorenza in which the author reports that Italy spent just under 2% of GDP in 2000 on defense. However, the Carabinieri comes out of that amount, so actual military spending may be significantly below 2 percent.

90   Sergio Mattarella (2001), "Italy's New Defence Model and its Contribution to CESDP," *The International Spectator*, 36 (1), Janaury-March. Note how this sentiment echoes Croci above.

91   Originally Italy, Portugal, France, Spain, Germany, the UK, Turkey, Belgium, and Luxembourg were partnered in the new airlift platform from the military division of Airbus. Subsequently, both Italy and Portugal dropped out of the program.

92   Nicolas Fiorenza (2001), "Southern Anchor," *Armed Forces Journal International*, 138 (6).

93   Italy (2001), "Italy: Current National Security Situation," Rome: National Intelligence Council.

94   Germano Dottori and Giovanni Gasparini (2001). "Italy's Changing Defence Policy," *The International Spectator*, 36 (4), October-December.

95   See Andy Nativi (2003), "Italian Aspirations," *Aviation Week and Space Technology*, 8 September, 37–38.

96   Roberto Aliboni (2003), "Neo-Nationalism and Neo-Atlanticism in Italian Foreign Policy," *The International Spectator*, 38 (1), January-March, 83 and 89.

97   Treacher.

98   Nuti. Andreatta and Hill also note that the first Berlusconi government of 1994–1995 was labeled as 'cool' towards EU integration, a feeling which may still linger in certain European political circles.

99   See Jean-Pierre Darnis (2003), "Atlanticism and Europeanism in Italy and France: A Critical Comparison," *The International Spectator*, 32 (2), April-June. Aliboni also mentions Berlusconi's business background and the thread of commonality that fact may provide to his affinity for Bush – and vice-versa.

100 Ratti, "Continuity and Consensus," 10.

101 Osvaldo Croci, (2002). "The Second Berlusconi Government and Italian Foreign Policy." *The International Spectator*, 37 (2), April-June.

102 Croci, "Italian Security," 19.

103 Croci, "A Closer Look," 483.

104 See Chantal de Jonge Oudraat (2002), "The New Transatlantic Network," *Policy Paper No. 20* of the American Institute for Contemporary German Studies, Johns Hopkins University.

105 Ratti, "Continuity and Consensus."

106 Hall Gardner (2003), "The Iraq Crisis and Its Impact on the Future of EU-US Relations: An American View," Cicero Foundation Lecture Series, 10 April.

PART TWO
NEW EUROPE

Chapter 7

In Search of Security: Bulgaria's Security Policy in Transition

Blagovest Tashev

Introduction

In the last several years Bulgaria's transition has been guided by its goal of achieving membership in NATO and the European Union. The content of its foreign and security policy, too, has been guided and determined by the two Euro-Atlantic institutions. Now that membership in NATO has been achieved, joining the EU is just a matter of time. Along with continuing the policies designed to prepare the country for accession, Bulgaria faces the challenge of formulating its security policy for the long run as a member of the Euro-Atlantic community. Accordingly, policy decision-makers are about to embark on planning for national security needs within the framework of the Euro-Atlantic institutional space, a process which will to a great extent determine Bulgaria's role in the new security environment. If the past 14 years are any indication, Bulgaria will face hard times during this process.

After the collapse of communism, new strategic thinking in Bulgaria slowly emerged. The relatively sluggish pace of the process is reflected in the late beginnings of real security and defense reform. Thus, until 1998 security sector reform was not guided by a vision and principles agreed upon by the political elite and the society at large. It must be noted that only in the last four years did the Bulgarian political elite reach a basic consensus on the Euro-Atlantic direction of Bulgarian foreign policy (especially regarding NATO). Not surprisingly, in lacking such a consensus in the early transition period, Bulgaria was unable to implement a comprehensive security and defense reform.

The chapter provides an overview of the slowly emerging political consensus on Bulgaria's security policy and the evolution of national strategic thinking. It also highlights some of the future challenges to the country's search for security in the context of integration in the Euro-Atlantic community.

Seeking Security after the end of Communism

The end of Soviet domination in Eastern Europe presented Bulgaria with fundamentally different security challenges. Bulgaria's entire security arrangement was based on the assumption that the Warsaw Pact, and the Soviet Union in particular, would provide unconditional assistance in the event of military conflict. Not surprisingly, the Bulgarian leadership was initially reluctant to let the Warsaw

Pact go. From early on, very few politicians, notably the Bulgarian President Zhelyu Zhelev, argued that the Pact was already a political corpse and insisted on closer ties with the West.[1] Zhelev made several visits to the West, including Western Europe, the United States and Japan in 1990–1991 to demonstrate the country's reorientation away from Moscow. While the governments in the first two years after 1989 were broadly supportive of this reorientation, they had difficulty contemplating an alternative to the existing security arrangements in a new security environment. Thus Bulgaria did not initially consider the unilateral dissolution of the Warsaw Pact as a viable option.[2]

When the end of the Warsaw Pact became inevitable in 1991, Bulgaria was at a loss to produce an alternative security policy. While acquiescing to the loss of traditional security guarantees, Sofia attempted to ensure national security by enhancing national military power, improving relations with neighboring states and nurturing a new, more equal relationship with the Soviet Union.[3] Although the government recognized that the new approach required good relations with NATO, it doubted Bulgaria would become a member of the Alliance.[4]

The loss of the traditional security framework which guaranteed Bulgaria's security in the context of fundamental political, social and economic transformation in the country coincided with the emergence of acute regional security challenges. The beginning of Yugoslavia's disintegration and the accompanying civil wars presented the country with unfamiliar threats and risks to which the leadership had no readily available responses. The Bulgarian leadership faced the necessity of formulating policies and strategies to address the challenges of a completely new international environment.

The conflicts of Yugoslavia's disintegration involved Serbia, among others, a state with which Bulgaria had a long history of rivalry, and Macedonia, a country which Balkan states have traditionally sought to possess or dominate.[5] Sofia feared that the conflict might spill over and engulf the entire region.[6] Feeling extremely vulnerable, Bulgaria's policy through 1996 of addressing the likelihood of a wider military conflict was to try to persuade its Balkan neighbors to avoid any involvement in the Yugoslav conflict. This policy explains why Sofia was the last state among the associated members of the EU to provide troops to various peacekeeping operations in the region. It considered such involvement risky with the potential to exacerbate conflicts among Balkan states.[7] Accordingly, Bulgaria was the first state to recognize Macedonia's independence in 1992, thus trying to prevent the repeat of past attempts by various Balkan states to dominate the area. The growing international isolation of rump Yugoslavia and Bulgaria's commitment to observe political, economic, and military sanctions against Belgrade denied Sofia opportunities to work with Serbia on any of the outstanding issues between the two countries and, in general, rendered impotent any Bulgarian attempts to affect developments in this part of the region.

The disintegration of the Warsaw Pact left Bulgaria alone to face Greece and Turkey, two states Bulgaria may have had to confront militarily in the event of war during the Cold War. Without external security guarantees, Sofia became increasingly concerned about military imbalances in the region. These concerns became more resilient as, in accordance with the Conventional Forces in Europe Treaty, excess weapons from NATO members in Western Europe, including advanced systems, poured into Greece and Turkey.[8] In addition, Sofia complained that Yugoslavia never signed the Treaty and thus was under no international obligation to limit its military power or participate in a confidence-building framework.

Consecutive Bulgarian governments adopted different policies to address the perceived threat. The short-lived first non-communist government of Philip Dimitrov in 1991–92 reoriented Bulgarian foreign policy toward greater cooperation with the West and Turkey. In this period, the Bulgarian leadership, with a few exceptions, did not actively seek NATO membership as a means of guaranteeing national security.[9] Dimitrov's policy led to improved ties with Ankara, which was pleased to see the changing treatment of the country's Turkish minority.[10] The two countries signed a Treaty of Friendship, Good-neighborliness, Cooperation and Security in May 6, 1992. Along with economic and social agreements, the governments agreed to develop bilateral confidence-building measures. Accordingly, Sofia and Ankara signed in December 1991 the Sofia Document on Mutually Supplementing Measures to Strengthen Confidence and Security and Military Contacts Between Bulgaria and Turkey, in which they agreed to give each other advance notice of military exercises taking place within 60 kilometers of the borders, an exchange of military observers, and so on. Military strength along the border was reduced on both sides. The Sofia Document was later strengthened by the Edirne Document on Some Additional Measures for the Strengthening of Security and Confidence and Military Contacts, signed in 1992.[11] The Edirne Document reduced the threshold for military activity notices and expanded the cooperation in military training and contacts.

Similar attempts were made to establish security ties with Greece. The Bulgarian-Greek Treaty of Friendship, Good Neighborliness, Cooperation and Security was signed in October 1991 to endure for 20 years. The two countries also signed in December 1992 a confidence-building agreement committed to lowering the Vienna Document's threshold on the number of troops, tanks and artillery pieces involved in military exercises.

Despite Bulgaria's early attempts to address its security concerns by seeking more extensive security ties with the West, in general, and regionally with Turkey and Greece, the Bulgarian leadership continued to see the country as dangerously exposed in an uncertain security environment. Political and military leaders continued to compare the national force structure and armaments with those of Turkey and Greece.[12] Discussions of the deteriorating state of the Bulgarian military and the increasing scope of military hostilities in Yugoslavia frequently evoked comparisons to the accelerated modernization of the Greek and especially the Turkish military forces as a result of the cascading transfer of weapons systems from Western Europe.

Although Bulgaria dramatically increased its ties with the West, the lack of security guarantees forced the country to fall back on previously tested security ties. In contrast to most other East European countries, Bulgaria did not see Russia as security threat to its independence and territorial integrity. Accordingly, in August 1992, Bulgaria and Russia signed a Treaty on Good Neighborliness and Friendly Relations, which went beyond similar treaties between Russia and its former

Warsaw Pact allies, as two of the articles in this treaty were security related. Article 4 states that consultations will be held if a particular situation endangers international peace and security, and Article 5 that "none of the contracting parties shall allow its territory to be used for military aggression or other violent activities against the other contracting party."[13] Some Bulgarian politicians interpreted the treaty as leaving the possibility of Russian military assistance to Bulgaria. Sofia was also highly encouraged by the fact that the treaty was signed during a visit of Russian President Boris Yeltsin to Sofia, his first visit to an East European country as a head of state. Yeltsin also promised his hosts more oil deliveries and greater access to the Russian market.

The signing of the treaty coincided with an increased sense of insecurity among the public. While in 1991 and 1992 the world closely followed developments in Yugoslavia, the Bulgarian public seemed preoccupied with the domestic transition process and disinterested in the disintegration of the neighboring state.[14] National media provided little coverage of the conflict and politicians found it only too convenient to avoid taking a stand on events over which the country seemed to have no control, influence, or interest.

Only in 1993 did part of the Bulgarian political leadership, notably the Union of Democratic Forces (UDF), begin to seek NATO membership as a guarantee for national security. After the Bulgarian Socialist Party (BSP) formed a majority government headed by Zhan Videnov in 1994, however, the issue of joining the Alliance became extremely politicized as the Socialists concluded that NATO was not the answer to national security concerns. Although the new government maintained formal relations with the Alliance, it was clear that the formal membership was not a foreign policy priority.[15] The Socialist government proved to be much more conservative in its foreign policy as it displayed a tendency to fall back on historically tested alliances and affinities. During the Cold War Bulgaria and Greece developed relatively close ties, an affiliation based on the shared mistrust of Ankara. Following the UDF government's recognition of Macedonia, which strained relations with Russia and especially with Greece, the Socialist government embarked on restoring ties with Moscow and fostering an even closer relationship with Athens. Thus Bulgaria tried to address its security needs by establishing closer relations with what it saw as historically tested allies while gradually isolating itself from the broader process of the East European countries' forging of increasingly extensive relations with the West. In fact, Bulgaria's shunning of NATO membership was accompanied by difficult relations with other institutions including the EU, the International Monetary Fund, and the World Bank.

Better relations with Moscow and Athens did not, however, translate into perceptions of more security on the part of the ruling elite. Politicians and military elites continued to compare the structure and power of the national military forces with those of neighboring countries.[16] At the same time, NATO was perceived to have encouraged an arms race in the Balkans, to Bulgaria's disadvantage, by further cascading weapons from Central Europe to Greece and Turkey.[17] This perception was shared not only by the Socialists but also by some in the opposition UDF.[18]

The Socialist government defined national security in narrow, traditional terms reflecting the government's preoccupation with external threats and risks. In the National Security Concept approved by the Videnov government on 13 July 1995, national security is defined as the lack of immediate threat of military aggression, political control, or economic coercion to the state and the society.[19] The Concept identifies international and domestic factors determining the state of national security. While the document recognizes the growing multiplicity of international threats and risks, it firmly identifies the traditional, specifically regional, hard-core threats – regional civil wars and their spill-over potential, historical conflicts among some Balkan states, serious asymmetry of institutional security guarantees among states, demands for territorial changes, and the emergence of new states after Yugoslavia's disintegration – as the most significant security challenges to national security. The document warns that the growing asymmetry between the military power of Bulgaria and most of its members may lead in the future to aggression against the country. Very significantly, the Concept fails to state that Bulgaria does not see an immediate threat to its territorial integrity and sovereignty stemming from the conditions existing in the region.

Although the Videnov government did not identify any country as threatening national security, it implicitly regarded Bulgaria's traditional enemies, especially Turkey and Yugoslavia, as posing a threat to national sovereignty. Although no country in the Balkans had declared any territorial claims to Bulgaria, the government and part of the society seemed to assume them.[20]

The document also contains an implicit criticism of the previous governments' policies which led to severe economic and social problems, in turn severely exposing the country to threats and risks. It points out that the country neglected traditional allies in its pursuit of integration in international institutions without regard for national autonomy and interests. According to the Concept, the state's goal is to guarantee its territorial integrity and sovereignty, to ensure the conditions for economic development and to guarantee the democratic character of the society, among others. The decisive way of achieving this is through the sustained process of increasing national power, active cooperation and coordination with international partners and stimulating the nation's patriotism and loyalty to the state through sustained economic and social prosperity. National interests can be protected by relying mainly on the national military forces. Moreover, military security is seen as determined by the strategic, political and military factors in the international environment, on the one hand, and national military capacities, on the other. Although the concept defines cooperation with international institutions and friendly states as an additional way to guarantee security, it makes no explicit commitment to seeking integration in NATO as a major foreign policy goal. Instead, it suggests that Bulgaria may seek NATO membership only after the Alliance transformed itself into one of the elements of a pan-European security framework in which Russia would have a major role. Accordingly, while membership in the EU and the WEU is defined as a priority, the relationship with NATO is seen as a partnership.

The Videnov government's Concept reflected the emergence of a deep division among the political elite over the nature of national security and how best to achieve it. While the Socialists perceived the issue in largely traditional ways, emphasizing the accumulation of mostly military power and the maintenance of alliance with friendly states, the UDF opposition insisted that integration in both the EU and NATO is both consistent with Bulgaria's quest to join a community of states sharing common values and the best way to guarantee the country's security and prosperity.[21] The BSP government, however, concluded that membership in both organizations is only a distant possibility and was skeptical of the organizations' ability and willingness to address the country's security needs.[22]

Early Relations with NATO

The beginning of Bulgaria-NATO relations was laid down by a decision of the Bulgarian government on 13 July 1990 to accept the invitation extended by the London Declaration of the NACC to establish diplomatic links with the Alliance. Compared to the other East European countries, however, Bulgaria remained ambivalent toward membership in NATO, as there was no domestic consensus on the foreign policy priorities of the country. The Socialist Party, internally split on foreign policy priorities, either insisted that the Alliance should first transform and even agree to accept Russia as a member before Bulgaria's accession to the Alliance or outright resisted any moves to establish long-term relations with NATO.[23] On the other hand, the pro-Western UDF also remained internally divided and ineffective in making the case for membership.

Bulgaria's ambivalence on relations with NATO between 1990 and early 1997 left the country unprepared for integration in the Alliance. The Parliament passed a declaration in December 1993 on the Euro-Atlantic orientation of the country and on 14 February 1994 the country signed the Partnership for Peace Framework Document.[24] The Socialist Party, however, undermined any attempts to establish a solid relationship with the Alliance: after its overwhelming electoral victory in 1994, the Socialists put the relations on hold. In 1996, after rounds of discussions with NATO in accordance with the PfP guidelines concerning prospective desire to join the Alliance, Bulgaria concluded that it did not want to pursue membership.[25]

Change of Course after 1997

The ascendance of the rightist UDF to power in early 1997 dramatically changed Bulgaria's approach to cooperation with and integration in the international community. Bulgaria saw membership in NATO, the EU and the WEU not only as a reliable source of security guarantees but also as a natural expression of the country's foreign policy orientations. Accordingly, the Kostov government not only reoriented the country's foreign policy but also altered its approach to security.

The National Assembly approved in April 1998 a new National Security Concept which reflected the new government's security policies and priorities.[26] Like the Concept of the previous government, the new one identifies both external and internal factors affecting and determining national security. Although the document sees a considerably decreased danger of direct military aggression against Bulgaria, it still emphasizes the importance of military and force factors in international

relations. In contrast to the previous government's approach, however, the new
Concept recognizes the inability of the country to ensure its security on its own or
to seek security through neutrality because of insufficient financial, economic and
military potential. Instead it identifies integration in international organizations and
participation in the globalization process as the means to address these
shortcomings. Along with identifying the national scarcity of security resources,
the document points out that national security is affected by world economic,
political, scientific and environmental processes as well as regional developments.
Thus it becomes very unlikely that unilateral decisions, including military ones, are
imposed in regional and bilateral conflicts. The Concept points out that these
developments – scarcity of national resources, the significance of certain world
processes, and the institutional, rather than unilateral, solution of problems –
prompts Bulgaria to seek security through transition to democracy and a market
economy and integration in Euro-Atlantic institutions, including the EU and
NATO. Significantly, the lack of security and stability until recently were caused
by the failure of the previous government to pursue these same policies. In other
words, it is not mainly the external threats that affected the state of national security
but the failure to advance reforms and the refusal to integrate in the Euro-Atlantic
institutions.

The new Concept, like the previous one, devotes much attention to threats in the
Balkans, especially the ones associated with the conflicts in Yugoslavia. The effects
of the crisis in the neighboring country are seen not in the form of a direct military
challenge but rather as the existence of conditions for the development of organized
crime and corruption and for the isolation of Bulgaria from the process of
integration in the Western institutions. These conditions jeopardize the stability of
the Bulgarian state institutions whose integrity is a precondition for national
security. In other words, the regional threats to national security are not in the form
of direct military challenges to the territorial integrity and sovereignty of Bulgaria
but in their effects on the capacity of the country to reform and integrate in Western
institutions. Bulgaria's perception of regional and limited threats to its national
security were also evident in its Military Doctrine, which did not envision any
direct military threat but defined any armed conflict in the Balkans as potentially
presenting the challenges already identified in the Security Concept.[27] Significantly, after the UDF's ascendance to power, political leaders and officials ended
their references to any military unbalances between Bulgaria and its neighbors as
Greece and Turkey were already seen as soon-to-be allies. Even the Socialists,
although fundamentally opposed at least until 2000 to a membership in NATO,
were unable to generate public support for their security and foreign policies. In
fact, while in opposition after disastrous electoral results in 1997, the BSP did not
develop any cohesive foreign policy vision of its own.

The new security concept was adopted shortly before a new escalation of armed
conflicts in the Balkans. In early 1999 NATO initiated air strikes against
Yugoslavia, the second such action in less than four years. This time the military
action was even closer to Bulgarian territory, in Kosovo and Serbia, and presented
an even more dramatic challenge to national perceptions of security. Both the
rhetorical and already institutional commitment to Euro-Atlantic integration, forced
Bulgaria to take a firm stand on the conflict. In contrast to the 1991–96 period,

when Bulgarian governments saw neutrality and noninterference as the best guarantee of national security, the Kostov government committed the country to the Alliance's strikes, including providing overflight rights, imposing sanctions on Serbia in accordance with EU associate members' obligations, and urging Belgrade to accept the international community's conditions.[28]

The crisis in Kosovo provided the biggest boost to Bulgaria's attempts to join the Alliance. Even before the beginning of the air campaign, the government intensified its consultations with NATO officials in anticipation of armed conflict.[29] President Petar Stojanov, elected on the UDF ticket, and Prime Minister Kostov also met with their Balkan counterparts and issued appeals to Serbia's leader Milosevic to accept NATO's plan for solving the crisis in Kosovo.[30] Later, during the air campaign, the government and the Parliament granted the Alliance the use of Bulgaria's airspace for attacks against targets in Yugoslavia. The government recognized that the Kosovo crisis, although posing numerous security challenges to the country, presented a unique opportunity to prove the irreversibility of Bulgaria's transformation, its choice to integrate in the Euro-Atlantic area, and more immediately, the strategic value of an aspiring NATO member.[31] Indeed, Bulgaria's support and cooperation with the Alliance significantly enhanced the country's standing, allowing it to catch up with the rest of the partners in their quest to gain membership. In return for its wartime support, the North Atlantic Council at the Washington summit in April 1999 extended a limited, in space and time, Article 5 guarantee to Bulgaria.[32] Even before this explicit statement of commitment, the Alliance on numerous occasions conveyed its interest in the security and stability of the country.[33] This was not lost on the Bulgarians and the government widely publicized any statement of support and commitment.[34]

The end of allied air strikes in Yugoslavia did not diminish the growing cooperation between NATO and Bulgaria. The need to maintain multinational forces in Kosovo and the beginning of a new conflict, this time in neighboring Macedonia, gave Bulgaria another chance to enhance its status among the aspiring membership candidates. In March 2001 the government agreed to sign an agreement allowing NATO forces to use Bulgarian territory, including the establishment of military bases, in the event of a Balkan crisis.[35] Remarkably, all political parties represented in the Parliament supported the agreement and it was approved without the usual resistance from the Socialist Party.[36]

It must be noted, however, that the government's decision to support the West in the conflict was taken over the public's disapproval of NATO's action and of the government's involvement in the conflict.[37] UDF was the only party which unequivocally supported the NATO air campaign, while the BSP strongly objected and frequently criticized the agreement between the Alliance and the government. Public resistance reflected the perception of an acute threat to national security and exposed the public's belief that neutrality to conflicts in the Balkans is still the best guarantee for Bulgaria's security.[38]

Although the perception of insecurity was widespread, the public did not exactly identify the nature of the threat posed by the Kosovo conflict. Yugoslavia did not issue any specific warnings about Bulgaria's support to NATO's action as Sofia's behavior did not substantially differ from the policies of the other Balkan countries, which provided political and practical assistance to the Alliance. Moreover,

Bulgaria did not turn into a destination for refugees leaving Kosovo, and aside from several stray American missiles landing on Bulgarian territory[39] the short war did not inflict any damages on the country.[40] Yet the public was afraid the country would be dragged into the conflict.[41] Despite government assurances that Bulgaria was ready to face any challenge with the assistance of Western Europe, and despite the widely publicized NATO commitments to national security, the public remained skeptical.[42] Conversely, the ruling elite saw the crisis as enhancing Bulgaria's security as it prompted Euro-Atlantic institutions to further assist Bulgaria's quest to join the West.[43]

In fact, the successful conclusion of the Alliance's air campaign against Serbia marked the transformation of the BSP's position on the country's membership in NATO. After a relatively short and uncontroversial intra-party debate, the Socialists decided to embrace NATO membership as the only politically attainable means to guarantee national security.[44] The change in the BSP's long-standing opposition to NATO was an attempt by the party leadership to transform the party into a modern social-democratic organization and position itself as a potential coalition partner ahead of the 2001 parliamentary elections.[45] Nevertheless, the Socialists remained the only party represented in the Parliament, which insisted that the country should hold a referendum on NATO membership. Even this condition, however, was dropped following the invitation to join NATO extended to Bulgaria at the Prague Summit. In any event, the Kosovo crisis may be seen as fostering the long-delayed consensus on the foreign policy orientation of the country, and more specifically, on the overall national security policy.

The collapse of the Socialist government in early 1997 marked not only the ascendance of the UDF but also a dramatic change in the country's foreign policy priorities. One of the first acts of the interim government of Stefan Sofiyanski was to declare Bulgaria's aspiration to join the Alliance.[46] After the UDF won the parliamentary elections and formed a stable majority government, the country became quite active in its quest to establish a strong relationship with the Alliance and ultimately gain membership. The government quickly established an infrastructure to catch up with the other candidates. On 17 March 1997 Bulgaria adopted the National Program for Preparation and Accession to NATO and set up an Intergovernmental Committee on NATO Integration. Yet, it was obvious that the country had lost valuable time and the final document of the Madrid Summit, which did not even mention Bulgaria as a potential future member, caused disappointment in the country but came as no surprise.

Indeed, political will aside, Bulgaria was hardly prepared to join NATO. While the country met some of the criteria listed in the NATO Enlargement Study, including democratization, protection of individual liberties, among others, and governmental control over the military, Bulgaria failed to take any substantial steps to reform the military. Until 1997 consecutive governments had not started the restructuring of the armed forces. Since the country did not seriously consider joining NATO, no efforts were made to achieve interoperability and train personnel for work with NATO members. No efforts were made to coordinate its defense budget, planning, and resource management.

The government of the UDF made a considerable effort after 1997 to implement wide ranging defense reforms, and more importantly, to end Bulgaria's self-imposed isolation and convince the Alliance of the benefit of the country's membership. Bulgaria approved its National Security Concept in April 1998, a Military Doctrine in April 1999, a Defense Plan in October 1999, and Partnership Goals in April 2000.[47] The government also established an inter-departmental structure, co-chaired by the foreign and defense ministers and an integration council in the Ministry of Defense, to coordinate NATO integration.

At the time of the UDF's ascendance to power in early 1997, the size of the military was still at pre-1989 force levels and structure. The new defense reform envisioned in the so-called Plan-2004 set out to cut the size of the armed forces from roughly 100,000 to 45,000 by 2004. It also called for restructuring of the forces and their gradual modernization to meet NATO standards.[48]

The Government of Simeon Saxe-Coburg Gotha: Staying the Course

The loss of the UDF in the parliamentary elections in 2001 and the ascendance to power of the Simeon II National Movement (NDSV) led by Simeon Saxe-Coburg Gotha – the former king of Bulgaria until the Communist takeover following World War II forced him into exile – did not change significantly Bulgaria's foreign policy priorities. NATO membership remained the foundation of the country's security policy. The victory in the presidential elections in late 2001 of leader of the BSP, Georgi Parvanov, did not seem to alter fundamentally what already appear to be the national and political consensus – integration in both NATO and the EU. What changed, however, was the international security environment. The terrorist acts in the United States on 11 September 2001 and America's changing military posture considerably enhanced Bulgaria's chances of actually joining the Alliance. It also posed new challenges to the country's ability to operate in a complex security environment.

The new government, including NDSV and the Movement for Rights and Freedoms (MRF), continued the reforms in the armed forces in accordance with Plan 2004 and the Membership Action Plan (MAP), and at the same time actively sought diplomatic support for Bulgaria's membership aspirations. In late 2001 and early 2002 it became apparent that NATO allies, and mainly the United States, were willing to welcome more states into the Alliance. On 22 November 2002 in Prague the NATO Summit decided to invite Bulgaria along with six more states. On 2 April 2004, Bulgaria, along with six other states, became a formal member of the Alliance.

In contrast to the first three post-Cold War members, the members of the new wave of NATO expansion seem better prepared to integrate into the Alliance and take on full responsibilities. Bulgaria's membership preparation takes place within the framework of three relevant basic processes – Membership Action Plan (MAP), Partnership for Peace (PfP) and the Planning and Review Process (PARP). The country is currently in the fourth cycle of the Annual National Program (ANP) under the MAP and it is expected to implement a fifth one as well. This process allows the invited countries to smoothly move from annual PARP to defense planning in the framework of NATO. Thus Partnership Goals will be substituted by temporary Target Force Goals or directly by NATO Force Goals. One of the big disappointments after the first wave of expansion was the inability of the three countries to meet their ambitious commitments under the Force Goals. This time MAP created the conditions for a more realistic assessment of each country's own capacities to meet newly formulated commitments. In other words, Bulgaria already has experience in the institutionalized process of negotiating force commitments and should have no problems participating in the NATO Force Goals process.

Despite the dramatic changes following 11 September 2001 and the invitation to join NATO, the government of Simeon Saxe-Coburg Gotha did not embark on changes to the existing National Security Concept. The impeding membership in the Alliance, however, prompted the initiation of the Strategic Defense Review (SDR), a process intended to analyze the national defense system and formulate the vision and programs for its future development.[49] In March 2004, the National Assembly approved the Political Framework of the SDR which, along with noting that the National Security Concept is outdated, identifies the main risks and threats to the security of the country, including international terrorism; organized crime; proliferation and use of weapons of mass destruction; instability of democratic processes in the conflict regions; illegal trafficking of strategic resources and technologies, weapons, drugs and people; destructive attacks on information systems; environmental pollution; economic instability; and, natural disasters and industrial accidents. Very significantly, Article 11 of the Political Framework notes that "the analysis of the security environment shows that in the next decade Bulgaria will most probably not face a threat of an interstate conventional military conflict to its territory." It appears that this conclusion had been one of the major contentious issues between the civilian and military leaderships in the Defense Ministry as the former insisted on its inclusion in the Political Framework, while the latter opposed the explicit reference to the lack of threats to the territorial integrity of the country.

The Political Framework points out that "Certain tendencies are taking shape and they are related to the emergence of challenges, risks, and threats that are hard to predict and for which the (existing) security and defense systems are not prepared." Accordingly, Article 14 concludes that "There is a need for a change of orientation – from the source of threat to a combination of preventive and proactive activities that requires the adoption of a flexible approach for strategic planning organized in a stable institutional mechanism that is able to join the international efforts for preventive building of security." More specifically, in fulfilling its missions, the armed forces must implement "capability-based strategies for the development of forces and troops."

The Political Framework of the SDR is heavily influenced by the dominant security thinking in the Euro-Atlantic area.[50] Indeed, the document considers Bulgaria's security as indivisible from the security of the entire Euro-Atlantic community, a radical departure from the thinking in the early 1990s. Yet, the country can hardly escape geography. Although recognizing the low probability of a traditional military conflict, the Political Framework points out that "certain parts of the Western Balkans continue to be relatively unstable with the potential for an increase in tensions that generates risks to national security." In addition, as in the security policies of the European states, the document identifies "the conflicts in the Middle East, the Caucasus region, Central Asia and North Africa" as having the potential to escalate and pose threats to Bulgaria's security.[51]

The Iraqi War

However, Bulgaria's membership in NATO and the upcoming membership in the European Union have brought not only better perspectives for the future, but new challenges as well. The trans-Atlantic tensions that became especially bitter during the last Iraq crisis exposed Bulgaria's precarious position as a country at the periphery of the Euro-Atlantic area – seeking the commitment of the United States to the regional security, while maintaining good relations with Germany and France.

During the Iraqi crisis Bulgaria, while fully devoted to its priority of joining the EU, reluctantly maintained a strong pro-American stand in the trans-Atlantic spat. Being a non-permanent member of the UN Security Council in 2002–2003, Bulgaria had no choice but to take public stands, which obviously contradicted the positions of France and Germany, two countries whose political support Bulgaria needs in the process of joining the EU. The relations between Bulgaria and France reached the lowest point in February 2003, when the country was warned by the French President Jacques Chirac that its pro-American position might endanger the prospects of attaining EU membership. Indeed, although all East European states were warned, Bulgarian and Romania received special attention in Chirac's public outburst. Unlike other criticisms coming from abroad, however, this one did not split the political parties and the society in Bulgaria. Almost unanimously, political leaders and the media, including those who opposed Bulgaria's support for the US in Iraq, condemned the French president's words.[52] President Georgi Parvanov even demanded explanations from the French ambassador to Sofia.

This unanimity in reactions to the French president's comments did not, however, hide the lack of political consensus on Bulgaria's position toward the crisis. Initially, responding to an American request, the parliament on 7 February 2003 provided over-flight rights, bases and non-combat troops to the coalition of states, which demanded Iraq meet its international obligations. Only the BSP's members of parliament and five independent MPs abstained during the vote.[53] In the Security Council of the UN, Bulgaria was one of the members which considered the use of force unless Iraq meet the requirements of Resolution # 1441. Domestically, however, not only the political parties but also state institutions were split. The government, supported by the UDF, insisted that the country is part of the coalition of the willing and while Bulgaria was participating in the attempts to find a peaceful solution to the crisis, whether there would be a war was up to the Iraqi leadership. President Parvanov, supported by the BSP, insisted that the decision of the parliament of 7 February did not make Bulgaria part of the coalition of the willing and in any event a war against Iraq without UN approval would be illegal.[54]

Indeed, the Iraqi crisis revealed the fragility of the political consensus on Bulgaria's security policies. While the ruling majority and the UDF supported the country's pro-American position, the president, the BSP and most of the society opposed the war. Thus, it appears that while there is consensus on the country's

Euro-Atlantic integration, political parties have quite different visions of Bulgaria's precise place and role in the community. For example, at the height of the calamity President Parvanov strenuously objected to the official Bulgarian position and criticized the American handling of the crisis. Literally hours after the beginning of combat activities in Iraq, President Parvanov appeared before the Parliament and stated "I do not accept this war."[55] Similarly, the BSP in the early February 2003 officially opposed the use of military force to solve the conflict and Bulgaria participation in any coalition than might go to war without UN mandate.[56] Very significantly, however, the Socialists did not exclude Bulgaria's participation in a war on Iraq with an explicit UN resolution.

The evident lack of political consensus on Bulgaria's position towards the crisis let to confusion and fears among the society. In the eve of the war, merely 2 percent of the public approved the use of force by the US and its allies without a UN resolution and just 10 percent approved of the Bulgarian government's handling of the crisis.[57] Yet, when the BSP decided to exploit the prevailing public sentiments, it did not gain much political advantage and its anti-war demonstrations did not gather much following. In the face of overwhelming anti-war attitudes, the government did not suffer significant domestic political losses pursuing its policy of support for the US in Iraq.

The Public's Security Perceptions in the Transition Period

In the early years of the transition, the public's security perceptions did not differ significantly from the official security perceptions. For example, in the same period the public did not see any great power posing a threat, and a very low percentage of the respondents said that a conflict between great powers was likely. Conversely, in 1992, 61 percent of Bulgarians perceived neighboring states as a threat to national security and in 1996 the percentage remained relatively high at 31. In other words, the beginning of the civil wars in Yugoslavia created a sense of insecurity while the intervention of NATO slightly decreased the fears of the public. The ethnic conflicts in the neighboring states also maintained the sense of fear among many Bulgarians that the minorities in the country pose threat to national security; in 1992–2000, between 37 and 46 percent of the respondents shared this perception.[58]

The public's perceptions of external threats were amplified by the growing sense of individual, economic and social insecurity among the majority during the transition from communism. In the first years of the transition, the national economy contracted, the unemployment increased dramatically, the incomes fell and the crime increased. The BSP's rule also coincided with the lack of satisfaction with the state of democracy and human rights, which additional increased insecurity in the society. Exactly in this period, the public began to perceive the effects of domestic developments as more significant in defining the state of national security. Perceptions of growing corruption at the highest level, the palpable presence of organized crime on the streets, unemployment, high inflation and the lack of economic reform came to dominate societal thinking about security; thinking of national security, citizens were considering personal security first and foremost, The Socialists, however, continued to perceive external factors as defining national security.

Widespread perceptions of external threats appeared again during the Kosovo crisis in 1999. The unwillingness of the public to support NATO's action was indicative that the majority saw neutrality in the conflict as the guarantee against eventual threats emerging in the Balkans. For example, 58 percent of Bulgarians believed that Kosovo was the most serious threat to national security.[59] The conflict also exposed the divergence between the political elite's perceptions of the crisis as ultimately contributing to the long-term national security, while the public saw it as posing an acute threat to the country's security in the short term.[60]

After 11 September 2001 there is once again an increase in the percentage of Bulgarians who see external threats to security as the most significant. Fears of external threats increased twice in the last two years, while the number of Bulgarians who see internal factors as the sources of threats fell.[61] Although nearly 60 percent of respondents did not see the existence of internal and external factors threatening national security, 36 percent pointed to global terrorism as a potential external risk. Twelve percent see tensions in the Middle East and 7 percent the situation in the Balkans as likely risks. At the same time, 17 percent of Bulgarians see economic crisis as the most serious internal threat, while 12 percent sees organized crime and 5 percent points to corruption.

This data is quite difference from the data from October 2001 when 48 percent of respondents considered internal factors as the main risk to national security; the percentage now is 34.[62] In 2001 merely 34 percent of Bulgarians perceived some external threats to national security, while in July 2003 the number reached 61 percent. It is interesting to point out that while right after 11 September 2001 merely 13 percent of respondents perceived international terrorism as a threat to Bulgaria, in July 2003 as many as 36 percent thought so. In other words, it can be argued that the Bulgarian society is globalizing in terms of its security perceptions.

September 2001 and the ensuing war on terrorism changed the dynamics in the Bulgarian public's security perceptions and at the same time exposed some major issues which required the attention of the political elite. For example, a public opinion poll conducted in February 2003 by the National Center for the Study of Public Opinion found that only 23.1 percent of respondents see the operations in Iraq as a part of the war on terrorism, while 53 percent took the opposite position and 23.9 percent had no opinion. Answering the question "Do you believe the US and NATO would protect Bulgaria in case of a war in Iraq?" 29 percent responded affirmative, while 50.3 percent had the opposite opinion. Answering the question "Are you afraid of terrorist attacks in Bulgaria if the country supports the US in Iraq?" 63.5 percent responded affirmative and 21 percent responded "no." Another question, "Do you believe the war in Iraq brings humanity closer to a new world war?" gives revealing results as according to 72.6 percent of the respondents this is correct. Merely 11.4 percent of Bulgarians believe that the war decreases the likelihood of a new world war, while 16 percent had no opinion.

In the transition years since 1989 public attitudes toward membership in NATO underwent radical change. While at the beginning of the 90s just 11–12 percent of Bulgarians supported membership, at the beginning of the new century the support stabilized at 50 percent.[63] This tendency was accompanied by a drop in the firm opposition to membership.

Despite the positive dynamic in the public support of membership, the Bulgarian society is not homogenous in its attitudes toward NATO. Positive attitudes toward the Alliance and Bulgaria's membership in it are prevalent among entrepreneurs, professionals, students, the college educated, people with high incomes, while the least support can be found among people earning low income and those with low educational level. Age is another variable as the greater support of NATO can be found among the young; the highest level of disapproval is among the older population. The divisions in the society in regards to NATO reflect the existing divisions among the political parties discussed in the previous sections. For instance, the electorates of the UDF, NDSV and the MRF have highly positive attitudes toward the Alliance and support the country's membership in it, while the supporters of the BSP tend to display negative attitudes toward NATO, although some of them accept the membership as a matter of pragmatic choice.

Here is the place to point out to one feature, common not only to Bulgaria but also most other East-European states. A great number of the supporters of membership in NATO are likely to waver during crises. For example, the Kosovo crisis, the Macedonian crisis at the end of 2000, the destruction of the remaining Bulgarian SS-23 missiles in the summer of 2002, and the war in Iraq at the beginning of 2003 led to a decline in support for NATO. Very significantly, the majority of BSP supporters disapprove of NATO and those who approve it see membership simply as politically expedient in the new security environment.

These results, along with many others, indicate that the existing foreign policy consensus, notwithstanding, the society is extremely susceptible to contextual developments and often reacts with heightened fears and sense of insecurity.[64] Public opinion studies prove the temporary duration of such mass reactions yet this does not make the problem less serious. As the Iraqi crisis well illustrates, the political elite has difficulty legitimizing its foreign and security policies. During the war, the public failed to see the connection between Bulgaria's participation in the collation of the willing and the pursuit of national security goals and interests. Even now, when close to 500 Bulgarian troops are serving with the coalition forces in Karbala, south of Baghdad, the public still has difficulty fully accepting the need of Bulgarian military presence in Iraq. Thus, despite the modern strategic thinking guiding Bulgarian foreign and security policy, the public is yet to embrace it and provide the backing which is essential for any sustainable and cohesive national policy.

Bulgaria's societal and political attitudes toward Russia require a place in this analysis as they have always been quite distinct compared to the prevailing and historically consistent attitudes in most other East European countries. During the Cold War, Bulgaria was considered to be Moscow's closest ally, while having no Soviet troops on its territory. Generations of Bulgarians have learned to consider Russia as the country whose war against the Ottoman Empire in 1877–78 restored the Bulgarian statehood. In contrast to attitudes in most other East European countries, the public does not see Russia as a threat to national security and only a small section of the society thinks otherwise.[65] Even the right-wing political parties almost never turn suspicions and fears of Russia into a political issue. Generally, the public shows little interest in the political processes in the Russian Federation. During the last parliamentary and presidential election in Russia, the leftist media in Bulgaria, including *Duma* and *Zemya*, as well as many other newspapers, displayed either a positive or neutral view of the electoral outcome. The leftist newspapers defined the growing concentration of power in the hands of President Vladimir Putin as a positive outcome and contrasted the current political and economic stability in Russia to the general uncertainty and volatility during the rein of former president Boris Yeltsin. Conversely, criticism of what is seen as growing authoritarian tendency in Russia and its possible negative effects on Bulgarian security was few and far between. For example, former Prime-minister Ivan Kostov warned that Russian influence in Bulgaria undermines its democratic foundations and threatens its national security.[66] Some political analysts, too, saw a Russian tendency of abandoning the direct opposition to Bulgaria's integration in the Euro-Atlantic community and instead of attempting to influence national politics and the society by establishing a powerful lobby to defend Russian interests and by penetrating the national economy.[67] Even foreign experts point out that the Bulgarian and Russian interests are incompatible and warn that Moscow may try to use the country in its policy of influencing the Balkans and undermining NATO and American interests.[68] All in all, however, the society and most political parties display no intense suspicion of Russian motives and policies toward the country.

Bulgaria's Contribution to Euro-Atlantic Security

Despite the high level of integration among the countries in the Euro-Atlantic community, particularly in the EU, the states are still facing different in nature and intensity threats and challenges. No degree of integration can change that. Thus, Bulgaria, too, is facing a specific set of threats and risks. They fall into several categories. First, Bulgaria is at the periphery of the Euro-Atlantic space, adjacent to regions of conflicts and threats including the Middle East, Caucasus, Central Asia and greater Asia. The appearance of terrorism, proliferation of WMD and organized crime as the most serious threats to international security inevitably turns Bulgaria into one of the likeliest victims of these threats. Furthermore, Bulgaria's continuing integration into the Euro-Atlantic space turns the country into a logical target and a place wherein these threats and risks materialize. Additionally, as a country in the periphery, Bulgaria is expected to contribute substantially to the policies aimed at preventing and eliminating the threats. This expectation is turning into a challenge to the ability of the political class and the society to define Bulgaria's role in the Euro-Atlantic security system and accordingly build political, military and societal capacities to fulfill it.

The second category of challenges is related to regional processes. Despite Bulgaria's continuing integration in the Euro-Atlantic community, the country cannot escape the fact that it is in the Balkans, a region, which after the cold war witnessed a series of civil wars and conflicts. Thus while the territorial integrity and sovereignty of the states in Europe face no challenge, in the last ten years the Balkans often witnessed violent changes to the political map of the region. Furthermore, the tendency of challenges to the territorial integrity still exists, however diminished. This tendency, although not directly threatening Bulgaria's territory and sovereignty, leads to numerous negative effects on the national security. The constant political instability in the region, the sometimes palpable lack of effective state authority and the proliferation of small arms increase organized crime groups' influence over the political process, arrest the process of economic cooperation between the countries in the region, and deter foreign companies from investing in the country and the region. One of the examples for direct negative impact is the repeatedly confirmed connection between organized crime in Bulgaria and the illegal traffic of humans, arms and drugs in the Balkans.

The third category of challenges is internal in its nature. Bulgaria is not only in an unstable region adjacent to serous sources of threats to the entire Euro-Atlantic area, but also a country which possesses relatively poor capacities and capabilities to face these threats. In other words, the country is in a threat-rich environment while having low capacity to achieve an acceptable level of security. According to the modern thinking, security is the delicate balance of threats and capacities. Following this logic, the main challenge facing Bulgaria is how to increase its national capacity while at the same time implement policies to better the security environment in the region. A country the size and capacity of Bulgaria obviously has no other valuable choice but to seek integration in institutions and communities which possess ample capacities to achieve security, particularly NATO and the EU. In the past, the traditional security policy sought the accumulation of military power as the only way to guarantee security. This, however, placed a huge burden on society, especially in countries with poor capacities. The modern security policy requires that countries with relatively scarce capacities seek integration in institutional frameworks, which not only abate the threats in the security environment but also increase national security capacities. Thus the best policy to guarantee Bulgaria's security is the integration in the Euro-Atlantic community. Therefore, threats to the process of integration are ultimately threats to national security.

The fourth category of challenges to Bulgaria is related to the processes within the Euro-Atlantic community. The end of the Iraqi war and the improving relations between the US and the European states opposing the war do not, however, eliminate future threats to Bulgaria's balancing act between the competing visions on both sides of the Atlantic. The proposal for the creation of an independent European defense identity formulated in early 2003 by France, Germany, Belgium and Luxemburg was yet another reason for Bulgarian decision-makers to worry about further tensions in the Euro-Atlantic community which would inevitably place the country in an uncomfortable position to once again make choices it wants to avoid. For now, however, the country continues its policy of providing support to the American war on terrorism while seeking a quick completion to accession negotiations with the EU.

Consistent with this approach is the Bulgarian leadership's recently expressed political will to host American military bases.[69] As a country adjacent to volatile regions, Bulgaria is compelled to formulate policy responses to dynamic developments and processes. It seems that Bulgaria sees NATO, and its perceived leader the United States, as the only robust security organization capable of providing security to the Euro-Atlantic space. Accordingly, from the very outset of the war on terrorism after 11 September 2001 Bulgaria has been a *de facto* American and NATO ally. The country granted blanket permit for the overflight of American aircraft taking part in the Enduring Freedom operation and hosted US Air Force refueling planes. Later Bulgaria sent a unit to participate in the UN mission in Afghanistan. The decision to support the United States in the standoff over Iraq was a natural choice given Bulgaria's need to secure the support for its membership aspirations of the most powerful NATO member. And although the decision of the government caused an internal political split and the loss of public support for its foreign policy, it came as no surprise for a country, which saw no other security institution as a valuable alternative. Consequently, the parliament decided to send up to 500 troops to support the allies after the overthrow of Saddam Hussein. What is remarkable about the Bulgarian participation in Iraq is that even though since late December 2003 the battalion gave total of 6 casualties and frequently engaged in violent confrontations in Karbala, its zone of operation, no political party in the parliament demanded the withdrawal of the Bulgarian troops. Even President Parvanov, who strongly objected to the war in Iraq and frequently criticized the Bulgarian government for its handling of the crisis, was quick to point out the withdrawing the battalion was not on the table. The Prime-Minister gave similar signals.[70] Yet the decision of Spain, Honduras and the Dominican Republic to withdraw their troops from Iraq increased the pressure on the government to reconsider the form of national participation and increased the chances a political party may use the anti-war sentiments both in Bulgaria and in Europe for political gain by demanding unconditional withdrawal.

In contrast to the other new NATO members, except Romania, Bulgaria is not compelled to define positions regarding the emerging European Security and Defense Policy (ESDP). As a country whose accession to the EU was deferred to 2007, Bulgaria is not formally involved in the process of defining ESDP. Indeed, neither the Ministry of Defense nor the Ministry of Foreign Affairs have attempted to formulate positions on the interplay of NATO and the EU security and defense institutions and policies and Bulgaria's place in it.[71] Not surprisingly, political leaders and officials limit their pronouncements on the complex politics of this issue to some general appeals for the need for coordination between the two organizations and assurances of Bulgaria's support to whatever the institutions reach as agreements. All in all, Bulgaria has no role in the debate on the interaction between NATO and the EU in the area of security and defense, except for its participation in the negotiations on the future constitution of the Union.[72]

Conclusion

Geostrategy defines Bulgaria as a state on the periphery of the Euro-Atlantic space, facing risks and threats emanating from the Balkans, the Middle East, the Caucasus, and the former Soviet Union. Threats and risks from these regions will influence strategic thinking in Bulgaria for many years to come. In fact, these security challenges are not specific to Bulgaria but to the entire Euro-Atlantic area. In other words, Bulgaria's integration in NATO and the EU will not diminish threats to national security but simply increase the country's capacity to face them.

Inevitably, being in the periphery is bound to dominate strategic thinking; in the near term, decision-makers are always tempted to formulate security policies for traditional threats and risks, thus ignoring developments and trends beyond the immediate security environment.

At the same time, Bulgaria faces risks and threats common to the Euro-Atlantic area including terrorism, organized crime, weapons of mass destruction, and mass migration. Indeed, in the last year three many Bulgarian citizens became victims of terrorist acts on several separate occasions and none of them took place in the country. Integration in the Euro-Atlantic area partially de-nationalizes Bulgaria's security policy as national security becomes a part of the community security. Thus, security policy must be formulated in close cooperation with allies and synchronized with the Euro-Atlantic community's security needs. In the short term, the great challenge facing the political elite and defense planners is to recognize that Bulgaria's integration in the Euro-Atlantic space to a great extent denationalizes the national security policy and accordingly change the national policy.

In addition to external threats and risks, Bulgaria faces numerous domestic challenges typical for all transition countries in Southeast Europe. Weak institutions, political instability, the slow pace of reforms, uneven economic development, social stratification, and organized crime and corruption are only some of the threats and risks challenging the ability of the states to provide basic security to its citizens. These threats were identified and widely discussed in the literature on democratization early in the post-communist period. However, while the countries of Central Europe proved capable of dealing adequately with most challenges and thus disproving the early pessimistic scenarios of the future of Eastern Europe, Bulgaria, in facing numerous threats and risks, has yet to demonstrate ability to deal with them effectively. In other words, Bulgaria's security policy faces the double-edged challenge of having to attain security in a threat-rich environment while possessing limited capabilities.

For very long in the post-communist period, the political elite did not achieve a consensus on the national interests and the ways to attain them. Compared to the other East European countries Bulgaria remained ambivalent toward membership in NATO as there was no domestic consensus on the foreign policy priorities of the country. Although it might be argued that the society and political elite have finally achieved a consensus on the place of the country in the world, it is still too early to discern any fledging consensus on Bulgaria's security needs, and especially on the policies to achieve security. In other words, the political elite and the society are yet to define what the country's role in the Euro-Atlantic security system ought to be.

There is a real danger that the political elite may conclude that NATO membership itself guarantees national security. If such a perception is to dominate strategic thinking, Bulgaria's security policy may lead to predominate investments in traditional, regionally-oriented security and defense capabilities while expecting the Alliance to add further resources to the national security capacity. In such thinking almost all of the future security risks and threats are of the traditional type, including conflicts between states. Such policy would turn Bulgaria into a consumer of security, which adds little to the security capacity of the Euro-Atlantic community. Indeed, despite almost four years of intensive defense reform, the armed forces are yet to change radically their structure, missions and capabilities. One of the consequences of the concluding Strategic Defense Review was to expose the tensions between the civilian and military leadership in the Ministry of Defense.[73] Most recently, for example, the minister of defense Nikolay Svinarov suggested that the armed forces should be downsized to 39,000 by 2015, down from the current 45,000, while the Chief of the General Staff General Nikola Kolev proposed an increase to 48,000. At the same time, despite the relatively large defense budget, reaching 2,6 percent of the GDP, the armed forces have difficulty preparing troops to serve in Iraq.

If no change in strategic thinking is to take place, Bulgaria will then assume a relatively low-profile in the Alliance, doing only the minimum required as a member and frequently refusing to take a firm stand on issues which do not appear to concern the narrowly defined national interest. Ultimately however, such strategic thinking and policy would not substantially enhance national security. In a security environment wherein most threats and risks would not very likely require allied actions falling under Article 5 of the Washington Treaty, the reliance on security policies translates into little added security. Therefore, it is extremely important for the sake of the future enhanced national security that the political elite and the society achieve a consensus on the thinking that more security in the Euro-Atlantic community is achieved through active participation in its future expanded security and defense policies.

Notes

1   "Pact Outlived Its Time" (1991), *CTK* in English, 1 February.
2   Foreign Minister Boyko Dimitrov rejected the idea that Bulgaria might join NATO and instead called for the simultaneous dissolution of both alliances. Ricardo Estarriol, "Foreign Minister Views European Issues," *La Vanguardia* in Spanish (date not given). Translated by the Foreign Broadcast Information Service (1990), *FBIS Daily Report-East Europe*, 29 March (PrEx 7.10: FBIS-EEU-90–061); 8–9.
3   Defense Minister Yordan Mutavchiev suggested that after the dissolution of the Warsaw Pact, Bulgaria must rely on its own defense forces and bilateral treaties with the Soviet Union. Zvyatko Belenski and Ivan Staevski (1990), "Our Military Doctrine is Defensive," *Otechestven Vestnik* in Bulgarian, 21 November.
4   See interview with Minister of Foreign Affairs Viktor Vulkov, Vikhra Rizova (1991), "Bulgaria Has Renounced the Satellite Syndrome," *Anteni* in Bulgarian, 26 June.
5   Joseph Rothschild (1993), *Return to Diversity: A Political History of East Central Europe Since World War II*, New York: Oxford University Press; Barbara Jelavich (1983), *History of the Balkans*, New York: Cambridge University Press.
6   On the Bulgarian perspective on military implications of the Yugoslav conflict see Michail Srebrev, "Southern Europe: Concerns and Implications from a Bulgarian Perspective," in Charles L. Barry, ed. (1993), *The Search for Peace in Europe: Perspectives from NATO and Eastern Europe*, Fort Lesley: National Defense University Press.
7   See interview with Acting Foreign Minister Dimiter Ikonomov, Ryszard Bilski (1993), "Stop the War," *Rzeczpolita* in Polish, 25 February, translated by the Foreign Broadcast Information Service (1993), *FBIS Daily Report-East Europe*, 4 March (PrEx 7.10: FBIS-EEU-93–041), 4–5.

8   See statement by President Zhelev in the daily *Balgarska Armia* (1991) in Bulgarian, 18 November, 1.

9   In his election address before the 1991 parliamentary elections, UDF leader and future Prime Minister Philip Dimitrov listed Bulgaria's integration in the EC as a number one foreign policy priority, but failed to even mention NATO; "Election Address" (1991), *Demokratsiya* in Bulgarian, 16 September.

10   Dunkan M. Perry (1992), "New Directions for Bulgarian-Turkish Relations," *RFE/RL Research Report*, 1, no. 41, 16 October: 33–40.

11   "Military Accord with Turkey" (1992), *RFE/RL Research Report* 1, no. 48, 4 December, 58.

12   Statements by President Zhelev and General Tsvetan Totomirov (1994), *Bulgarian Telegraph Agency*, 2 October.

13   Kyril Haramiev-Drezov (1993), "Bulgarian-Russian Relations on a New Footing," *RFE/RL Research Report*, 2, no. 15, 9 April: 33–38.

14   Kjell Engelbrekt (1994), "A Vulnerable Bulgaria Fears Wider War," *RFE/RL Research Report*, 3, no. 16, 22 April: 7–12.

15   "Lecture of the Prime Minister of Republic of Bulgaria, Zhan Videnov Before the Atlantic Club in Bulgaria, 4 April 1995," available from the Atlantic Club in Bulgaria.

16   Vasil Lyutskanov (1995), "Army Needs Urgent Modernization, Or We Will Be Hopelessly Behind in One or Two Years," *Sofia Trud* in Bulgarian, 6 February.

17   Liubomir Denov (1994), "At One Stroke, NATO Pushes Us Into a New Arms Race," *Sofia 24 Chasa* in Bulgarian, 27 October, 10.

18   Nikolay Slatinski, former Chairman of the National Assembly's National Security Committee, worried in early 1995 that the Conventional Forces in Europe Treaty exacerbated an already great regional imbalance to Bulgaria's detriment by allowing modernization of weapons system and cascading of military hardware to Greece and Turkey. Given the economic and social crisis in the country, Bulgaria was seen as unable to compete and keep up with these countries. See Nikolay Slatinski and Marina Kaparini (1995), "Bulgarian Security and Prospects for Reform," *NATO Review*, no. 2, March: 28–32.

19   Council of Ministers of the Republic of Bulgaria (1995), *National Security Concept of the Republic of Bulgaria*. In Bulgarian, Sofia.

20   In an interview with the *Kontinent* daily, Turkey's president Suleyman Demirel was asked to assure the Bulgarian public that his country had no evil designs on Bulgaria or the Balkans; "Suleyman Demirel, Interview" (1993), Sofia *Bulgarian Telegraph Agency* in English, 10 December.

21   On the UDF's view of Bulgarian membership in NATO in 1994 see interview with then Deputy Defense Minister and a future Defense Minister in the Kostov government, Boyko Noev; Lyubomir Denov (1994), "Boyko Noev: The Time for Neutrality Has Passed," *24 Chasa* in Bulgarian, 11 March.

22   The Socialists' mouthpiece *Duma* commented that the signing in 1994 of a memorandum by the Bulgarian government and visiting US Defense Secretary William Perry was serving America's strategic interests in the Balkans, but none of Bulgaria's; "Bobi Michailov is Not Guarding the State's Goal" (1994), *Duma* in Bulgarian, 20 July.

23   See Videnov, 3–5; Council of Ministers of the Republic of Bulgaria, *National Security Concept*, 34.

24   Nikolay Slatinski and Marina Kaparini (1995), "Bulgarian Security and Prospects for Reform," *NATO Review* n. 2, March: 28–32.

25   Jeffrey Simon (1998), "Bulgaria and NATO: 7 Lost Years," *Strategic Forum* no. 142, May, online at http://www.ndu.edu.

26 Government of the Republic of Bulgaria (1999), *National Security Concept*, June, online at http://www.md.government.bg.
27 The military doctrine was approved on 8 April, 1999. Council of Ministers of the Republic of Bulgaria (1999), *Military Doctrine of the Republic of Bulgaria*, June 1999, online at http://www.md.government.bg.
28 In a sharp reversal of previous Bulgarian policy of neutrality toward Yugoslavia, President Stoyanov stated that Bulgaria's long-term interests did not coincide with the interests of today's leadership of Yugoslavia and described the conflict as "a collision between the democratic community and the last communist regime in Europe." "Bulgaria Sides with NATO Over Kosovo" (1999), *Agence France-Presse*, 16 April. In an interview for *Le Monde*, President Stoyanov noted that in the past seven years Bulgaria had been a hostage of Milosevic's policies and that it is time to solve the Serbia problem; *Bulgarian Telegraph Agency*, 5 May, 2001. In an interview for the daily *Trud*, Prime Minster Ivan Kostov stated that Bulgaria cannot have a neutral policy toward the Kosovo crisis for neutrality would bring about more threats to Bulgaria; Valeriya Veleva (1999), "You Stop Violence with Violence," Sofia *Trud* in Bulgarian, 3 May 1.
29 "Bulgaria-NATO Consultations" (1998), *Bulgarian Telegraph Agency*, 13 October.
30 "Bulgaria, Romania Urge Milosevic to Accept NATO Force" (1999), *Agence France-Presse*, 22 February.
31 Anatoly Verbin (1999), "Bulgarian Government Tested Over Kosovo," *Reuters*, 19 April; in a interview, Ivan Krastev, a Bulgarian political scientist, argued that the "crisis in Kosovo makes Bulgaria a real candidate for NATO membership"; "Kosovo Crisis Made Bulgaria Visible" (1998), *Kapital* 13, 5 April.
32 In a "Statement on Kosovo," the NAC committed the Alliance to the security and territorial integrity of the countries challenged during the crisis by Serbia's regime; quoted in Jeffrey Simon (2000), "NATO's Membership Action Plan (MAP) and Prospects for the Next Round of Enlargement," Occasional Paper no. 61, Washington D.C.: Woodrow Wilson International Center For Scholars, November, 9, online at http://www.wilsoncenter.com.
33 Steve Holland (1999), "NATO Vows to Guard Border States from Serbs," *Reuters*, 25 April.
34 Interview of foreign minister Nadezhda Michailova (1998), "NATO Extends its Security System Over Bulgaria," *Kapital* 41, 19 October. In an interview, Prime Minister Ivan Kostov said that NATO Secretary General Javier Solana had sent a letter stating that "NATO is ready to guarantee the security of Bulgaria in a case of attack by Yugoslavia" (1998), *Bulgarian Telegraph Agency*, 13 October.
35 "Deal Will Let NATO Forces to Use Bulgarian Territory" (2001), *Reuters*, 29 March.
36 "Socialists Decide to Vote for Ratification of Agreement with NATO" (2001), *Bulgarian Telegraph Agency*, 4 March.
37 In March 1999, 72 percent of the public was against NATO military intervention in Yugoslavia and 77 percent were against NATO equipment and personnel crossing Bulgaria; "Bulgaria–Survey–Kosovo" (1999), *Bulgarian Telegraph Agency*, 23 March.
38 In the same survey, 58 percent of the public viewed the conflict in Kosovo as the worst threat to national security. While one-third considered NATO guarantees a reliable protection only 59 percent said Bulgaria would be better protected if it did not allow its territory to be used in a possible attack on Yugoslavia; ibid.
39 "Fifth Stray NATO Missile Hits Bulgaria" (1999), *Agence France-Presse*, 7 May.
40 During the air campaign the Bulgarian military was not placed on higher alert although some special security measures were implemented, including additional security for the

nuclear plant in Kozloduy. Galina Sabeva (1999), "Bulgarian Leaders Work to Grant NATO Request," *Reuters*, 19 April.

41 Anatoly Verbin (1999), "Bulgarian Government Tested Over Kosovo," *Reuters*, 19 April.

42 During the crisis Bulgaria and the Alliance held intensive consultations, and in late 1998, NATO Secretary General Javier Solana sent a letter, which, according to Prime Minister Kostov, provided security guarantees to the country; "Bulgaria–NATO Consultations" (1998), *Bulgarian Telegraph Agency*, 13 October.

43 The Kosovo crisis was one of the main reasons the EU decided to initiate accession negotiations with Bulgaria. For the political elite's view see President Stoyanov's interview with *Le Monde* (2001); *Bulgarian Telegraph Agency*, 5 May.

44 "BPS Declares Itself in Favor of Active Partnership with NATO," *Bulgarian Telegraph Agency* (7 March, 2000); "Ex-Communist Socialist Back Bulgaria's NATO Bid," *Reuters* (6 March, 2000).

45 "Socialists Break with Past, Back NATO" (2000), *Reuters*, 7 May.

46 Council of Ministers of the Republic of Bulgaria (2000), *17 February 1997–Decision of the Council of Ministers for Full NATO Membership*, November, online at http://www.md.government.bg.

47 See Simon, "NATO's Membership," 10.

48 Bulgaria, Ministry of Defense (2001), *Military Doctrine of the Republic of Bulgaria*, online at http://www.md.government.bg; Bulgaria, Ministry of Defense (2001), *Plan 2004*, June, online at http://www.md.government.bg; Jeffrey Simon (2000), "Transforming the Armed Forces of Central and East Europe," *Strategic Forum*, no. 172, June, online at http://www.ndu.edu.

49 Bulgaria, Council of Ministers, *Political Framework of the Strategic Defense Review*, online at http://www.md.bg.

50 As in other East European countries joining NATO in the last wave of enlargement, Bulgaria makes a wide use of Western expertise in the formulation of the basic security-related documents and concepts. Civilian and military officials and experts from NATO countries participate in all phases of the soon-to-be completed SDR.

51 The Political Framework of the Strategic Defense Review is not intended to provide a comprehensive review and assessment of security environment, but considering that the current National Security Concept is hopelessly outdated, the document inevitably devotes some attention to the various threats, risks and challenges facing Bulgaria. Logically, the government of Saxe-Coburg Gotha is currently considering the formulation of a National Security Strategy to replace the old National Security Concept.

52 "Members of Parliament: Paris Must Apologize" (2003), *Standart* in Bulgarian, 19 February, 2; Petyo Tzekov (2003), "Our Politicians and Sociologists: The French President Doesn't Bother Us," *Sega* in Bulgarian, 19 February, 3.

53 The mouthpiece of the BSP, Duma described the vote as a decision for participation in war; Georgi Georgiev (2003), "Bulgaria Goes to War," *Duma* in Bulgarian, 8 February, 3.

54 "The Position on Iraq is Split Into Two Blocs with the BSP and the UDF" (1993), *Dnevnik* in Bulgarian, 19 March, 1.

55 "Parvanov and BSP Against Participation with the US Without UN Mandate" (2003), *Mediapool.bg* in Bulgarian, 5 February, online at http://www.mediapool.bg; "Statement by President Parvanov before the National Assembly" (2003), *Bulgarian Telegraph Agency* in Bulgarian, 5 February; "The President Objected to Bulgaria's Participation in the Coalition" (2003), *Dnevnik* in Bulgarian, 21 March, 1.

56 Krastina Krasteva (2003), "The Socialists Against War in the Gulf," *Trud* in Bulgarian, 3 February, 4.

57 Public opinion poll conducted by Gallup International – Bulgaria; "Just 2% of Bulgarians Approve of War Without the UN" (2003), *Sega* in Bulgarian, 18 March, 1.

58 Christina Haerpfer, Claire Wallace and Richard Rose (1997), *Public Perceptions of Threats to Security in Post-Communist Europe*, Glasgow, Scotland: Center for the Study of Public Policy, University of Strathclyde, 15; Alfa Research.

59 See "Bulgaria–Survey–Kosovo," *Bulgarian Telegraph Agency* (23 March, 1999).

60 In its 1999 report the European Commission summed up the prevailing view among the member states that "one of the key lessons of the Kosovo crisis is the need to achieve peace and security, democracy and the rule of law, growth and the foundations of prosperity throughout Europe. Enlargement is the best way to do this. There is now a greater awareness of the strategic dimensions of enlargement." Accordingly, despite the lack of full compliance with the economic requirements for the start of accession, the Commission recommended that Bulgaria be accepted as a candidate at the Helsinki summit on 10 December 1999. Thus, paradoxically, the Kosovo crisis increased Bulgaria's chances of joining Europe sooner; European Commission (2000), *Composite Paper 1999: Reports on Progress Toward Accession by Each of the Candidate Countries*, Supplement 2/99, Luxemburg: Office for Official Publications of the European Communities, 5.

61 Public opinion poll conducted by BBSS Gallup International. Information published in mediapool.bg, online at http://www.mediapool.bg.

62 See Zhivko Georgiev (2003), "Public Attitudes Towards NATO Membership," in Security Sector Reform Coalition, *Report #5: Bulgaria's Preparedness for NATO Membership*, Atlantic Club in Bulgaria: Sofia, July: 60–63.

63 Ibid.

64 Antoni Galabov (2003), "Public Perceptions of Threat, Risk and Security," paper presented at the Risks and Threats to the Regional and Euro-Atlantic Security round table in Sofia, organized by the Institute of Euro-Atlantic Security, 12 June.

65 In 1992 only 6 percent and in 1996 just 5 percent of the public perceived Russia to be a security threat to Bulgaria's security; Haerpfer, Wallace and Rose, *Public Perceptions of Threats*, 6.

66 Ivan Kostov (2004), "Russia and Our Security," *24 Chasa* in Bulgarian, 4 February.

67 Evgeniy Daynov (2004), "The Russian Interest Eats the Bulgarian Interest Like Snake Eating the Frog," *24 Chasa* in Bulgarian, 13 February, 14.

68 Interview with Janusz Bugajski of the Center for Strategic and International Studies, Washington, D.C.; "Bulgaria Presents a Special Interest to the Russian Espionage" (2004), *24 Chasa* in Bulgarian, 25 February, 17.

69 *Bulgarian Telegraph Agency* (16 October 2003); Jim Garamone (2003), "US to Consult Allies on American Military Presence," *American Forces Press Services*, 25 November; on the transformation of American military posture see speech by Douglas Faith (2003), Undersecretary of Defense for Policy, at the Center for Strategic and International Studies, Washington, D.C., 3 December, online at http://www.csis.org.

70 "Bulgaria is Firmly Staying in Iraq" (2004), *24 Chasa* in Bulgarian, 25 March, 4.

71 Interviews of the author with officials from the Ministry of Defense and the Ministry of Foreign Affairs.

72 However, there is already an emerging debate in the non-governmental expert community. For instance a book by the former Prime-Minister Philip Dimitrov (2004), *The New Democracies and the Trans-Atlantic Relations*, in Bulgarian, Sofia: Siela and Konstantin Dimitrov, ed. (2004), *Implementation of Bulgaria's Membership Commitments. The Road after Prague*, Sofia: Procon.

73 Panaiot Angarev (2004), "The Armed Forces Enter NATO Still Having its Soviet Structure," *Dnevnik* in Bulgarian, 28 January, 1.

Chapter 8

The Dilemma of 'Dual Loyalty': Lithuania and Transatlantic Tensions

Dovile Budryte

Introduction

The 21 November 2002 was one of the most festive days in Lithuania's recent history. Lithuanians learned that they were offered membership in NATO. The celebration continued two days later, when President George W. Bush announced to a cheering crowd in Vilnius that there would be " ... no more Munichs ... no more Yaltas in the future. Lithuania's enemies will be America's enemies." Bush's speech was followed by a short-lived public celebration of the "End of Yalta." "Having heard these [Bush's] words, we can be sure that the future of our state will be secure," wrote Audrius Baciulis, a political commentator.[1] Many could identify with this sentiment. Coupled with an expectation to join the EU, the dream of a secure and prosperous life seemed to be within reach.

However, Lithuania's prospective membership in NATO and the European Union has brought not only bright visions of the future, but new dilemmas as well. The transatlantic tensions that became especially acrimonious during the recent Iraq war made it clear that in the near future Lithuania's policy makers will have to balance their actions to achieve two goals. The first is to remain a reliable partner of the United States. The second is to remain committed to the process of European unification.

During the 1990s, membership in NATO and the EU were Lithuania's major strategic goals, rarely questioned by Lithuania's political elite. Having received invitations to these dream clubs, Lithuania's political elite became engaged in a discussion about the future of Lithuania's security policies and what actions would be required to pursue them. Some argued that Lithuania should be an active small state and aspire to become a regional leader. Close cooperation with the United States would be one way to achieve this vision. Others argued that Lithuania should focus on economic prosperity, trying to become "a golden, or rich and boring, backwater of Europe." Accordingly, these theorists believed that impartiality was primary for Lithuania's prosperity.[2]

Questions about the future contours of Lithuania's security policy cannot be answered without describing the threats that Lithuania currently faces and identifying Lithuania's core security priorities. Recently questions about these priorities were addressed in the 2002 National Security System and Security Expansion Report presented by Linas Linkevicius, Lithuania's Defense Minister, to Lithuania's Parliament on 17 June 2003; National Security Strategy ratified by the Lithuanian parliament on 28 May 2002 as well as in The 2002 White Book published by the Defense Ministry. The Ministry of Foreign Affairs reiterates the country's foreign policy priorities – being able to contribute to a strong and prosperous Europe, maintaining NATO's viability, building a stable international system based on the rule of law, and promoting economic interests – on a regular basis.[3]

Threats and National Security Priorities

There is general agreement that Lithuania has recently been enjoying an unprecedented level of security. This feeling of security is shared by many and it was created by Euro-Atlantic integration. According to a public opinion poll, as many as 39.4 percent of respondents said that NATO membership made them feel more secure.[4]

Currently the state does not face any immediate military threats. Not a single country, not even Russia, is identified as an enemy in its national security documents. Euro-Atlantic integration helped the state to mend fences with Poland and Russia, its neighbors and former enemies. In 1994, hoping for membership in NATO, Lithuania signed the Good Neighborhood Treaty with Poland. Later, numerous intergovernmental institutions, such as the Parliamentary Assembly of Lithuania and Poland and the Government Cooperation Council of Lithuania and Poland, were created. Currently 351 Lithuanians serve in LITPOLBAT, a Lithuanian-Polish peacekeeping unit.[5] Since August 2003, 45 soldiers from the motorized infantry battalion patrol serve in Iraq in the Polish-controlled sector.[6]

Official Lithuanian-Russian relations improved following the terrorist attacks of 11 September when Russia weakened its opposition to Lithuania's NATO membership and agreed to resolve the transit issue to Kaliningrad.[7] On 1 July 2003, Lithuania successfully implemented a new visa policy for the residents of Kaliningrad, an exclave of Russia bordering Lithuania. Residents of Kaliningrad can now obtain free transit visas in order to travel to Russia proper. In June of 2003, Russia finally ratified a border treaty with its western neighbor, thus removing a major sticking point in Lithuanian-Russian relations.

Despite this positive trend in official Lithuanian-Russian relations, the elites as well as the public constantly express their fears about Russia.[8] The elites' discourse analysis suggests that the "East" is still perceived as a threat to the nation and the sovereign state.[9] Reactions to several recent developments – the overwhelming victory of pro-Putin "Yedinaya Rossiya" (United Russia) party in the Russian Duma elections in December 2003 and the 2003–04 Lithuanian presidential crisis – are cases in point. For example, on 9 December 2003, when the Russian election results became public in Lithuania, an editorial in the leading Lithuanian daily "Lietuvos Rytas" claimed that the Putin-style "managed democracy" is creeping into Lithuania. President Rolandas Paksas and his party of liberal democrats were responsible for this development. They were supporting Russia's interests in Lithuania, and their rule started to resemble Putin's rule.[10]

Such claims became much more pronounced during the height of the so-called "Paksas-gate" (the presidential scandal) in November, December 2003 and in

January 2004. On 1 December 2003, a parliamentary inquiry found that President Paksas' advisers were linked to organized crime, and that Paksas himself was close to Yuri Borisov, a Russian born dealer in helicopter parts who sponsored Paksas' election campaign. Borisov was thought to be linked to a Russian lobbying firm tied to Russia's security services.[11] He was seen as an agent of Russian influence with Paksas ready to help him. According to the findings of the inquiry, the President "was, and still is, vulnerable. Taking into account the special status of the President, his responsibility and role in domestic and foreign policy, this poses a threat to Lithuania's national security."[12]

Naturally, during the "Paksas-gate," commentators and politicians made numerous claims about "the return of Russia," arguing that only those who are naïve can't see how Russia attempts to control not only "our economics, but also our deep political processes."[13] For example, Romanas Sedlickas, a member of the Liberal Center Party, who observed the parliamentary elections in Russia, suggested that "Russia still harbors imperial ambitions, and it hopes to regain its influence in the post communist countries through investment."[14] The public shared his concerns. According to a public opinion poll, in 2003 Russia was considered to be the most threatening country to Lithuania's security (42.3 percent). Belarus came next (19.7 percent).[15]

Militarily, Belarus does not pose a threat to Lithuania. However, Lithuania cannot ignore its eastern neighbor's failure to democratize and develop economically. President Alexander Lukashenko's continued harassment of the opposition and the independent media is of concern to some politicians and policy analysts. Jonas Cekuolis, a Lithuanian MP and chairman of a subcommittee on Belarus in the European Council, described Lithuanian-Belarus relations: "Economically and culturally speaking, Lithuania and Belarus enjoy normal relations, but as far as political relations are concerned, they are not good."[16] Like other EU countries and the EU candidates, Vilnius has been boycotting President Lukashenka's regime. Since 2000, there have been no official Belarusian-Lithuanian meetings above the level of deputy ministers.

However, some dialogue has been taking place. To build trust, in 2001 Lithuania signed a bilateral agreement with Belarus to exchange information about military exercises on a regular basis. Such exchanges have been taking place since 2001.[17] Since 2002, the two neighbors have been engaged in cultural exchanges. Vilnius has an interest in participating in these cross-border programs since there are 18,000 ethnic Lithuanians in Belarus. To help them keep their ethnic identity, the Lithuanian government built two secondary schools to teach Lithuanian in Belarus. On the other hand, the Belarusian government is interested in developing relations in trade, transportation and cross-border exchanges with its Western neighbor because Lithuania and Latvia provide access to the Baltic ports.[18] (Belarus is landlocked.) Lithuania is one of Belarus' main trading partners, exporting oil and its products and importing minerals.[19]

Before EU expansion in May 2004, Belarusian-Lithuanian relations have been pursued on a strictly bilateral basis. Neither the EU nor Moscow was directly involved. Needless to say, this will change when Lithuania joins the EU. There are fears in Belarus that expansion of the EU will reduce Belarus' exports to Lithuania since Belarusian trucks will not meet EU standards and will not be allowed to enter the country. Visas may become prohibitively expensive, which will reduce the number of social and personal contacts. Some have argued that these developments may in fact strengthen the authoritarian rule in Belarus.[20] Concerns about Belarus' future sparked a debate in Vilnius in October 2003. Vytenis Andriukaitis, deputy chairman of the ruling party of Social Democrats, suggested that it may be time to rethink the current Lithuanian-Belarusian relationship, since the current policies "were not yielding good results." Andriukaitis went on to argue that it may be beneficial to try to persuade the EU to allow Lithuania to establish relations with high Belarusian officials, including President Lukashenka.[21]

Andriukaitis' proposition did not receive a lot of support. In fact, it was strongly criticized by the right wing politicians.[22] Instead, there has been an emerging consensus that Lithuania is going to cooperate with the other EU members to create a common policy toward Belarus. Since 2003, Lithuania has been participating in the planning processes of the EU New Neighbors Initiative. Some believe that given its size, Lithuania is unlikely to be as important as Poland in the future EU-Belarus relations.[23] Yet Vilnius has a clear idea of what it would like to see in Belarus in the future. Belarus should be prevented from a further consolidation of authoritarian rule and closer relationship with Moscow. The "expanding east" – closer Belarus-Russia union – is still perceived as a potential security threat in Vilnius.

Thus, although facing no direct threats from nation-states right now, Lithuania is far from being free of worry about its security environment. National security documents suggest that Lithuania is worried about transnational threats, such as international terrorism, and trafficking in drugs and people. Furthermore, national security strategists warn that "too much dependence" on imports of strategically important materials, such as petroleum, and capital from one "potentially unstable country" may become a threat to Lithuania's national security in the future.[24] Even though the EU has become the leading market for most of Lithuania's export products (Russia received only 5.2 percent of Lithuania's exports in 2002),[25] Lithuania remains dependent on Russia for petroleum and other raw materials.

Last but not least, in addition to traditional and nontraditional threats, Lithuania's security environment is affected by domestic economic developments. In 2002–03 Lithuania experienced unprecedented economic growth. Its GDP growth was 6.7 percent in 2002 and 7.7 percent in the first half of 2003. In July 2003 it had the fastest-growing economy in Europe, growing exports, zero inflation, a steady currency, and shrinking unemployment.[26] During the second half of 2003, average GDP growth was approximately 8.3 percent.[27] The unemployment rate dropped from 17.4 percent in 2001 to 13.8 percent in 2002. It 2003, it continued to decline.[28] In mid-2003, the unemployment rate was 9.4 percent, and it was expected to fall in the second half of the year. This economic growth started in 2000, and it is expected to last for the next few years.[29] Compared with the current EU members, however, Lithuania is still poor. According to the Economist Intelligence Unit, it may take as many as 53 years for Lithuania to reach average income per person in the "old" EU countries.[30] As a matter of fact, by some estimates, as many as 16 percent of Lithuania's residents live in poverty, earning less than $100 per month. Poverty has been difficult to eradicate, contributing to feelings of political apathy. If left unattended, poverty could become a challenge to democratic processes.[31]

Uneven economic development is related to another problem – corruption. According to a survey conducted in Lithuania by Transparency International in 2002, 75 percent of respondents thought that bribing helps to "solve problems." One third was ready to give a bribe.[32] One out of every three businessmen who participated in the survey admitted to bribing a government official. Corruption was recognized as a "threat to national security" as early as 1994, but has proven to be very difficult to eradicate. One corruption scandal in July 2003 involved seven diplomats in the Foreign Ministry. Accused of taking bribes in exchange for issuing visas, they were forced to resign.[33] Most recently, the "Paksas-gate" exposed the links between the top officials and organized crime.[34]

There are some indications, however, that the level of corruption is going down. According to a survey conducted in 1999, 60.4 percent of respondents were ready to give a bribe.[35] In 2002, this number was approximately 39 percent. State institutions are also becoming stronger and better at fighting corruption. Nevertheless, corruption among politicians and government officials remains a major problem.[36] In a recent parliamentary hearing on national security, three ministers in the current government – Linas Linkevicius, the Minister of Defense, Antanas Valionis, the Minister of Foreign Affairs, and Virgilijus Bulovas, the Minister of Internal Security – identified corruption and organized crime as potential threats.[37] The presidential impeachment proceedings brought corruption of the government officials to everyone's attention.

It is generally agreed that in the domestic sphere, achieving security means fighting corruption, obtaining guarantees of political and social stability as well as further economic growth. On paper, the main challenges to Lithuania's security are transnational, such as organized crime, people/drug trafficking, but in practice, significant changes in the international system, such as US detachment from Euro-Atlantic community or the creation of a large-power-only directory in Europe, are seen as the real threat. Historically, Lithuania was most vulnerable to traditional military threats – that is, invasion and occupation by its neighbors, such as Germany and Russia. Lithuania's history is marked by constant insecurity from external aggression. It is difficult to forget the 50-year occupation by the Soviet Union. The National Security Strategy and the 2002 White Book still mention the remote possibility that Lithuania may have to deal with a "demonstration of military power, provocations, and threats to use this power" by an unnamed nation-state in the future.[38]

Given these perceptions of insecurity and weakness, it is understandable that Lithuania wanted to get into an American-led NATO as soon as possible. It did not see any alternatives to this alliance led by the benevolent hegemon. This hegemon, the United States, is seen as the only power that is capable of preventing unfair *diktat* by big and powerful European powers. Based on historical experiences, the Lithuanians want to live in a security environment in which Munich-like agreements are unthinkable.[39] France, Germany and other Western European states are seen as incapable or unwilling to deliver such environment. In fact, some perceive them as ready to betray Lithuania's interests to Russia. Sometimes Germany is portrayed as a country that has been long opposed to Lithuania's dream of membership in NATO. France is portrayed as being preoccupied with keeping its influence in Europe and willing to make ad hoc coalitions with Russia.[40] Thus, naturally, Lithuania is more than willing to accept an all-powerful America in Europe. America is seen as the only power capable of helping Lithuania secure its territory. Since the country borders Belarus and Kaliningrad, it is likely to remain preoccupied with the territorial defense in the nearest future, which will also make Lithuania into a pro-Atlanticist member of the alliance.

Consequently, the government and the Lithuanian parliament identified the following core security priorities:

- Strengthen domestic political, social, and economic stability;
- Prevent threats and develop a reliable defense;
- Integrate successfully into the Euro-Atlantic community while preserving the transatlantic link.[41]

The third priority is the most important. There is general agreement that without Euro-Atlantic integration, long term security and prosperity will remain elusive. It is expected that EU membership will bring increased economic growth by attracting more foreign direct investment and by doubling Lithuania's exports.[42] Furthermore, "Euro-Atlantic integration" has been a politically correct term for reducing Lithuania's dependence on Russia. Lithuania now prefers to conduct its relations with Russia, not on a bilateral or a regional basis, but within the Euro-Atlantic framework.[43] "Euro-Atlantic integration" also refers to a sense of belonging. It has already become a cliché in the popular discourse that NATO and EU membership will bring Lithuania "back to Western civilization" and re-unite Lithuania with the countries that share the same values and the same threats as Lithuania.

The recent war in Iraq, however, shattered the myth of a united "Western civilization" with the same perceptions of threats and the same values. In January 2003, Lithuania's politicians were faced with a question whether to back the United States' decision to use its military muscle in Iraq or whether lend its support to France and Germany who opposed the war. On 5 February 2003, together with the other members of Vilnius-10 group (ten aspiring NATO members) and several other European countries, Lithuania expressed its support for the United States. On 25 March, the Lithuanian parliament decided to send a small support task force consisting of ten servicemen and logistics specialists as well as six medical officers for a six-month "humanitarian mission" in Iraq. Three months later, the number of Lithuanian troops to be sent to Iraq was increased to 130, and the length of the mission was increased to 18 months.

Why did Lithuania Support the US in Iraq?

A debate about Lithuania's role in Iraq started in February when it became clear that the opinions of different NATO and EU members regarding this crisis had irreconcilable differences. Jacques Chirac's comments referring to the "childish" behavior of Central Eastern European states as well as the decision of the European Union to exclude the representatives of these states from the simultaneous EU Summit dealing with the crisis fueled this debate. Some, although they were the minority, argued that Lithuania should have remained "neutral" because its support for the United States may endanger Lithuania's EU membership and actually help to increase the already existing transatlantic tensions. The majority thought that Lithuania should support the United States. The cruelty of Saddam Hussein's regime and the possibility that this regime possesses weapons of mass destruction was the main argument put forward by those who defended the latter point of view.

A closer analysis of this debate helps to identify the main reason – historical memory – behind Lithuania's initial knee-jerk support for the United States. The participants of the debate remembered that during the major crises of the post-independence period (since 1991), the United States has always supported Lithuania.[44] Furthermore, during the Soviet times, the United States did not recognize *de jure* the incorporation of the Baltic states into the USSR. In 1993, the United States helped to negotiate the withdrawal of the Soviet army from Lithuania and supported Lithuania's membership in the European Union and after 9/11 in NATO. Unlike the USA, France and Germany took what the Lithuanians viewed as a more "pro-Russian" position arguing that Lithuania's membership in the Euro-Atlantic community should not make Russia insecure. Other "betrayals" of Central Europe by Western Europeans, such as Munich, were remembered as well.[45] It was argued that Lithuania, as well as other Central and East European states, suffer from a victim's syndrome. These nations have experienced numerous abuses by big powers in the past. As long as this syndrome remains in collective memory, Lithuania will invite a friendly power (that is, the United States) to balance against Russia.[46]

The main reason behind Lithuania's support for the United States during the Iraq crisis was summarized by MP Egidijus Vareikis: "I trust security guarantees (extended to us) by the United States and NATO (not France and the EU)."[47] The need for American-backed security guarantees was more sharply perceived when it became clear that President Putin supported the French and the Germans. MP Rasa Jukneviciene argued that Russia's support for the German and the French position was consistent with its desire to increase its power vis-à-vis the United States and eventually regain its full influence in the former Soviet territories. Therefore, Lithuania had no other choice but to pursue a pro-American foreign policy.[48] Vytautas Landsbergis, a former leader of Lithuania's independence movement, expressed a similar opinion, arguing that Russia was trying to maximize its potential gains from these transatlantic tensions, thus hoping to increase its sphere of influence. Consequently, supporting the United States was a logical choice for Lithuania.[49] On 20 March, the Lithuanian Ministry of Foreign Affairs released a statement declaring that "Lithuania expresses its regret that Saddam Hussein's regime did not take the last opportunity. In our belief, the operation launched by the coalition is the last resort step aimed at Iraq's disarmament, which was envisaged by the UN Security Council Resolution 1441."[50]

The pro-American sentiments felt by Lithuania's political elite were by and large shared by the public. According to the public opinion polls, the Lithuanian public was one of most pro-American nations in Europe during the Iraq crisis. For example, according to a survey conducted by public opinion research firm Vilmorus in February 2003, 75 percent of Lithuania's population felt that Iraq was a threat to the world. Only 5.4 percent disagreed with this statement. 26.5 percent of respondents suggested that their country should not help the United States if there was a military conflict.[51] The respondents believed that the United Nations, NATO and the EU were the "most reliable" actors in this drama. Only 0.5 percent believed that Iraq was a "reliable" actor, and only 5.7 percent believed that Russia could be trusted. In comparison, according to a poll conducted between 14 March and 20 March by market and public opinion research firm Latvijas fakti and released by the Latvian Ministry of Foreign affairs, 78.2 percent of Latvia's population believed that the threat of terrorism has increased and that Saddam's regime had to be disarmed of its WMDs. In Latvia, however, 61.3 percent of those polled did not support the use of military means to disarm Iraq.[52] Antiwar demonstrations took place in all three Baltic states. On 30 March, Estonian police detained 83 protesters in front of the US Embassy in Tallinn.[53] Around the same time, there was a demonstration in front of the US Embassy in Vilnius organized by an NGO "Sviesos lyga" (The League of Light). High school students, several left wing politicians and MP Rolandas Pavilionis, the former rector of Vilnius University, participated in the demonstration.

On 25 March 2003, the Lithuanian parliament started a debate on what was already known as "the dilemma of dual loyalty." The Lithuanian parliamentarians had to decide how to please the United States (that is, whether to send its troops to help to rebuild Iraq), while at the same time trying not to upset the Europeans. The future of Lithuania's relations with the EU in general, and France and Germany in particular, was the dominant theme in this debate. Algirdas Gricius, speaking on behalf of the center-right United and Liberal Faction, argued that the regime change in Iraq was necessary for global peace and that Lithuania should support the change. Furthermore, Lithuania should support the United States, its reliable "strategic partner." Some leftist parties, such as social liberals and the ruling social democrats, supported the proposal to help the United States in its war in Iraq. The opponents were primarily from the left (Socialists, the new democrats, and so on.) MP Kazimiera Prunskiene, speaking on behalf of the "The New Democracy" party, a leftist party in the ruling coalition, argued that Lithuania was tempted to give too much support to the United States and did not give enough support for the "most important partners in the EU" – France and Germany, thus endangering the future of Lithuania's economy. Her opinion mirrored the arguments of those who argued against Lithuania's support for the United States: By supporting the US, Lithuania was going to tarnish its reputation as a "good EU member."[54]

The text of the final resolution tried to accommodate these two positions. According to this document, Lithuania's involvement in Iraq was a "humanitarian mission" (that is, Lithuania was not getting engaged in war directly). The goal of this mission was merely to help the victims of the conflict, not to participate in combat. The document included a reference to the Resolution of the European Council dated 20 March 2003 that asked for humanitarian help for Iraq and for the involvement of the United Nations. In other words, Lithuania was supporting the United States, but not ignoring the position of the EU. According to Linas Linkevicius, Lithuania's Defense Minister, the final (25 March) version of Lithuania's standpoint regarding Iraq had a "European" accent that was missing in the previous Vilnius-10 declaration.[55] In spite of this "European accent," 13 out of

74 parliamentarians still voted against the resolution which approved a mission of sixteen Lithuanian specialists. Three months later, on 29 May 2003, 10 out of 73 parliamentarians voted against sending 130 troops to help the United States to keep peace in Iraq.

The Iraq crisis made it clear to many there was no Europe speaking with one voice – not yet. France, Germany and Belgium were perceived as speaking with a clear anti-American accent, while Great Britain, Italy, Spain, Portugal and Denmark spoke with a pro-American one.[56] Importantly, the Iraq crisis created a perception that the European Union was far from developing a common security policy.[57] There was general agreement that these intra-European and transatlantic tensions caused by the Iraq crisis were severely hurting Lithuania's security. It was hypothesized that the most devastating impact of the war in Iraq on transatlantic relations would be NATO's transformation into a toothless OSCE-like organization. In February 2003, the Lithuanians were traumatized by the decision of the governments of France, Germany, Luxemburg and Belgium to impede NATO support to Turkey if the latter were attacked by Iraq. This started a debate about the future role of NATO. Some argued that NATO was on its way to extinction because it is torn by "identity crisis" and virtually "meaningless" in a new post-Cold War security environment when threats are less discernible and can't be dealt with military force.[58] This could mean that NATO would not be able to provide any significant security guarantees to Lithuania.[59] Although similar worries were voiced before the Iraq crisis, the transatlantic and intra-European disagreements over the use of force in Iraq and over Turkey's defense gave some currency to those who argued that Lithuania should try to develop closer security cooperation with the United States because "neither the EU nor the changing NATO will be able to give security guarantees to Central and Eastern Europe."[60] Predictably, the emerging European security structures were remembered, although in-depth, informed discussions about Lithuania's role in them took place.

Lithuania's Security after the Dual Enlargement: Roles for the ESDP (European Security and Defense Policy), NATO and the US

Since 2002, Lithuania has supported the EU's Common Foreign and Security Policy (CFSP) and contributed to the development of this policy. Specifically, in 2002, Lithuania was particularly interested in promoting cooperation between the EU member states and the "new" Eastern neighbors of the EU – the former Soviet republics of Belarus, Russia, Moldova, and Ukraine. After the enlargement, Lithuania is a "borderland state" of the European Union neighboring non-EU states of Belarus and Russia. Consequently, Lithuania has supported the "wider Europe" initiative which proposes fostering better relations with the EU's eastern and southern neighbors.[61] In this respect, Lithuania's position is similar to that of Poland: Both countries stress a need for deeper dialogue with the former Soviet republics and a need for long-term strategic thinking regarding the EU's eastern neighbors.[62] This could prevent tensions between the future "ins" (new EU members such as Lithuania) and "outs."

Since Lithuania faces transnational threats such as organized crime and trafficking of drugs and people, it will be interested in cooperation with the EU in justice and home affairs. Lithuania has already received a lot of help from the EU to control its borders. Strengthening border control with Belarus and solving the Kaliningrad visa issue are two cases in point. The Lithuanian government wants the EU to be able to prevent conflict and manage crises successfully. It is ready to contribute 100–150 troops and equipment, such as helicopters Mi-8 and airplanes An-26, to the European Rapid Reaction Force. In May 2003, Lithuania offered to add one squadron of special operations to this force.[63]

The willingness to contribute to the European Rapid Reaction Force may suggest that the country fully endorses the development of the Common European Defense and Security Policy (ESDP). Its support to the ESDP, however, is not without reservations. Lithuania has carefully followed the evolution of the ESDP since 1999, and voiced several concerns. Vilnius did not like the fact that in the past the would-be EU members were not invited to participate in the dialogue about the future of the ESDP.[64] Other reservations included the lack of political will in Western Europe to put more money toward the development of the European military power and the lack of commitment to common European defense. The Western European leaders are seen as incapable of increasing their military expenditures significantly because such decisions would not be popular in the eyes of their publics. Furthermore, US military power instinctively gets more respect. The elites are aware that the Europeans have spent several decades to create a security and defense identity, and these efforts did not bear much fruit.[65] Consequently, Lithuania does not see the ESDP as a substitute for NATO. It supports the ESDP only to the extent that it complements NATO. The Lithuanian forces that are planned for the European Rapid Reaction Force are also ready to participate in NATO operations.

Interestingly, the Belgian initiative supported by Germany, France, and Luxembourg to speed up the development of the ESDP by creating a European Defense union with a separate planning headquarters independent from NATO has actually strengthened Lithuania's skepticism regarding the ability of the Europeans to create a reliable defense organization any time soon. Analysts in Lithuania dubbed the proponents of the Belgian initiative as "the opponents of war against Saddam Hussein's regime" (read: anti-American).[66] They noticed that Great Britain, a major European pro-American country, did not support the Belgian initiative. It was argued that the four proponents of this union could not afford to become the leaders of European defense because of their meager (except for France) defense budgets. The idea behind the Belgian initiative was seen as an attempt to speed up the development of the ESDP at the expense of NATO, thus drawing another dividing line between the "stubborn and ambitious Old Europe" and the "New Europe" which has been trying to preserve the transatlantic link.[67]

The Lithuanian official reaction to the Belgian initiative took shape in the second half of May 2003, when Linas Linkevicius, Lithuania's Defense Minister, attended a meeting of European defense ministers in Brussels. Linkevicius argued that Lithuania does not support the development of European military capabilities that would duplicate the existing NATO capabilities. Relying on the reformed NATO would help to avoid unnecessary competition and expenses.[68] He re-iterated

Lithuania's perspective regarding the ESDP during Vilnius Roundtable on Northeast European Security in June 2003: "Various mini summits, quartets and two speed Europe ideas do anything but strengthen European security and cooperation between NATO and the EU. As [the] future members of both organizations we have a stake in the success of this cooperation. The outcome of the ESDP project must not in any way compromise the role of NATO as the cornerstone of Euro-Atlantic security but [it must] strengthen it." In December 2003, Linkevicius' position was echoed by Foreign Minister Antanas Valionis during the meeting of NATO foreign ministers in Brussels. NATO should remain the basis of collective defense and the main forum on transatlantic security issues. The ESDP should add to NATO, but not compete with it.[69]

Instead of whole-heartedly supporting what is perceived as anti-transatlantic and anti-American defense initiative, Lithuania has remained faithful to NATO. The Lithuanian strategists argue that NATO should transform itself from "an immobile defense alliance in the heart of Europe into a flexible and rapidly reactive force capable of intervention wherever needed to prevent a conflict rather to stop one that has already started." According to their statements, the country has been adjusting to its new vision of NATO by "dropping [the] outdated territorial defense posture" and modernizing its military capabilities.[70] Vilnius believes that NATO should remain a strong collective security alliance capable of defense against unpredictable new global threats such as terrorism. To achieve this goal, the Europeans should be willing to find funds to modernize their armies, thus helping to bridge the "capabilities gap" between the Europeans and the United States. NATO members should simplify decision making procedures to make the organization as effective as possible. At the same time, Lithuania supports keeping NATO's doors open to new candidates such as Croatia and Georgia.

The official documents suggest that after joining NATO, Lithuania will support a more active NATO engagement with Russia.[71] It is argued that bringing Russia as close to NATO as Russia wants to come will be one of Lithuania's security priorities after the dual enlargement. Official suggestions on how to bring Russia closer to NATO include common NATO-Russia training projects in Kaliningrad and attempts to achieve force interoperability for peacekeeping missions.[72] Currently, the official position of Lithuania is to welcome a closer NATO-Russia cooperation through the NATO-Russia Council. The policy makers probably realize that the NATO-Russia council enhanced Russian rights of consultation and relaxed Russian attitudes toward expansion of the alliance to include the Baltic states. Conceivably, a tough Russian response to the second wave of NATO expansion could only have made Russian relations with the US and Europe tense; this would not have been beneficial for Vilnius. In December 2001, Poland and the Czech Republic, not the Baltic states, tried to persuade the United States to block a British initiative to institute a closer relationship with Russia.[73] By arguing that Lithuania wants to bring Russia closer to NATO after the second wave of enlargement, the Lithuanian diplomats are probably trying to relieve lingering Russian fears about NATO's advance to Russia's borders and what is perceived as isolation of Kaliningrad. Outside of diplomatic circles, however, the Lithuanian-Russian relations still suffer from the lack of trust. According to Ceslovas Laurinavicius, a political commentator, the Lithuanians are still confused on how to treat Russia. Some view it as a monster eager to swallow this small country any time. Others see Russia as a big and influential friend with whom they know how to communicate and make deals. Most, however, still do not treat Russia as a trustworthy partner.[74]

It is understood that after the dual enlargement, Lithuania will have to balance its commitments to NATO and to the EU. Consequently, Lithuania would like the EU's security and defense policy to become a pillar of NATO instead of developing into a separate defense alliance.[75] Lithuania could balance these two sets of commitments better if there are no serious intra-European tensions in the future and the United States remains involved in Europe. As a matter of fact, keeping America actively involved in Europe is one of Lithuania's most important strategic goals. This is why since June 2003 Lithuania has welcomed establishing NATO (or, as Linas Linkevicius, the Minister of Defense, said *"American* or NATO") military bases or training facilities in its territory.[76] Lithuania is also interested in helping to enhance security in the Caucasus and Central Asia because after 9/11 the United States has a growing interest in those areas. Furthermore, Lithuania is hoping to increase the volume of US investments. For example, in July 2003, Lithuania hosted a conference of Lithuanian American businessmen to achieve this goal. In 2003, the United States was the fifth largest foreign investor in Lithuania, accounting for 8.7 percent of all foreign direct investments.[77]

The United States is regarded as the main strategic partner of Lithuania and also the main partner of European security.[78] The adjective "partner" is significant: Lithuania would like to see the United States engaged in a close predictable relationship with Europe strengthened by expanding security, economic, and cultural ties. Lithuania believes that Europe and the United States should remain together in a security community with shared values such as commitment to democracy and common interests such as facing unpredictable global threats. It is in Lithuania's interests to see more unity in Europe and that the United States address Europe as one actor instead of dealing with one issue and one country at a time. *Ad hoc* coalitions with separate European countries weaken the transatlantic alliance and threaten one of the core security priorities of Lithuania.[79] Ideally, the United States should be prepared to accept multilateral restraints on its actions, and the Europeans should be prepared to help the United States, especially in conflict prevention and postwar nation-building. In such a relationship, both sides would have roles that are both essential and complementary.[80]

Although Lithuania remains fully devoted to preserving the transatlantic link, it cannot afford to ignore its Western European partners and their reactions to Lithuania's attempts to solve the dilemma of "dual loyalty." So far, the Lithuanian-EU relations (or, rather, the Lithuanian-French relations) reached the low point in February 2003, when Lithuania and other pro-American EU candidates were "warned" by the French President Jacques Chirac that their pro-American position may endanger the prospects of getting EU membership. The French-Lithuanian relations warmed up two months later, when the EU members along with the would-be members were getting ready to discuss a new draft constitution for Europe. On 29 April, Lithuania's Foreign Minister Antanas Valionis was invited to discuss the EU Convention on the Future of Europe at an international conference "Europe and the Baltic states after Prague and Copenhagen." In Paris, Valionis reconfessed his country's devotion to transatlantic cooperation, but at the same time he re-iterated "the real need" to develop the CFSP further.[81] However, not transatlantic cooperation, but certain common European interests – the European Constitution, the future of the EU-Russia relations, and plans to modernize the transportation system in Lithuania – were the topics of the French-Lithuanian conversations after Iraq.[82] One reason why France does not engage in meaningful conversations about the European security structures with Lithuania is probably because France continues to believe that foreign and defense policy must remain the exclusive realm of the largest European states. Temptations to establish a directory of large European states to address security issues are felt by some French politicians.[83] Seen as a small pro-American state, Lithuania would probably not be invited to be part of this arrangement.

There have been times when Lithuania has compromised its generally pro-American outlook in foreign and security policies. In June 2003, Lithuania, together with the other Central and Eastern European states, experienced pressure from the United States. Lithuania had to decide whether to support the common European position regarding the International Criminal Court (ICC) or face the threat that the United States will suspend its military aid. The common European position was to resist signing bilateral agreements with the US pledging not to surrender each other's citizens to the International Criminal Court. In this case, Lithuania managed to solve its "dilemma of dual loyalty" quite well. On one hand, it expressed its support for the EU position by refusing to sign a bilateral agreement with the United States. On the other hand, it struck a deal with the Americans. On 30 June 2003, one day before the US officially suspended the aid to those countries that did not sign the bilateral agreements, the Lithuanian Defense Ministry signed a $12 million military aid agreement with the US officials, and went on to purchase 69 Humvee vehicles as well as other American-made equipment for its armed forces.[84] On November 21, 2003, six countries, including Lithuania, were cleared by President Bush to have US military assistance reinstated to help the future NATO members to integrate into this organization better as well as to support US-led operations in Iraq. In the future, however, deciding on the merchant (the Europeans or the Americans) of the equipment for Lithuania's armed forces is likely to raise the "dilemma of dual loyalty" again.[85]

Lithuania's Contributions to Transatlantic Security

After regaining its independence from the Soviet Union in 1991, Lithuania had to create its armed forces from zero. Its priority has been to develop a small, but well-trained, easily deployable armed forces. It started the process by adhering to NATO standards. Lithuania, a country with 3.5 million people, today has a 12,000 strong army trained under Western standards. The Lithuanian military is basically compatible with NATO, and it has participated in a wide range of NATO programs and operations as well as other international missions.

As of 2002, Lithuania spends approximately 2 percent of its GDP on defense. In comparison, the average for NATO candidates is 2.1 percent GDP. In June 2003 the Lithuanian politicians renewed their commitment dating back to 2001 to an annual defense spending of no less than 2 percent of Lithuania's GDP.[86] Lithuania's defense budget has been increasing since 1995, from 0.57 percent of GDP in 1995 to 2 percent in 2003.[87] This data, as well as the agreement, suggest that Lithuania will remain committed to maintaining an efficient army that will serve its national security interests as well as contribute to transatlantic security.

Currently Lithuania's contributions to transatlantic security fall into three broad categories: 1) participation in international missions run by NATO, the United Nations and the OSCE, 2) developing useful niche capabilities within its military, and 3) regional cooperation initiatives. So far, the country has participated in seven international missions. As of November 2003, 270 military personnel are deployed abroad. Currently they are in Afghanistan, Kosovo, Iraq, Bosnia, and Macedonia. Since 2000, one officer has participated in the OSCE-led mission in Georgia. The goal of the mission was to observe the movements across borders between Georgia and the neighboring areas of the Russian Federation.[88]

Since 1994, Vilnius has contributed to several missions in the Balkans. Almost 1,000 Lithuanian soldiers took part in various peacekeeping missions in the region.[89] In 1994–95, the Lithuanians participated in the UNPROFOR-2 mission in Croatia. Since 1996, they were part of IFOR (Implementation Force) and SFOR (Stabilization Force) in Bosnia-Herzegovina, and in 1999 – AFOR in Albania. Since 1999, one platoon has served in Kosovo (KFOR) as part of a Polish battalion. Since 2001, Lithuania has also contributed transport aircraft with crew in KFOR and SFOR missions. Currently, 95 servicemen are deployed with the Danish forces as part of NATO-led SFOR in Bosnia.[90]

Lithuania has supported the US – led war against terrorism. Since autumn 2002, 40 members of Lithuania's special operations forces have been deployed alongside the US troops in Afghanistan in Operation Enduring Freedom. The government came up with a 50,000 Litas (approximately $17,000) financial aid to the Afghani refugees. Since August 2003, 45 troops support the Polish-controlled sector in Iraq. 54 soldiers serve in the British sector together with the Danes, maintaining social order in the northeast Basra area.[91]

In late summer and early autumn 2003, these commitments abroad became a topic for a public debate and a debate in the Seimas. On 20 August 2003, following the meeting between Defense Minister Linas Linkevicius and President Paksas, the daily "Lietuvos zinios" reported that Lithuania may have to rethink its participation in various peacekeeping missions.[92] A heated debate in the Seimas followed. Some parliamentarians argued that the taxpayers do not receive any immediate benefits from sending peacekeepers abroad and that although Vilnius has committed itself to spending at least 2 percent of its yearly GDP on defense, if it continues to spend money on the peacekeeping missions, less money will be left to make training and operations at home better. According to the Presidential spokesman Rosvaldas Gorbaciovas, "decisions had to be made concerning the mission in Afghanistan."[93] Alvydas Sadeckas, chairman of the National Security and Defense Committee in the Seimas, managed to convince the Seimas to continue the participation in Afghanistan. His argument was that this was the way for the Lithuanian troops to gain hands-on experience and to be respected among other nations. His arguments were supported by the Defense Minister Linas Linkevicius who argued that the future NATO member should be able to be a security provider, not just a security consumer, and be willing to fight military threats with its allies.[94]

The decision makers in this small country realize that it can make the most meaningful contributions to transatlantic security by developing useful niche capabilities within its military. Lithuania has been working together with Latvia and Estonia on numerous "BALT" initiatives to develop such capabilities. BALTRON and BALTBAT initiatives were praised in the past by NATO experts. BALTRON is a joint Baltic squadron of naval vessels with mine-clearance capabilities. Three to four ships are constantly available for immediate use. BALTNET is a Regional Air Surveillance and Control Center in Karmelava. This surveillance system supplies data for both military and civilian authorities. It is already prepared to exchange information with NATO. BALTDEFCOL is an international training college in Tartu, Estonia, created to prepare officers and other Baltic security specialists. BALTBAT was a joint Baltic infantry battalion of 666 troops capable of performing peacekeeping operations. (It was closed in 2003.) This battalion was created for NATO-led operations following NATO's Partnership for Peace Program under the Danish leadership, but it is going to be replaced by trilateral cooperation of land forces getting ready to conduct joint operations and participate in international missions.[95]

Since 2001, using the BALTBAT model, Lithuania has been developing a national battalion LITBAT (a.k.a. The Grand Duke Algirdas Battalion).[96] This 700 strong battalion is ready to join NATO missions. It is planned that in the future Lithuania will be able to deploy Algirdas Battalion for longer (six months and beyond) international operations using rotating reinforcements from the Iron Wolf Brigade, an action-ready infantry brigade.[97] Furthermore, Lithuania plans to increase its cooperation with Latvia and Estonia in international operations in order to save money and rotate troops efficiently.[98]

To ensure the interoperability with NATO, Lithuania has purchased weapons and equipment for its armed forces from NATO members, mostly from the United States. In 2002, to strengthen its mechanized infantry, the country purchased JAVELIN anti-tank systems from the United States. In the same year, Lithuania agreed to purchase Stinger antiaircraft systems from the same manufacturer. To upgrade the army's data and communication systems, Lithuania has been purchasing radio systems that are manufactured jointly with the United States. (Lithuania manufactures handheld tactical radio stations by itself.) Aided by the US, Lithuania established a cartography center which produces NATO-interoperable maps.[99] Vilnius is also engaged in scientific cooperation with NATO. Currently Lithuanian scientists participate in NATO projects focusing on the application of lasers and biotechnology.[100]

Last but not least, Lithuania's contributions to transatlantic security include regional initiatives. Lithuania has managed to develop good relations with its neighbors. Now it is ready to expand the zone of stability to the South Caucasus and Central Asia. Lithuania has been helping Georgia, Armenia, Azerbaijan, and Uzbekistan to educate their military officers, to identify the ways in which civilian control over the military could be established, and to reform their militaries. Since Georgia and Azerbaijan have recently officially expressed their interest in joining NATO, Lithuania has promised to help those countries to prepare for their membership.[101] "Spreading security to the South" helps Lithuania to see itself as a bridge between the Euro-Atlantic Community and Eurasia.[102]

Conclusion: Security Implications of Transatlantic Tensions for Lithuania

Vilnius refers to the Euro-Atlantic integration as the "backbone" of its security. It hopes to serve as an active and respected member with full rights and duties in a functioning security community. For this hope to be fulfilled, Lithuania needs the United States to stay involved in European affairs. Vilnius wants NATO to be as strong and effective as possible, ready to intervene wherever and whenever needed to prevent a conflict. It opposes forging separate European security structures that could serve as a balance against the American power.

It is not entirely surprising that the elites and the public supported the US during the crisis in Iraq. Almost instinctive pro-Americanism, especially when it comes to national security and foreign policy, has become an important part of Lithuanian identity. Lithuania's history has been strained by constant insecurity and aggression from its European neighbors. The US is seen as the only power that has supported the country's search for lasting security arrangements. The Western European countries have not been viewed as fully reliable allies. Furthermore, there is a popular belief that the US, less elitist than the Western European countries, is more likely to include post-communist countries, including Lithuania, in transatlantic security arrangements and policy making process. Like many other post-communist countries in eastern central Europe, this Baltic nation has accepted the notion that it cannot provide for its own security; thus, the most logical and the most attractive decision is to give full support to the hegemonic role of the United States – in Europe as well as elsewhere in the world.

Lithuania's lingering preoccupation with defense of its territory is not likely to go away any time soon, although economic, political or even security cooperation with Russia in post-enlargement Euro-Atlantic zone is not ruled out. On the contrary, in appropriate international settings security elites reiterate their country's willingness to establish friendly and predictable relations with Russia. At the same time, the Lithuanian mass media is quite sensitive to any developments that are interpreted as imperial hangovers of the big neighbor. Russia's reprimands about the "mistreatment" of ethnic Russians in Latvia and the ongoing Chechen predicament are cases in point.[103] Russia's search for identity, its ambivalent attitude toward the expansion of the Euro-Atlantic zone as well as its spotty record in democratization coupled with unwillingness to admit the past wrongs contribute to Lithuania's sense of insecurity. These are some of the reasons why the Lithuanians have developed of what appears to be a schizophrenic attitude toward Russia: on one hand, the eastern neighbor is seen as a familiar partner with a great promise for future cooperation, but on the other hand, it is still seen as a potential threat.

A strong, US-led NATO is seen as the only actor in the current international system capable of delivering a security environment that reduces this old-fashioned fixation on territory. Further American detachment from Europe would be the worst case scenario for Lithuania. This could happen if the United States relied on unilateral action, ignoring the EU. More unilateral actions may be an incentive for some European states to create their own directory-like security arrangement, probably consisting of big powers. Russia may be invited to participate in such an arrangement, which would be an anathema to a truly "common" European security structure that includes smaller European states. Lithuania's historical memory warns against "security" arrangements that include Germany and Russia but exclude the United States.

The future development of the European Union and Russia will affect the ways in which Lithuania solves its "dual loyalty" dilemma in the future. The best case scenario for Lithuania, of course, would be to become part of a united Europe that is treated as a reliable global partner by the United States. Globally, Europe and the United States would be engaged in a complementary relationship with a clear and mutually agreed upon labor division. For example, the Europeans would be helping the US in nation building, while the Americans would lead military interventions having consulted their European allies. In this rosy scenario, Lithuania would cooperate more closely with Russia within the framework of transatlantic institutions.

However, the intra-European divisions that manifested themselves recently in debates over Iraq, the future shape of Europe (that is, the European Constitution), and common European security structures (the Belgian initiative) suggest that there will be no clearly organized union in the near future. The United States may be tempted to establish temporary ad hoc deals with individual European countries, which would hinder internal European integration. Under such conditions, Lithuania is likely to cling to its pro-American stance. It is likely to continue to further pursue its strategic relationship with another strongly pro-American country – Poland. In fact, the transatlantic tensions over Iraq and recent domestic scandals may have in fact strengthened the pro-American orientation of Lithuania's security elites who are committed to the country's participation in international operations, including America's war against terror. The commitment to transatlantic security, however, needs domestic support. If the country fails to secure its economic growth, curb corruption and reduce its vulnerability to organized crime, the US and its allies may lose interest in being Lithuania's security partners. A painful scenario indeed.

Notes

1   Audrius Baciulis (2002), "Puse simtmecio lauktas zodis," *Veidas*, 28 November, 23.
2   Vaidotas Urbelis (2003), "Skirtingi ir pavojai, ir JAV interesai," *Lietuvos Rytas* (Rytai-Vakarai), 11 January, 2.
3   For example, see address by Foreign Affairs Minister Antanas Valionis at the annual meeting of ambassadors accredited to Lithuania, Vilnius, 17 February 2003, online at www.urm.lt.
4   "Lietuva pakvietus i NATO lietuviai eme jaustis saugiau" (2002) *Veidas*, 12 December, 8.
5   Lietuvos Gynybos Politikos Baltoji Knyga (2002), Vilnius: Lietuvos Krasto Apsaugos Ministerija, 16.

6   54 Lithuanian soldiers serve in the British sector. Lithuanian Ministry of National Defense (2003), Fact Sheet, November, online at www.kam.lt.

7   Some argue that President Putin's speech during a joint conference with the Finnish President Tarja Halonen before 9/11 was a breaking point in Baltic-Russian relations. During this speech, Putin said "It is their choice, although we can't see an objective reason for NATO's expansion." Quoted in Marko Mihkelson (2003), "Baltic-Russian Relations in Light of Expanding NATO and EU," Demokratizatsiya, Spring, 277.

8   For example, recently Vytautas Landsbergis, a former Chairman of Lithuania's Parliament, publicly expressed his concern that Russia may do "something undesirable" before Lithuania is officially admitted to NATO and the EU. "Konservatoriu politikas raginamas islisti is alegoriju olos" (2003), Lietuvos rytas, 24 July, online at www.lrytas.lt.

9   Inga Pavlovaite (2003), "Paradise Regained: The Conceptualization of Europe in the Lithuanian Debate," in *Post-Cold War Identity Politics: Northern and Baltic Experiences*, eds. Marko Lehti and David J. Smith, London: Frank Cass, 199–218, esp. 201.

10   Laiko zenklai (2003), *Lietuvos rytas*, 9 December 2003, online at www.lrytas.lt.

11   "Muddling on" (2004), *The Economist*, January 10, 46.

12   "Commission Concludes That President's Vulnerability Threatens Security," RFE/RL Baltic States Report, 19 December 2003.

13   Eugenijus Gentvilas (2003), "Lietuvos misija – tramdyti Rusija," *Veidas*, 4 December, 39. The phrase "the return of Russia" is attributed to Romualdas Ozolas, quoted in Andrius Kubilius (2003), "Rusija grizta. O ar ji buvo isejusi?" *Veidas*, 27 November, 35.

14   "Rinkimu rezultatai Rusijoje gali atsiliepti ir Lietuvai, teigia juos stebejes Seimo narys," *Baltic News Service*, 10 December 2003.

15   "Lietuvius stingdo baime likti Europoje antrarusiais," *Veidas*, 5 June 2003, 8.

16   Quoted by Steven Paulikas (2003), "Lithuania Uneasy about Relations with Belarus," *Baltic Times*, 22 July, online at www.baltictimes.com.

17   White Book 2002, 20.

18   Leonid Zaiko (2003), "Belarus: Give a Dog a Bad Name," in Ambivalent Neighbors: The EU, NATO and the Price of Membership," Anatol Lieven and Dmitri Trenin, eds., Washington, D.C.: Carnegie Endowment for International Peace, 96.

19   "Lietuvos ir Baltarusijos santykiai," 23 October 2003, online at www.urm.lt.

20   Zaiko, 102.

21   Arturas Rozenas (2003), "Kaip Lietuva keis Baltarusija?", *Veidas*, 30 October, 40.

22   For example, Vytautas Landsbergis (2003), "Rytu kaimynysteje nieko nauja," *Veidas*, 30 October, 41.

23   Political scientist Raimundas Lopata, quoted in "Kaip Lietuva keis Baltarusija?", 41.

24   Nacionalinio saugumo strategija, 5, also White Book 2002, 7.

25   *Lithuanian Macroeconomic Review*, Vilniaus Bankas, April 2003, 20.

26   "Baltic Tiger," *The Economist*, 19 July 2003, 41.

27   "Laiko zenklai," *Lietuvos Rytas*, 7 January 2004, online at www.lrytas.lt.

28   *Macroeconomic Review*, 23.

29   It is possible that the Russian financial crisis (1998–99) turned out to be a blessing in disguise for the Lithuanian economy because it forced the Lithuanian businesses to reorganize themselves and become more competitive at the micro level. *Macroeconomic Review*, 4.

30   "When East Meets West," *The Economist*, 22 November 2003, 4 (Survey of EU Enlargement).

31 Sonata Maciulskyte (2003), "Skurdo veiksnys Lietuvos politikoje," *Politologija* (1), 50.

32 "Apklausa parode bauginancius korupcijos mastus," *Lietuvos rytas*, 6 March 2003, 4.

33 "Laiko zenklai," *Lietuvos rytas*, 29 July 2003, online at www.lrytas.lt.

34 The Lithuanian State Security Department clandestinely recorded conversations between Remigijus Acas, an Adviser to Rolandas Paksas, the President of Lithuania, and a representative from an organized crime group in Russia. Reportedly, these conversations mentioned debts owed by President Paksas to the Russians.

35 Audrius Skaistys (2002), "Korupcijos poveikis nacionaliniam saugumui," presentation at a conference "Ar baimes akys dideles: Netradiciniai saugumo aspektai," Vilnius, Atlanto sutarties Lietuvos bendrija, 21 March 21, online at www.nato.ot.lt.

36 Arguably, one of the major reasons for corruption is the absence of system that would give funds to political parties from the state budget. When trying to find funds to win the election, politicians are tempted to ask for money from groups and individuals with links to organized crime. See Algimantas Sindeikis (2003), "Auganti ekonomika be politines visuomenes," *Veidas*, 24 July 24, online at www.veidas.lt.

37 "Didziausia gresme ivardinta korupcija," *Lietuvos rytas*, 18 June 2003, 3.

38 National Security Strategy (2002), 5; White Book 2002, 7.

39 Raimundas Lopata (2003), "Etapas iveiktas, priesaky – naujos paieskos," *Lietuvos Rytas*, 24 April 2003, 4.

40 For example, see "Laiko zenklai," Lietuvos Rytas, 13 August 2003, online at www.lrytas.lt.

41 These priorities are listed in the National Security Strategy ratified by the Lithuanian Parliament on May 28, 2002. These priorities are the cornerstone of the National Security Policy pursued by the Lithuanian government. They were reiterated in "2002 Nacionalinio Saugumo Sistemos Bukles ir Pletros Ataskaita," 3.

42 Aktualus klausimai ir atsakymai apie Lietuvos stojima i Europos Sajunga, Vilnius: Europos komitetas prie LRV, 2003, 7.

43 Arnas Lazdauskas (2003), "A Future NATO and EU Member," *Lithuania in the World*, 11(3), 11.

44 This argument was put forward by Raimundas Lopata, the leading Lithuanian political scientist. "Nato vidaus nesutarimai-blogas zenklas Lietuvai," *Lietuvos Rytas*, 13 February 2003, online at www.lrytas.lt.

45 "Proamerikietiskosios salys," *Veidas*, 27 February 2003, 37.

46 Vykintas Pugaciauskas (2003), "istorija europieciams vel tapo svarbi," *Lietuvos Rytas*, 1 March, 2.

47 Ibid.

48 Quoted in "Atlantizmas ir Lietuva," *XXI amziaus horizontai*, 19 February 2003, 8.

49 Vytautas Landsbergis (2003), "Europoje yra geriau," *XXI amzius*, 30 April 2003, 10.

50 Quoted in Max Olson, "The Baltic States Involvement in the Iraqi Conflict: Security and Diplomacy," working paper, online at dept.washington.edu/Baltic/papers/iraq_war_olson.htm.

51 "Dauguma lietuviu isitikine, kad Irakas – gresme pasauliui," Lietuvos Rytas, 19 February; and "Lietuviai-didziausi JAV kariniu operaciju remejai," *Lietuvos Rytas*, 16 May 2003, 4.

52 Olson, 4.

53 Olson, 4.

54 "Seimo nutarimo 'Del Lietuvos kariu dalyvavimo Jungtiniu Amerikos Valstiju vadovaujamoje tarptautineje operacijoje Persijos ilankos regione' projekto svarstymas ir priemimas" stenograma, *Krasto Apsauga*, 8–22 April 2003, 3–11.

55 Ibid., 4.

56   "Kokia bus Siaures Atlanto sutarties organizacija, kai i ja istos Lietuva?," *Lietuvos rytas*, 13 February 2003.
57   Vytaute Smaizyte (2003), "Pasaulio savaite," *Lietuvos Rytas*, 8 February, 11.
58   Algis Klimaitis (2003), "Lietuvos interesas-Europa," *Veidas*, 21 February 2003, online at www.veidas.lt.
59   "NATO vidaus nesutarimai-blogas zenklas Lietuvai," *Lietuvos Rytas*, 13 February 2003, online at www.lrytas.lt.
60   "Kokia bus Siaures Atlanto sutarties organizacija, kai po metu i ja istos Lietuva?," *Lietuvos Rytas*, 13 February 2003, online at www.lrytas.lt.
61   Ataskaita, 11.
62   For a good summary of Polish attitude toward CFSP, please see Jacek Saryusz-Wolski (2003), "Poland: The View from a Candidate Country," Simon Serfaty, ed., *The European Finality Debate and Its National Dimensions*, Washington, D.C.: CSIS, 227.
63   Baltoji knyga, 19 and Rita Grumadaite (2003), "Dideja Lietuvos indelis i Tarptautines karines pajegas," *Krasto Apsauga*, 20 May-9 June, 7.
64   Linas Linkevicius (2002), "Stabilumo palaikymas Baltijos regione: Ateities Perspektyvos," *Krasto Apsauga*, 12–25 July, 2.
65   Latvia and Estonia have similar attitudes. Zaneta Ozolina (2003), "The EU and the Baltic States," Anatol Lieven and Dmitri Trenin, eds., *Ambivalent Neighbors: The EU, NATO and the Price of Membership*, Washington, D.C.: Carnegie Endowment for International Peace, 211.
66   "Laiko zenklai" (2003) *Lietuvos Rytas*, 25 March, 4.
67   Tomas Janeliunas (2003), "ES ateities vizija temdo jos nariu ambicijos," Rytai-*Vakarai* (Lietuvos Ryto priedas), 3 May, 2.
68   "Europos karines pajegos vis dar primena miraza," *Lietuvos Rytas*, 21 May 2003,8.
69   "Lietuva remia Europos gynybiniu iniciatyvu pletra ir siulo nedubliuoti NATO strukturu," *Krasto apsauga*, 8–22 December, 5.
70   Linas Linkevicius (2003), "Northeast European Security after the 2004 Dual Enlargement: The End of History?," Keynote Speech, Vilnius roundtable "Life after Enlargement," Vilnius, 6 June 2003. Also see Povilas Malakauskas (2004), "Pagrindiniai issukiai desimciai ateinanciu metu," Speech, Seminar "Survey of Baltic Strategic Defense," 9 January, online at http://www.kam.lt.
71   This goal is mentioned in "Lietuvos ateities raidos strategija" [A Strategy for the Future Lithuanian Development] ratified by the Parliament. See "Lietuva imasi ambicingo plano-kurti geroves valstybe," *Veidas*, 28 November 2002, 31.
72   Linkevicius, "Northeast European Security . . . ."
73   Karl-Heiz Kamp (2003), "The Dynamics of NATO Enlargement," in Lieven and Trenin, 196.
74   Quoted in Eugenija Grizibauskiene (2003), "Lietuva-Rusijos pinigu placdarmas," *Veidas*, 13 November 2003, 21.
75   CSIS (Washington, D.C.) and Institute of International Relations and Political Science (Vilnius) (2002), "Lithuania's Security and Foreign Policy Strategy: White Paper." Published in *Lithuanian Foreign Policy Review*, 1, 131.
76   Linkevicius, "Life after Enlargement." Also see "Aljanso bazems-atviros durys," *Lietuvos Rytas*, 3 June 2003, 3.
77   Vakaris Deksnys (2003), "JAV lietuviai bus ikalbinejami atverti pinigines," *Lietuvos Rytas*, 5 July 2003, 14.
78   "National Security Strategy," 10.
79   If the United States addresses the major issues by calling on separate countries in Europe, Moscow is expected to do the same. The voice of small countries is not likely

to be heard under such conditions. Audrius Baciulis (2002), "NATO iesko naujo veido," *Veidas*, 23 May, 35.

80 For a full description of a functioning transatlantic alliance based on "complementarity," see Andrew Moravcsik (2003), "Striking a New Transatlantic Bargain," *Foreign Affairs* (July/August), 74–89.

81 Edita Urmonaite (2003), "Issibares Paryzius grizta prie mandagumo," *Lietuvos Rytas*, 3 May, 9.

82 Arnoldas Pranckevicius (2003), "Po keliones I Paryziu-pliuso zenklas," *Lietuvos Rytas*, 15 May, online at www.lrytas.lt.

83 Philippe Moreau Defarges (2003), "The View from France: Steadfast and Changing" in Serfaty, 128.

84 RFE/RL (2003), *Baltic States Report*, 28 July.

85 Interview with Robertas Sapronas (2003), Lithuanian Defense Ministry, 1 July.

86 "Sutarta toliau krasto apsaugai skirti 2 proc. BVP," *Baltic News Service*, 19 June 2003. The agreement was made by the representatives of most political parties in Lithuania.

87 "Krasto Apsaugos Ministerijos 2003–05 metu sutrumpintas strateginis veiklos planas," *Krasto Apsauga*, 24 February-10 March 2003, 8.

88 Lithuania, Ministry of National Defense (2003), Fact Sheet, November, online at www.kam.lt.

89 Valdas Adamkus (2002), "Lithuania's Contribution to the Euro-Atlantic Security," *Lithuanian Foreign Policy Review*, 9.

90 Lithuania and NATO: Military Contributions, Factsheet 2002, online at www.kam.lt.

91 "Lietuvos kariai jau vykdo uzduotis Irake," *Krasto Apsauga*, 24 June-14 July 2003, 9.

92 RFE/RL (2003), "International Peacekeeping Missions May be Reduced," *Baltic States Report*, 28 August.

93 Ibid.

94 Quoted in Steven Paulikas (2003), "Missions Continue," *Lithuania in the World*, 11(6), 18.

95 Lithuania, Ministry of National Defense, "Baltic Military Cooperation Plans to be Discussed in Tallinn," Press Release, 11 December, online at www.kam.lt.

96 White Book 2002, 14–16.

97 Matt Kovalick (2003), "No Time for Complacency," *Lithuania in the World*, 2, 11.

98 "Baltijos salys galvoja apie bendrus karinius junginius," *Krasto Apsauga*, 20 May–9 June, 7.

99 Lithuania and NATO Factsheet 2002.

100 Adamkus, 10.

101 "Krasto apsaugos ministras lankesi Azerbaidzane," *Krasto Apsauga*, 20 May–9 June 2003, 5.

102 Linas Linkevicius (2002), "Stabilumo palaikymas Baltijos regione: ateities perspektyvos," *Krasto Apsauga*, July 12–25, 3.

103 For example, Arturas Rozenas (2004), "Rusijos sokis prie Baltijos," *Veidas*, 29 January; or Eugenijus Gentvilas (2004), "I ES ir NATO, bet Rusijos uzantyje," *Veidas*, 5 February, online at www.veidas.lt.

Chapter 9

Czech Republic's Role with Regard to the Trans-Atlantic Security Challenges

Petr Vancura

Introduction

The 1990s in the Czechlands were full of hopes. Soviet Communism had collapsed and, with the weakening of Russian influence, a wave of democratization swept through the country, as it did around the world. Now, in the first years of the new century, things no longer look as rosy as in those heady days: terrorism, proliferation of dangerous weapons, organized crime, and government-level corruption have intensified, and the world is gripped by insecurity again.

In the Czechlands, as a part of this sobering awareness, we see that democratization has so far not led to respectable democracy. Behind the facade of democratic institutions, organized clans often rooted in the Communist secret services wield political power, corruption grows every year, the law-enforcement system is far too feeble against high-level criminality,[1] and the population has again resigned in the face of renewed domination by a powerful elite, whose motivations are not benevolent.

The United States, attacked by a still unidentified enemy, has declared a war against terrorism, and toppled two evil regimes which had most obviously been involved in spreading such insecurity, the Taliban in Afghanistan, and Saddam Hussein's dictatorship in Iraq. But the roots of the trouble have proven to be deeper than just a loose terrorist network (al Qaeda), and a couple of rogue regimes. Tenacious resistance against the allied forces in Afghanistan and in Iraq has developed, and the threats of further terrorist attacks, proliferation, organized crime and corruption around the world continue.

With regard to this new war on terrorism, the United States has been left almost alone in the first two years of the fight. Now, the tide is slowly turning, as a more acute awareness of the implications of terrorism awakens in Western Europe and elsewhere. NATO has now taken over some of the responsibility in Afghanistan, and speaks about doing the same in Iraq, even if most of the burden, especially the military operations, still rests on the US.

The Czechlands, as has most of Central Europe, with its wobbly moves towards democratization and joining the Western Alliance, has so far not reached a position to take a more significant part in these larger contests. Here, the main struggle is an internal one of whether the natural wishes of the population to become a part of the democratic and affluent West will overcome the corrupt and criminal influences, mostly rooted in the Communist past, with strings still attached to the former Moscow masters. Before Central Europe could move towards being a helpful ally for the West, it would have to deal with its post-Communist ills of organized crime, corruption, spiritual decline and ambiguity, human indifference, subversive mischief, intransparent public service, all underlined by simple human folly, and, equally important, it would have to cut the strings to Russia. In these efforts, the demands and conditions of EU membership, underpinned by the executive powers of the European Commission and the judicial power of the European Court, are by far the most effective instrument of change.

The Czech population knows well what it desires, and confirms its desires in poll after poll: democracy, rule of law, security, defeat of corruption and crime. But the political elite is now almost exclusively post-Communist, that is, composed of former Communists, their former collaborators, and others enrolled after 1989 on the grounds of sharing in the benefits of power. For these elite, corruption and amoral pragmatism are the way of life. The old tools of power are again used, especially the manipulation of public opinion, and many indications point to Russian influences behind these factions.[2]

For these reasons, the Czech Republic has so far not been a truly reliable ally. The Czech governments have provided some relatively valuable help in a number of peace-keeping missions, but the political resolve for such help is diminishing. The Czech public, influenced heavily by all kinds of propaganda, often anti-American, mostly view the broader international security challenges as remote, largely irrelevant to their lives. The burnt down twin towers of the World Trade Center were, for most, a horror of the TV screen only, and the American campaigns in Afghanistan and Iraq remain largely uncomprehended.

The Czechlands – Security Analysis

Throughout the 1990s, the Czech desire in international security was clear, and was also expressed relatively unambiguously by most, though not all, leading Czech politicians: strong NATO, US involvement in Europe, strong European Union, and strong security cooperation between the US and Europe. The driving motivation was fear of Russia, even if it was not voiced, and the ostensible attitude was that Russia no longer threatens anyone. But, by now, most of the individuals who represented such clear desire have either left the political scene, or been pushed out from political prominence, and while no one has dared to put these policies in doubt yet, the messages emitted by Czech politicians have become far more ambiguous.[3]

Czech security policies are exclusively in the hands of the few politicians directly concerned with them at the government level and in diplomacy. The quality of understanding the main issues of international security among these people is now, however, mostly mediocre. In addition to this, foreign policy decision-making is often based on motivations which emerge from the leadership's political background, and its reasoning and conclusions then remain unexplained.[4] To learn what the West can expect from the Czech Republic, it is indispensable to try to dissect and understand the inner workings of Czech politics.

The Czech Political Environment

After 1989, the two top priorities of Czech international policy became membership in NATO and in the European Union. These priorities were articulated by a few members of the Czechoslovak Parliament already early in 1990, and there was little opposition to them among the democratic MPs[5] (that is, all except the Communists, who continue opposing them even now). After the June 1990 elections, these two priorities were confirmed in the new Government Declaration. The experience of Russian oppression of the Soviet days was still painfully fresh, and no one argued against policies aiming to protect the country against a repetition of that dreadful experience.

At the same time, the average Czech citizen has not been quite clear about these foreign policy priorities. In fact, the average citizen has, to a large extent, been left to guess what the adopted priorities of his country are. Although the policies found no opposition in the Parliament, political leaders never made the effort to explain them to the public in a convincing way, and the media reporting was, and remains, weak. Doubts about NATO have often been raised from various directions, and even the old Communist propaganda about NATO as the main enemy of peace has occasionally been voiced. The real reason for joining the West – the fear of Russia – was very soon accepted to be taboo in the public discourse. Such unclear reporting continues and, if anything, the pro-Russian and anti-Western bias returns, as the experience with Communism recedes into the past.

Another detrimental influence must also be considered: intentional misleading propaganda, apparently conducted by the Russians themselves. Many people refute such considerations as conspiratorial or paranoiac, but there is convincing evidence about these forces' activities. Most authoritatively, the October 2001 public report of the Czech counter-intelligence agency, BIS, released the shocking information that Russian secret services organize disinformation campaigns in the Czech media. This is not really surprising – manipulation of public opinion and deception were among the main and most successful arts of the Communists ever since Lenin.[6]

Under normal conditions, one would expect the country's public servants to make appropriate provisions to prevent such foreign penetration, and would inform people accordingly. No such thing has happened, however. The politicians said not a single word, and the media, after the first two days of excited headlines, followed suit. The BIS information, which also stated that the Russians are expanding their influence networks and penetratation of government agencies all the way from government ministries down to local administration, was to be forgotten. No public debate about the Russian penetration, nor about the curious and frightening silence of Czech politicians has ever taken place.[7]

A strange picture emerges. The official foreign policy priority of the country has consistently been participation in the Western Alliance, most probably ensured by the momentum of public desire. But while this priority apparently cannot be thwarted, at least not yet, many Czech politicians and media are ambiguous about active participation. Some of them occasionally promote Russian interests, or act against the interests of the Western alliance in other ways. As a result, the public is confused, as can be seen from the results of opinion polls, which show only lukewarm public support for both NATO and the European Union. The United States and its anti-terrorist campaigns have hardly any support at all.[8]

Importantly, the two most powerful Czech politicians of the period after 1989 were politicians with anti-Western and anti-American attitudes, and, not surprisingly, also undemocratic attitudes. They are the two former Prime Ministers and chairmen of the two largest political parties, Václav Klaus and Milos Zeman, in whose hands tremendous power was put, partly by the Czech proportional voting system.

Václav Klaus

The former federal minister of finance in 1990–92, Prime Minister from 1992 to 1997, Chairman of the Chamber of Deputies of the Parliament from 1998 to 2002, and chosen by the Parliament to serve as the country's President in March 2003, Václav Klaus probably influenced the direction of the country after 1989 most.

A son of a prominent Communist,[9] Václav Klaus was allowed by the Communist regime to study in the US during the period of the fierce clamp-down after the Prague Spring of 1968, when other Czech students in the West had either to emigrate, or to return. After these studies he became a clerk at the Czech National Bank in Prague, but since 1985 he was employed by the Prognostic Institute of the Czechoslovak Academy of Sciences, an institution whose sole customer was the Central Comittee of the Communist Party. Several of the most prominent political leaders after 1989 were also former employees of this Prognostic Institute, and all of them contributed significantly to leading the country down the path of corruption, privatization fraud, and neglected rule of law. Klaus's role model at the Prognostic Institute was reportedly the famous KGB agent Karel Köcher, who was released from US prison in 1986, and exchanged for several prominent Russian dissidents (among them Nathan Shcharansky).[10]

Klaus' attitudes to foreign policy and security issues have been questionable at best. In his first coalition government, appointed in June 1992, his partners had to threaten to leave the coalition to force him even to agree to a meeting to start discussing government priorities in foreign policy. When this meeting finally took place in December 1993, according to reports by at least two participants, he voted against NATO membership, the lone dissenter among the eleven participants. In the years of applying for NATO membership, it was a whispered worry at the Czech foreign ministry that the foreign minister, Josef Zieleniec, and President Václav Havel had to push through the NATO membership policy against Klaus's strong resistance.

Later, these attitudes continued. When the Dayton Agreement was concluded, Klaus hurried to be the first foreign statesman to visit Slobodan Milosevic in Belgrade. When NATO decided to bomb Serbia in 1999, Klaus protested loudly, and organized the signing of his new book at the Prague Yugoslav Embassy.[11] He asserted that negotiating options had by far not been exhausted, and the attack against Serbia was "terribly wrong." His stand with regard to Afghanistan was similar, and when the US entered Iraq in 2003, Klaus, by then the President of the Czech Republic, refused to "support any of the powers,"[12] and even reportedly asked the US Ambassador in Prague, Craig Stapleton, to have the Czech Republic deleted from the list of countries supporting the United States.[13] Later, Klaus felt the urge to speak out against the consideration of an American base in the Czechlands.[14] Outgoing President Havel had tried to save such embarrassing weaknesses of Czech politicians. In his public statements, he had showed a confident understanding of global issues, unique in the Czechlands,[15] and had, on his last day in office, signed the well-known "letter of eight," which expressed support, even if rather reserved,[16] for the United States, in the face of the French and German vaccilation. But with this letter the unambiguously pro-Western stands from Czech politicians ended.

Some of Klaus's other attitudes in foreign policy also deserve to be noted. Next to his opposition to NATO, Klaus, in the last few years, also opposes further integration of the European Union, although it was he, then Prime Minister, who signed the EU membership application in 1996. Noticeably, his change of attitude came at about the time when Russia finally decided to change its stand with regard to the EU, and shifted from supporting the EU membership of the post-Communist countries of Central Europe "rather than NATO membership," to opposing both NATO and the EU outright. Now, Klaus is the fiercest opponent of the EU in the Czechlands.[17] His party, ODS, which parrots Klaus's anti-EU tirades, is now having difficulties in being accepted into the all-European right-of-center European People's Party.[18]

For reasons never explained, Klaus, as Prime Minister, always arrogantly ignored the Visegrad cooperation, a promising initiative in its early days, and the split has since not been properly healed.[19] After the 1998 elections, in which Klaus's ODS lost, Klaus began playing the nationalist tune, utilized until then by the extremist Republican Party of Miroslav Sládek. He was ridiculed in the press for attempting to attract Sládek's electorate, and the policy may have contributed to one more election defeat of his party in 2002. It is a curious coincidence that the Hungarian Prime Minister of the time, Viktor Orbán, expanded his nationalist policies around the same time as Klaus, and then also lost the 2002 parliamentary elections. Together with his nationalist turn, Klaus, then chairman of ODS, a party which likes to describe itself as "conservative" and right of center, also adopted the policy of cooperation with the Communists. He then became the President of the Czech Republic thanks to the 20 percent of Communist votes in the lower chamber of the Czech Parliament.[20]

Milos Zeman

In June 1998, a minority Social Democratic government was formed, although the Social Democrats (CSSD) had only about one third of the seats in the Chamber of Deputies, which appoints the government. This was made possible by an odious agreement hatched by the chairmen of the two strongest parties, Milos Zeman of CSSD and Václav Klaus, which they called "Opposition Treaty." The agreement put into Zeman's hands the power of a grand coalition, in a situation when the nominally center-right parties were in majority in the Parliament.

Milos Zeman became Prime Minister and the country took a clear turn for the worse. Corruption grew and culminated in several highly visible scandals.[21] But the most important and damaging change he brought about was the return of

Communists into the state administration, practically everywhere. These changes were made with the full support of Klaus, with whom he was reported to meet regularly for consultations.[22] Already in the fall of 1998 the Ministry of Interior and the Czech Police were purged of people who were enrolled after 1989, and two years later thorough purges were made also at the Ministry of Defense. Less obviously, steps were also being taken to purge the intelligence services. These steps continue even during the present government of Vladimír Spidla, under the management of Stanislav Gross, who was Minister of Interior in Zeman's government, and retained his portfolio.[23] The director of BIS who submitted the report which contained the information about Russian influence was fired in the summer 2003, for reasons unrelated to the 2001 report. At the Police unit combatting organized crime, practically the whole department combatting Russian-speaking mafias was dismissed in the fall of 1998, with the Director, Zdenek Machácek, put into custody for three months on false charges in September 1998. When his trial took place at last, three years later, he was fully cleared of the accusation. However, the rest of the Police marked the message: do not touch Russian criminals, the government does not wish it.[24]

Zeman's Foreign Minister became Jan Kavan, another controversial figure of Czech politics after 1989. Kavan is considered by the intelligence community to be a "typical" double agent, for Russia and the United Kingdom, although this suspicion cannot, of course, be verified. His acts, however, speak volumes. For example, when NATO decided to liberate Kosovo from Milosevic, Kavan prepared a policy proposal which included the demand to stop the bombing of Serbia. His partner was the Greek foreign minister, and for the signing and announcement of the proposal they chose, of all places, Beijing. The Czech-Greek plan was met with incredulity and icy silence. In December 1998, when an Iraqi diplomat defected in Prague with information about planned terrorist attacks against Radio Free Europe, Kavan, with a simpleton face, announced it publicly the next day, which sent the frightened Iraqi packing for London. At the time when the Czech Republic's accession to NATO was being decided, in 1998, Kavan's query was whether it is possible to leave NATO. His right-hand man whom he brought to the Foreign Ministry as the "General Secretary," a position created for him, a military intelligence agent who had served in the Communist secret services, was recently sentenced for an attempted murder of an inconvenient journalist, and is still being investigated for corruption at the foreign ministry. Kavan also infuriated the US Government when he proposed a UN Human Rights Commission resolution condemning the United States for the embargo against Cuba. When the Ministry employees came to replace his personal safe, authorized by him, they found a heap of cash, in various denominations, which he left there by mistake. The report about the finding was later lost, and the unfortunate employee, director of the department of special tasks, Mr. Pavel, who was in his forties, died a couple of weeks later of burst aorta during a ministry assignment in Lithuania. Jan Kavan was then sent by the Czech government, for the 2002/2003 term, to serve as the Chairman of the General Assembly of the United Nations.

While post-Communism took firm hold in the Czechlands under Zeman's government, and corruption and organized crime continued to grow largely unchecked, the country became a member of NATO in the spring of 1999, and

Zeman's government largely fulfilled the conditions for EU accession. The two foreign policy priorities of 1990 were formally not put into doubt by Zeman, nor by any other of the post-Communist politicians. At the same time, the political will for Eastward enlargement has been strong enough in both NATO and the European Union to overlook the post-Communist frailties, and ignore the possibility that the post-Communist countries might serve as Russian Trojan horses in both organizations.

Vladimír Spidla's Government

Milos Zeman had pledged in 1998 that he will retire from politics after one term as Prime Minister. He kept his pledge, and picked Vladimír Spidla as his successor, his deputy both in CSSD and in the Government. Spidla introduced himself with far-left rhetoric, but then seemed to proceed to act in a relatively decent way. After he had become Prime Minister in June 2002, he resisted the pressures to continue the "Opposition Treaty" arrangement with ODS, and formed a coalition with the two small right-of-center parties, Union of Freedom and the People's Party. While corruption thrives under this government, too,[25] Spidla yet found at least the courage to cancel some of the most offensive corrupt deals of Zeman's government (in which he was Vice-Chairman), like the purchase of Swedish fighter airplanes, or a construction deal to have a section of a highway built by a company of Russians with Israeli passports, under incredibly disadvantageous conditions for the Czech state. Sadly, after the public outrage about these huge corrupt deals has quieted down, the government is returning to the plan to acquire the unneeded and NATO-incompatible Swedish fighters, thus corroborating the suspicion that it has some unrevealed obligations to, or deals with, the Swedes.

In foreign and security policy, Spidla has steered a cautious course. Although his party has a strong majority in the government, he gave the Foreign Ministry to the People's Party, which prefers pro-Western positions, often very different from the positions of Spidla's own CSSD. When his own party conference voted against supporting the United States in the Iraq campaign in the spring of 2003, Spidla more or less ignored it.[26] This was a situation when Václav Klaus was openly against supporting the United States, and the Czech Parliament voted to provide such support only if the second UN resolution in support of the US military intervention were accepted. This left Spidla little wiggle room, yet, with the Czech military hospital and chemical unit grounded by the Parliamentary decision in Kuwait, he somehow managed to keep the overall impression that the Czech Republic supported the United States.

But Spidla's days are numbered. The public support for CSSD has declined below that of the Communists, and the next election will almost certainly see the return of ODS to power, most likely in coalition with the People's Party. Spidla was made CSSD chairman by Zeman, but has no constituency of his own within the party. The party is now seriously divided, for various reasons, partly thanks to Spidla's attempts to start at least some reform of the public finances, which have been sent into a nose-dive by his predecessors, Klaus and Zeman.[27]

Corruption and Blackmail Replace Communist Party

The key to understanding post-Communism is the phenomenon of corruption. The international assessments of corruption have shown a steady growth of corruption in the Czechlands and some of the other post-Communist countries of Central Europe. Only Russia and Ukraine are now assessed to be more corrupt than the Czechlands, which has descended to the level of countries like Bulgaria, Romania or Albania. This is unpleasant in itself, but it is only a part of the picture.

Transparency International carefully measures what it calls "Corruption Perception Index", that is, it is making relatively responsible opinion polls of people's perception about bribery. The corruption we are concerned with here, however, is not just bribery, it is the abuse of delegated authority for the purposes of power in general. In principle, these are situations in which individuals pledge to serve others, usually described as "interest groups," in exchange for various benefits. Parliament and local elected council seats, desirable positions in public administration, or lucrative contracts, are awarded to those who are willing to support such interest groups, no questions asked. Without such pledges, the benefits are unattainable.[28]

This is despicable, obviously against the interests of the people, it puts power into the hands of the worst individuals, and it will most likely turn against the interests even of those who allow themselves to be corrupted in this way! And yet, this is the reality of post-Communism. The corrupt networks of power have gradually been formed, by influences nesting partly in business, and partly also in the political sphere which, already in the early 1990s, was penetrated by these post-Communist interests. The mechanism of state-level corruption stands on well-positioned individuals, and on sufficient supplies of money. The individuals in positions of power hand out appointments in exchange for faithful service. People who get such appointments but disappoint, don't obey, or wish to implement their own ideas, are eventually dismissed.

Money is needed to win elections. Since decent people in post-Communist situations have no money, they are excluded from the political contest. Those who tried in the first years after 1989, and perhaps succeeded for a while in the beginning, have by now been pushed out of politics. A number of tools have been used against them vigorously and successfully: their political parties were penetrated, some of the individual politicians were discredited, others corrupted (bribed!), when they borrowed money they went bankrupt, often helped on the way down by people around them. Those who made it all the way to a chance to govern were shown for fools – on the one hand, they were not well prepared, on the other hand, all the instruments of subversion were used against them by the post-Communists.

This kind of corruption creates mafia-type pyramids of power in which just a few individuals at the top and in some other key positions are needed to manage the whole structure. The post-Communist management top need not be the government: While it can be imagined that Václav Klaus belongs to it, generally it could very well be individuals or groups unknown to the public, who stand behind the politicians and have access to financial resources and authority over the mechanisms of influencing public opinion.[29] Minister Gross could well be one of the politicians subservient to such influences.[30] The various parts of the structure have their own pragmatic motivation to serve in their positions and, in case of need, they can effectively be held in place and obedience by blackmail. The system is wonderfully effective, as there is no need to run complicated party structures for oversight – a breath-taking improvement of the mechanisms of evil. Various private companies with opaque origins exist around post-Communist politics, having mushroomed after the fall of Communism. They control large sections of the economy, particularly in the strategic areas always considered most important by the Russians: energy, arms industry, financial services, and media.[31]

Another important aspect of the whole scheme, observed all over the post-Communist world, be it Central Europe, the Caucasus, or Russia itself, is that there are always a number of such corrupt/criminal groups competing for power. From the point of view of a master conductor, such an arrangement has only advantages: The various groups can be played against each other, those who can best be used to serve at a given moment can be given the opportunity to prevail, but then they can later be pushed out of power again, according to the needs of the orchestrator. In the case of post-Communism, the orchestrator would be sitting in Moscow, most likely in the dark recesses of Lubyanka.

The system is devilishly perfect: Decent people never get a chance because they would not participate in corrupt schemes but, just like under Communism, promotion is only available through corruption. Greed without principles has replaced ideology. The public outrage at the unprecedented levels of corruption does not lead to their appreciation of democracy, because there is none around. Instead, the high moral ground becomes occupied by the unrepentant Communists who say, "Look how the capitalists behave, our rule was by far not as corrupt." They are wrong, but the public accepts their message. So far, the post-Communist societies have no mechanisms to escape these devious webs, certainly not in the Czechlands.

The Democratic Momentum

It is truly a wonder that under these conditions and with such politicians the Czech Republic has still kept its initial foreign policy priority of joining the Western Alliance. After President Václav Havel stepped down, none of the leading Czech politicians can really be trusted to mean what they say. And yet, the pro-Western priorities appear to hold, despite the wavering caused by people like Klaus, Zeman, Gross, or Kavan, and despite the clearly very strong Russian influence, with its continued quest to bring down the United States.

The main reason why the pro-Western priorities are maintained is probably the momentum of public desire. The public is confused but, for the most part, people know that they wish to be a part of the rich West rather than a part of the desolate, criminal East. This, after all, is true also of most of the politicians. Those few who, for some reason, play the Eastern game, like Klaus or Kavan or Gross, can only afford to do so indirectly, while at the same time paying explicit lip-service to the participation in the Western integrative bodies and its culture.

Another positive influence in the Czechlands is the long cultural tradition. Here, much like in Western Europe, people have been developing respect for rule of law and for the traditional European norms of social behavior for centuries. Communism eroded this respect considerably, but not fatally. Unfortunately, the changes since 1989 have not succeeded in bringing about a return to proper rule-of-law governance. Law-enforcement is still unreliable and large-scale and organized crime, as already observed, can operate without much challenge. Moral integrity continues to decline.

The expectations of NATO and the requirements of the European Union also contribute positively to the overall political direction of the country. So far, the post-Communist politicians do not oppose the minimal democratic requirements of the West. Yet, there is a sense that the wavering democratic direction of the country could crumble with a change of wind, particularly if the world of Western democracy should be further weakened, and the space for Russian influence should further open.

All these impulses, cultural rather than political, translate into the language of the official "Security Strategy of the Czech Republic," approved in May 2001. Since the draft document was submitted to wider discussion in the security community, the text was eventually made acceptable. The document still stresses territorial integrity and sovereignty excessively, but the concept of Allied cooperation has now also received due prominence. In the previous Security Strategy of 1999 NATO cooperation fared much worse. Now, NATO cooperation comes as the first-mentioned "strategic interest" of the Czech Republic, after the "vital" interests of "existence, sovereignty, territorial integrity, the principles of democracy and a legal state, and the creation of the fundamental conditions for the lives of citizens."

Czech Republic as an Ally

Given the described political situation, neither clear-cut decisions, nor long-term reliability should be expected from the Czech Republic. Among the actors who do have clear ideas about international security in the Czechlands, the people with anti-Western and anti-American leanings appear to be gaining on those who would wish to cooperate fully with the Western Alliance. The poor showing in Iraq was one indication, but perhaps most revealing are the dismal developments in the Czech Army.

In the Czech armed forces, years of ever changing and never implemented reform plans have resulted in a situation where the Czech military is incapable of any meaningful military action even if the politicians brought themselves to the decision. According to informed military observers, and even public statements of top Czech army officers, this situation is likely to last for quite a few years to come, especially when no promising solutions appear on the horizon as yet. Capable officers have mostly left the armed forces, and underqualified officers have filled their spots in the Ministry of Defense and the General Staff. In the process, the principle of civilian control of the army has been abandoned. Billions of crowns have been misused, and many useless pieces of outrageously expensive equipment have been purchased, in large part on credit, so that army investment money has, in fact, been spent for many years in advance.[32] All the good intentions promoted over the years by quite a few well-meaning and capable officers have come to nothing.

The good officers were fired, and the intentions were swept away, first in the years of the Klaus governments, and then, with some finality, during the Zeman minority government supported by Klaus.

There can only have be two reasons which could have led to the feebleness of the international security policies of the Czech Republic, despite all the Western help available since 1989 but for the asking: The Czech governments and the armed forces management:

1   have been incredibly incapable, and lacked good will with regard to theWestern Alliance, and/or
2   they have been under Russian influence.

All of this means that the future performance of the Czech Republic within the Alliance will depend primarily on the immediate configuration of the domestic political establishment, and on the relative strength or weakness of the Alliance. When pro-Russian politicians prevail, disruptive policies will likely gain strength, when less corrupt politicians ascend, less dependence on the Russian-connected power networks will be had. With Politicians such as Vladimír Spidla in CSSD, or perhaps Mirek Topolánek in ODS, the country will be more responsive to the Alliance needs.

The unreliability of the Czech political elites does not correspond to the general attitudes of the Czech public, nor to the wishes and tendencies in the Czech society. Admittedly, Czech people are confused. But their uncertainties are more the result of inadequate information than of some ambiguity about where they belong: There is little doubt that they see themselves squarely in the mainstream of European, or Euro-Atlantic, democracy.

The confusion in people's minds about international affairs partly mirrors, unfortunately, the confusion we find elsewhere in the Western world as well. Talking to people about international affairs shows quite clearly that people are also poorly informed, and are strongly influenced by anti-Western and anti-American propaganda. There are two main ways such propaganda is spread here in the Czechlands – through the media, especially television, and then by "shouters" and whisperers in all kinds of informal settings. Analysts and commentators who bring balanced information and opinions do get some space in the more serious newspapers and on some radio stations, but they are read and heard by only relatively few, usually the few whose opinions are well balanced anyway.[33]

The key to understanding the behavior of countries like the Czechlands would be to decipher what exactly are the incentives and motivations of people like Václav Klaus who work so doggedly against the creation of decent public service in the country, against its desire to become a well running and well integrated part of the world of Western democracy, and on behalf of the Russian interests. With the personal history and the performance observed over the years, the most likely explanation is again that some of these people are either directly on the Russian (KGB/FSB) payroll, or are obliged to respond to some demands through blackmail.

Whatever the power mechanisms of the post-Communist influences, the fruit of their labors can be observed by all: Fourteen years after 1989 very few democratic reforms have been accomplished. The principle of "legal continuity" allowed the

Communists and their helpers to escape responsibility. They proceeded to gain economic power, and to gradually return into many positions in public administration. Law-enforcement has never quite made it, although some good points have been scored, and serious economic criminality and corruption have gone largely unpunished. Middle class has not been given a chance to reestablish itself. Education lags with little meaningful reform even in sight. There is the worrisome tendency towards a society where power is in the hands of a narrow layer of mafia-type rich, who can bend law and law-enforcement to their purposes. Politicians like Klaus or Zeman have been primarily responsible for this development, and they and others like them, or who do their bidding, still seem to have the upper hand. Thus, the Czech Republic cannot be expected to be a reliable ally, even if Czech units, formed *ad hoc* from hired volunteers, have so far performed with good results in the international peace-keeping missions, and despite the fact that, individually, Czech people view themselves as part of the West, and, in principle, are willing to do their part in protecting their own, and the West's, security.

Implications for Western Security Policies

The presented facts and considerations imply that the Czechlands, as most other post-Communist countries of Central and Eastern Europe, cannot be relied on as allies as yet. The "New Europe," mentioned by US Secretary of Defense Donald Rumsfeld in some frustration over the French and German behavior with regard to Iraq, is by no means more pro-American than Western Europe. West European countries may have some foolish and irritating politicians, seen as such by the US as well as by many of its own citizens, but they are settled, well-established democracies with functioning rule of law, and they have been trustworthy allies for over a half-century. On the other hand, the post-Communist countries, deeply corrupt, and to some extent under Russian influence, have a long, long way to go yet. At the moment, they may, in fact, be moving away from the Alliance rather than towards it, thanks to the political ascent of Communists in many of these countries.

Under these circumstances, the further building of the Western Alliance should be seen as a shared task of the Western trans-Atlantic Allies. A task not only of defining the new challenges and new responses to them, but also of dragging a new Central Europe, first to democracy, and also to being true allies in the full sense of the word. It must be understood and accepted by the West that the adversary in this process of making Central Europe part of the Alliance is, in fact, Russia. Russia, through its influence networks which have been preserved from the Communist days and have now been revived and expanded,[34] will do everything to prevent the meaningful integration of Central Europe into the Western Alliance. Subversion, penetration, chaos, destabilization, driving wedges between allies, discreditation, sabotage, corruption, all these have ever been and remain the methods and tools of the Soviet/Russian strategists. The use of these strategies can best be studied in the countries of Russian "near abroad," expecially Ukraine and the Caucasus. Then we can wonder to what extent they are also used elsewhere, the West including.

The present estrangement between the United States and France, and to some extent still also among other Europeans, is unpleasant, and needs to be faced with utmost seriousness. The West, besieged by the terrorist onslaught, cannot afford to fall prey to its own contentions. The differences which occur must be faced and overcome, much as they used to be faced during the Cold War. The old proverb should be heeded, that pride precedes fall. If the Western Alliance is to have a future, it must continue to be built on the joint strength of the United States and Western Europe.

The citizens of the Czechlands, as well as of the rest of Central Europe, desire to participate on the power of such a united democratic Alliance. But their countries still first need to become secure democracies, respecting the traditional values of honesty, rule of law, and transparent and accountable public service. Only after this democratic goal is achieved, in spite of the detrimental influences of the Russian fifth column, can the further goal of becoming true allies also be tackled. The security of the Western Alliance thus rests, in the first place, on the protection and development of its democracy.

Notes

1 See note 31.
2 The most important public media is television. In the Czechlands there are now two private and two public TV channels, and the public TV has, for years, been under strong pressure by Václav Klaus and others to be privatized. The private TV station NOVA has most viewers, and has acquired enormous influence on public opinion. But its ownership is unclear, hidden in a maze of some 60 interlinked companies, which also own the other private channel, PRIMA, and they may well be owned by Russians. The station was originally financed by the American businessman Ronald Lauder. But in 1999–2000 the director of the station, Vladimír Zelezný, in effect stole the TV from the Americans, which resulted in an international arbitrage and, in 2003, the international arbitration court sentenced the Czech Republic to paying Ronald Lauder's company almost 11 billion Kc. In the many investigations of Zelezný and his dealings, enough information has been uncovered to give a sense of the machinations around the station. When Zelezný started his "new NOVA" in 2000, part of the money for his one-billion loan from the IPB bank arrived from Switzerland, from Russian companies "linked to organized crime," according to the police. In connection with the TV NOVA takeover, a company owned by former StB members and members of Russian secret services called "Interconex" also lent three billion Czech crowns to the IPB bank which provided the loan for the start of "new NOVA." The criminal investigation has never been concluded, and has, by now, disappeared from public eye. Similarly, multiple complaints from viewers about lack of objectivity of TV NOVA have never led to any penalty by the responsible TV Council; see *Respekt*, 5 February 2001.
3 So, for example, before the final step of becoming NATO members on 12 March 1999, Czech leaders averred that they do not seek only security for the Czech Republic, but wish to actively help towards security for others. But when NATO struck at Serbia in the Kosovo conflict, the Czech government tried to excuse itself saying the attack was decided without Czech participation. While it had given its explicit consent in Brussels, at home Prime Minister Zeman denounced the attacking pilots as "troglodytes" and "primitives." Throughout the war Zeman and Klaus, then Chairman of the Chamber of

Deputies of the Czech Parliament, used every opportunity to distance themselves from the Allies, and express disagreement with their conduct. Klaus stated that the Albanians are not expelled from their homes by Milosevic but by NATO, and his shadow foreign minister, Jan Zahradil, called President Bush and British Prime Minister Blair "warmongers," and appealed for their resignation. Prime Minister Zeman visited Moscow in mid-April 1999, but instead of using the opportunity to expound the principles and motivations which led to the NATO intervention, he reached an agreement with the Russian foreign minister Ivanov that what was happening in Kosovo is a humanitarian catastrophy, with no word on who was responsible; *Respekt*, 3 January 2000.

Czech politicians easily reach agreement with the Russians, often in contradiction to the Alliance policies. After Russian President Putin denounced the American/British attack against Saddam Hussein as an "unjustifiable act and regrettable mistake," the Chairman of the Chamber of Deputies, Lubomír Zaorálek, visited Moscow and, after his meeting with the Communist Chairman of Russian Duma Seleznev, announced that "Czech and Russian positions have come significantly closer to each other," *Respekt*, 24 March 2003.

4   This feature of post-Communist politics was rampant under Prime Ministers Klaus and Zeman, but continues even in the present government of Vladimír Spidla. A recent example was the nomination of Milos Kuzvart as a European Commissioner. Kuzvart, a Social Democratic Parliament Deputy and former Minister of Environment, is a weak, ineffective, but relatively well-meaning young politician, and was pushed through by the Prime Minister, to the amazement of all. After his first interview with Romano Prodi, however, Kuzvart resigned disgracefully, blaming the Czech diplomatic mission and the foreign minister for insufficient support. Media reported that he had language difficulties, and when he was asked by journalists in Brussels what he thought about the European Constitution, the only answer he could offer was, "I am very optimistic. 'What do you mean?' I am very optimistic;" see, for example, *Lidové noviny*, 22 February 2004; or *Respekt*, 23 February 2004.

5   The Czech Parliament has two chambers, the lower one, which has most of the parliamentary powers, called the 'Convent of Representatives,' usually translated into English as 'Chamber of Deputies,' and the Senate, with equal powers only in constitutional amendments, electoral laws, and the election of the president of the country. The Chamber appoints the government, and approves the country budget.

6   A recent controversy about a vulgar program on the private TV station NOVA brought a revealing public debate. In an article titled "Jílková and Caban evade the merit of the matter," Vladimír Just illuminates the manipulative nature of NOVA programs: " ... identity of interests between the representatives of power and the tabloids, in their clientelistic coalition against free criticism. ... warns about the merging of private media, politics and economic cartels. ... no court is capable of defining the legal status of the broadcaster of our most watched TV station [NOVA] ... this intransparent beast, having escaped control, produces something directly opposite to what it got its licence for. The punishment we all pay has the size of the 11-billion debt [the penalty Czech Republic had to pay, by a decision of an international arbitration court, when NOVA TV station was stolen from its former American owner, Ronald Lauder] ... on NOVA, they never speak about the out-of-court agreement Klaus-Zelezný [an agreement after which NOVA stopped all criticism of Klaus, and Klaus withdrew a law-suit against NOVA for an incorrect report that Klaus owned a house in Switzerland – there apparently is a house owned by his sister, at a time when other top ODS politicians revealed that ODS owns a secret account in Switzerland, an accusation they, too, were unable to substantiate]; they are silent about the fact that the results of the last elections

conspicuously corresponded to the appearances of politicians on NOVA half a year before the elections. They do not speak about the fact that, although we have roughly 300 legislators, on NOVA they consistently rotate only about twelve of them, which is a specific form of Czech corruption. ... "; *Lidové noviny*, 2 March 2004.

7 Czech media are still relatively free, but some extent of "self-censorship" which protects the corrupt politicians exists. The Czech Republic has now also experienced two cases of direct intimidation of critical journalists. In the first case, a high-level official of the Czech government was sentenced to eight years in prison for a botched attempt to have a journalist murdered, after the would-be murderer informed the police, in the second, the editor-in-chief of the weekly Respekt was beaten up by two thugs, and had to spend a week in hospital; *Lidové noviny*, 24 Janaury 2004.

8 According to the February 2004 opinion poll of the Czech Center for Public Opinion Research 75 percent of Czech population opposed the deployment of Czech soldiers in Afghanistan. Only 17 percent agree with the deployment. The Czech Republic, a NATO member, is now, in March 2004, sending all of 108 soldiers to help the Americans in Afghanistan, but only for half a year; *Lidové noviny*, 6 March 2004.

9 According to contemporaries, Klaus's father was the Director of one of the state monopolies created by the Communists after 1948, Mototechna, responsible for car parts trade. The family of Klaus Sr. comes from Ruthenia, where it lived under the name Pruzhinsky. Ruthenia was annexed by the Soviet Union in 1945. Klaus Sr. died early, in 1954, and Klaus Jr. never speaks about him.

10 Very little information about Karel Köcher is available, due to his intelligence involvement. He continues to keep a low profile even now. Born in 1934, with extremely high IQ, he was enrolled by StB, Czechoslovak Communist intelligence service, already while student at the Mathematics/Physics Faculty of Charles University. Later he was sent to study at the Columbia University in New York, and here he was hired by CIA. In CIA, he eventually became a leading officer in the Eastern Europe section. His identity was in the end revealed to CIA by Oleg Kalugin after his defection in 1984. It is reasonable to believe that he continues to play an important role for Russian secret services. A photograph was printed in Czech press in the early 1990s showing two identically-looking men, with the caption reading, "Václav Klaus and his double, Karel Köcher."

11 Few people bother to read Klaus's books, often ridiculed for lack of ideas.

12 *Lidové noviny*, 11 April 2003. In another prominent Czech daily, *Mladá fronta Dnes*, 25 March 2003, Klaus was quoted as saying, "The notion of the supporters of the attack against Iraq that democracy can be installed by military power is, for me, like from another universe."

13 *Lidové noviny*, 10 April 2003; and an interview with Ambassador Stapleton, *Lidové noviny*, 25 April 2003.

14 Klaus compared the idea of an American base to the former Soviet garrisons in Czechoslovakia, and said: "New deployment of foreign troops would likely not be welcome;" *Lidové noviny*, 3 May 2003.

15 In an interview with the weekly *Respekt*, published on January 13, 2003, he explained that, as he understood from his talks with Egyptian President Mubarak and other statesmen, Saddam's regime was terrible, genocidal and dangerous. In his view, "America" (the US) was "a country of ideals, and often of such an enthusiastic drive on behalf of ideals which Europe could only envy." To reduce US politics to no more than strategic interests was a vast simplification for him.

16 The language of the letter, originally drafted by the Spanish and the British governments, was diluted upon the insistence of the Czech Government and the other Central European signatories.

17   "What interests me is whether we shall have to face the attempt to build a continental state with the ambition to rule over Europe from one center, or shall work on the basis of national states," Klaus said in Berlin in April 2003, at the occasion of one of his first foreign trips as President; *Lidové noviny*, 11 April 2003. On February 14, 2004, Klaus published an article, "Why I am not an Europeist," *Lidové noviny*, supplement "Orientace," 14 February 2004. In an interview given to *Lidové noviny* (which spent two-and-a-half pages and a special supplement in what feels like a cult-creating promotion of Klaus), Klaus spoke about "incredible, centralizing, bureaucratic, directivist, autocratic tendencies, rolling upon us from that European Union;" *Lidové noviny*, 27 February 2004, special supplement 26 February 2004. (Speaking of cult-creating, another major Czech daily, *Mladá fronta Dnes*, published a 12-page supplement as a celebration of Klaus's first year as President, 12 photographs of Klaus in its magazine on February 26, and, finally, a two-page interview. Within the year, Klaus's public support rose from low twenties to almost 70 percent; the campaign in both these major daily newspapers is reminiscent of the cult-making of Vladimir Putin in Russia. Both papers are owned by the same obscure German-registered publisher. The country has only two other daily papers, Právo (far left, the descendant of the Communist "Red Law" daily) and Hospodárské noviny, both with smaller readership.)

18   *Lidové noviny*, 28 February 2004.

19   Explained in detail in an article by Lubos Palata (2003), *Lidové noviny*, 5 April 2003.

20   For analysis see, for example, the excellent article by Martin Weiss (2003), *Lidové noviny*, 2 May 2003.

21   In the four years of Zeman's government, CPI (corruption perception index) fell from an already poor 4.9 to the European low of 3.9. The worst corruption cases revealed were the proposed purchase of the Swedish fighter airplanes, Gripens, its price estimated at 100 to 170 bn Kc, the deal failed in the Chamber of Deputies of the Czech Parliament by one vote one day before the government stepped down; the construction of highway D 47 by a Russian/Israeli firm Housing Construction with no experience in building highways, which was approved by the government in the last week of its term, only to be canceled by Spidla's government at a cost of some 700 million Kc; the 4 bn Kc government project of providing computers for schools, in which a major part of the funds was embezzled; and the sale of a part of the Russian debt, about 100 bn Kc, to an intransparent Czech-registered Swiss/Russian company, Falcon Capital. Falcon is obviously well connected, but without even an office and a telephone in the Czechlands. Although the Russian government released 50 bn Kc for the deal, only 20 bn Kc made it into the Czech treasury, having traveled through the accounts of some other firms, for example the French branch of Russian bank AKB Eurofinance, then an American bank, Deutsche Bank, and only then to the Czech government. Why so many transactions have remained a mystery for the public. 100 bn Kc from the Russian debt of about 130 bn Kc was thus erased. The deal caused a scandal both in the Czech Republic and in Russia, where the money apparently first traveled to Chubais's RAO JES, and helped to repay its debt to the Russian government. In Russian media interviews RAO JES managers spoke about a 9-billion provision for Falcon, which was supposed to finance "some programs of the Czech government." Now, the government of Vladimír Spidla has signed another deal with Falcon to sell the rest of the Russian debt. These transactions have the appearance of money-laundering in reverse by both the Czech and the Russian governments, which might be providing huge amounts of money for the organized-crime and terrorism underworld. All these cases received wide coverage in the media, but the government ignored the criticisms; see for example *Lidové noviny*, 23 January 2003, and *Respekt*, 18 March 2002.

22 According to press reports, Klaus and Zeman met secretly since as early as January 1998.

23 Minister Gross, who was just over 30 years of age when he first became government minister in 2000, not only continues the purges but also surrounds himself with people linked to the former regime, to Communist secret services, and to murky Russian influences. Soon after his appointment in January 2000, Gross appointed into the position of First Deputy to the Director of Czech Police Mr. Václav Jakubík, a former Communist prison guard. Upon press inquiries he said that Jakubík possessed the necessary security clearance, which was not true. But Jakubík never really got the required clearance, even though the National Security Office (NBU) fired the responsible officer, Mrs. Smídová. In the end, he got a lower degree clearance based not on the proper screening process, but on the political decision of the Director of NBU. Gross's own first deputy was a pre-1989 prison guard, Petr Ibl, now a Parliament Deputy for CSSD. Also notorious are Gross's contacts with influential business figures who are former StB agents or employees of Communist foreign trade companies. Gross strongly opposes the opening of the StB files, and consistently demands greater powers for police, which sends shivers down many people's spines; see, for example, *Respekt*, 15 October 2001.

After Jakubík's appointment as Deputy Police Director, the management of Czech Police underwent a complete coup, with six of the eight of the managing officers replaced by policemen with long Communist police experience. The then chairman of the Parliamentary Committee for Defense and Security, Petr Nečas, described the situation for the press in these words: "Some British and American experts have indicated to me that if this continues they will cut us off from their information about crime." President Havel himself stood up in defense of the police services. He visited until then very respected Agency for Combatting Organized Crime, and stated: "Somebody is making an attempt to destabilize these units, and thus paralyze the investigation of crimes. The center of the destabilizing forces is apparently outside the Police, but it is clear that one or two of these people are former police officers." In another statement President Havel specifically accused Josef Doucha, a former criminal police officer, who was then employed by a law firm specializing in the defense of people suspected of participation in Russian criminal mafias; *Respekt*, 26 January 2001.

24 See *Respekt*, 17 December 2001.

25 In the latest Transparency International (TI) assessment, the Czech Republic has scored 3.9, in the 54th to 56th place, together with Brasil and Bulgaria, below Belorussia. The chairwoman of the Czech TI, formerly the head of the government Czech Statistical Office, explained: "...beside bribes, other forms of corruption are spreading. ... Clientelism or nepotism, when friends, acquaintances, or relatives are appointed into lucrative positions with the expectation that they will then be beholden. What is perhaps even worse for this country is this influencing and dominating of the state, and lobbyism. Completely uncontrollable lobbyism, which results in considerable social losses, and a limitation of the effectivity of the markets. And this means both the economic ones, and political ones. ... International researches show ... high occurance of corruption in public administration, infrastructure, and construction business. But when you look at the researches which inquire where the situation is most in need of change, the answers are, in the judiciary, police, and customs service;" *Lidové noviny*, Special Supplement, 24 February 2004.

Prime Minister Spidla is clearly well aware of the menace of corruption: "Unless we manage to wipe out the influence of grey and criminal economy on this country, it will not matter in the least who will govern," he uttered in front of journalists in the fall of 2003. Reported, for example, in a thorough analysis in *Respekt*, 9 February 2004.

Respekt comments: "This is logical: for 500 billion crowns, decisive influence on any administration can be bought." Czech Police estimates that the yearly profit of criminal economy is around 500 bn Kc.

26   The conference resolution included the following: "The Conference of CSSD (Czech Social Democratic Party), taking place in Prague on March 28–30, 2003, expresses its disapproval of the war conducted by the USA, Great Britain, and the so-called Alliance Against Iraq, which was started without the agreement of the international community of the UN, and is therefore, in the opinion of the Conference, conducted in breach of international law;" *Lidové noviny*, 31 March 2003.

27   The total public debt has now surpassed the Czech GDP, with the 2003 deficit of public finances expected to be around 195 billion Kc, some 12 percent of GDP. The Government misleadingly operates with what they call "state debt," which does not include the deficits of the various government agencies like the Fund of National Property, and the deficits of local administration.

28   See note 25.

29   Klaus, for example, tends to spend his vacation with his sponsors: In August 2003 he chose a Russian-owned hotel in Karlovy Vary (Karlsbad), a city now practically owned by Russians – *Lidové noviny*, 15 August 2003. When the fact was reported in the press, he moved to another hotel, explaining that he did not know the hotel was owned by Russians (!); in the past he was reported to spend a vacation with his sponsor Peter Kovarcík in Kovarcík's private villa on Mallorca.

30   Stanislav Gross, an engine driver by profession, in his low thirties, is, by the testimony of a Social Democratic insider, Jana Volfová, the most powerful person in CSSD;. see an interview with Jana Volfová (2003), *Lidové noviny*, 19 April. Reportedly, he has no friends in the Parliament, and does not consult his policies with his colleagues. Leaks from police recordings of telephone conversations of criminals under investigation have revealed that he apparently keeps contacts with some unsavoury business figures, who can call his cell phone even late at night.

31   One of these companies is the mysterious PPF which recently acquired 66 percent control of the most influential Czech TV station, NOVA. PPF also owns majority control of the largest Czech insurance company, the formerly state monopoly Ceská pojistovna, and several banks and other financial institutions, and is believed to be contemplating the purchase of Czech Telecom. It expands its activities also to Slovakia and Russia;. *Lidové noviny*, 20 December 2003. Its owner, Petr Kellner, another of the powerful youngsters who have appeared in Czech post-Communism, never speaks to media. His company, PPF, is owned by another company, PPF Group, registered in the Netherlands, whose owners it is impossible to identify; *Lidové noviny*, 28 February 2004. Another example is a mysterious American, reportedly Delaware-registered, company called Appian Group, which owns the largest Czech machine factory Skoda Plzen and one of the largest Czech coal companies. The company is believed to be dominated by former StB, Communist secret police; *Respekt*, 23 December 2003 and 23 February 2004. As with PPF Group, it has been impossible, even for the Czech Police, to identify the real owners of Appian. For months now, journalists have followed the largest privatization sale of the last two years, of North Bohemian Coal Mines, for which Appian has from the beginning been the government's favorite. Public outrage has now made the deal too sensitive for the government, and it canceled the privatization for the moment, most likely only to wait for another opportunity to hand the mines over to Appian, much as it did with the purchase of the Swedish fighter airplanes Gripen.

    Russian power in the Czechlands is ominous, and is beginning to be spoken about even by some of the highest government officials. The 'Supreme State Prosecutor,'

Marie Benesová said in a recent interview for Hospodárské noviny: "I have grave signals about very dangerous criminal activities, for example in Karlsbad, where there is an influx of Russian money of uncertain origin. ... The breakdown is already so huge that something must be done. ... Karlsbad is a dangerous region. Policemen cover up their crimes, abduct and beat up people. The Russians build unauthorized buildings and no one does anything against it. They dominate the city and the security services are incapable of finding out where their money comes from. It is a fascinating contempt of law." Unfortunately, Czech law-enforcement agencies are apparently helpless against the Russians, most likely because they do not have the necessary support from the highest levels of the Ministry of Interior and the Czech government. The reasons may be the same as indicated in the subchapter on Milos Zeman. The new director of the special police department combatting Russian-speaking mafias, Jan Svoboda, says that his department is underfunded and practically helpless against the Russian criminals. An excellent recent overview of Russian criminal involvement in the Czechlands was published in *Respekt*, 1 March 2004.

32 The largest of these orders were the purchase of 72 subsonic fighter trainer airplanes from the Czech company Aero Vodochody which the Czech Air Force does not need, and the order for the modernization of 350 T-72 tanks in 1995 for 13 bn Kc, when it now appears that the Czech Army will only need 30 of them, *Respekt*, 23 February 2004. Another strange procurement is the newly conceived purchase of Russian helicopters *Lidové noviny*, 14 February 2004, which, incomprehensibly, drags the Czech Republic back into dependence on Russian suppliers, a phenomenon that can be observed all over post-Communist Central Europe.

33 See note 2.

34 As asserted by the BIS report of October 2001 mentioned above.

Chapter 10
Poland's Security and Transatlantic Relations

Andrzej Kapiszewski with Chris Davis

Introduction

Which European head of state was first greeted in Washington by newly elected President George W. Bush? The Polish President. Which country in the world is the most pro-American, at least according to *The New York Times* columnist Thomas L. Friedman?[1] Poland. Who did Tony Blair and Gerhard Schröder try to convince to become next Secretary General of NATO? Polish President Aleksander Kwaśniewski.[2] Which country was called by the German press the American Trojan horse in Europe for supporting the US intervention in Iraq? Poland.[3] Was *The Economist* correct when it wrote on 10 May 2003: "Is Poland America's donkey or could it become NATO's horse? Polish-American diplomacy may be deepening the divisions in Europe – or paving the way to a post-Iraq rapprochement." How has Poland – a country that not so long ago was just one of many Soviet satellite states – become such an important though highly controversial country? Is it becoming an asset or a burden for a transatlantic alliance?

Additionally, what are the current threats to Polish security? Do old enemies continue to endanger Poland? And is Poland important again for European and Western security, as in the past when it protected the continent against Turkish or Russian invasions? Recall the Battle of Vienna in 1683 and the Battle of Warsaw 1920 – both won by Polish armies and considered two of the most important battles for Western civilization.[4] To answer these questions, one has to consider the following: the consequences of the 1989–1990 revolutions in Europe, the position of Poland in East-West relations, and its memberships in NATO and the European Union.

Since 1989, and for the first time in centuries, Poland has developed good relations with all its neighbors. Moreover, since becoming a member of NATO and the European Union, Poland has secured crucial political and military guarantees for all dimensions of its security. Joining these organizations has involved Poland in out-of-region conflicts. Finally, integration with the international community has introduced the country to complex political relations between Europe and America.

The understanding of security has changed significantly during the last few decades. In the past, security referred to the condition whereby a state and its people either were not threatened by outside aggression or were capable of repelling threats that did exist. Today, Poland's security is affected by economic, social, ecological, cultural, and ethnic issues. These are further linked to energy supplies, population migrations, environmental protection, religious freedoms, and cultural values. Moreover, the dynamic of security is more global in scope and is often characterized by uncertainty and the absence of a clearly defined aggressor. Poland remains in transition. Some of its policies are still based largely on the traditional concept of territorial defense rather than a modern security rationale, but Poland's approach to security continues to evolve.

Between East and West: Poland's Security Challenges in a Historical Context

Poland is a Central European country with 320 thousand square kilometers of territory and a population of thirty-nine million. It is smaller than the European 'key four' – Germany, France, Great Britain, and Italy – but largest among Central European countries joining NATO and the EU. The country is often described as the 'heart of Europe' due to its key geopolitical location and special position in East-West relations.[5] Geographically, Poland can be described as an East European country but in every other sense its strongest links have always been with the West.[6] This is where Polish culture has its roots. In centuries past, all of its elected rulers came from Western Europe. In the Middle Ages, due to its loyalty to the Roman Catholic Church, the powerful Polish kingdom was the 'Bulwark of Christendom,' a defender of Europe against eastern invaders. According to Norman Davies, "The Poles are more Western in their outlook than the inhabitants of most Western countries."[7] In later years, Poles fought to liberate a number of nations, especially in the nineteenth and twentieth centuries. During World War II, Poles fought Nazi Germany not only in Poland, but also in France, Britain, Norway, North Africa, Italy, Holland, and Belgium, before arriving in Berlin. In the last decades of the twentieth century, Poland also led the fight against communism.

At the same time, Poland's strong attachment to the West has usually been unreciprocated. Rarely have Western powers assured Polish security. This had dire consequences for Poland when it lost its independence at the end of the eighteenth century, when it led uprisings against Russians in the nineteenth century, and when it was assailed by Germany and Russia in 1939.

Situated along the strategic and historical East-West axis (Moscow-Berlin-Paris-London), Poland has throughout its history been ruined by the wars of great European powers. Whether Poland itself was invaded or its territories were used as corridors or frontlines for others, the Polish people have born the brunt of battle. Neighboring powers have always pushed hard against Poland's borders – and have sometimes succeeded in erasing them from the map. From the seventeenth century onwards, the Polish-Lithuanian commonwealth was in constant conflict with the Russian empire over the control of lands between the ethnic Polish and ethnic Russian territories. This typically resulted in Poland's defeat. For over a century, between 1795 and 1918, Russia, Prussia, and Austria occupied Poland. Soon after regaining independence in 1918, it was invaded by the Red Army. In September 1939, Germany and the Soviet Union invaded and occupied Poland again. During these events the country's infrastructure was destroyed, millions of Poles lost their lives (six million dead in World War II alone), and even more were deported or forced to emigrate. The Yalta and Potsdam Conferences of 1945 determined the post-war order and the fate of Poland. Stalin, Roosevelt, and Churchill moved Poland's borders west. Though Poland gained German territory to its west, it lost a third of its pre-war eastern territory to the Soviet Union. During the liberation of Poles from Nazi occupation in 1944 and 1945, the unwelcome ideology of communism was brought in on the backs of Russian tanks, replacing one form of oppression with another. The country fell into the Soviet sphere of influence and once again lost control over its sovereignty, this time for almost half a century.

Because of its turbulent history, even minor security issues have been treated as mortal undertakings for nearly every generation of Poles throughout Poland's thousand years of statehood. Poland's location between two powerful neighbors, Germany and Russia – both of which, historically, were hegemonic and imperial – has always determined Polish security policies. Any analysis of contemporary Poland is impossible without first understanding its past. In Poland's long history, "attachment to historical clichés has always been a feature of discussions about Poland's security."[8]

Poland's Security in the Aftermath of the 1989 Revolution

The year 1989 brought radical changes to Poland's political and economic system, to its notion of sovereignty and security, and to the daily lives of its people. After almost a decade of the 'Solidarity' movement, which culminated in the 'Round Table' talks between communist authorities and the democratic opposition, the totalitarian system crumbled. A new, non-communist government was formed following free and fair elections. The Soviet Union, where Gorbachev's *perestroika* was already under way, decided against military intervention in the rebellious country. This contrasted with past Kremlin reactions to similar pro-democratic movements, when punitive intervention was exacted on insubordinate countries. The subsequent collapse of communist regimes across Eastern Europe brought the dissolution of the Warsaw Pact, the Soviet's multinational military structure that facilitated control of its empire. One by one, newly liberated countries, led by Poland, demanded the prompt withdrawal of Russian troops from their territories (this task was accomplished in Poland by August 1993). By the late 1990s, as a consequence of the fall of the Berlin Wall, the two German states were unified. The disintegration of the Soviet Union at the end of 1991 enabled Lithuania, Ukraine, and Belarus to emerge as newly independent states on Poland's eastern border. To the southwest of Poland, Czechoslovakia split into two independent states. Thus, in a few short years the number of states bordering Poland increased from three to seven – all of which were new political entities.

These complex events forced Poland to quickly develop a new national defense policy. On 2 November 1992, Lech Walesa, then-Polish President, signed the 'Guidelines on Poland's Security Policy,' which emphasized cooperation with Western military and security organizations and rapprochement with neighboring states.

Poland's comprehensive new security doctrine took into account new threats and alliances in post-communist Europe, but also reflected the country's civilian economic priorities and budget constraints. To be effective, it had to address the sources of the region's security vacuum post-1989: the collapse of the old order and the absence of a new one, border disputes between new countries, and civil strife and armed conflict close to Polish territory. In particular, formulation of the Polish defense doctrine had to account for war in the Balkans, instability in Russia and Ukraine, and the possible return of Belarus into the Russian sphere of influence. It also had to tackle the domestic political and economic developments affecting the country's overall stability, such as the penetration of foreign intelligence into Polish government and the country's utter dependence on Russian oil.

A new doctrine, 'The Policy on Security and Defense Strategy of the Republic of Poland,' was eventually adopted by the government in January 2000. It stated that the country's primary goals were the protection of Poland's most vital interests, which include national security, the right to live in peace, state sovereignty and independence, and territorial integrity.[9] It also emphasized the unchanging character and inviolability of borders as the premise of European peace. Furthermore, the document asserted that Poland's security should become linked indispensably to the security of NATO and EU members. While recognizing the importance of international commitments and mutual assurances, the document underlined the role that Poland's economy needed to play to guarantee Polish security.

Poland also devised new national military policies that accounted for the dissolution of the Warsaw Pact and the closure of a Europe that had been divided into rival military camps. These policies recognized the limitations of adopting Russian military doctrine and training standards and put forth measures to overcome them. A reform program streamlined the Ministry of National Defense and the military's administration, and ultimately brought the military under civilian rule. Term limits in commanding positions were introduced and Parliament gained control over the defense budget. Attempts were also made to restore the armed forces to a national institution separate and above politics. Its prestige had been lost during communism because it was used to crush opposition reform movements. Post-communism, the paramilitary forces used by the Ministry of Internal Affairs to suppress civil unrest in the totalitarian state were either dissolved or redirected in order to manage Poland's genuine security threats. Within a decade Poland reduced its total number of troops from 400,000 to 150,000. It changed the composition of its armed forces by cutting conscript service from twenty-four months to twelve, with the goal of creating a fully professional contract army in a few years. By 2003, half the Polish Army had already been staffed with professionals. Structural reorganization followed: seventy-three garrisons were eliminated, forty percent of military property was relinquished, and a substantial portion of outdated inventory was decommissioned.[10] Polish troops have been deconcentrated along Poland's western borders and relocated to the east. To guarantee stable defense spending, the Polish Parliament adopted in May 2001 the Program of Restructuring, Technical Modernization, and Financing of the Polish Armed Forces in the Years 2001–2006. It provides for the continued scaling down of the Polish military in order to finance the upgrading of its crisis-management troops. The program reduces the units dedicated to territorial defense while increasing the number of units deployable for out-of-area crisis management. It also aims for one-third of the Polish armed forces to achieve full interoperability with NATO. The planned spending level would account for 1.95 percent of GDP.

To bring its armed forces up to NATO standards, successive governments in Warsaw have decided to replace Soviet-era armaments and equipment. In the early 2000s, Poland purchased eight Spanish EADS/CASA C-295 medium-range transport aircraft; 48 US-made F-16 fighter jets ($3.8 billion deal secured by the US long-term loan and off-set programs); 690 AMF Patria armored personnel carriers from Finland ($1.2 billion); and Israeli anti-tank 'Spike' missiles ($350 million). Modernization has been underway on the Polish fleet of aging MiG-29s and Su-22s jets, as well as its Mi-24 helicopters. Poland's military infrastructure has likewise been enhanced. Longstanding NATO members have offered assistance to new members in the education and training of its military personnel. They have also transferred excess military hardware in the form of grants. In what were the most significant security-assistance transfers to any new NATO member, the United States presented Poland with two decommissioned Perry Class frigates, four Sea Sprite helicopters, and six transport planes. Germany gave Poland twenty-three former East German MiG-29 fighter jets and over one hundred Leopard 2A4 tanks. Poland also obtained a Koben-class submarine from Norway.

It is worth mentioning that the Polish Army did not oppose the systems change and the pro-Western policy reorientation, despite having a majority of Russian-trained officers. General Wojciech Jaruzelski, long-term head of the Polish Army and the first President of the new Poland, did not block Poland's transformation. In the middle of his term, he even stepped down voluntarily to allow a fully democratic election of the next president. In 1990, Polish intelligence authorities – at that time still controlled by old, Soviet-linked officers – offered assistance to the US during the Gulf War.

Polish security after 1989 was closely connected to political changes within the country, its new relationship with the Western world, and the geopolitical reorganization of its region, which led to a swath of newly independent countries – and new relationships – that emerged along Poland's eastern borders.

Poland and Russia

One of the most important changes since 1989 has been Polish-Russian relations. Russia has finally admitted—albeit under Polish diplomatic pressure – that the Soviet Union committed crimes against Poland, especially during World War II. Under Stalin's orders, the murder of 4,000 Polish prisoners of war in a forest near the town of Katyn has negatively affected relations for years. President Boris Yeltsin, after assuming power in Russia, acknowledged Poland's sovereignty. This was noteworthy, considering it came from the leader of a country that had long considered Poland only a region in its empire. Russia became territorially distanced from Poland as the dissolution of the Soviet Union brought about the independence of three of its republics – Ukraine, Lithuania, and Belarus – forming a buffer between Poland and Russia. This resulted in improved affairs with Russia, more so than at any time since the eighteenth century.[11]

Nevertheless, some developments post-1989 still adversely affect Polish security. For example, Poland and Russia maintain a common border with the enclave of Kaliningrad, which is located on the Baltic Sea between Poland and Lithuania but has no land link to Russia proper. Kaliningrad is actually farther west than Warsaw, a strategic importance for Moscow. Poland's proximity to Russia has had considerable consequences. In 1995 Russian media and politicians began discussing (in their view) the necessity of building an 'extraterritorial' road through Poland, connecting the Kaliningrad enclave to Russian-linked Belarus. For Poles, this evoked Germany's demand in 1939 for a similar link to East Prussia through Polish territory. Hitler used Poland's refusal as a pretext to invade Poland and start World War II. What concerns Poland most about Kaliningrad is that it is a heavily militarized area. When in 2001 American media reported on the suspected presence of Russian nuclear weapons in the enclave, a national security crisis of sorts occurred in Poland, despite the fact that these weapons posed no genuine military threat to Poland's security.[12] Furthermore, Kaliningrad serves as a contact point between Russia and two new members (Poland and Lithuania) of NATO, the organization Russia historically perceives as hostile.

The collapse of the Soviet Union did not end Moscow's traditional policies toward its so-called 'near abroad.' For centuries, Russia believed that the need to defend itself justified controlling its neighboring states, whose complete sovereignty Russia was never ready to recognize.[13] All post-Soviet states in Russia's 'near abroad' have been formulated into Russian security policies. Currently, it is unclear whether Poland belongs in this zone. But in the early 1990s, Russian protests against NATO expansion suggested that Poland and several other East European states certainly were. Later, de facto Russian acceptance of NATO expansion required the Kremlin to modify this view. Nevertheless, some Russian political forces, such as Vladimir Zhirinovsky's nationalist party, have not abandoned the position. This continues to be a source of concern for Poles.

Other tensions in Polish-Russian relations developed over the 1990's. Poland's broad public support for the Chechens – which culminated in protests against Russian intervention in Chechnya – strained the Polish-Russian relationship even further. Also, Poles were highly critical of the treatment of Polish Catholic priests working in Russia. There were many complaints about the difficulties in recovering old Polish churches there and establishing new ones. In turn, the Russian Orthodox Church loudly criticized what they perceived as Polish attempts to spread Catholicism in Russia. Finally, Russians continued to block the access of Polish ships to the Baltic Sea through the Pilawska Strait and blocks Polish fishermen from operating in the Okhotsk Sea. In the second half of the 1990s, disagreements arose as Moscow tried to neutralize NATO's enlargement by proposing certain adaptations to the European Conventional Arms Reduction Treaty. These adaptations would have limited the previously agreed-upon reduction of Russian troops. Russia also criticized the establishment of the Polish-German-Danish corps located in the city of Szczecin. In 2000, relations deteriorated further when Poland expelled nine Russian diplomats accused of spying. In 2004, Russia expressed unease when Washington began consultations with Warsaw on establishing military bases in Poland. Poles have been reminded by Moscow that it agreed to German unification in exchange for Western assurances that any large bases would not be establish in Eastern Europe. In February 2004, Russian Defense Minister, Sergei Ivanov, told the 40th Annual Security Conference in Munich that the Treaty on Conventional Forces in Europe (CFE) "in its actual form cannot uphold stability and the balance of interests of the signatory states considering the actual military and political developments in Europe."[14] Ivanov complained that NATO was poised to start operating "in a zone of vitally important interests of our country," even though the Baltic states had not yet officially joined NATO (they are expected to join by May 2004). The Minister requested that Russia should have monitoring facilities at NATO bases "to verify the fact that the uses of those facilities, as we are told, pose no threat to Russia." Ivanov said the construction of NATO bases in Romania and Bulgaria may be justified for antiterrorism operations in the Middle East but asked what terrorist threat necessitates NATO bases in Poland and the Baltic states.

Another important issue in Polish-Russian relations has been Poland's energy security.[15] Most oil and gas consumed by Poland is imported from Russia. A 1996 gas deal between the two countries guarantees Poland's long-term purchase of large quantities of gas from Russia on the basis of payment-on-delivery. Despite its current demand and requests for cutbacks, the agreement locks Poland into buying these large amounts of gas well into the future.

In order to make deliveries more secure and to earn revenue from transit fees, Poland built through its territory a pipeline linking the enormous Russian Jamal gas fields with the Western European pipeline system. For even broader energy security, Poland would like to diversify its sources of imported energy. In the 1990s, Poland discussed with Norway the possibility of building pipelines to import gas from the Nordic Sea, but the project was economically unviable and eventually shelved. This project was revisited in 2004 when Russia stopped gas deliveries for a day due to a quarrel with Belarus, the transit country.

Polish-Russian oil and gas issues have remained problematic. From late 1999, the Kremlin pressed Warsaw to build a pipeline connecting Belarus to Slovakia instead of constructing the previously agreed upon second Jamal pipeline through Ukraine. In doing so, Russia wanted to diminish the role of Ukraine in the transit of Russian gas, a highly beneficial enterprise for Kiev. This put the Polish government in a delicate political situation, as Poland did not want to jeopardize its relations with either Russia or Ukraine. In the end, Russia ditched the project in exchange for more compliant, pro-Russian policies from Ukraine.

As a result, Poland began to criticize the unprofitable 1996 gas deal with Russia. Renegotiation of the agreement in early 2000 has done little to improve matters. Also in that year, a scandal arose with the discovery of a large fiber-optic line being built along the Jamal gas pipeline, hitherto unknown to Polish authorities.

Several times in the post-1989 era Poles have felt threatened by closer cooperation between Russia and key Western countries, especially when Poland was not consulted. Historically, there has been an inverse relationship between Poland's security and the West's cooperation with the Russia – this is to say, the more the West collaborates with or appeases Russia, the less secure Poland becomes. Still vivid in Poland are memories of the German-Soviet Non-Aggression Treaty of 1939 (the Ribbentrop-Molotov Pact), which partitioned Poland between the two powers. The Yalta Agreement let Poland fall into the Soviet camp after the war. Because of this, along with its "chronic distrust of the world," Poland protested its exclusion when the United States, France, England, and Russia began talks in 1990 about German reunification. Poland also lobbied hard to maintain NATO after the fall of communism when France seemed to yield to Russian demands that the Alliance be dissolved. More anxiety was generated when Poland and Lithuania began to prepare themselves for EU membership and re-introduced visas for Russians. Moscow strongly objected to having to request visas in order to cross Polish and Lithuanian borders on the way from Kaliningrad to the Russia proper. France took up the cause on Moscow's behalf, and Poland promptly criticized French President François Mitterrand's support of President Putin's request for special visa status for the citizens of Kaliningrad. Despite general improvements in perceptions of one another, a certain level of mistrust remains between Poland and Russia.[16] Russians are still reminded in schools that in the seventeenth century the Polish Army intervened in Russian affairs and captured Moscow. To this day, school children commemorate the Russian victory that drove them out. In turn, the numerous Russian invasions of Poland have been burned into Polish consciousness. Warsaw's victory over Russia when it invaded in 1920 is today commemorated as Polish Army Day. Recent events have done little to help Poles overcome their historical sensitivities. Russia has been painfully slow in coming to terms with the past and acknowledging its offenses to nations subjected to their rule.[17] It also continues to interfere in the internal affairs of the countries within its 'near abroad,' such as Belarus, Ukraine, or the Baltic states. This is perceived in Poland as further proof of Moscow's imperial ambitions in Eastern Europe.

Because of these memories and other more current observations, many Poles continue to believe that their country's independence is threatened by Russia.[18] At the beginning of the new millennium, Poles view Russia – and Vladimir Putin in particular – with deep suspicion. These misgivings have heavily influenced Polish security and defense policies and explain why Poland still attaches primacy to its territorial defense. It also complicates Poland's relation with West European countries and the US, which view such an approach to Russia as anachronistic.

Poland and Ukraine, Belarus, and the Baltic States

Ukraine and the Baltic states, especially Lithuania, impact Polish security not only because they share a border with Poland, but also because they affect Polish-Russian relations.

The appearance of an independent Ukraine, the largest country in Eastern Europe, with considerable military potential and a strategic geopolitical location, has had enormous implications for the region. This can be summarized by the axiom: "an independent Ukraine = a non-imperial Russia."[19] Poland, with vital interests in an autonomous and stable Ukraine, was the first country to recognize Ukraine's independence in December 1991. Since then, both countries have maintained close ties, often characterized as a 'strategic partnership.' Poland, out of its own self-interest but also in the broader interest of the West, has tried to help Ukraine establish a democracy. Poland would also like to see Ukraine eventually join NATO and the EU, though Russia has tried desperately to keep this country out of the Western sphere of influence.

Ukrainians themselves have been indecisive about their direction, and their politics have lacked consistency and assurance. Consequently, the West has often been discouraged by the government in Kiev and Poland has had to redouble its efforts to help Ukraine to reform and become a pro-Western country.[20] When NATO established in 1997 a 'special partnership' with Ukraine, Poland – even before it become a formal NATO member – actively participated in the activities of the NATO-Ukraine Commission. In the second half of the 1990s, Poland and Ukraine formed a military battalion, which began in 2000 its mission in Kosovo. There have also been instances when Poland has acted as an important third party in relations between Ukraine and the West – which soured in the Fall of 2002 when Ukrainian President Leonid Kuchma was accused of authorizing the sale of sophisticated military radars to Iraq. Relations further deteriorated in late 2003 when Ukrainian authorities took undemocratic steps to allow Kuchma to seek a third presidential term. In each instance Poland faced the dilemma of either hampering its relations with the Ukraine or, by continuing to court Kuchma, risking a reproach from the West. Poland attempted to resolve this dilemma when it organized the conference, "Ukraine in Europe." It attempted to help Ukrainians find consensus over domestic political issues by bringing together representatives of the Ukrainian government and its opposition, and included the EU's Foreign and Security Policy Chief, Javier Solana.

Overall, since 2002, Poland has been disappointed with Kiev's inability (or unwillingness) to deepen political and economic transformation and reorient itself westward. At times, it has even chosen to move closer to Moscow. Despite Poland's positive engagement with Ukraine in the international arena and the close ties that exist between the highest authorities of both countries, relations have often been spoiled by bitter memories of Polish-Ukrainian clashes during both world wars and their aftermath. Polish public opinion turned sharply when authorities in the city of Lvov (a place significant in both Polish and Ukrainian history) blocked the opening of the renovated Polish cemetery – an event the presidents of both countries had agreed to long in advance.

Poland's relations with Belarus after 1990 have been in the context of Polish security.[21] Clearly, Poland desires a border with another democratic, pro-market country in the East. The victory of autocratic forces in Belarus in 1994 and the pro-Moscow policies of President Alexander Lukashenko have set the country back. Unwilling to sever contacts with its strategically situated neighbor, Warsaw has maintained a 'critical dialogue' with Minsk. Poland has preserved contacts at lower levels while criticizing Belarus for its human rights abuses and stifling of democracy.

On the contrary, changes that occurred in Lithuania and other Baltic states have actually reinforced Poland's security. These countries refused to join the Russian-crafted Commonwealth of Independent States and decided instead to apply for NATO and EU membership. They also abandoned an earlier one-way course that would have enhanced links exclusively to Nordic countries. Collaboration in security matters has strengthened the Baltic's ties with Poland. Most important has been the relationship between Warsaw and Vilnius. Poland endorsed the establishment of an independent Lithuania determined to join Western institutions. As with Ukraine, however, Polish-Lithuanian relations have suffered from a troubled, shared history. The source of most disputes is the minorities living in both countries. Fortunately, these tensions have not been detrimental. The establishment of a Polish-Lithuanian combined military battalion (LITPOLBAT) in 1997–1998 symbolized their friendship and mutual trust.

As a consequence of joining NATO and the EU, Poland's role vis-à-vis some of its Eastern neighbors has become more problematic. Ukraine's relations with these institutions remain distant and there is no indication that they will change in the foreseeable future. Belarus will likely isolate itself further from the West. Poland's transition to democracy and a market economy is near completion, though similar reforms in the Ukraine and Belarus have not yet been undertaken. Thus, as Poland continues to advance at a pace far greater than its eastern neighbors, it will be even more difficult for Poland to build bridges between these countries and the West.

Poland and Germany

Equally important to the security of Poland – and to Europe as a whole – has been the reunification of Germany. The establishment of a very powerful country in the middle of the continent has been a challenge for many in Europe.[22] The question for Poland was whether or not a unified Germany would finally accept Poland's borders and the impact they would have on Europe's territorial order. (The Potsdam Conference in 1945 readjusted Poland's borders ostensibly to compensate the Poles for lands lost in the East. This effectively shifted Poland westward into traditional German territory, demarcating the Oder and Neisse Rivers as the new Polish-German border until a final peace treaty could be signed.) The border dispute had been the longest-standing political quarrel between Poland and Germany since the end of World War II. Fortunately, Poland had little to fear this time. As early as November 1990, Poland and Germany signed a permanent border agreement. In June 1991, the comprehensive treaty on 'Good Neighborliness, Friendship, and Co-Operation' was signed, which addressed matters such as the status of the German minority in Poland and the Polish minority in Germany.

Bordering Germany has now become a historic opportunity for post-communist Poland. In only a few short years Germany has become Poland's most valued neighbor. It is Poland's greatest trading partner and it strongly promotes Polish access to Western organizations, especially the European Union.

The two countries' opinions of one another are generally much improved since 1989. However, because Poland's accession to the EU will open up the country to unrestricted flows of people and capital, many Poles – especially those living in territories that belonged to Germany before World War II – worry that Germans will return and reacquire their old lands. On the other hand, Germans have expressed fears about the potential influx of low-wage Polish laborers that could worsen German unemployment.

Considering the burden of Polish-German history, and the fact that they still considered each other as enemies even during communism, relations in the 1990s were highly constructive. They have rightly been compared to the earlier transformation in Franco-German relations, which became a cornerstone of European peace and stability. Nevertheless, some issues have remained unresolved: Germany has been reluctant to implement the agreed-upon changes to its history curriculum and teaching materials, making them more objective; German refugee organizations have continued to demand compensation for the private property confiscated from Germans expelled from the territories transferred to Poland after the war; both countries have disputed the restitution of art and state treasures found on either side of the border in the aftermath of the war; and they have disagreed over quotas allowing Polish laborers to work in Germany.

Unfortunately, the level of trust began to change by the end of the 1990s. This resulted from the challenges faced by Poland's negotiations on EU accession and the emerging controversies concerning the future of transatlantic relations, which both countries have approached differently.[23] In 2003, Polish-German relations further deteriorated over Poland's participation in the US campaign against Iraq. German Defense Minister Peter Struck reacted angrily to the Polish proposal to commit German troops to the Polish-led international division in Iraq.[24] More problems surfaced over the EU constitution and a project that was backed by the Bundestag to establish a Center of the Expelled in Berlin. This commemorates the Germans forced to leave the aforementioned territories given to Poland after World War II. Poles view this as an attempt to allay German guilt for the war.

Poland and the United States

Building strong ties to the United States has become the most important goal of Polish foreign policy in post-1989 era.[25] Polish governments, unconvinced that Polish security could be guaranteed by European partners, have placed their trust in America. For the US, Poland's success with democratization and the introduction of a free market economy represented a victory in the lengthy war against communism. In addition, Poland and America have parallel political interests. Both consider the North Atlantic Alliance a crucial element for security in Europe. They also agree that maintaining the Alliance's cohesion and efficiency is a prerequisite for all other security initiatives. In these circumstances, Poland has become for the US a close ally in Europe. At times Poland has been trusted even more than some of the older members of the transatlantic alliance. Poland even represented American interests in Saddam Hussein's Iraq. Poland's standing in the US was bolstered during the war in the Balkans, and because of the anti-Western trends of Russian politics. This state of affairs convinced the first Bush and the Clinton administrations to expand the area of stability and security in Europe by strengthening their positions in Central and Eastern Europe. Poland, the largest and most pro-American country in the region, was well-suited to play a special role in these endeavors. As a result, the 1990s witnessed an improvement in what were already close bilateral ties between Poland and the US. The two countries also undertook several regional initiatives, including the Polish-American-Ukrainian Cooperation Initiative.

The most important security goal for post-communist Poland was obtaining membership in NATO, which required US support. Early on, Washington was cautious about NATO's expansion eastward because the Kremlin was adamantly against it. But Poland and other Central European countries pushed hard for membership. The unstable situation east of Poland and in the Balkans made NATO expansion logical. The "Partnership for Peace Program" was initially perceived in

Poland as a delaying tactic proposed by the US, but in fact it enabled both sides to better prepare for the decisive move. Finally, in 1997 the Clinton Administration paved the way for Poland, Hungary, and the Czech Republic to join NATO. The decision to expand the organization was approved by all its members in 1999. In the process, American authorities offered Poland substantial military aid. To modernize its armed forces in order to comply with NATO standards, Poland obtained a $150 million loan from the US. In addition, Polish officers were allowed to study at US military academies. Washington lifted a number of trade restrictions, which enabled Poland to purchase the latest generation of armaments. The US has since become a major supplier of military equipment to Poland.

Another key factor in US-Polish relations is the large Polish ethnic group – over nine million – living in the US. Poles have been a part of American history from its very beginning. They were among the founders of the first colony in Jamestown. They also fought in the War of Independence and in the War of Secession, during which time Polish heroes – Generals Tadeusz Kosciuszko and Kazimierz Pulaski – played important roles. Later, waves of Polish immigrants helped build America's powerful economy. Polish-Americans continue to send remittances back to Poland. In Washington, Polish-Americans have lobbied successfully for Poland's interests abroad.

Historically, US governments have always advanced the Polish cause. The reclamation of Polish independence in 1918 was aided by President Woodrow Wilson's position on Polish statehood – despite the many obstacles created by European powers at the time. After World War II, many West Europeans criticized the prolonged stationing of US troops in their countries; Poles, on the contrary, valued this not just as a guarantee against further Soviet imperialism, but also as the continent's best chance to expel communism. During the Cold War period, Americans did much to sustain the Polish people, especially by assisting Polish underground movements and the 'Solidarity' trade union. Crucially, America's stand with Poland may well have prevented a Russian invasion in 1980. After 1989, Washington encouraged the economic and political transformation of Poland.

Given this history, Poles are unafraid of the US becoming the world's sole superpower, and are ready to support it as a guarantor of democracy and freedom. This attitude was confirmed by President Kwasniewski during his visit to the US in January 2003. He applauded America's leading role in the world, stating that it is "unquestionable" and that it "should be exercised."[26] Polish political elites, like their US counterparts, are generally skeptical about the efficacy of multilateralism in *all* cases, and are concerned about the redundancy of additional multilateral security institutions that could diminish the role of NATO and to some extent the UN.[27] Poles believe that the policies and impotence of the League of Nations encouraged the development of German revisionism, which subsequently led to World War II. Similarly, they partly blame the United Nations for leaving Poland on the wrong side of the Iron Curtain. Consequently, and unlike West European states, Poland does not seek to restrain American supremacy; in fact, Warsaw contends that its interests are best served by the preservation of American strength in the world. Moreover, most of Poland's political elites, influenced by the country's traditional 'strategic' and cultural predispositions, are not averse to the concept of preemptive engagement when confronted by a threat to regional stability. Poles remember well the costs of West European pacifism, of France and Britain's appeasement of Hitler and their subsequent failure to defend Poland in September 1939.

Some politicians, like the American ambassador to Poland, Christopher R. Hill, go even further, arguing that "the Poles and Americans have similar attitudes towards security and foreign policy in general."[28] As Zborowski and Longhurst noted, "interestingly, the sources of this concord are quite different for each of these two states. In the case of America they result from its power; in the case of Poland they are rooted in its relative weakness."[29]

In Poland, Atlanticism has become dogma and European anti-Americanism is greeted with suspicion. President Kwasniewski once asked rhetorically who would defend Poland in times of crisis, the United States or the Weimar Triangle (Poland's three-way partnership with Germany and France)? Opinion polls support such views. In 2001, among persons convinced that Polish independence is threatened, twenty-four percent believed that Poland could count on the United States, with twelve percent trusting Germany, and ten percent France.[30]

It is interesting to note that Polish-American cooperation in the post-communist era began with Iraq. When in 1990 Saddam Hussein unexpectedly attacked Kuwait, American CIA operatives in Iraq were caught by surprise and failed to evacuate in time. With the operatives' lives at risk, Washington turned to Poland. This was not such an obvious move at the time – the communist system had barely started to come apart. The Polish people already had their democratically elected Prime Minister, but the President of the country and the crucial Ministers of Internal Security and Defense remained communist. Nevertheless, the Polish intelligence apparatus decided to help the Americans. With Polish passports in hand, together with Polish construction workers, the CIA agents were smuggled out of Iraq. Following this, Poland supplied Americans with detailed maps of Baghdad that had previously been created by Polish cartographers at Iraq's request. In so doing, Poland contributed to some of the coalition's military actions during Operation Desert Storm in 1991. In exchange, Washington helped Poland repay some of its communist-era debts.

After 9/11, fighting terrorism became a priority of the Polish-American security agenda. Without hesitating, Poland backed the US campaign in Afghanistan, even sending Polish troops. In November 2001, Warsaw organized a Central and East European summit devoted to fighting terrorism. The Polish government began to work closely with the US on such matters as blocking the financing of terrorist's organizations and restricting the movement of suspected terrorists.

Since 2001, the military partnership between Poland and the US has strengthened considerably. Poland was among the few European states that supported Washington's missile defense program, and offered its territory for missile defense radars and launch pads. The two countries also established the Military Cooperation Working Group in 2002. It enhanced joint training; provided greater interoperability in nuclear, biological, and chemical weapons defense; increased work on missile defense; and helped to modernize Poland's defense-acquisition process.[31] In July of 2002, following a state visit by President Kwaśniewski, a joint statement with President Bush was released. It reaffirmed "the deep friendship and vibrant alliance between the United States and Poland" and stated a willingness "to expand cooperation between [their] armed services both to deepen [their] military-to-military relations, and in particular to promote needed transformation in [Polish] defense."[32]

In March 2003, as the political strife in the Security Council between the US and the Franco-German-Russian alliance was nearing its climax, Poland – along with seven other European countries – sent a letter to President Bush supporting his policies on Iraq.[33] Though the "Letter of Eight" was signed by the British, Italian, Spanish, Portuguese, Danish, Czech, and Hungarian prime ministers, France and Germany singled out Poland for criticism. They were infuriated that a country so dependent on them for EU admission had not followed their lead, but had instead proclaimed an independent and pro-American foreign policy. Several commentators in France and Germany once again labeled Poland as America's Trojan horse in Europe, or as a country bought by the US in order to advance American interests on the continent. Jacques Chirac undiplomatically criticized Poland as a newcomer to world politics, saying that in serious debates it should know its place and keep quiet.[34]

Despite this, Poland resolved to stay the course and to send its soldiers to Iraq. Poland contributed the largest contingent of troops after the US and Great Britain, almost 2500 soldiers. British newspapers, such as *The Times* and *The Guardian*, rightly compared Polish policy toward the US to that of Tony Blair's: acceptance of a leading but not dominant role of the US in the world; convergence of values and interests; and a readiness to cooperate, stopping short of subordination.

Throughout the war, the Bush administration praised Polish participation in what became knows as the 'Coalition of the Willing.' President Bush, in his address to the Polish people during his visit to Krakow in May 2003, declared that "America will not forget that Poland rose to that moment."[35] Nevertheless, involvement in the Iraqi campaign caused the US to lose some of its support in Poland. Positive views of the US have fallen to 50 percent in March 2003 – from nearly 80 percent six months earlier.[36]

In Iraq, Poland has been given the task of running one of four administrative zones. A Polish General now commands an international division of stabilization forces in that zone. Marek Belka, the former Polish finance minister, has been appointed deputy head of the American-run Office of Reconstruction and Humanitarian Assistance and the Chairman of the Council for International Cooperation for the Reconstruction of Iraq. These were important tasks and appointments, seen as confirmation that Poland's position in the international community was indeed growing.

Goodwill and partnership between the United States and Poland have been possible because Poles have always had a special (and typically uncritical) esteem for the US. On the 150th Anniversary of America's Independence, Poland presented to US President Coolidge "A Polish Declaration of Admiration and Friendship for the United States of America." The 111 volume gift, containing the signatures of some 5.5 million Polish citizens – one-sixth of the total population at the time – was probably the largest expression of affection one nation ever made to another. In public opinion surveys, Poles have always viewed Americans most favorably. In a 2003 survey, 58 percent of Poles declared sympathy toward Americans, with 51 percent toward both the French and British, and 28 percent toward Germans.[37] American presidents have likewise garnered positive opinions in Poland. In polls conducted in July 2002, 73 percent of Poles had a positive view of George W. Bush. Only 8 percent had a negative view, in strong contrast to opinions of him in Western Europe.[38]

Nevertheless, a few problems remain despite the partnership's success. There is a major disagreement over US visa policies for Poles, who are frustrated at having to apply for a visas to America. In addition, Polish firms have not won contracts for the reconstruction of Iraq. Some pundits in Poland have even predicted an impasse between the two countries if they cannot resolve these matters soon.

Poland and France and Great Britain

Relations between Poland and France in the post-1989 period, although generally friendly, have been in the opinion of many Poles rather disappointing.[39] Close historical ties do exist between the two countries. French royals became kings of Poland, and many Poles fought in Napoleon's armies. In the nineteenth and twentieth centuries, Paris welcomed Polish emigrants and political and economic refugees. During World War II, Polish troops fought alongside the French. Despite these ties, in the early 1990s French President Mitterrand treated Poland as a country within the German sphere of influence. He was one of the very few European leaders that did not find time to visit the new Poland. France was opposed to quick enlargement of NATO and the EU, seeming to care little for the security interests of Europe's newly liberated states. The Weimar Triangle was not as productive as Poland would have liked, primarily because France lacked interest in the partnership. In the late 1990s, anxieties between France and Poland intensified as Poland voiced concerns about the European Defense and Security Initiative (ESDI) and supported America's plan to develop a missile defense system. Poland's stance on both these initiatives was seen in Paris as anti-European—or even worse, pro-American. In a characteristic move, France did not sign the final declaration of the "Community of Democracies" ministerial conference in Warsaw in 2000—a conference organized by Poland and the United States and attended by 107 countries. Given their history of mutual assistance and peaceful coexistence, it is surprising that most of the existing problems in Franco-Polish relations derive from differences over of European security.

Conversely, relations between Poland and Great Britain in the 1990s were healthy and productive. The two countries collaborated closely during World War II. Polish forces actively participated in the Battle of Britain and fought alongside British forces on all fronts while the Polish government in exile resided in London throughout the war. After the Cold War, both governments agreed on NATO's importance to European security. Consensus between the two governments led to closer ties, especially after the Labor Party came to power in 1997.[40] British advisors began working in the Polish Ministry of Defense and with the General Staff. British forces also used firing ranges in Poland and soldiers from both countries fought in Afghanistan and in the Balkans. Warsaw and London – the two leading European countries supporting the US position on Iraq – cooperated further during the military campaign to remove Saddam Hussein. As a result, Great Britain remains one of Poland's most important allies in Europe. The only concern Poles have about London is it often neglects other East European states and instead promotes greater contact between Moscow and NATO, a move not always favored by Warsaw.

Poland's Perception of its Security

Polish politics in the post-1989 era focused on linking the country with the democratic West.[41] However, Poland's successful reintegration depended on the attitudes of key Western countries. These countries were caught by surprise at the speed of East European revolutions and the disintegration of the Soviet bloc. Many Western governments feared the collapse of communism could revive the ardent nationalism in Europe. Interstate conflicts, border disputes, and ethnic tensions were also legitimate concerns. In response, they tried – often unsuccessfully – to exert influence on Central and East European politicians to ensure stabilization. The Russian factor was also critical. Western politicians did not want the events in Eastern Europe to jeopardize Russian interests. They seemed to acquiesce to the Kremlin doctrine that required a "historically justified Russian security zone," forgetting who had historically threatened whom.

Polish political and economic reforms obtained necessary support from Western Europe and the United States. Washington seemed to understand more clearly than some of its European partners the historical implications of the Polish-inspired revolutions. The US championed the politics of the new Polish government and after initial reservations engaged itself in the security arrangements for Central and East Europe. At the same time, Washington worked successfully with Russia – an essential task for global and regional security, since Russia remained a nuclear power.

In the early 1990s Germany was preoccupied with reunification and remained unsure about the benefits of including Central and East European countries in NATO, preferring instead some form of Russia-NATO association. Later on, however, the German government became convinced (more so than many others) about the importance of spreading democracy, prosperity, and stability farther east. Despite costs of its unification, Germany provided Poland with substantial economic aid during the 1990s.

The attitude of other West European countries toward changes in Central and East Europe was often indifference. During the Cold War, Western Europe achieved high levels of growth and prosperity – and it did so without involving eastern part of the continent. Many in the West had serious doubts about Eastern Europe's ability to adapt quickly to capitalism, western business practices, and liberal-democratic politics, all of which had take the West many decades – if not centuries – to cultivate.

As a result of friendly cooperation with its neighbors and eventually joining NATO, Poland enhanced its security considerably in the 1990s. Yet some Poles remained convinced that the independence of Poland was not fully secure.

Table 10.1   Year/percentage of respondents who believed that Poland's independence was threatened

1991	1992	1993	1994	1995	1996	1997	1998	1999	2000	2001
44	28	22	21	33	27	19	16	27	13	19

Source: Public Opinion Research Center, "Sytuacja Polski na arenie miedzynarodowej" [Poland's Situation in the International Arena], July 2001.

Soon after transformation had begun, during the re-unification of Germany and collapse of the Soviet Union, as many as 44 percent of Poles believed that Poland's independence was still threatened. That percentage decreased over the next four years, only to spike again as a result of crises in the Balkans during 1995 and 1999, and 9/11 in 2001. Most respondents mentioned Russia as the country to fear most (64 percent in 2001—to only 12 percent that feared Germany). Poles also maintain the conviction that Russia will attempt to regain its influence in Central and Eastern Europe.

Table 10.2   Year/percentage of respondents believing that in the future Russia will try again to regain its influence in Eastern Europe

1993	1994	1995	1996	1997	1998	1999	2000	2001	2004
39	53	72	69	63	59	53	60	68	48

Source: Public Opinion Research Center, "Sytuacja Polski na arenie miedzynarodowej" [Situation of Poland on the international arena], July 2001 and February 2004.

Poland in the European Union: the Security Dimension

As Poland and other Central and East European countries integrate themselves into western political and military structures, they have been increasingly attentive to the development of a common European defense. After the revolutions, Warsaw in particular sought to expand and institutionalize Poland's contacts with the West European Union (WEU), perceived at that time as a potential European pillar of NATO. In June 1992, the WEU and eight Central European states established a Consultative Forum to discuss issues of European security. In 1994, Poland became an 'associate partner' of WEU, and in 1999 became an 'associate member.' Achieving this status allowed Poland to participate in certain WEU activities, including military exercises.[42]

Poland's official security strategy viewed participation in the EU's security structures as important for the country as its membership of NATO. But Poland was skeptical and unenthusiastic about Union's defense initiatives, especially the common European Security and Defense Policy (ESDP). Poles were afraid that ESDP could undermine NATO in the future, and that Europeans would soon be reluctant to back US positions abroad. This would allow Russia to gain more influence over European security, jeopardizing Polish interests. Poles argued that the EU should develop their defense capabilities within NATO's European Security and Defense Identity (ESDI) scheme; otherwise, the structures would be duplicated, and competition between them would weaken the Alliance. Moreover, authorities in Warsaw were unhappy that the planned ESDP excluded from the actual decision-making process those European NATO members that did not yet belong to the EU. For Poles, NATO's Partnership for Peace Program, and other initiatives involving members and non-members of the organization, should serve as a proper model for security cooperation. Polish ministers on different occasions criticized the EU's plans as unclear and lacking military and operational viability.[43] It was only the EU summit in Portugal, in June 2000, which accepted Poland's proposal to include six non-EU European NATO members into the ESDP discussions. These six were also given an opportunity to participate in the Political and Security Committee, a liaison body between the ESDP and CFSP. Poland was also able to establish contacts with the EU Military Committee.[44]

While trying to present Poland as a nation committed to European integration and to alleviate concerns of some EU member states, President Aleksander Kwaśniewski was able to say in 2001 that "ESDP is a commendable effort, guided by vision, and implemented with courage, that Poland salutes."[45] Similar pro-ESDP statements were made at that time by the Polish Foreign Minister, Wladyslaw Bartoszewski, who argued that Poland should be actively engaged in European security developments—that failing to do so could cost the country dearly, as in the past.[46] Characteristic of contemporary Polish declarations on security, however, are statements declaring that the EU should never attempt to substitute for the Atlantic Alliance.[47]

In the years that followed, Poland has confirmed its preparedness to contribute to the EU's Rapid Reaction Force and the EU's civilian instruments for crisis management. Poland contributed to the first EU autonomous police mission in Bosnia and Herzegovina, which the UN handed over on 1 January 2003. Poland has participated in a series of UN (SFOR, KFOR, and ISAF) and OSCE peacekeeping and observing operations. Furthermore, Poland has passed its own legislation and ratified international conventions in response to terrorism, and has aligned itself with the EU's Action Plan and the Common Positions. Poland also complies with sanctions regimes imposed by the UN and the EU, and its legislation adheres to the EU *Acquis Communautaire* and the EU Code of Conduct for Arms Exports.

Poland's EU membership will enable Poland to use the units it has assigned to NATO intervention forces as units serving under the EU flag. Thanks to the cooperation of neighboring countries, Poland will be able to deploy a contingent of up to 8000 soldiers under EDSP.[48] This affords Poland the political and moral rights to help make political decisions under the EU's Second Pillar. It also gives Poland – despite its economic weakness – a greater say in the funding of EU programs.

Poland will enter an EU whose military spending has been declining for years, especially in relation to the US, Russia, and China. The reality is that Poland is not simply acceding to a west European political structure, but also (though in degrees) to a more socialist, anti-war west European political culture. In terms of foreign and security policy, this political culture increasingly promotes the application of 'soft power' and the redirection of military expenditures to offset spending on social programs and international aid. This spending has resulted in large budget deficits for Poland. But the EU Growth and Stability Pact will require Poland to limit public deficits to three percent of GDP. As Poland also aspires to join the euro, it will have to maintain fiscal discipline in order to meet the economic criteria of the Euro-zone. To accomplish all of this while transforming and modernizing its military will be extremely difficult.

Poland and a Transforming NATO

NATO expansion eastward reflects a radical change in the dimensions of European, American, and global security. In merely a decade the world witnessed the collapse of the Berlin Wall and the Soviet Union, the dissolution of the Warsaw Pact, and the germination of democracy in Central and East Europe. Initially, some politicians in Poland considered neutrality or nonalignment, modeled principally on Switzerland or Austria. But such ideas proved unrealistic. Poland bordered several newly independent states formed from the remnants of the Soviet Union, including a nuclear-armed Ukraine and a highly unpredictable new Russia, prone to coup attempts and economic calamity. For Poland, the scope of political realities east of the so-called Curzon Line was impetus enough to reorient itself westward.

In July 1994, in Warsaw, President Clinton declared that the time had come to discuss NATO's future. Contacts between Poland and NATO were increased and Polish military successfully cooperated with NATO forces in Bosnia. The Clinton's administration sent strong signals about the possibility of enlarging the transatlantic alliance.[49] Secretary of State Madeleine Albright referred to enlargement as "an essential part of a broader strategy to build an undivided, democratic, and peaceful Europe."[50]

Not everyone in the US supported this approach, however. George F. Kennan wrote in *The New York Times* on 5 February 1997, that a decision to expand NATO "would be the most fateful error of American policy in the entire post-cold war era" and "may be expected to inflame the nationalistic, anti-Western and militaristic tendencies in Russian opinion; to have an adverse effect on the development of Russian democracy; to restore the atmosphere of the cold war to Eat-West relations; and to impel Russian foreign policy decidedly not to [US] liking."

In contrast to Kennan's arguments, David Kay noted the strong geostrategic premise for including Poland in transatlantic structures: By "extending American power through NATO between a rising unified Germany and a declining post-Soviet Russia, the historic risk of great power competition over this strategic area could be reduced."[51]

Membership in NATO has required the transformation of Poland's own military in order to achieve interoperability within the alliance. By signing on to NATO's Defense Capabilities Initiative (DCI) and the Prague Capabilities Commitment

(PCC), Poland has committed itself to improving its ability to respond to twenty-first century global threats. Until recently, Poland's military has been predicated on Cold War, continental strategic scenarios and outfitted with dated Soviet technology and hardware. Some reforms are underway already. Even so, Poland has recently had problems with fulfilling its NATO commitments, namely its readiness to provide at least two brigades for a single NATO mission.

From a Polish perspective, the transformation of NATO – and for that matter, the existence of NATO – is still a variable in the calculations of its national and regional security interests. The constant is America's commitment to the stability and organization of Europe, including a military presence.

On the other hand, a strong Poland in a strong NATO complicates an increasingly separatist continental European security policy, led mainly by France and Germany. Fearing a duplication of resources and marginalization in an increasingly centralized European superstate, Poland has a vested interest in a revitalized, relevant NATO. Such a NATO, with Poland in it, could strengthen Poland within its region and on the continent. In this context, Poland has been a staunch supporter of a further eastward enlargement of NATO.

On 12 September 2001, Poland and every other NATO member invoked Article 5 concerning common defense. Shortly thereafter, these members placed resources at US disposal in order to combat terrorism. On 22 November, the Polish government approved the participation of Polish troops in 'Operation Enduring Freedom' in Afghanistan. While Poland was not threatened directly by terrorist attacks, it nevertheless felt that its values – and Western civilization – had been assaulted. Furthermore, 9/11 had broader implications for European security. Although Polish participation in this particular campaign has not been large-scale, it has been appreciated by all members of the Alliance.[52] When NATO took over the responsibility for the Afghanistan's operation, Poland continued to participate in it.

The year 2003 brought further cooperation between Poland and NATO: a joint force training center was established in the city of Bydgoszcz; Adam Kobieracki became the Assistant Secretary General of NATO for Operations; and Poland obtained NATO intelligence and logistical support for its mission in Iraq. Warsaw hopes that NATO will eventually assume command of Poland's multinational division in Iraq.

Poland and the Transatlantic Alliance Post-9/11

Divisions have opened up across both Europe and the Atlantic. If 9/11 buried once and for all the anachronistic, Cold War strategic thinking in Europe and America, then the war in Iraq destroyed the hopes of rebuilding a common, strategic world view. Warner Weidenfeld notes that, "where it was once fashionable to speak of a paradigm change, one now soberly acknowledges paradigm atrophy."[53]

Poland insists that choosing between Europe and America is a false choice. In terms of its security, both now and in the future, keeping America engaged in Europe is more important for Poland than developing a common European defense. European-wide integration has already lost much of its thrust. Forging a supranational entity on par with the US is less likely now than before the war in

Iraq. Inasmuch as the events leading up to the war created divisions within Europe, they revealed many more. As Poland knows all too well, this is because "Europe has no common perception of war and peace – each nation's own historical trauma is too different to permit such a shared basis."[54]

Perhaps the most accurate view of Poland in the context of transatlantic relations post-Iraq is that of a country *between* power and weakness.[55] Though Robert Kagan's thesis begins a new discourse on transatlantic relations, it presumes that Europe is unified – or that it remains something more like the old WEU. This takes for granted the role a country like Poland already plays in the EU's global affairs, especially since the Union lacks a viable CFSP. Though Poland is economically a net beneficiary of the EU budget and is not yet a political powerbroker within Europe, the US can still accord it coequal status in its dealings across the Atlantic. Though it has virtually no economic leverage, Poland does possess a degree of political leverage: Poland's dissent from Paris and Berlin, especially in times of crisis, and especially when allied with Britain, can alter the present course of the European project.

Against the US, by contrast, Poland likewise possesses a degree of political leverage: its participation in Iraq, its support for US missile defense, and its support for Bush's global war on terrorism. Already, authorities in Warsaw are testing their relationship with the US on the matter of US visas for Polish nationals. Though the US has demonstrated willingness for unilateral action, coalition building – with real partners, not on paper but on the ground – will be vital to an overstretched US military and an administration increasingly isolated and resented abroad. Poland can play here an important role as a 'regional leader.'[56]

America naturally expects Europe to project a united strength in defense of Western interests and ideals. Increasingly, however, Poland's greatest security threat is being dragged by the US into a conflict abroad. This complicity with the US could make it a terrorist target. As well, belligerence abroad could undermine tranquility at home, especially if such a campaign is perceived abroad as American imperialism.

Conclusion

Poles entered the twenty-first century with a greater sense of security and with the conviction that they are no longer destined to be dominated by their powerful neighbors, Germany and Russia.[57] Reconciliation with long-time foes has allowed Poland to exorcise its past ghosts and to establish fruitful cooperation within Europe. Polish-German relations at the beginning of the new century have been better than at any other point in history. Poland has also established strategic alliances with Ukraine and Lithuania and continues to work with Russia. Relations with Czech Republic, Slovakia, and Hungary have remained traditionally close, and Poland continues to serve as an important contact in the west for Belarus.

In this context, Poland has become a bridge connecting east to west. This has enabled Western Europe to access essential new markets and resources, and has paved the way for Eastern membership in EU and NATO membership. Poland has fostered political stability and security not only of the region, but also the whole of Europe and beyond.

In the larger sphere of European security, Poland officially supports both the strengthening of CFSP and the development of ESDP. However, it retains certain doubts about these issues. Poland remains dedicated foremost to NATO and the transatlantic alliance, on which its external security depends entirely. As such, movement toward ESDP would have to solve two basic dilemmas for Poland. The first dilemma is reconciling its national sovereignty with European political integration. Having spent three quarters of a century under a Soviet imperial yoke, Poles find harnessing a Western one simply unacceptable. EU expansion will place direct pressure on Poland's eastern borders. Illegal immigration, along with drug and human trafficking, will add new security challenges for a country that now delineates a new and extended European Union. For Poland, maintaining its tactical relationship with Washington is fully acceptable and considered the only guarantee against a resurgent Russia, a destabilized Belarus or Ukraine, a re-ignition of violence in the Balkans, or, conceivably, a radically Islamicized Bosnia. With such challenges, Poles perceive the US as the partner that can offer the most assistance without jeopardizing Polish sovereignty.

The second dilemma that ESDP poses for Poland is the reconciliation of a more centralized European Union – in terms of strategic decision-making and resource allocation – with a strong and permanent NATO. Reconciling NATO with a French-inspired ESDP will have enormous implications on the transatlantic partnership and limit Poland's ability to act independently.

The challenge for Poland is to increase its political leverage within the EU, thereby contributing to the future of the Union – and by extension, its own future. Despite a lifeless CFSP to date, one of Poland's greatest fears is that an EU driven by France and a willing Germany will increasingly function as a counterweight to Washington. The accession of Poland and other Central and Eastern Europe countries predisposed to supporting US-led global initiatives may have some sway in this balance – particularly so in times of global and regional crises. This, however, will depend on Poland's willingness to occasionally break rank with Paris, Berlin, and, increasingly, Moscow. It remains to be seen whether disagreement or dissent can generate sufficient political capital for Poland, especially when allied with the other Central and East European countries or with other, more independent-minded nations on the union's periphery.

Despite signing the "Letter of Eight," the gravity of Brussels may prove insuperable. The Czech Republic, Hungary, and even an instinctively pro-American Poland may ultimately disparage the idea of serving as America's Trojan Horse in Europe. Even the former pro-American Spanish Prime Minister, José María Aznar, ruefully notes that the fashion in Central Europe is to be "leftist, federalist and anti-American."[58] Poland's political and economic integration with the EU may someday reduce the necessity and value of American allegiance. In addition to this, the collective memory of successive Polish generations is fading. Past dependency on the Soviet Union, its occupation of Central and Eastern Europe, the repercussions of Warsaw Pact membership, and the legacy of US assistance from Wilson to Reagan (Yalta notwithstanding) will have less and less relevance to Poland's post-Cold War generations.

The Bush administration's approach to national security and foreign policy – perceived by most in Europe as unilateralist – could further erode America's standing in many corners of the world. Meanwhile, Europe's political elites, shaped by the continent's postmillennial pacific culture, will continue to view the EU as the natural progression in the liberal democratic order. Poland, as always, lies somewhere in between. But to decision-makers in Brussels, serving as America's most reliable ally is tantamount to serving as America's proxy. The outcome of the Iraq war, in which Poland participated and a number of Central and East European capitals endorsed, will have enormous consequences for the development and utility of CFSP and ESDP. Should NATO take over the Polish sector in Iraq, the prospects of an autonomous, intra-European defense scheme – and Poland's role in it – will be further diminished. Equally significant for Poland will be the political climate vis-à-vis the rise and momentum of European conservatism and anti-Eurocentrism in Western and Southern Europe. Poland sees the future of the Union, and it's place within it, hinging on a number of key issues currently being fought between those favoring greater centralization and political union and those fighting for decentralization and the preservation of national sovereignties. Poland is vying for a more equitable distribution of power in Europe and for a plurality of voices to chart the EU's course. To many Poles it is ironic and disturbing that France and others predicate their policies and behavior in the international arena on an almost religious adherence to strict multilateralism, decrying the accumulation of disproportionate amounts of power in global affairs by any one nation or coalition of nations.

For Poland, fear of marginalization in Europe may indeed offset the legacy and prospect of US assistance, thwarting any designs on emerging as a US-backed powerbroker in the EU. However, the promise of a grand and unified Europe is far from assured. In fact, it is increasingly in question. Europe as a single polity may not facilitate the end of the American era, as some have predicted, but instead prove to be no more than an expanded free-trade zone with a single currency and a common law. In this case, Poland's long-term national goals and aspirations, its strength in the region, and its place not just in Europe but in the world, might be served better by its alliance with the US and NATO. In this scenario, Poland can be a key player in the stabilization and democratization of the east, and help newly independent states wean themselves from mother Russia.

The US will likely remain at the apex of global power into the foreseeable future. So long as antipathy toward America does not engender resentment of Poland and make it a diplomatic or terrorist target, greater cooperation with the US will improve Poland's military, enhance its position in NATO, and give it the opportunity to play a leading role on the international stage. This could hold it in good stead in the coming years – especially if a country's power and influence in the emerging international order will be a function of its significance to the US and not to Europe. Regardless, Poland's endeavor is to become an indispensable partner to both continents – bridging east and west.

Notes

1   Thomas L. Friedman (2003), "There U.S. Translates as Freedom", *The New York Times*, 28 December 2003. Friedman quoted Michael Mandelbaum, the Johns Hopkins

University foreign specialist, who remarked after visiting Poland: "Poland is the most pro-American country in the world–including the United States."

2   As revealed by Kwaśniewski himself in the TV interview in July 2003.

3   For example, *Suddeutsche Zeitung*, May 2003.

4   Norman Davies (1982), *God's Playground. A History of Poland*, New York: Columbia University Press, vol. I, 399–400; vol. II, 481–6.

5   Norman Davies (1984), *Heart of Europe. A Short History of Poland*, Oxford: Oxford University Press.

6   Ibid., 343.

7   Ibid., 345.

8   Olaf Osica (2002), " 'The Past as an Excuse': The Role of History in Polish Security Policies", *Yearbook of the Polish Foreign Policy 2002*, Warszawa: Polish Institute of Foreign Affairs.

9   Marek M. Siwiec (2001) [Poland's National Security Bureau chief], "Poland's Security at the Outset of the 21st Century," *Yearbook of the Polish Foreign Policy 2001*, Warszawa: Polish Institute of Foreign Affairs.

10 Rafał Domisiewicz (2003), "Modernisation of the Armed Forces in Polish Foreign Policy," *Yearbook of the Polish Foreign Policy 2002*, Warszawa: Polish Institute of Foreign Affairs; Andrew A. Michta (2003), "Modernizing the Polish Military," *Defence Studies* (Summer).

11 Richard Pipes (1994), "Rosja po szoku" [Russia after the shock], *Rzeczpospolita*, June 4–5; Jakub Karpiński (1996), "For Poland, More Distance Leads to Less Enmity," *Transition*, (23) 15 November.

12 Adam Kobieracki (2002) [Assistant Secretary General of NATO for Operations since 2003], "Poland's Security in the Year of Unconventional Threats," *Yearbook of the Polish Foreign Policy 2002*, Warszawa: Polish Institute of Foreign Affairs.

13 Karpiński: "For Poland."

14 Online at http://www.armscontrol.org/act/2004_03/MilitaryBases.asp.

15 Andrzej Karbowiak (2002), "Poland's Energy Security," *Yearbook of the Polish Foreign Policy 2002*, Warszawa: Polish Institute of Foreign Affairs.

16 Karpiński: "For Poland."

17 Marcin Zborowski and Kerry Longhurst (2003), "America's Protege in the East? The Emergence of Poland as a Regional Leader," *International Affairs*, 79 (5), 1021.

18 For example, in a 1995 survey, 32 percent of Poles worried about security of the country. Out of this, 36 percent viewed Russia as a potential threat to Poland's independence, with only nine per cent perceiving Germany as a threat. "Polacy o bezpieczeństwie kraju po zjednoczeniu Niemiec i rozpadzie ZSRR" [Poles on Poland's Security after German Reunification and the Breakup of the USSR], Public Opinion Research Center (CBOS), July 1995.

19 Marek Menkiszak and Marcin Andrzej Piotrowski (2002), "Polska polityka wschodnia [Polish Eastern Policy]," in Roman Kuźniar and Krzysztof Szczepanik (eds), *Polityka Zagraniczna RP 1989–2002* [Polish Foreign Policy 1989–2002], Warszawa:ASKON publ., 214–275.

20 Roman Wolczuk (2003), "Polish-Ukrainian Relations: A Strategic Partnership Conditioned by Externalities," *Defence Studies* (Summer).

21 Menkiszak and Piotrowski: "Polska polityka wschodnia."

22 Stanisław Michałowski (2002), "Nowa jakość w stosunkach z Niemcami" [A New Quality in Relations with Germany], in Kuźniar and Szczepanik, *Polityka Zagraniczna RP*, 146–162.

23 Andrzej Sakson (2000), "Crisis or Normalcy? Reflections on Contemporary Polish-German Relations," *Yearbook of the Polish Foreign Policy 2000*, Warszawa: Polish

Institute of Foreign Affairs; Marcin Zaborowski (2002), "Power, Security and the Past: Polish–German Relations in the Context of EU and NATO Enlargements," *German Politics* (August), 165–168; Kai-Olaf Lang (2003), "The German-Polish Security Partnership within the Transatlantic Context–Convergence or Divergence?," *Defence Studies* (Summer).

24   "Berlin Feathers Ruffled over Iraq Force," *BBC News*, 6 March 2003.

25   David Dunn (2002), "Polska – nowy model sojusznika Ameryki?" [Poland – a New Model of An American Ally], in Olaf Osica and Marcin Zaborowski (eds.), *Nowy członek "starego" sojuszu. Polska jako nowy aktor w euroatlantyckiej polityce bezpieczeństwa* [New Member of the Old Alliance. Poland as a New Actor In Euroatlantic Security Policy],Warszawa: Centrum Stosunków Międzynarodowych,129–160; Jadwiga Stachura (2002), "The Role and Importance of Bilateral Relations with the United States," in Kuźniar and Szczepanik, *Polityka Zagraniczna RP*, 126–145.

26   Speech at West Point Military Academy, online at www.president.pl/ser/index.php3?-tem_ID = 5382&kategoria = Last%20month.

27   As Zaborowski and Longhurst rightly pointed out; "America's protege in the east?," 1013–14.

28   Interview in *Gazeta Wyborcza*, 22 December 2002.

29   Zaborowski and Longhurst: "America's Protege in the East?," 1012.

30   Public Opinion Research Center (2001), "Sytuacja Polski na arenie międzynarodowej" [Poland's Situation in the International Arena], July.

31   U.S. – Poland Military Cooperation Initiative (2002), The White House, Office of the Press Secretary Washington, D.C., 17 July, online at http://www.state.gov/p/eur/rls/fs/11902.htm.

32   US, White House (2002), Joint Statement by President George W. Bush and President Aleksander Kwasniewski, Office of the Press Secretary, 17 July, online at http://www.whitehouse.gov/news/releases/2002/07/20020717-4.html.

33   Subsequently, a further group of 16 European states supported the US's Iraqi policies.

34   *Le Monde*: online at http://www.lemonde.fr/article/0,5987,3218–309684-00.html.

35   Remarks by the President to the People of Poland (2003), Wawel Royal Castle, Krakow, Poland, 3. May, online at http://www.usinfo.pl/bushvisit2003/wawel.htm.

36   The Pew Research Center Report of 18 March 2003, online at http://people-press.org/reports/display.php3?ReportID = 175.

37   "Czy Polacy lubia inne narody?" [Do the Poles Like Other Nations?] (Public Opinion Research Center [CBOS], January 2003).

38   "Stosunek Polaków do wybranych postaci ze świata polityki zagranicznej: [The Poles' Attitude To Selected Politicians Active on the International Scene] (Public Opinion Research Center [CBOS], July 2002).

39   Stanislaw Parzymies (2002), "Bilateral Relations with Selected West European Countries. France," in Kuźniar and Szczepanik, *Polityka Zagraniczna RP*, 163–175; Vanda Knowles (2003), "Security and Defence in the New Europe: Franco-Polish Relations – Victim of Neglect?", *Defence Studies* (Summer).

40   Witold Sobków (2002), "Bilateral Relations with Selected West European Countries. Great Britain," in Kuźniar and Szczepanik, *Polityka Zagraniczna RP*, 175–182; Silke Pottebohm (2003), "Poland and Britain: The Future of an Atlanticist Partnership in Europe," *Defence Studies* (Summer).

41   Roman Kuźniar (2002), "Ewolucja miedzynarodowych uwarunkowań polskiej polityki zagranicznej po 1989 roku" [The Evolution of International Determinants of Polish Foreign Policy after 1989], in Kuźniar, Szczepanik, *Polityka zagraniczna RP*, 58–66.

42   Anna Kurylowicz-Rodzoch and Stanislaw Parzymies, "Unia Zachodnioeuropejska," online at www.acn.waw.pl/zgroszek/uze.htm.

43   Zaborowski and Longhurst: "America's protege in the east?," 1017.
44   EU (2002). 2002 Regular Report of the EU Commission on Poland, COM (2002) 700 final, SEC (2002) 1408, chapter 27, Brussels, Belgium, 9 October.
45   "Intervention" (speech, special meeting of the North Atlantic Council, NATO HQ, Brussels, Belgium, 13 June 2001), online at http://www.nato.int/docu/speech/2001/s010613k.htm.
46   Speech delivered at Warsaw University, 11 May 2001, online at www.msz.gov.pl.
47   For example, Polish Foreign Minister Wlodzimierz Cimoszewicz, addressing Polish Parliament on 14 March 2002, stated that one of the tasks of Polish foreign policy concerns "the harmonised development of the European Security and Defense Identity within NATO and the ESDP within the EU" assuming "that NATO will maintain its leading role in he area of security policy," online at http://www.msz.gov.pl.
48   Andrzej Harasymowicz, Przemyslaw Zurawski vel Grojewski (2003), "Costs and benefits of Poland's Accession to the EU in the Area of the Common Foreign and Security Policy and the European Security and Defense Policy," in *Costs and Benefits of Poland's Membership in the European Union*, Warsaw: Centrum Europejskie Natolin, 214.
49   Steve Weber, "NATO Expansion," online at www.ciaonet.org.
50   US (1998), US Department of State Dispatch 9, no. 2, 13–19.
51   Sean Kay (2003), "Putting NATO Back Together Again," *Current History*, 102 (662) (March), 106.
52   Kobieracki, "Poland's Security", 8.
53   Weidnfeld, Warner (2003), "A New Order, New Partners," *Naval War College Review* 56(4), 153.
54   Ibid.
55   Zaborowski and Longhurst: "America's protege in the east?," 1012.
56   Ibid., 1009.
57   Bronislaw Geremek [Polish Minister for Foreign Affairs, 1997–2000], "Poland's Geostrategic Opportunity."
58   Quoted in William Safire (2003), "Baudelaire's Birds," *New York Times*, 10 September.

Chapter 11

Slovakia

Ivo Samson

Introduction

An absolute majority of the Slovaks have traditionally (since 1993) supported the integration of their country into the EU (contrary to NATO) and waves of skepticism towards NATO existed in the past. This pessimism towards NATO (and the Transatlantic link) became visible especially in times of crises (Kosovo crisis in 1999, Iraq crisis in 2003). In spite of this, both Slovak governments, which came out of elections in 1998 and 2002, expressed an unreserved support both for the transatlantic link, and explicitly for the US in its military campaigns not only in Kosovo and Afghanistan (here Slovakia did not differ from the rest of Western Europe), but also in Iraq.

Slovak Security Priorities

Slovakia became an independent state after the division of Czechoslovakia in 1993 and its security orientation were not clearly transparent at that time. During 1993–1994, opinions were voiced in Bratislava that economic and political developments could be separated. The example of the "Asian tigers" was often mentioned as a possible model for Slovakia's transformation. The "Eastern alternative" became a standard part of Slovak policy following the division of Czechoslovakia, especially as the authorities came under increasing Western criticism of their policies. As in November 1994 Slovakia applied for NATO membership and for the EU membership in June 1995, the country was paid more attention by both organizations. The EU started to criticize Slovakia for democratic deficits[1] NATO and US leaders repeated the criticisms expressed by the EU. Washington admonished Bratislava for the policies of the Meciar[2] government, which threatened progress in democratization and economic reform and thus Slovakia's prospects for crucial US support for NATO integration. Developments inside Slovakia had significant international dimensions as they began to endanger the two most important goals of official Slovak foreign policy: membership in the EU and NATO. Many experts in Slovakia regarded membership in the EU as equally important to NATO accession. With no direct military threat, some analysts and politicians argued that the EU was even more significant than NATO.

During NATO's Madrid summit in the summer of 1997, Slovakia was not only bypassed in the first wave of enlargement; it was not even mentioned (unlike Slovenia and Romania) among the most-likely candidates for a possible second round. Neither were developments in Slovakia an invitation for better relations with the West European Union (WEU), of which Slovakia was an associate partner. On 12 May 1997, the WEU parliamentary speaker expressed discontent with Bratislava. Slovakia, therefore, faced a threat to its plans to become a member of all three Western security institutions (NATO, EU, and the WEU).

It was the political instability arising mainly from Bratislava's policies and the resulting bitter political feud between the prime minister and the president that created a bad image for the country. In addition, Slovakia maintained extremely good relations with the Russian Federation, which occasionally aroused criticism in the West. Although neither the EU nor NATO openly condemned the close relationship between Bratislava and Moscow, it clearly became a source of concern.

The United States and NATO positively viewed the makeup of the new Dzurinda[3] government. The new prime minister's first official trip was to Brussels, to the EU and NATO headquarters, thus symbolizing the new orientation of Slovak foreign policy. NATO secretary general Javier Solana asserted after meeting with Dzurinda that Slovakia was a solid partner for NATO. But he could not set any concrete date for eventual NATO admission. Premier Dzurinda highlighted the argument that Slovakia had once been on the same starting point as the Czech Republic, Poland, and Hungary for NATO accession.

Alliance representatives were reasonably impressed by arguments about the positive attitudes of the public toward membership and the compatibility of the Slovak army with Allied forces. They repeated the principle of the "open door policy" and confirmed this approach at NATO's Washington summit in April 1999. However, it became clear that catching up on four lost years and reversing Slovakia's exclusion from the group of leading NATO candidates would be much harder than was initially envisaged by Bratislava.

Despite the difficult international context, between 1998 and 2000, Bratislava began to repair some of the deficits. By the end of 2000, following the December EU summit in Nice, the door to Slovakia's integration into the West was still not opened completely. However, nor was it closed. Slovakia expects further evaluations of its activities and progress, including the positive results of reform in the armed forces.

In June 1999, the Slovak government reacted to NATO's MAP (Membership Action Plan) by adopting the Program of the Preparation of the Slovak Republic for NATO (PRENAME). An effective coordination of this program has been supported by a resolution of the Slovak government in 1999. A specialized National Program of the PRENAME (NP PRENAME) was followed by the NP MAP (October 1999). In this way, an instrument for implementing the MAP was created, and conditions for monitoring from NATO's side were met.

An evaluation of Slovakia's progress in implementing the MAP was made at the NATO-Slovakia North Atlantic Council (NAC) meeting held under formula $19 + 1$ in Brussels on April 20, 2001. NATO ambassadors judged that Slovakia had made significant progress in implementing the MAP over the last two years in the areas of legislation, communication strategy, security planning, and military reform. The Slovak parliament passed an important amendment to the constitution on February 23, 2001, which regulated deployment of foreign troops on Slovak territory and the deployment of Slovak troops abroad. On March 27, 2001, the Slovak parliament passed a basic document on the Security Strategy of the Slovak Republic by an overwhelming majority. Eighty-seven percent of members of the Slovak parliament voted in favor of the document, which supported Slovakia's NATO membership.

What followed was the adoption of the Military and Defense Strategy of the Slovak Republic, which specify in detail the concept of security and military reform in Slovakia. Still prior to the NATO Summit in Prague (November 2002), Slovakia was able to adopt some additional laws, which were necessary to fill the gap in the Slovak legislation, and which were a prerequisite for Slovakia's NATO membership. In November, 2002, Slovakia was invited to become a NATO member together with six other post-communist countries of Central Eastern Europe. Starting with April, 2004 Slovakia became full-fledged NATO member.

Despite the politically problematic period between 1994 and 1998, Bratislava's relations with NATO have deeply influenced the process of developing Slovakia's security and military planning as well as military reform. Slovakia joined the Partnership for Peace (PfP) program in 1994, and Slovak troops took an active part in several joint exercises with NATO troops. Slovak peacekeeping battalions are deployed in Bosnia-Hercegovina and Kosova, and the government opened up Slovak ground and airspace for NATO logistic transports to the Balkans during the Kosova crisis in the spring of 1999. This demonstrated the posture of Slovakia as a de facto NATO member. Following the Operation Afghani Freedom in 2001, Slovakia keeps a unit of 40 men in Afghanistan and following the end of the operation Iraq Freedom in May 2003, Slovakia send a unit of about 70 men to Iraq, which was increased to the strength of 105 men in 2004.

On the basis of an intergovernmental agreement, the US Air Force uses the air base in Kuchyna in western Slovakia for its exercises. Military-to-military relations are well developed, and Slovakia's relations with NATO have been well established especially since 1999.

Slovak Security Policy before the Iraq Crisis

The security policy of the Slovak Republic following the big political change after 1998 has abandoned tactics and assumed firm features of a long-term strategy. Although Slovakia was not admitted to NATO in Washington (NATO Summit in April 1999),[4] it proclaimed the foreign policy strategy saying that it "will behave as if it were NATO member". Reflecting this strategy, as well as the new security environment in the region and in the world, the *Security Strategy of the Slovak Republic*[5] was created to define reactions to security challenges and risks, and to bring Slovakia near to membership in collective defense organs and other international organizations.[6] The document has four chapters, which describe Slovakia's security environment, state its security risks and security threats, outline its security policy principles, and set the criteria for its security system.

The Security Strategy – a documents Slovakia entered NATO in 2004, reflects the collective efforts of the domestic security community, and makes use of the experience of foreign experts in security. It focuses on Slovakia's integration into NATO and EU. Both areas are relatively balanced from the point of view of quality and content. In terms of the development of security theory, the definition of Slovak national interests and important interests is a significant one. The document for the first time in the history of independent Slovakia:

- officially defines Slovak security policy;
- describes the Slovak security environment;
- defines the security system.

At the same time, it puts Slovakia on a more active footing towards the international security environment.

Besides of "security risks" official Slovak documents worked also with "security challenges". On the other side, the document does not work with "security vulnerabilities", which might have presented an obstacle in defining the difference between "prevention" and "pre-emption" in connection with the discussion on the European Security Strategy in the second half of 2003. One of the crucial challenges was the participation of Slovakia at the forming of European Security system. Other "challenges" have been formulated in a very standard and general way as follows:

- active participation in Central Europe in the sphere of establishing and developing good neighborhood relations;
- using the chances of cooperation within the Visegrad Group;
- strengthening of democracy, legal state and fundamental human and civic rights;
- social-oriented and environment-oriented market economy;
- transition of Slovakia from an industrial to an information society.

National Interests of the Slovak Republic

National interests of the Slovak Republic have been formulated in the document, too. Slovakia, like other states, discerns between "vital" and "important" national interests. Four "vital interests" have been specified:

- Guaranteeing the security of the Slovak Republic, its sovereignty and integrity.
- Safeguarding and developing the democratic fundaments of the state, its domestic security and domestic order.
- Securing the lasting economic, social, environmental and cultural development of the society and protecting the important infrastructure of the state.
- Preserving peace and stability in Central Europe and spreading the zone of democracy, security and prosperity, including the full membership of Slovakia in NATO and EU.

In addition to the "vital interests", there exist six "important interests":

- Preserving peace and stability in the world and prevention the tensions and crises, eventually their solving by peaceful means.
- Good relations with direct neighbors and development of mutually advantageous cooperation.
- Domestic stability based on a corresponding social consensus concerning vital and important interests of Slovakia.
- Transformation of the Slovak economy to an environmentally balanced market economy.
- Safeguard of social peace and stability based on the equality of all citizens regardless of political orientation, religious affiliation, gender, ethnicity and social classification.
- Reaching of environmental security within the framework of domestic and international structures.

From the enumeration of national interests of the Slovak Republic and their formulation there ensues that the security decision makers, policymakers and politicians were not able to get deeply into the problems and to avoid generalizations and cliches. They approved such a formulation and division of national interests that results partly in overlapping of goals, partly in clearly tautological definitions.[7]

Security Risks

The document summarizes and defines the security risks that can be faced by the Slovak Republic at the time of NATO integration in 2004.[8] The main risks have been summarized as follows:

- the probability of a global war has remained very low;
- in a long-term perspective, however, the risk of a large-scale armed conflict cannot be excluded;
- regional conflicts in unstable regions;[9]
- terrorism; non-controlled migration, international organized crime; criminalization of social relations; activities of foreign intelligence services; excessive dependence of the Slovak Republic on Russian energy sources;[10] negative demographic development; environmental threats.

As to the most sensitive issues of today – threat of international terrorism and the Transatlantic relations, Slovakia did not differ from other new democracies in the course of 2003. During the Iraq crisis it consequently supported (within the Vilnius Group – the group of ten NATO candidate countries) the USA, politically and militarily. The official position towards the ESDP can be summarized as: yes, but not at the cost of effective Transatlantic relations.[11] This is the position of the government not corresponding, however, to the stance of opposition political parties, which have enjoyed the support of absolute majority of citizens in the opinion polls in 2003/2004.

Contributions – Armed Forces as Planned Commitments towards NATO

Already in 2002, Slovakia made the following commitments towards NATO:[12]

- Mechanized battalion (838 professional troops);
- Engineer company (90 professional troops);
- SHORAD battery (58 professional troops) with readiness period 10 days and supplies for 7 days;
- Military police platoon (46 professional troops);
- One sub-flight of combat helicopters;
- One sub-flight of transport helicopters;
- Field mobile hospital (111 persons).

Armed Forces Abroad

Due to their character and umbrella organisations, several categories of the SR Armed Forces foreign missions may be identified:

- UN operations (Cyprus, Eritrea-Ethiopia, East Timor, Golan Heights);
- NATO operations (KFOR, SFOR);
- European Union operations (FYROM);
- Crisis management operations (Afghanistan, Iraq).

In 2003 the SR Armed Forces were involved in the following operations:

- UNFICYP (Cyprus) – one battalion, 277 troops;
- UNMEE (Eritrea, Ethiopia) – 199 troops;
- UNTAET (East Timor) – field hospital, 35 troops;
- UNDOF (Golan Heights) – 99 troops;
- KFOR – 96 troops (in the joint Czech-Slovak Battalion);
- SFOR – two transport helicopters Mi-17 deployed in this mission under the Dutch command;
- ISAF (Afghanistan) – one engineer unit consisting of 40 troops.

The participation of the Slovak Republic in two smaller UN missions is only symbolic:

- UNAMSIL (Sierra Leone) – 2 troops;
- UNTSO (the border of Lebanon and Syria with Israel) – 2 troops.

Iraq Crisis in 2003: Between May and June 2003, 74 troops were sent to Kuwait (Camp Doha) as part of the NBC unit. In September 2003, the engineer unit in strength of 40 troops started to deploy in Iraq and became part of multinational division under the Polish command. After the assessment of security situation the SR Ministry of Defense decided to strengthen these forces by a special unit that should protect dislocated units. After completing this, the total number of Slovak troops in Iraq achieved 105 troops at the beginning of 2004.[13]

Table 11.1 Development according to CFE limits[14]

	Limit as to CFE	1.1. 1994	1.1. 1995	1.1. 1996	1.1. 1997	1.1. 1998	1.1. 1999	1.1. 2000	1.1. 2001	1.1. 2002	1.1. 2003	1.1. 2004
Battle tanks[15]	478 323 (since 2004)	745	644	478	478	478	478	275	272	272	271	268
Armored combat vehicles[16]	683 643 (since 2004)	944	749	683	683	683	683	622	622	534	524	526
Artillery systems[17]	383	813	632	383	383	382	383	383	383	374	374	373
Attack helicopters[18]	25 40 (since 1998)	19	19	19	19	19	19	19	19	19	19	19
Combat aircraft[19]	115 100 (since 2004)	122	116	114	113	113	94	82	82	79	71	65
Personnel	46.667	54223	52015	45832	45483	45483	44880	44519	38929	32366	26436	23197

Armaments – CFE I/IA Limits

The CFE-I-Treaty (Conventional Forces in Europe) allows Slovakia the limit of 46.667 soldiers, 478 battle tanks, 683 armored combat vehicles, 383 artillery systems (caliber over 100mm), 115 combat aircraft, 25 attack helicopters. Slovakia, however, successfully asked for a rebalancing: Instead of 115 combat aircraft 100 of them and instead of 25 helicopters 40 of them. Following the Istanbul (OSCE) Summit in 1999, since 2004 this ceiling was to be further reduced in battle tanks (323 since 1 January 2004) and armored combat vehicles (643 since 1 January 2004).

Thus, the contribution of Slovak armed forces to NATO-led missions (as well as for missions within other organizations) has its natural limits.

Structural Development and Changes

Over recent years, clear objectives have been established to "westernize" the armed forces (Army of the Slovak Republic before 2002) and ultimately join the NATO Alliance. Downsizing has occurred and several attempts at systemic reform were initiated. This process proved very difficult, so much so that assistance was requested from a number of western countries to help focus the effort and accelerate achievement of results. As part of this assistance a number of western assessments were accomplished: each cited serious deficiencies in many areas; all provided very similar recommendations.

First of all, the Government of the SR requested assistance from the United States Government to provide services necessary to plan and support government defense modernization efforts. The US Department of Defense selected Cubic Applications, Inc. to provide this support. The contribution consisted of a "top-to-bottom" assessment of the current defense posture within the Slovak Republic. Referred to as the "Defense Review", its principal focus was to address the current status, practices, legislation, regulations and policies, and to provide prioritized recommendations.

Alongside of the Cubic Applications Inc., British, French, and German assistance was provided for Slovak Armed Forces. This was very important especially during works on new defense model.[20] All advisors functioned in area of their expertise inside of five working teams. Along with providing advises and consultations, foreign experts organized few workshops and seminars related to defense reform and development of essential documents needed for faster approach to our membership. The cooperation with NATO experts resulted in the shape of the future active force that will consist of ground and air elements as well as a consolidated training and support capability. Command and control will be provided through a streamlined Ministry and General Staff. This latter aspect has already been established. One of the revolutionary steps is the professionalization of military service. By the end of 2006 conscription will end as the gradual transition to a professional force is completed. It means that after 138 years, the compulsory military service is to be abolished.[21]

According to the reform:[22]

- Ground elements will include both mechanized and light infantry capability of brigade size.
- Separate battalions for task organizational needs of the force.
- The brigades will have additional organic combat support capability such as artillery and engineers.
- Ground combat equipment for the near term will include T72 Tanks and BMPs as well as both self-propelled and towed artillery.
- Modernization of selected items is planned.
- Air Force elements include two wings of aircraft.
- Fixed wing combat requirements will be satisfied with a new multi-role fighter.
- All (former) Warsaw Treaty Organization vintage fixed wing fighters will be retired.
- Existing attack and transport helicopters will be retained in limited numbers for the near term modernization and upgrade will occur for these systems.
- One air defense brigade will be retained.
- The Training and Support Command will be responsible for all initial entry and advanced individual training and will control most of the training bases throughout the country.
- The central logistics system and associated bases will also be the responsibility of this command, as will the Bratislava Garrison and strategic communications in support of the armed forces.
- Included in the logistics structure is a joint multi-functional organization to augment organic capability of the Land and Air Force and to support deployed forces.

This is a tight organization: duplication and redundancy have been allegedly[23] eliminated.

Transatlanticism in the Reflection of Central Eastern Europeans: Slovakia as Model Case?

Traditionally, since the changes in 1989/1990, the countries of the former Soviet bloc – Slovakia included – have received a number of names: post-communist countries, countries in the process of transformation (transforming countries), Central Eastern Europeans, Central Europe, Eastern Europe, former communist countries. Due to the double integration process of "Central Eastern Europeans", that is due to the integration both into NATO, and the EU, these labels seemed to be increasingly obsolete. Especially after 1999, that is after the Czech Republic, Hungary and Poland became NATO members, the general designation of these countries produced question marks. It became obvious that one cannot, over and over again, call these countries "post-communist".

In the past years, the Slovak security and foreign policy has been tied more to NATO membership than to the European Security and Defense Policy (ESDP) within the framework of the EU. Nominally, Slovakia has always supported the idea of a collective European defense but practical steps have been oriented at NATO as the only realistic supplier of the Slovak security.

It was especially Slovakia that might have been meant in the report of the US Senate Committee on Foreign Relations on NATO enlargement in 2002: "Finally, we were convinced, as have been many US Government officials, that the seven countries seriously under consideration for NATO membership, in addition to the three new members of NATO, are more committed Atlanticists (with the possible exception of Slovenia) than many of the current NATO allies."[24]

It should be noted, that following the pro-US letter of 8 NATO countries calling for a support of the USA in the war against Iraq, Slovakia was the first (altogether 9th) country that joined the "gang of eight".[25] The strongly pro-US foreign and security policy of Slovakia might have been the reaction to a period of an almost anti-US foreign policy of the Slovak Republic in the 1990s. The years 1994–1998 meant a relatively anti-American foreign policy position assumed by the populist-nationalist-leftist government. After the parliamentary elections of 1998 Slovakia turned to be strongly pro-US in the following four years. Thus, 1998 brought to an end a period in which the US Government had openly criticized the policy of the Slovak Government and had limited the official contacts with Slovakia to a minimum. In the official Report on Meeting the Goal of the Slovak Foreign Policy for 2001 with the Outlook to 2002, USA is already seen as a strong ally.[26] In the Report the relations between Slovakia and the USA are described as having reached the "best level in the hitherto history of bilateral relations" and the relations of Slovakia to USA "will preserve their foreign policy priority".[27] The pro-American orientation was formulated in several ways:

1   In the practically de facto foreign policy doctrine of the Slovak republic expressed by the new prime minister Mikulas Dzurinda at the end of 1988 and repeated after the Washington Summit in 1999.[28]
2   In the strong support of the NATO Kosovo campaign in spite of strong anti-American (more than anti-NATO) reactions of the absolute majority of the population.
3   In the strong condemnation of the terrorist attacks against the USA after September 2001.
4   In the participation at the operation Enduring Freedom in Afghanistan In the participation at the operation Iraq Freedom.

After the parliamentary elections in September 2002 the pro-US foreign policy has been confirmed and intensified. The reason is that the government was formed of the right-of-the-center parties that have claimed partly a strong pro-US orientation before. With the exception of KDH (Christian Democratic Movement), which is strongly anti-communist, but not explicitly pro-US, the other three parties either not focus on foreign policy (liberals from ANO – Alliance of New Citizens) or support openly a pro-US course (SDKU – the Slovak Democratic and Christian Union and SMK – Party of Hungarian Coalition).

There exist at least five reasons, why Slovakia has been in favor of US foreign policy (and, implicitly, supported the war on Iraq):

1   In the election programs, the (now) governmental parties (especially SDKU) emphasized the participation in the fight against international terrorism[29] and have never doubted the Bush Doctrine following 11 September 2001.

2   The SDKU, as the strongest part of the four-Coalition, has been the strongest supporter of a good Slovakia – US relationship during the last years.

3   The SDKU has occupied all three positions that shape security and foreign policy of the country: position of the prime minister (Mikulas Dzurinda), of the Minister of Foreign Affairs (Eduard Kukan) and of the Minister of Defense (Ivan Simko, who was replaced by Juraj Liska in 2003).

4   Additionally, the Head of State (president Rudolf Schuster) has always supported official US foreign policy. The new president of Slovakia, although a representative of the oppositition (officially the supreme commander of the armed forces), who was elected in April 2004, expressed also his conviction that the Slovak troops should continue their mission in Iraq despite the terrorist threats in Europe.

5   The leading government representatives of the present (after the September elections of 2002 until April 2004), if asked by the media, have never expressed any objections as to an attack of US against Iraq.

After the NATO Summit in Prague, the Slovak PM said in an official statement: "Now, Slovakia has a government that will not hesitate to take a principal attitude, if the question of values is in the game".[30] Practical steps – sending a unit of Slovak soldiers to Kuwait – followed at the beginning of 2003.

The Minister of Foreign Affairs manifested several times a future pro-American stance of Slovakia in the Iraq issue. Addressing Iraq directly, the Minister said meeting the requirements of allowing the UN arms inspectors to enter the country is not enough: "Iraq has to fulfill all the previous UN SC resolutions".[31] As to the Minister of Defense, after taking the office, on 21 October 2002, he presented his "seven priorities", two of them touching the US-Slovakia relationship. The first has been the ESDP, but "strictly within the framework of NATO" (which openly means preferring the European Security and Defense Identity – ESDI), the second priority being the participation of Slovakia in the fight against international terrorism and participation in peace-keeping missions. The new Minister of Defense has not changed these priorities after he took office in the summer of 2003.

After 2000, the relationship between the Slovak Republic and the USA has been defined as "strategic partnership" in a variety of government documents published by the Slovak Ministry of Foreign Affairs.[32] One can easily identify the reasons for this kind of partnership, as well as the implications for the security policy of the country. As NATO membership became a crucial foreign policy priority of the Slovak government after 1998, logically, the country too the pro-US orientation. The reasons were obvious: *first*, the USA has been the hegemonic leader of the Alliance; *second*, the enlargement of NATO depended, first of all, of the US decision; and *third*, Slovakia, like other Central Eastern European countries, stresses the hard security guarantees and is not ready to victimize them to their "soft" equivalent, which some Western European NATO members have preferred. The whole process of a new attempt at the reform of the armed forces (see the sub-chapter above: Structural Development and Changes), the definition of vital Slovak national interests, as well as the political initiative of the Slovak Ministry of Foreign Affairs in connection with the adoption of the European Security Strategy (see the sub-chapter below: "European Security Strategy and Slovakia") betrays this focus on hard security guarantees. This emphasis explains best the inclination of government elites to a transatlantic policy. As victims of the Cold War, Slovakia, like other Central Eastern Europeans, cannot afford to forget that the US-led NATO was able to respond to the security threats posed by the Soviet Union. The direct implication of this lesson learned is that Slovakia, like other post-communist countries in the region, has backed a Europe with Euro-Atlantic orientation and disapproves of "building a stronger EU as a counterbalance to the US".[33]

The question is, however, how durable this development might be. One can suppose that at least until the parliamentary elections (if held in ordinary term in 2006) Slovakia will stick to the pro-Atlanticist and pro-US orientation. It this trend is to be continued even afterwards, depends of two factors: *first*, the composition of the new government coalition and, *second*, of the development within the EU as to CFSP and ESDP. Like in the neighboring Czech Republic, in Slovakia, too, the leftist political parties "instinctively" prefer rather a European-autonomous than a transatlantic dimension of the security and foreign policy. If these parties,[34] together with Slovak nationalists[35] win a strong position in the Parliament and are able to form the government (which is not excluded at all), one can expect a shift of the country's security and foreign policy in a Euro-autonomous direction. If, on the contrary, the Central Eastern Europeans stick to their transatlantic course, in the long term they will be able to influence the CFSP/ESDP in the pro-Atlantic dimension, too.

Of course, the attitude of the population is one of important factors, which can have impact on the future political landscape of Slovakia. The public's attitude does not correspond, however, to the position taken by the government. In spite of a clear disagreement of the population with the government, the voters are able repeatedly to cast their votes for those political parties, which take a different position in foreign and security policy matters.[36]

The highest support for NATO in the history of independent Slovakia was reached in March 2002, when it exceeded the 60 percent limit. Public opinion polls conducted after the 2002 elections signalled a decline in public support for NATO integration. In spring 2003, the Alliance's popularity dropped to the level of 34 percent. This was triggered by the Iraqi crisis.[37] On the other hand, most respondents endorsed *generally* a participation of Slovak troops in NATO peacekeeping missions. The commitment to send Slovak troops in defense of another member state earned a near equal amount of endorsement and disapproval. As for other possible Slovak contributions, including the participation of Slovak troops in the fight against international terrorism in Afghanistan and Iraq, disapproval prevailed over endorsement in 2003.[38]

Especially the Iraqi crisis became an important domestic political issue. Public opinion on this problem showed certain discrepancies. Although two in three Slovaks (67 percent) viewed the regime of Saddam Hussein as a possible international threat, only one third of them acknowledged the right of the international community to defend itself against dangerous dictatorship regimes. Of available tools, respondents clearly preferred soft, non-military ones, such as political and economic pressure, negotiations, and so on. Before the start of the Iraqi operation (public opinion poll in February 2003), the military operation was perceived as very dangerous (77 percent) and unjust (49 percent).[39] At the turn of March and April 2003, three in four Slovak citizens (74 percent) viewed it as wrong. The Slovaks appreciated the approach of those countries that opposed the military intervention (France, Germany).[40]

As to the attitude of the public to the dichotomy between transatlanticism and ESDP, no specific public opinion poll was taken, because for a large part of the population the notions of "transatlantic link" versus "autonomous European defense" are not fully understandable.

"New Europe's" Reactions to the Iraq Crisis[41]

The openly pro-American language of the Vilnius Group[42] declaration on Iraq at the Prague summit that reportedly shocked some European governments, notably France and Germany,[43] was subject to vivid discussion in the Slovak media. A four-day delay the government took in making the declaration public led to speculations about whether or not the Prime Minister signed an automatic commitment to military engagement if a US-led attack takes place. Meanwhile, reports from other V10 members showed no sign of controversy in their countries. There were some negative reactions that the Prime Minister had not consulted the parliament before making "binding decisions". These statements reflected a lack of knowledge of international law and government-to-parliament responsibilities and sometimes revealed personal aspirations and political frustrations of their authors. There was even some petty confusion as to whether the Prime Minister actually signed anything or made his pledge by word. However, there have also been more consistent signals across the board that the legislative branch should be more involved in NATO integration, bearing in mind the upcoming parliamentary ratifications in NATO member countries.

More importantly, the brief exchange that flared up may have also brought the germs of a healthy debate on the principles, values and overall orientation of Slovak foreign policy. To date, when the Iraq war is militarily at its close, both extreme pro-American, and anti-American (not necessarily pro-European) views dominate in Slovakia, which is promising from the point of view of breaking the passivity of the public relating to Slovakia's place in Europe.

The policy of the government is generally viewed as distinctly pro-American and seems to express best the US view how "New Europe" should behave in times of crisis. Prime Minister Mikulas Dzurinda has had strong statements of support for US policy. With regard to possible solutions to the Iraqi crisis, at a time of European hesitation prior to the Prague summit, the head of Slovak government said: "*Slovakia is and will be a firm, strong ally of the United States of America. In any case, under any circumstances.*"[44] From this point of view, the Slovak foreign and security policy has showed a rare continuity and is a model example of behavior of "New Europe" the US administration has dreamt of. How far this position is compatible with the future membership of Slovakia in the EU and with the implementation of both Common Security and Foreign Policy (CFSP), and ESDP, which form a part of the *Acquis*, remains a question.

European Security Strategy and Slovakia

Due to the reshuffling of expert staffs at the Ministry of Defense and at the Ministry of Foreign Affairs following the parliamentary elections in 1998, relatively young people assumed leading expert positions at both ministries. It means that the official declarations of ministers and state secretaries of these ministries could correspond to expert analyses, which supported the declamatory Transatlantic foreign and security policy course of the country. This attitude was reflected by the Slovak reaction to the draft of the European Security Strategy.[45] Since the beginning of the following discussion about the "Solana Paper" to the final (and modified) product,[46] the Slovak experts proposed a lot of changes. In spite of the fact that these proposal were hardly reflected in the final (Brussels) version, one can win, at least, an insight into the official Slovak position as to the Transatlantic relationship. All EU candidate countries were invited to three expert discussions about this paper and their views could be heard at pre-enlargement joint EU security policy forums.[47]

In July 2003, the Slovak Ministry of Foreign Affairs elaborated a reaction to the European Security Strategy, where it combined a combination of critical remarks and recommendations for the final version.[48] In the official remarks, the Slovak Republic, of course, welcomed the "paper" as a document, reflecting the increased interest of the EU for the field of security as well as the need for an enhanced coherence in this sphere. In the Slovak position, one emphasizes the need of a document being relevant for 450 million people. For this reason, Slovakia demands the discussion about form, structure and substance of the European Security Strategy.[49] Less successful was the proposal that all involved countries (that is all 25 EU member countries plus candidate countries with *de jure* membership after May 1, 2004) should exchange position papers before.

In the Slovak paper, sometimes unrealistic, or, as the case may be, in details only general demands have been expressed, summarized as follows:

- Slovakia welcomed the idea to adopt the European Security Strategy – its elaboration reflects an enhanced role of the European Union in the field of security, as well as the will of the European Union to reach more coherence in this field;
- European Union needs such a strategy in order to confirm its will and efforts to act as a global actor and a partner in other global actor's effort, sharing responsibility for global security with other players;
- The paper prepared by the Secretariat and introduced by the SG/HR J. Solana "A secure Europe in a better world" is a good starting point for discussion;
- Elaboration of a solid document, which is relevant to nearly half a billion of people, requires a thorough discussion on its form, structure and substance;
- Slovakia welcomes the proposal to hold seminars on specific topics that would provide contribution to the drafting process;
- Exchange of national positions/papers at the outset, as well as comments by other organisations, would be helpful;
- The strategy should bring to Europe a common perception of an overall security environment in Europe and beyond, and also a harmonization, to a

certain degree, of their so far individual pursue of national security interests, as well as of the tools for tackling them;

- This new strategic document should be the key document for formulation and implementation of the CFSP and ESDP;
- The strategy should reflect all positives of relevant strategic security documents and concepts not only of EU Member States but also of non-EU NATO countries and relevant partners in accordance with a broader concept and understanding of security;
- Discussion on the strategy could contribute also to elimination of differences of view within Europe, and in transatlantic relations between Europe and the US – we believe that based on shared fundamental values both Europe and the US should share common perception of security threats and challenges and should act as partners;
- The Strategy should fully exploit the existing EU capabilities in all areas of CFSP/ESDP;
- The Strategy should offer guidelines for an EU engagement in an operation under the ESDP;
- The UN, NATO, OSCE, and other regional and sub-regional structures and initiatives, including various think-tanks, could be consulted in the process of elaboration of the Strategy;
- The role of NATO as the main pillar of the European security should be reconfirmed. NATO is not only "an important expression of transatlantic relationship", but "an essential pillar" of the European security, stability and prosperity, which should be preserved and further fostered;
- The Strategy should be a living document, understandable to the citizens of the EU Member States;
- The Strategy should reflect the changing security environment and offer a security concept for a 3–5 years period;
- The Strategy should be a comprehensive document and flexible enough to respond to a wide variety of contingencies, although not an exhaustive one.

Structure or form:

- Descriptive/narrative parts should be shortened as much as possible;
- The Strategy could be developed further in specific areas in action plans (weapons of mass destruction, arms exports, arms trafficking, money laundering terrorism, illegal migration, and so on);
- Main parts of the European Security Strategy (no priority or order) could be:

  - security glossary;
  - security environment analysis/regional and wider view;
  - defining vital interests;
  - assessment of security threats and challenges;
  - specifying strategic goals, objectives, priorities and basic principles;
  - analysis of resource requirements, means and capabilities for implementation of the Strategy;

- measures to address the threats and root causes of the threats;
    building strategic partnerships/security dialogue and consultations with
    key partners such as the USA, Russia, China, Japan and Ukraine;
- defining level of cooperation/engagement with other regional structures;
    policy outline towards world regions, namely with the W. Balkans,
    Middle East, Mediterranean, Africa, Asia;
- establishing annual review conference.

Substance:

- The strategy should cope with recent as well as emerging threats to peace and
  security, and should address root causes of the threats, not their symptoms,
  namely terrorism, proliferation of weapons of mass destruction, extremism,
  religious fundamentalism, ethnic tensions, uncontrolled migration, world
  poverty, scarcity of resources, and so on;
- Military and non-military crisis management should be emphasized;
- The Strategy should specify the goal of Europe to effectively resolve crises,
  not only politically maintain 'peace of weapons' (as it is the case of frozen
  conflicts);
- The concepts of deterrence and active countering of possible threats should
  be further explored and accounted for in the strategy; we support the
  proposed wording "outside our borders, within the framework of prevention
  and projection-action, we must be able to identify and prevent threats as soon
  as possible. Within this framework, possible pre-emptive action should be
  considered, where an explicit and confirmed threat has been recognized."
  International community, including the EU should be ready to act when rules
  of international organisations and treaties are ignored or broken. The EU
  should stand ready and willing to take necessary early action on the
  protection of the principles of democracy, fundamental human rights,
  individual liberty and the rule of law;
- The strategy should spell out that an effective implementation of the strategy
  requires an increase of expenditures in security and defense sectors and the
  most effective use of them respecting principles of cooperation, non-
  duplication, and exploring possibilities of role specialization in building of
  high-tech capabilities;
- Strategy has to be realistic in threat assessment – we hesitate to use
  expressions as "Europe has never been so secure", "distant threats to
  Europe"; It is hard to distinguish between "internal and external threats",
  "military and non-military threats", and "police and military action";
- Handling and resolving of existing 'frozen conflicts' in Europe vicinity
  should be addressed appropriately;
- In the context of the fight against terrorism we do not recommend to
  highlight "traditional terrorist organisations" – we should avoid to
  differentiate between good and bad terrorists; the threat is terrorism as
  such, not only terrorism with international links and influence; the respective
  part lacks a future outline;

- The part on "failed states and organized crime" should be divided because an organized crime is not only the problem of failed states; furthermore failed or rogue states are frequently also a source of terrorism, arms exports, trafficking or even arms production, WMD proliferations, and so on;
- The term "effective multilateralism" should be very carefully detailed. Unfortunately, building an international order unfortunately does not always guarantee security if the breeches of the UN SC resolutions are met with ineffective response by international community or when international community is divided on interpretation of an UN SC resolution. The instruments of the international order should no doubt be strengthened, its implementation made more efficient.

One can see that the general orientation of the employees (analysts) at the Ministry of Foreign Affairs have been relatively positively oriented towards transatlanticism and slightly critical of a low transatlantic standard in the EU in 2003–2004.

Conclusion

At the time being, the leading elites in Slovakia take a strong transatlantic position. There remain reasons enough, however, to a precaution. The absolute majority of the population reject the participation of the Slovak troops in Iraq and according to the opinion polls at the beginning of 2004, the opposition (which oppose both the support of the USA in Iraq, and the strong transatlantic link) would win the elections, should they take place at the beginning of 2004 (January – April). Slovakia also depends of Germany, economically. Germany is by far the biggest foreign investor in Slovakia and due to the natural connection between foreign and economic policy, it can exercise a pressure on Slovakia. In the framework of the government parties, there does not exist a unanimous position. Especially the Christian Democratic Movement (KDH), reflecting the negative stance of the Pope to the war in Iraq, urge a withdrawal of Slovak troops from there.[50]

Notes

1 Especially the failure to meet the EU Copenhagen criteria of 1993, namely the stability of democratic institutions and the democratic division of power between the government and the opposition after the parliamentary elections in the Fall of 1994.
2 Vladimir Meciar, the Prime Minister of the Slovak Republic in 1991, 1992–1994 and 1994–1998.
3 Mikulas Dzurinda, the Prime Minister of the Slovak Republic after the elections in the Fall of 1994 (1994–1998) and the second time after the elections in 2002 (2002–).
4 As Slovakia was convinced – following the elections in autumn 1998 – that it met political criteria, some politicians believed in the so called format 3 + 1, namely that Slovakia will be additionally invited to NATO to become a full-fledged member together with other Visegrad countries in 1999.

5   Slovakia, Ministry of Defense (2001), Security Strategy of the Slovak Republic / *Bezpecnostna strategia Slovenskej republiky*/, Bratislava: Ministry of Defense.

6   *Slovak Parliament Resolution No. 1312*, 27 April 2001.

7   Ivo Samson (2004), *New Security Environment in Slovak Security Documents*. Proceedings from the PfP EASSG conference, Bratislava, 12–13 January. Forthcoming: PfP Consortium of Defense Acadamies and Security Studies Institutes.

8   At the time this document was elaborated, the time of the NATO admission was not known to the authors, of course.

9   The document has localized this risk in the regions of South-eastern Europe and of the Caucasus, 7–8.

10 This risk has not been mentioned explicitly by name.

11 Ivo Samson (2003), *Discussion on Transatlanticism in Slovakia*, in *After Prague and Copenhagen: Iraq Impacts on the Euro-Atlantic Security Issues*, Proceedings of the 15th Meeting of the Euro-Atlantic Security Study Group, PfP Consortium of Defense Academies and Security Institutes, 92–95.

12 Vladimir Kmec (2002), *Security of the Slovak Republic and Integration to NATO and European Union*, Bratislava: Institute of Public Affairs.

13 Slovakia, Ministry of Defense (2004), "Exchange of Engineering Units in Iraq" (*Striedanie zenistov v Iraku*), online at www.mod.gov.sk.

14 Slovakia, Ministry of Defense (2004), "Overview of the National Level and Real Numbers According to the CFE in Europe" (*Prehlad narodnej urovne, skutocneho stavu a pocte osob podla Zmluvy o KOS*), Bratislava: Ministry of Defense, January.

15 Type: T-72 M.

16 Types: BMP-1; BMP-2; OT-90; BRDM-2; BPsV.

17 76 D-30A (122 mm); Zuzana (howitzers, 155 mm); 2S1 (122 mm); Dana (M-77, 152 mm); RM-70 GRAD (122mm); surface-to-surface missiles; surface-to-air missiles.

18 Type: Mi-24D.

19 Type: MiG-21; MiG-29; Su-22; Su-25.

20 Under the much cited name: *Armed Forces of the Slovak Republic – Model 2010*.

21 The compulsory military service was introduced in the former Austria-Hungary in 1868 and since then it has been lasting at the territory of Slovakia.

22 Slovakia, Ministry of Defense (2002), *Armed Forces of the Slovak Republic: Force 2010*, Bratislava: Ministry of Defense, 2002.

23 See many discussions in Slovak military journals, especially in the bi-weekly *Obrana* ("Defense"), and in the quarterly *Slovak Army* (published in English).

24 US, Congress (2002), *Report of the United States Senate Committee on Foreign Relations*, Washington D.C., 30 August, 3.

25 The Slovak PM called the Spanish PM Aznar – the official head of the pro-US initiative – on 30 January 2003 and asked for the permission for Slovakia to be added to the list. It should be emphasized that Slovenia (together with Latvia) that was mentioned with reserves in the Report of the US Senate Committee on Foreign Relations of 30 August 2002, joined the pro-US initiative the following day.

26 Slovakia (2002), "Report on Meeting the Goals of the Slovak Foreign Policy in 2001 and Goals in 2002" (*Sprava o plneni uloh zahranicnej politiky Slovenskej republiky za rok 2001 a zameranie na rok 2002*), in Report of the Government of the Slovak Republic no. 1419.

27 Ibid., 6, 14.

28 "Although we are not members of NATO, we will behave as if we were NATO members." In Slovakia, it should be noted, NATO is largely identified with the leading position of the US.

29 Ivo Samson (2002), "International Security, NATO Integration, Defense Policy, Army," in *The Foreign Policy of the SR in Election Programs of Political Parties*, Bratislava: SFPA, 7–22.

30 M. Dzurinda (2002), online at http://www.sdkuonline, 10 November.

31 The Speech by E. Kukan (2002) at the UN General Assembly, 19 September.

32 http://www.foreign.gov.sk.

33 Serena Giusti, "Visegrad – Balancing between United States and European Union?", Marek Stastny, ed. (2002), *Visegrad Countries in an Enlarged Trans-Atlantic Community*, Bratislava: Institute for Public Affairs, 99.

34 First of all the left of the center party SMER.

35 First of all the SNS – Slovak National Party.

36 One can give as an example the negative attitude of the public opinion to the government's support of the NATO-led military operation against the former Yugoslavia (Kosovo crisis) in 1999. In spite of the fact that about 70 percent of the population disagreed with the pro-NATO stance of the government, they repeatedly voted for the same political parties in the parliamentary elections in 2002.

37 Grigorij Meseznikov and Miroslav Kollar, eds. (2004), *Slovakia 2003: A Global Report on the State of Society*, Bratislava: Institute for Public Affairs, 208.

38 Ibid.

39 Vladimir Krivy (2003), "Vztah slovenskej verejnosti k USA" ("The Relation of the Slovak Public to the USA"), in *USA a transatlanticka spolupraca* ("The USA and Transatlantic Cooperation"), Bratislava: Institute for Public Affairs, 21.

40 Ibid.

41 The following findings are partly based on the analysis by Mario Nicolini from the Ministry of Defense of the Slovak republic, published immediately after the Prague Summit on 11 December 2002; Slovakia, Ministry of Defense (2002), *News Analysis*, MoD SR, 11 December.

42 Vilnius Group was established as a group of nine NATO candidate countries in 2000. In 2001 the group was enlarged by Croatia and since then it has been also called "Vilnius 10" Group.

43 "German leaders were reported struck by the bluntly pro-American tone of a recent initiative of the so-called Vilnius Group, 10 former Soviet bloc countries, presenting themselves as part of a potential coalition committed with the United States to the disarming of Iraq. A declaration by the group, virtually all EU candidates, coinciding with the NATO summit meeting in Prague in November, showed them to be ahead in terms of support for the Americans than many of the EU's senior member states", John Vinocur (2002), "The Big Winner in the EU Expansion: Washington", *International Herald Tribune*, 9 December.

44 Press Conference of the US Secretary of Defense Donald Rumsfeld (2002), Bratislava, 22 November.

45 Javier Solana (2003), *A Secure Europe in a Better World*, Thessaloniki: European Council, 20 June.

46 Javier Solana (2003), *A Secure Europe in a Better World*, Brussels: European Council, 12 December.

47 An expert meeting in Rome on 20 September, 2003, under the auspices of the Aspen Institute. An expert meeting in Paris on 6–7 October under the auspices of the Institute of the Security Studies of the EU. And an expert meeting in Stockholm on 20 October under the auspices of the Swedish Institute of International Studies. At all three meetings, representatives of the Ministry of Foreign Affairs of the Slovak Republic participated.

48   Slovakia, Ministry of Foreign Affairs (2003), "Slovak Non-Paper" (as to European Security Strategy), Slovak Ministry of Foreign Affairs, July.
49   In between, this demand has been met thanks to announced experts meetings of EU and EU candidate countries in Rome, Paris and Stockholm.
50   This demand was expressed by the Minister of Justice (Christian Democrat – KDH) of the Slovak Republic officially on 26 April 2004.

Chapter 12
Hungary
László Valki

Introduction

Hungarian security priorities – or threat perceptions – have undergone considerable changes since the end of the Cold War. A long time has passed since the beginning of the fundamental social changes of 1988–1999. It seems as if Hungary – together with some other countries – has also shifted its geographical location. An 'East' European country became a 'Central' European one. This was due not so much because of a move toward the west, but because of the emergence of independent, autonomous states east of Hungary following the break-up of the Soviet Union. After a while, Hungary ceased to regard itself as a state on the continent's periphery, and defined its position as somewhere in the middle of Europe. It was not easy to have this fact accepted in political thinking, but eventually it was. At the same time, initial Hungarian perceptions were greatly determined by the disappearance of the bipolar system. In the beginning, this fact entailed considerable uncertainties.

Threat Perceptions and Uncertainties Following the End of the Cold War

The West in the second half of the Cold War was by no means a rigid entity under the leadership of a single superpower. Bipolarity was composed of a comparatively rigid East, and a relatively loose Western military-political bloc. On the Western part of the world, some sort of multipolar system existed with the priority of a superpower. After the Cold War, the opposite formation emerged. The West seemed largely an integrated military-political system, while Central and Eastern Europe (CEE) became fully disintegrated. It seemed that the international situation in CEE resembled that after World War I. Empires and federations were similarly dissolving and new small states arose that felt unsafe under the new conditions. "East Central Europe is littered with potential mini-Weimar republics, each capable of inflicting immense violence on the others. Paradoxically, while heavily armed, these countries nonetheless lack the ability to defend themselves against major outside aggression," wrote analysts of Rand Corporation.[1]

Indeed, small countries gained independence after 1989 that would have been unable to successfully counter a considerable threat individually. The potential threat was posed at the time by the Soviet Union. No one knew how long Gorbachev would remain in power and what dangers a possible restoration would involve in the former Soviet sphere of interest. Many thought that given such an opportunity, Moscow could not resist the temptation to restore its former empire. It was similarly an undecided question whether the political differences among CEE countries would not lead to unpredictable consequences.

All politicians were looking for some sort of order that could provide security for the countries in the region. Some described the situation after the dissolution of the Warsaw Pact as a power vacuum. They said that the disappearance of a hegemonic power in the region would once again open the way for armed conflicts among the smaller states. Others held a different view. First, because the notion 'power vacuum' suggests that the vacuum would exist for a short time, after which it will be condensed by massive external either pressures, or filled by a new regional power. Those who were saying this mixed the characteristics of the international regime with a domestic one. A state by definition cannot exist without central power, while the international community – also by definition – can. Nobody in CEE was looking for a massive external pressure or an emerging regional power.

The Transitory Socialist Government (November 1988 – May 1990) realized it. In those years Hungary still belonged to the Warsaw Pact – Soviet troops were stationed on Hungarian soil, and the country was a member of the Comecon. However, as early as November 1998 then Foreign State Secretary Gyula Horn of the Socialist Party addressed a meeting of the Political Committee of the Parliamentary Assembly of NATO. Later, in February 1990 – already as Foreign Minister – at a meeting of the Hungarian Association for Political Sciences Horn said the following: "A close relationship should be established with NATO, and I personally do not find it unlikely that Hungary would join its various political organs."[2] The Foreign Minister must have been referring to the North Atlantic Assembly but did not go into details. The speech caused some sensation, the more so because it was mistakenly presented by television coverages. Reporters said that Horn spoke about the possibilities of joining NATO. The Soviet Government did not like to see Hungary making approaches to NATO and expressed its concerns through diplomatic channels. However, at the time of the speech, Moscow had already promised Hungary to withdraw the Soviet troops and the inter-state agreement on this had already been drafted and ready to sign in March 1990.

The demand for relying on NATO was becoming ever stronger. After the withdrawal of the Soviet troops from Hungary by June 1991, many regarded NATO as the only military power with a deterrent force and the only possible ally in the region. Both experts and politicians were aware that in case of a Soviet restoration of imperial ideals, Hungary could hardly count on either the UN or the Conference on Security and Cooperation in Europe.

After the first free elections in May 1990, the conservative Prime Minister József Antall conducted a more cautious policy. He did not speak about the possibility of a Hungarian membership in NATO. Moreover, he found it would be more advisable to draw away from NATO and approach the European Communities instead. However, in July 1990, Antall was the first Central European prime minister to visit NATO headquarters and hold unofficial talks with Secretary General Manfred Wörner. In October, he paid an official visit to the NATO headquarters and gave a speech at a NATO meeting. He said the Hungarian Government believed that Hungary's membership in NATO would be an unfounded goal for the time being:

We [still] hold it very important that NATO should consider it its duty to show determination against aggression and the violation of frontiers. ... NATO is the guarantee for stability in Europe. We highly appreciate the international agreements, the Helsinki Final Act, and the Organization for Security and Cooperation in Europe but hold NATO the only efficient organization for security.[3]

On 1 July 1991, the WP was dissolved and at the end of the year, the Soviet Union disintegrated. It was a promising statement on the part of NATO, and something that satisfied Hungary's expectations, when NATO foreign ministers declared on the third day of the attempted coup in Moscow in August 1991 that their security was "inseparably linked to that of all states in Europe, particularly to that of new democracies. We expect the Soviet Union to respect the integrity and security of all states in Europe."[4] This was an explicit warning for Moscow.

However, the aggression of Iraq against Kuwait in the previous year and the outbreak of the war in Yugoslavia in 1991 called the attention of the Hungarian political elite to the fact that the end of the Cold War did not automatically lead to lasting peace. At the same time, the spectacular victory of the coalition in the Gulf War created the impression that the West had at last decided to bring about a New World Order. Moreover, the war revealed such a superiority of western, more specifically, American military technology that it was felt in Budapest to be more than enough to prevent a crisis anywhere in the world. However encouraging the role of the West in the Gulf War had been, what the western powers did or left undone in Yugoslavia was disappointing. The Hungarians living along the southern borders felt an increasing threat of escalation of war in their neighborhood. The situation demanded continuous contact with NATO Headquarters in Brussels. When the Security Council introduced a no-fly-zone over Bosnia, NATO invited the Hungarian Government to agree to AWACS planes continuously performing reconnaissance flights in Hungarian air space. The activities of these specially equipped planes diminished Hungary's anxiety as they would have given warning about a possible Serbian attack.

By 1993, the Hungarian Government had concluded that Hungary's security could be guaranteed only within the framework of NATO. From then on, it strove to reach this goal by all possible means. In April 1993, the Resolution adopted by Parliament on the principles of national defense declared the following: "The aim of the Republic of Hungary is to join existing security organizations, that is, NATO and the Western European Union as a full member."[5] Accordingly, Hungary applied for NATO membership.

Next, the socialist-liberal coalition under Prime Minister Gyula Horn pressed the United States and other NATO members even more vigorously to admit Hungary and the other two 'Visegrad Countries', Poland and the Czech Republic, into NATO. The desire of the political elite – with the exception of the far right wing Hungarian Party of Justice and Life[6] – was self-evident: joining NATO and EU would put an end to the perception of insecurity. Joining NATO was, of course, the first priority since after a while the Hungarians understood that admission into the EU would be a much more difficult and lengthy process than they initially thought.

Hungarians also felt that membership would help to handle conflicts among the new member states themselves. Indeed, after having got rid of the Soviet occupation, the conservative Antall Government set another priority in its foreign policy *vis-a-vis* the neighbors of Hungary, namely the protection of human rights and the improvement of the living conditions of ethnic Hungarians beyond the frontiers. József Antall probably made the most frequently quoted statement. He said on many occasions after the first free elections "he would like to be the Prime Minister *in spirit* of 15 million Hungarians." Since the population of Hungary did not reach 11 million, Antall obviously spoke about those who lived beyond the frontiers.[7] Although Antall was always stressing the key words: 'in spirit', both the press and the politicians in the neighboring countries quoted him as if he was talking about his will to be the Prime Minister of *all* Hungarians in Central Europe. It was also usual to refer to possible 'peaceful' changes of borders as a reference to the respective paragraph of the Helsinki Final Act, according to which the borders cannot be changed but in a 'peaceful way'. This formula had been interpreted in the neighboring countries in a negative way, that is, that Hungary did not exclude the possibility that the borders might somehow be changed in the future. It was extremely difficult to explain to the Romanian or Slovak Government why Hungary was not ready to recognize the common borders of a so-called basic treaty concluded between Bucharest and Bratislava. These contributed to a growing threat perception in the neighboring countries, even if the Hungarian behavior has never gone beyond rhetoric. Although no big Hungarian army units have ever deployed close to the borders, no planes violated the territorial integrity of Rumania or Slovakia, it was still a problem in need of solving.

Hungarians did not perceive any conventional threat posed by its neighbors. The latter, however, were concerned about official Hungarian speeches and documents. In fact, none of the states has ever mobilized their armed forces close to the Hungarian borders and no specific border dispute has ever emerged between Hungary and the two countries. This was reflected in the Parliamentary Resolution on Fundamental Principles of Hungarian Security Policy of 1993.[8] The Resolution stated flatly, "the Republic of Hungary does not have any enemy perception."[9] The sources of danger lie only in "the economic backwardness, the difficulties of transforming the command economy to a free market society, ... the psychological legacy of dictatorships, the problems related to the shaping of new democratic systems, ... the situation of ethnic minorities, [and so on.] ... All that may contribute to a political and social instability in the region."[10] Another Parliamentary Resolution passed a month later on the Principles of Defense Policy listing the same sources of instability.[11] It referred also to the dangers that could arise from the civil wars and other military activities of neighboring countries. In such conflicts, one or the other party might cross Hungarian territories, including airspace, in order to achieve a better military position against its enemy. These threat perceptions – the Resolution called 'risks' – were clearly connected with the Yugoslav crisis (1991–1995). Indeed, during the crisis, there were some Serbian overflights in Hungarian air space, and some troop movements occurred in border areas. However, the Hungarian army and air force – acting very carefully – has never engaged in any military conflict with either parties. Yet both Resolutions "refused *forceful* border changes," implying that peaceful changes might be welcome by Hungary. The legacy of 'centuries-old' conflicts was kept in the mind of some Hungarian conservative politicians. The public was preoccupied with every day problems, like inflation and bad infrastructure and frankly did not care too much about its fellow Hungarians living beyond the borders.

The solution to the problem of Hungarian ethnic minorities (and borders) was brought about by the socialist-liberal coalition elected in 1994. It sharply rejected all forms of nationalism and racism in its domestic and foreign policy. It started out from the concept that living conditions of Hungarian minorities could only be improved if intergovernmental relations were normalized first. This corresponded with the interests of the West, and those of the neighboring countries. The Government was prepared to sign a basic treaty with them. Before beginning negotiations, it laid down demonstratively that it had no territorial claims whatsoever against its neighbors, nor would it make such claims in the future, furthermore, it was prepared to include a provision to this effect in the treaty without any preconditions. Hungary negotiated and signed the Basic Treaty; first with the Ukraine in 1993, then with Slovakia in 1995. Finally, after nearly two years of prolonged and difficult negotiations, the Basic Treaty was signed with Romania in 1996. Western diplomatic pressure put on Romania was decisive in the conclusion of the treaty.

Had Hungary not signed the two treaties, it would have never made it into the first circle of NATO and EU enlargement negotiations. Never has Hungarian foreign policy received so much appreciation from the international community as it did in connection with the conclusion of these treaties. This time the West finally believed that Hungary did not represent a potential source of conflict in the region, and that it was really prepared to do anything to solve its disputes, and that it would not be Hungary's fault should it fail to reach an agreement with its neighbors. Because of this, Hungary became a member of NATO in 1999.

In the meantime, negotiations on Hungarian admission to the European Union ended successfully also. Budapest accepted the so-called *aquis communitaire*, in other words it incorporated all legal rules made by the Community in the past and – with some exceptions[12] – joined all policies, including the Common Foreign and Security Policy (CFSP) and the European Security and Defense Policy (ESDP). As of 1 May 2004, Hungary – together with nine other countries – became a member of the European Union.

Around Hungary, the political, economic and security landscape has completely changed. It was, of course, not a result of only two formal legal actions (admissions) but of a continuous process. In the second half of the 1990s, Hungary became more and more integrated into Euro-Atlantic structures. It participated in the Partnership for Peace programs, sent troops to the IFOR, SFOR and KFOR, after the Dayton Accords provided a military base for the American forces in Taszár, and opened its land and air space for NATO military operations in Bosnia and, during the Kosovo conflict, Yugoslavia.

Recent Threat Perceptions in Hungary

Threat perceptions that characterized the first half of the 1990s have completely disappeared. Although Russia struggled with a number of severe economic and political problems throughout the decade, they did not lead to the turmoil that

Hungarians feared. The Russian Government did not try to influence Hungarian domestic and foreign policy in any way except, of course, its opposition to NATO enlargement, which was, however, successfully neutralized as a result of US diplomatic efforts. No longer did the elite or the 'men of the street' think there was any threat to Hungary from the East. Thus, the elite and the public shared the same views – not any more hostile – with regard to Russia. Normal relations between the two countries have been gradually restored. Only the volume of trade has remained very low, but vital Russian oil supplies have been unaffected.

Relations with the neighboring countries have also definitely normalized. The situation of Hungarian minorities in Romania and Slovakia improved, and, today, their parties are either part of the government coalition or supported it, enabling them to take part in the political decision-making of the respective countries. After the basic treaties were signed, territorial disputes of any kind ceased to arise, except in the case when, during the NATO air campaign against Yugoslavia, the above mentioned extreme right-wing Hungarian Party for Justice and Life demanded that, taking advantage of the situation, Hungarian settlements along the border be reannexed to Hungary. Both the Government and opposition parties dismissed the demand labeling it distasteful.

Ultimately, by the end of the nineties, Hungary had no direct threat perception remaining. The Parliamentary Resolution on the Basic Principles of Hungarian Security and Defense Policy that came into force on the date of NATO accession in 1999 also reflected this.[13] The Resolution stated that during recent years a fundamental change has taken place in the security of Hungary, essentially because of the achievements made in the field of Euro-Atlantic integration. Compared to the period of a bipolar international system, the threat of a global armed conflict has been reduced to the minimum. At the same time, however, the scope of risks and sources of danger have significantly increased and become more complex. Hungary's security is now, the Resolution added, influenced primarily by the security of the Euro-Atlantic region and the political, social and economic processes taking place in that part of the world. The proliferation of weapons of mass destruction and their means of delivery and the possibility of attacks on information systems present an increasing challenge and danger. This was followed by an important statement in the Resolution:

> The Republic of Hungary can maintain its security most effectively as a member of NATO. ... Hungary considers transatlantic co-operation a cardinal factor of European security in the long run as well. In the framework of intra-Alliance co-operation, Hungary supports the development of a European Security and Defense Identity. ... As a result of the [ongoing] negotiations with the European Union ... [Hungary] would take part in the shaping and implementation of the Union's Common Foreign and Security Policy.[14]

In other words, the Resolution established that, overall, the above risks and threats do not directly affect Hungary's security. Since Hungary has become a member of NATO, threat to its security is perceived in a broader context. In other words, any threat to the Alliance also affects Hungary, and Budapest is under obligation to contribute to joint actions carried out within a NATO framework. Hungary fulfilled this obligation when, in wake of the 9/11 terrorist attacks, the

United States launched its counterstrike against Afghanistan. Although NATO was not involved in this, in the interest of restoring the peace, Hungary joined other NATO member states that supported the United States in the fight against terrorism. Hungary contributed by sending a medical team.

The Government did not see any contradiction between "Euro-Atlantic" and "European" security. Budapest did see that some tensions emerged occasionally between the European allies and the United States, it knew that the Europeans made efforts toward establishing a European Security and Defense Identity, that from time to time they tried to revive the Western European Union, and that subsequently they wanted to integrate the latter into the EU. However, the question did not even arise that some day Budapest would have to choose between "Atlantic" and "European" cooperation. Hungarian politicians were aware of America's position as first among equals, but they attributed this mainly to the fact that during the Cold War the US was, and, in fact, has remained ever since, by far the strongest military power in the world, spending twice its GDP on armament than the European allies. In addition, at the time of passing the above Parliamentary Resolution, the Hungarian Government already considered admission to NATO settled and, at the same time, continued the negotiations on EU accession.

As regards the role of international institutions and international law, the Parliamentary Resolution stressed that Hungary wishes to realize its security goals in accordance with the norms of international law, with special regard to the principles and obligations enshrined in the Charter of the United Nations, in the documents of the Organization for Security and Co-operation in Europe, the Council of Europe, and in the North Atlantic Treaty.[15] This meant that, in accordance with Article 24 of the UN Charter, Hungary started out from the primary role of the Security Council.[16]

However, the Study on National Security – prepared after the war against Iraq – put the emphases elsewhere.[17] The reason for this was that the war against Iraq has changed the Hungarian security policy, and that Hungary joined the EU in 2004. The Study no longer accorded priority to the rules of the UN Charter, and only subsequently referred to the primary responsibility of the UNSC. The Study established first that the fundamental guarantee of Hungary's security lies in cooperation in NATO and the EU. "Hungary is not threatened by military aggression, and the risk of other conventional threats is minimal." According to the Study, the Hungarian National Security Strategy has to comply with the Strategic Concept of NATO of 1999 and the European Security Strategy of the EU of 2003. According to the Study, the primary Hungarian interests are the following:

- the extension and deepening of integration realized within the framework of the European Union;
- increasing the efficiency of the Common Foreign and Security Policy, strengthening the European Security and Defense Policy serving as the means of CFSP;
- continuation of NATO's central role in the Euro-Atlantic security system;
- adjustment of NATO's activity to the changed security environment of the 21st century, including the military presence and active role of the United States in Europe.

The study stated that the terrorist attacks against the United States on September 11, 2001 have become a strategic threat to the security of the Euro-Atlantic region. Terrorism exerts a destabilizing impact on international relations. It undermines the operation of states and the international system. The study said that the United States occupies a prominent position in the system of international relations. Hungary – similarly to other member states of the European Union – shares traditionally common values with the United States.

The UN is mentioned only after the previous statements, and expressed with some criticism. The study stated that the maintenance of international peace and security remains the primary, but not exclusive, responsibility of the UN Security Council. "In wake of the events in recent years, there is increasing demand among international actors that the legal and institutional bases of the international community are brought into compliance with the new challenges, and that the UN becomes more efficient."[18] The Study also takes a stand on the question of "Euro-Atlantic" and "European" cooperation:

> It may considerably increase the success of conflict management in the Euro-Atlantic region and its environment if NATO and the European Union strengthen their strategic partnership in the field of crisis management and development of capabilities. ... It is in Hungary's interest to have an expanded, strong, and unified Europe that maintains a stronger transatlantic partnership, where small countries like Hungary *are not compelled to choose between Europe and the United States*. In the European Union, Hungary's aim is to be America's strategic partner, and in NATO to be an ally that strengthens European commitment.[19]

The last sentences express the essence of the recent Hungarian way of thinking. The division with regard to the war against Iraq between the United States and Great Britain, on the one hand, and the rest of allied countries, on the other, put a severe strain on the Hungarian political elite that also became divided over the Iraqi conflict. The elite would not like to see this happen again.

Finally, the Study refers to Russia by saying that its geographical extension, resources, and military potential, especially its nuclear weapons, continue to make it an important actor in international politics. At the same time, it notes with satisfaction that Russia established partnership with NATO and the EU, that it applies European values in its internal development, and that the aim of cooperation with NATO and EU came to the forefront of its foreign policy. According to the study, the dangers arising from internal instability of Russia diminished but did not disappear completely. It serves mutual interests that Russia and the states and organizations of the Euro-Atlantic region are stable and predictable partners for each other. Among the other neighboring countries, the study refers only to the states belonging to former Yugoslavia without naming them. It observes that, due to the presence of foreign forces, the security situation in these countries gives no reason for concern for the time being, but their economic and democratic development is too slow. For this reason, Hungary also takes part in the efforts that serve this development.

The conclusions of the study concur with the Hungarian political elite's view, though there may be differences in emphasis, sequence, and details. As already mentioned, these differences were far more pronounced before and during the Iraqi war.

The Iraqi Crisis

The view of the Hungarian political elite on the issue of the war against Iraq was polarized. The socialist-liberal Government – particularly Foreign Minister László Kovács – firmly supported the statements and objectives of the United States from the beginning. On the other hand, the conservative opposition did not express an opinion at first, but later took the stand that a peaceful solution should be achieved. The part of the intelligentsia sympathetic to the Government was itself divided, although along different lines. Certain liberal journalists, writers, and public figures sided with the American position, while others – socialist and liberal voters, academic circles – expressed disapproval. On the conservative side, nobody supported the invasion of Iraq. As regards public opinion, the overwhelming majority strongly opposed the attack against Iraq.

The Government's view was determined primarily by the following:

1 *Sympathy toward America.* There is considerable sympathy toward Americans not only in the administration but also among the people, which was only enhanced by the US support to the NATO enlargement and its military intervention in Bosnia. Although public opinion resented the 78-day long NATO air campaign against Yugoslavia, the administration knew that Milosevic had to be halted at all cost, and that land invasion would have involved heavy burdens and great risks for Hungary too. The coalition parties believed that in case of a possible emergency they could count mainly on the United States.

2 *US policy toward Hungary.* During the previous election period, between 1998 and 2002, America formed an increasingly negative picture of the conservative Hungarian Government. In order to maximize its votes, the Government formed an alliance with the extreme right and was 'indulgent' of its anti-Semitic, nationalist manifestations. Moreover, many considered even the coalition nationalistic. The American ambassador publicly condemned the events seen in Hungary, and President Bush refused to receive the Prime Minister Viktor Orbán during his visit to the United States. The socialist-liberal coalition Government – elected in 2002 – had nothing to do with nationalism or racism, and, thus, was welcomed by the Republican administration. Relations between the two countries became rather friendly. The socialist-liberal coalition wanted to maintain its good relations with Washington even at the time of the Iraqi conflict. Besides this, the coalition deeply sympathized with the American people after the 9/11 terrorist attacks.

3 *Evidences of WMD and al Qaeda connections.* The Hungarian Government accepted the confidential American and British evidences concerning WMD, and felt that the Saddam regime had to be removed because it posed a threat to

international security. Everyone knew of the previous breaches of international law by Saddam Hussein, the war against Iran and Kuwait, and the deception of UNSCOM inspectors.

4   *Division of Europe.* The Government perceived that Europe became deeply divided on the question of the war. The EU was not in a position to form its own policy concerning Iraq, therefore, Hungary had to choose between the war coalition and the states opposing the war, and not between America and Europe. Declaring "neutrality" was politically impossible.

5   *Historical perceptions.* The Government was well aware of the fact that during both world wars the United States rushed to the assistance of Europe and that during the Cold War it made considerable sacrifices in conducting the policy of containment against Soviet expansion.

6   *EU attitude at the accession negotiations.* The CEE countries – including Hungary – expected the 15 member states to show a more generous attitude at the negotiations on accession. Although they knew that the EU was preparing for the simultaneous – consequently, difficult – admission of 10 countries, they nevertheless hoped that they would get the same support from the various EU funds as Portugal or Spain had earlier. Their attitude was characterized by some disappointment.

All these were reflected in the Hungarian political statements. For instance, Foreign Minister László Kovács said in September 2002 after he listened to the speech of President Bush:

> I fully agree with the thrust of the message in the speech delivered by President Bush in the UN General Assembly this morning. ... Saddam Hussein and the present Iraqi regime pose a threat to peace in the region and in the rest of the world. ... We give priority to measures that are supported by a UN resolution. *But we are aware of the danger of not taking action if that action becomes necessary in order to prevent Saddam Hussein from producing and using weapons of mass destruction.*[20]

Thus, the foreign minister presumed as early as September 2002 that the members of the Security Council would not reach a resolution on armed intervention against Iraq, and stated that the regime change in Iraq would have to be carried out even if no decision is made by the UNSC. The opposition harshly criticized the minister, saying he evidently disregards the rules of the UN Charter which prohibit the use of force unless in self-defense or with UNSC authorization.

However, the first unanimous UNSC resolution was passed in November and the UNMOVIC inspectors began their work. After this, events followed a normal course for a while, until Donald Rumsfeld made his notorious statement on "the old and the new Europe." This was followed by the initiative that came to be known as the Letter of the Eight. The British ambassador called on Prime Minister Péter Medgyessy and handed him a draft of the letter. The Prime Minister decided to sign the letter providing there was agreement on a few changes.

As regards the agreement between America and Europe on the authorization to use force against Iraq, the Prime Minister used a different language. He emphasized the importance of the participation of Europe in the decision making and passing a second resolution. He stated in Parliament that:

> Europe must take part in the resolution of this question. ... The declaration signed by eight countries contributes to the possibility of a peaceful resolution and prompts the framing of a common European stand. ...It is my belief that there is a need for a real Common Foreign and Security Policy in Europe. Today, there is no approved common standpoint even on the question of Iraq. ... According to our standpoint, after the evidence of the existence of weapons of mass destruction are presented, the Security Council should be reconvened, and pass the necessary [second] resolution on this issue.[21]

On another occasion, a reporter asked if Medgyessy approved of the American standpoint that "those who are not with us, are against us." His response was:

> I think that for the reason that you've just mentioned it would not be good if the US sought to resolve every problem alone. And if the US would be left to himself, it might try a [unilateral] solution. If the dialogue between the United States and Europe is successful and a common standpoint is accepted, it will become clear that [Washington] needs Europe. ... Europe must make itself heard, but first it must work out a common standpoint.[22]

As the debates in the UN continued, Medgyessy said again that he hoped for a second SC resolution authorizing the use of armed force against Iraq. "The Americans should make public all information they have on the Iraqi weapons of mass destruction, and if there is evidence of such weapons and Iraq does not agree to disarmament, the Security Council must pass a new resolution."[23] The Foreign Minister, who unconditionally supported Iraq's invasion, did not make a similar statement. Commenting on Colin Powell's speech in the Security Council on 5 February 2003, Kovács called it an important and favorable development that the American Secretary of State laid before the Security Council the evidence showing that Iraq was not cooperating with the UN weapons inspectors, that it was obstructing their work, and was trying to mislead them and, through them, world public opinion.[24] By this, he wanted to indicate that according to the Foreign Ministry the attack has to be launched whatever happens, irrespective of passing or not a second resolution.

Prior to launching the attack against Iraq, the American government turned to the Hungarian Government on two occasions for permission to use Hungarian territory for military purposes. In the first case, the request involved possible assistance to Turkey. Since NATO backed this request, the Government's proposal, following a debate with the opposition, was unanimously approved by Parliament, moreover, it decided that Hungary too would send to Turkey various protective equipment in case of chemical attack. In the second case, a few days before the planned invasion, the United States requested permission for overflights in Hungarian airspace. However, due to the conservative opposition's objection, it was feared that the Government's proposal would not receive the necessary two-thirds majority vote in Parliament. Fortunately for the Government, a Parliamentary Resolution, in force since 1998, provided, without setting a deadline and naming any state, that the

Government may exercise its competence without consulting Parliament "in case of implementing Security Council resolutions against Iraq."[25]

On the day the attack was launched, Foreign Minister Kovács made the following statement: "Since the start, Hungary has urged the peaceful political resolution of the Iraqi crisis. Unfortunately, the possibilities have been exhausted, and Saddam Hussein's obstinate opposition left no choice but to press Iraq to disarm by the use of force." Responding to a question, he stated that it was not surprising that the American President spoke about coalition in his speech announcing the launching of the attack. He referred to a remark of Bush who said that 35 states backed the United States, in various ways supporting the preparation for the use of force, and Hungary was one of them. Kovács also stated that the President's speech did not mean that Hungary became in a state of war with Iraq. By way of justifying the Government's step, he also said that Germany and France, neither of which supported the invasion, allowed for all American and British troop movements and overflights.[26]

Every time the members of Government explained their position on the intervention, they spoke about the confidential evidence disclosed to them regarding the presence of weapons of mass destruction in Iraq. There were only passing references to Saddam's dictatorship, the violations of human rights, and the presumed terrorist links. Not one Hungarian politician used the term "liberation" or "regime change," and none said that the liberating forces were expected to be greeted by celebrating crowds in Baghdad.

The smaller conservative opposition party, the Hungarian Democratic Forum, stated that authorizing the use of airspace was in violation of the Hungarian Constitution. It considered it shocking that "the Government, referring to a 1998 Parliamentary Resolution and bypassing Parliament, exercised its own competence in authorizing the use of airspace in case of a war against Iraq. The HDF does not approve of any act of war, and therefore, does not support any troop movement, including the use of Hungarian airspace in connection with a possible war against Iraq."[27]

The bigger opposition party, Fidesz, released the following statement:

> The key question, deciding the legitimacy of this particular military intervention, is whether the operation has international authorization or not. Fidesz is of the opinion that the operation does not possess the necessary international legitimization. ... The series of steps taken by the Hungarian Government in support of the American-British unilateral military intervention in Iraq, most notably co-authoring the letter which torpedoed a common EU-stand on the Iraqi crisis late January, will certainly affect Hungary's EU-accession process and the country's position therein following accession. Opposing this intervention does not at all mean siding with the Iraqi dictator.[28]

As far as Hungarian public opinion is concerned, the overwhelming majority opposed any military intervention in Iraq. In February 2003 Gallup asked: "Do you approve or oppose that the United States carry out military operations against Iraq?" Of those who gave answers, a very high ratio, 74 per cent, opposed military intervention by the United States and only 15 percent approved. The rest did not express an opinion.[29]

As regards post-war events, on 25 April 2003, the United States asked Hungary to take part in the Iraqi peacekeeping operation. The Government believed that it would not serve Hungary's prestige if it were to shirk participation, since almost every NATO member state and a number of countries desirous of joining already indicated their participation in the stabilization. In addition, the participation of Hungarian firms in Iraqi reconstruction also raised (futile) hopes. This notwithstanding, serious debates preceded the decision to send Hungarian troops. The Government proposed the sending of a 300-strong military police unit. This decision also required a two-thirds majority vote. Due the differing opinion of opposition parties, the Parliamentary debate on the peace mission dragged on for weeks.

Fidesz leaders said that while there was no obstacle to Hungarian non-military humanitarian assistance, they insisted that international legitimacy provided by the Security Council, NATO, or the European Union as to the legal status of the stabilization force in Iraq is a precondition to Hungarian military contribution. The other opposition party, the HDF, expressed the same view. Fidesz rejected the Government's proposals to send a military police unit to Iraq, while being supportive of humanitarian assistance. By way of compromise, the Government introduced another motion under which Hungary would contribute a 300-strong military transport and logistics unit with self-defense capabilities to the stabilization of the situation in Iraq. Fidesz rejected this motion, too. The Government had been insisting that Hungary must make its contribution even without a legal authorization, because that would not take place. The Security Council passed Resolution 1483, recognizing the United States and Great Britain as occupying powers, and providing international authorization for the stabilization of Iraq. Accordingly, Fidesz approved the sending of a 300-strong military transport and logistics unit with self-defense capabilities.

On 28 May, the parliamentary parties reached an agreement in principle on sending a 300-strong military transport battalion to Iraq. Finally, on 2 June, Parliament unanimously approved it. On 18 August, the first Hungarian soldiers arrived at al Hilla, south of Baghdad, where they joined the international forces under Polish command. Defense Minister József Juhász declared that if the situation in Iraq were to escalate into a war again, he would recall the troops, because they were going to Iraq to assist in the stabilization process and not to fight. Naturally, Juhász did not mean guerilla attacks, but the emergence of a grave situation.[30] Many criticized the Minister for this statement, although it was, in fact, a responsible declaration made at a time when no one could foresee what would happen in Iraq.

The majority of the Hungarian public opinion did not support even the sending of a military unit. In September 2003, Gallup asked the following question: "Do you support or oppose that the Government has sent a transport unit of professional soldiers to Iraq?" 67 per cent of the respondents opposed it, and only 23 percent were in favor. The rest gave no answer. It is interesting to compare these data with those of the public opinion surveys following the close of the Bosnian war. In December 1996, 58 percent supported Hungarian participation in the Bosnian peacekeeping operations, and only 25 percent were against. Due to Hungary's and Bosnia's closeness, public opinion showed greater empathy toward the peaceful resolution of that conflict. The majority took a personal interest in having the

Bosnian situation stabilized and did not deem participation dangerous. On the other hand, many deemed the Iraqi intervention an unlawful, not legitimate operation that Hungary has nothing to do with, and which also puts Hungarian troops in danger.[31]

Several months after Saddam Hussein's regime was overthrown, when the interim Iraqi Governing Council was already working, and no WMD was found nor any trace of al Qaeda links, Gallup again asked the question of what people thought of the military attack against Iraq by the United States and Great Britain. The majority, 65 percent, continued to oppose the intervention, and the ratio of supporters did not exceed 21 percent.[32] This shows a slight shift in opinion in favor of the war after Saddam's capture, but not an essential change. It was under these circumstances that the Hungarian Government had to maintain its position concerning the intervention. The decrease in the number of those against the war is due primarily to the fact that during 2002 and 2003 the Government pursued essentially a low profile policy in respect of Iraq. Although the statements by both the Government and the opposition, cited in this paper, were made public, the politicians seldom addressed the public on this issue. It was not the politicians but the media that discussed the questions of the war.

A significant part of the independent security-policy experts, international lawyers, members of the likewise independent media and certain well-known intellectuals were among the opponents of the Iraqi intervention, as was the author of this paper. In the course of their deliberations they started out primarily from the following:[33]

1   The first dossiers containing the evidence (the IISS and the British Government dossiers in September and the CIA dossier in October 2002) were not convincing. They asserted merely that Iraq failed to account for the WMD it possessed during the 1991 war, and this corresponds with the findings of the last UNSCOM report of 1999. No one ruled out Iraq possessing such weapons, but no one believed that it could deploy them against neighboring countries, much less against distant ones. The statement in the British dossier, according to which Saddam would be able to deploy its weapons within 45 minutes, also seemed dubious. Subsequent reports by inspectors led by Hans Blix and elBaradei actually indicated that Iraq could have only very few WMD, or perhaps none at all, since the question was only whether Iraq could prove having destroyed the weapons it still had in 1991.

2   There was no evidence of any link between Saddam and al Qaeda. The only information referring to such (Mohamed Atta's meeting in Prague with an Iraqi intelligence officer) was refuted before the war. Only "retired" terrorists (Abu Nidal and Abu Abbas) had been given refuge in Iraq.

3   A war against Iraq would weaken the war on terrorism. After the attack against Afghanistan – which was lawful, launched with SC authorization – the United States should not use its full force against Iraq. The campaign against terrorism is a very complex activity extending to many states and carried out primarily by the intelligence services, and it should not be conducted simultaneously with a conventional war.

4   It seems unlikely that during the 12-year long embargo Iraq would have been able to continue its arms development programs like the ones carried out

unchecked before 1990. Moreover, experts presumed that American satellites and American and British reconnaissance planes over the two no-fly zones – and perhaps U-2 planes flying at great altitude over the central Baghdad area – were capable of keeping track of Iraq's possible development programs, therefore, they had to know what was really going on there.

5   Iraq cannot be compared to post-war Germany or Japan. It is impossible to create the first Arab parliamentary democracy in history by the use of cruise missiles. Subsequent events proved that this cannot in fact be done – at least not in the short run.

6   International conflicts – with a few exceptions such as the one in Kosovo – cannot be resolved by the use of force, not even if it involves the world's biggest power.

7   A 'preventive' war launched without Security Council authorization creates the impression as if the fundamental norms of international law were no longer in force, that is, that any one state can take a similar action against another. Although the New World Order that came into being after the Cold War was unipolar, adequate multilateral cooperation among the world's leading powers based on the UN continued during the first ten years. It was this that the Iraqi war broke off, notwithstanding that after 9/11 the world stood behind the United States in unison never before experienced.

8   By launching the war against Iraq, the United States would lose its allies. As early as November 1991, Germany and France expressed their objections concerning the war, and European – including British – public opinion was very much opposed to the war. Irrespective of the manner in which the Germans and the French expressed their criticism, there was a danger that not only the UN but also NATO would become marginalized.

9   Meanwhile, it came to light that American neoconservatives occupying leading positions in the administration for years urged attacking Iraq and also vindicated rights on the basis that after the Cold War the United States remained the sole military super power in the world.

10   At the same time, it also became known that leading American experts in international security sharply opposed the war and phrased a number of convincing arguments before the war.[34]

Those, who on the liberal side supported the attack against Iraq mentioned mainly moral reasons, the necessity of overthrowing Saddam's bloody dictatorship, and made no reference to weapons of mass destruction. They said that the US is carrying out a humanitarian mission when it removes regimes of this type that disregard human rights and murder hundreds of thousands by ordering the torture and execution of people. The liberals agreed with and defended in every respect the arguments presented by the US and Great Britain.[35]

Hungarian Approach

The Hungarian Government supported the position of those who thought the split in NATO and the EU in wake of the Iraqi war must be brought to an end. However, it was also clear that few things depend on a small member state like Hungary.

Hungarian politicians, in speaking at international meetings and bilateral conferences since the end of the war, consistently argued in favor of cooperation. They expressed the wish that the leading NATO and EU powers come to an agreement on global security policy. One of their frequently made statements was that for Hungary, *cooperation within NATO cannot mean less Europe and joining EU cannot mean less America*. As already mentioned, Hungary would not like to choose among its allies, either between the members of the EU, or between the EU and the US.

Hungary would welcome the further strengthening of CFSP and ESDP in the EU. The Hungarian political elite was pleased to see that Germany, France, and Great Britain who became adversaries over Iraq, felt the need to restore unity, or at least to begin regular high-level consultations in the field of security policy. Hungary also deemed it important that in the midst of the conflict EU members were able to agree on three missions, specifically, on the EU police mission in Bosnia and Herzegovina, the peace operation in Macedonia (Concordia) and in the eastern part of Congo (Artemis). Finally, Hungary appreciated that an agreement was reached on the European Security Strategy, which may boost common European strategic thinking. In the spring of 2003 Hungary did not support the idea of four EU member states that a common European command be established, because it believed that it would lead to a needless duplication of institutions and infrastructure, and would be costly. Hungary does not support the multi-tiered Europe concept in this respect either, because it feels that it would cause a split among the member states of the Union, and Hungary would immediately be classified among second-class members. The Hungarian Government believes that institutions such as the NATO-EU Capability Group should play an important role in transatlantic relations. The two organizations should not compete against each other instead, they should develop compatibility. In this area, the Prague Capability Commitment (PCC) should be brought into compliance with the European Capability Action Plan (ECAP). Cooperation between NATO and the EU should be based on Berlin plus and extended to the fight against terrorism and the proliferation of WMD. At the same time, there is no reason for rewriting the Strategic Concept of NATO, because the situation has not changed all that much since 1999, moreover, it would only provide an opportunity for NATO and EU members to renew their debates over theoretical questions. Instead, emphasis should be laid on pragmatic cooperation.

As a first step, the Hungarian Government complied with a request that had been a source of problem in the execution of NATO missions on a number of occasions since the country's accession. Due to its geographical location, Hungary has been an important military transit country since the beginning of the 1990s; overflights were carried out by allied military planes during the first Gulf War, as well as during the subsequent conflicts in Bosnia and Kosovo. As already mentioned, any foreign troop movement on Hungarian territory and overflight in Hungarian airspace, as well as the sending of Hungarian troops abroad required a two-thirds majority of Parliament. Due to the differences among the parties, this regulation remained in force even after Hungary joined NATO. Before the onset of the Iraqi war, the debates among them became particularly harsh on the question of providing assistance to Turkey. But, finally, a compromise was reached. At the end of 2003, the Government submitted a proposal on the amendment of Article 40 of the Constitution according to which the Government would have the power to issue permission without the consent of Parliament, but only if

1   the decision on the *use of force* by Hungarian or foreign armed forces is made by the North Atlantic Council, and
2   the decision on *any other troop movements* of Hungarian and foreign forces is based upon a NATO decision.[36]

In other words, any decision on the use of force – including troop movements or overflights for that purpose – must be made by the NAC itself. In all other cases other NATO bodies, like the Defense Planning Committee, may ask the Hungarian Government to issue the necessary permission. Of course, if only the United States or only a few NATO allies request permission for transit movement or overflight, the old rules apply, that is, the Government has to take the case before Parliament. In December 2003, Parliament accepted the amendment. If the EU would reach a development in respect of ESDP, Parliament would again confer on the Government the same powers as it had in the case of NATO.

Progress was made on other points, too. On 7 January 2004, the Government decided that until 31 December 2004 Hungary would take part in the NATO Reaction Force with 150 soldiers making up a reconnaissance battalion. Hungary would send the same military unit to the European Rapid Reaction Force. This is not primarily a question of principle, but of finance. At the moment, approximately 1000–1100 Hungarian soldiers perform peacekeeping or similar operations from Bosnia (SFOR) through Afghanistan (ISAF) to Iraq.[37] Although the UN covers the costs of some peacekeeping operations (Cyprus), the stationing of Hungarian units abroad nevertheless considerably burdens the Defense Ministry's budget. It is impossible to foresee how relations among the leading NATO member states will develop in the future. At the time of writing this paper it seems that the same type of conflict would not emerge again between those who invaded Iraq and the rest of NATO. Whether George W. Bush would be elected in November 2004 or not, the US elite had probably come to the conclusion that such a war must not be repeated any more. The Bush administration must have realized that this war had no adequate preparation, the information provided by the intelligence and the Iraqi emigrants were misleading, and the stabilization and "democratization" of Iraq is an extremely difficult goal. Moreover, the war contributed to a split among allies, to degradation of multilateral cooperation, to loosing faith in international law, the UN and NATO. It forced CEE countries to choose between their friends. There is a serious hope among most Hungarians that among allies and other major countries the same level of cooperation and mutual respect would be restored as in the immediate aftermath of 9/11.

Notes

1   Ronald D. Asmus, Richard L. Kugler, and F. Stephen Larrabee (1993), "Building a New NATO," *Foreign Affairs*, 72 (4), 29.

2   Lajos Pietsch (1998), *Magyarország és a NATO* (Hungary and the NATO), Euroatlanti Könyvtár, Budapest, 10–11.
3   "Különleges elbánást a 'Visegrádiaknak'. Antall József a NATO-nál" (Special treatment for the 'Visegrád countries,' József Antall at NATO), *Népszabadság*, 29 October 1990, 3.
4   NATO, NAC (1991), *The Situation in the Soviet Union*. Statement issued by the North Atlantic Council Meeting in Ministerial Session at NATO Headquarters, Brussels, NATO Press Communique, 21 August.
5   Hungary, Parliament (1993), Parliamentary Resolution No. 28/1993, 29 April.
6   Magyar Igazság és Élet Pártja.
7   According to the estimations in the beginning of the 1990s around 2 million ethnic Hungarians were living in Romania, and a further 800,000 in Slovakia, Vojvodina (Serbia), and the Ukraine.
8   Hungary, Parliament (1993), Parliamentary Resolution No. 11/1993, 12 March.
9   'Ellenségkép' – Literary translation of the German term *Feindbild*.
10 Parliamentary Resolution No. 11/1993.
11 Hungary, Parliament (1993), Parliamentary Resolution No. 27/1993, 23 April.
12 Like joining the euro-zone.
13 Hungary, Parliament (1998), Parliamentary Resolution No. 11/1998, 17 February.
14 Ibid.
15 Ibid.
16 Article 24 states: "In order to ensure prompt and effective action by the United Nations, its members confer on the Security Council primary responsibility for maintenance of international peace and security. ..."
17 Study on Hungarian National Security. SVKK (Reseach Center for Strategy and Defence), Budapest, February 2004 (manuscript).
18 Ibid.
19 Emphasis added.
20 Comment by the Hungarian Foreign Minister, Mr. László Kovács (2002), on Iraq, 12 September (emphasis added), online at www.kum.hu/Archivum/Korabbiszovivoi/2002/kovacsl/0912KLirak.htm.
21 Address by Prime Minister Péter Medgyessy to the Parliament, 4 February 2003, online at www.miniszterelnok.hu/archivum.php?tipus = beszed.
22 Ibid.
23 Interview with Prime Minister Péter Medgyessy, Katimerini (Greece), 15 January 2003, online at www.miniszterelnok.hu/archivum.php?tipus = interju&ap = 1.
24 5 February 2003, online at www.kulugyminiszterium.hu/Kulugyminiszterium/HU/Miniszterium/Szervezeti_egysegek/   Szovivoi_iroda/Miniszteri_beszedek/2003_februar/030205_Powell_beszed.htm.
25 Hungary, Parliament (1998), Parliamentary Resolution No. 11/1998, 17 February, online at www.kum.hu/szovivoi/2003/02/szov0213_1.html 13 February.
26 16 March 2003, online at www.kum.hu/szovivoi/2003/KovacsL2003/0316%20KL.htm.
27 *Népszabadság*, 17 March 2003.
28 The position of Fidesz on the recent military intervention in Iraq, 20 March 2003, online at www.fidesz.hu/index.php?MainCategoryID = 54&SubCat = 46.
29 Gallup Hungary, 29 February, online at www.gallup.hu/Gallup/release/irak030926.htm.
30 Online at www.taszar.com/?clicked = 7&page = archivum.php.
31 Ibid.
32 Ibid.
33 Some examples: László Andor (2003), "Háború – de miért?" (War: But for What Reason?), *Népszava*, 15 February; László Andor (2003), "Féligazságok háborúja" (The

War of Half-Truths), *Magyar Hírlap*, 22 February; László Andor (2003), "Tony Blair drámája" (Tony Blair's Drama), *Európai Szemle*, No. 3–4, Autumn; Endre Gömöri (2002), "A terroristák vigyorognak a sikátorban" (Terrorists Are Sneering in a Back Street Alley). *Népszabadság*, 31 October; Endre Gömöri (2004), "A bizonytalan harsona esztendeje" (The Year of Uncertain Trumpet), *Népszabadság*, 3 January; István Eörsi (2003), "Egy kérdés és egy válasz" (A Question and an Answer), *Népszabadság*, 31 March; László Kasza (2003), "A szuperhatalom és mi, többiek" (The Super Power and the Rest of the World), *Népszabadság*, 18 July; László Szocs (2003), "Hogyan nyerjük meg a békét?" (How to Win the Peace?), *Népszabadság*, 2 August; László Valki (2002), "Kit fenyeget Irak?" (Who is Threatened by Iraq?), *Népszabadság*, 18 September; László Valki (2003), "Irak és a neokonok" (Iraq and the Neocons), *Élet és Irodalom*, 19 September.

34   See Karl Kaysen, Steven E. Miller, Martin B. Malin, William D. Nordhaus, John D. Steinbrunner (2002), *War with Iraq – Costs, Consequences, and Alternatives*, Cambridge: American Academy of Arts and Sciences.

35   Dávid Meiszter (2002), "Preventiv csapás és túszdráma?" (Preventive Strike and Hostage Drama?), *Népszava*, 19 November; László Seres (2003), "Az igazság pillanata: szabadelvu érvek Irak megtámadása mellett" (The Moment of Truth: Liberal Arguments in Favor of the War Against Iraq), *Népszabadság*, 17 March; "Imre Kertész az Amerika-ellenességet bírálta" ([Nobel-Prize Winner in Literature] Imre Kertész Criticised the anti-Americans [in Germany]). *Népszabadság*, 3 April 2003; László Seres (2003), Hírsikkasztás: Avagy az Irak utáni médialegendák (Obfuscation of the News: Or Post-Iraq Media Legends), *Élet és Irodalom*, 20 June.

36   Hungary, Parliament (2003), Act of Parliament No. CIX on the Amendment of the Constitution of the Republic of Hungary, 8 December.

37   The total personnel of the Hungarian defense forces will be reduced to 35,000 in the course of the modernization program.

Chapter 13

Romania's Position Towards the Evolution of the Transatlantic Link after 11 September 2001

Mihail E. Ionescu

Introduction

The terrorist attacks of 11 September decisively influenced world politics and the evolution of the international security system. All of a sudden it was internationally understood that a new security threat had appeared, one which is not state-centric, has no definite territory and is fundamentally transnational in its way of action.[1] Most nations strongly condemned the terrorist activities and accepted the challenge in forming the widest alliance ever seen in history, a US-led coalition against global terrorism and its state-sponsors.

The tragic events of 11 September 2001 were seen be Romanian leaders and the population as a critical test for our country in order to demonstrate its willingness and capacity to act as a responsible de facto member of the western security community. Therefore, after 11 September, Bucharest broadened its activities toward achieving its national interests, meaning the accelerated integration with the West, namely joining NATO and the EU.

But has Romania's foreign policy really been influenced by the tragic events of 11 September? What kind of impact on the international stage have these events played for the Romanian position? As history teaches us, security in time of danger depends on the robustness of the bilateral/multilateral security agreements which one is part of and on a vigilant monitoring of the global and regional security environment to act according to one's vital national interests. After the collapse of the Soviet bloc and the end of the bipolar rivalry, the world was more stable and peaceful in comparison with the previous era, the risk of a great war being substantially diminished. Immediately after the end of totalitarian rule, Romania decided to choose those national strategies and security policies which could make it part of the free and democratic world, a place we traditionally call 'the West.'

Romania Moves Towards the West

Romania's perspective on the European security architecture at the beginning of the 1990s, when the Soviet Union still existed, was focused on the Conference on Security and Cooperation in Europe launched in 1972 at the top point of the 'détente' between the Soviet and American blocks. The focus was on the CSCE Helsinki Final Act signed by the states within the two rival blocs in 1975, a document which had sanctioned the political and territorial *status quo* in Europe after the Second World War. In exchange for the recognition of the current borders, the Soviet Union had to agree with a platform devoted to the respect of human rights, while hoping to infringe upon them without any punishment. The dissident anticommunist groups in Eastern Europe immediately took advantage of this legal document and made stronger pressures toward the respect of human rights.[2] This fact is one of the reasons explaining the gradual collapse of Soviet power, a decline arising especially from the inner sphere. In March 1989, months before the end of the communist regime in Romania, in the framework of the CSCE, arms control negotiations opened in Vienna, between the 23 member states of NATO and the Warsaw Treaty Organization, on the reduction of the amount of conventional forces in Europe, the final result being the Treaty on Conventional Forces Reduction in Europe (CFE).

In November 1990, the CSCE Summit Meeting of Heads of State and Government of 34 member states adopted the Charter of Paris for a New Europe and in the following years, the CSCE, renamed to OSCE in 1994, set up instruments for preventive diplomacy for use in regional crises management. But because of the decision-making process requiring unanimity and the divergences among member states, OSCE has become a discussion forum with a reduced capacity for enforcing security in Europe. Therefore, emphasizing the paramount role of CSCE was understood in Bucharest as a guarantee against possible strengthened Soviet hegemony over Romania, or at least hegemony over Eastern Europe.

On the other side, the importance attached by the Romanian leadership to CSCE/OSCE immediately after the end of the Cold War is explained by the fact that the Helsinki Final Act was the guarantee for the maintenance of the current state boundaries in face of the perceived growing threats of ethnic separatism/irredentism illustrated within the Yugoslav civil war. We should not forget that prior to the final disbandment of the Warsaw Pact, the Soviet Union maintaining it theoretically.

As these domestic and foreign tensions gradually diminished (we shall mention the Western constructive involvement in the Balkans crises and the fact that NATO had launched a new "out of area" approach toward the former communist countries, illustrated by the formation of the NACC in 1991), Romania began to look for a wider security framework in order to move closer to the West. Because the Soviet Union and its instrument, the Warsaw Pact, did not exist any longer, the former communist states began to try to actively join NATO. Romania, for its part, had a historically proven record that showed a typical Eastern and Central European trend for having a common geopolitical destiny.

Romanian leaders and civil society understood that the new European security framework (consisting preponderantly of the Western institutions like the EU, the WEU, NATO, the Council of Europe but also the UNO more effective after 1990) had at its core the North Atlantic Treaty Organization, gathering the Western states which stand together, during the Cold War, in face of the Soviet threat. NATO was not only a military alliance for collective defense but a structure built on common values, principles and norms (democracy, world security, peace, respect of the human rights), and therefore a much more efficient international player. As a demonstration of its will to establish closer links with former communist states, NATO created the North Atlantic Cooperation Council (NACC) in December 1991 which brought together the allied states and nine states from Central and East Europe, adding another two former communist states in 1992. NACC creation was in accordance with the Strategic Concept of NATO, adopted in November 1991 at the Rome Summit, a document which kept a collective defense as the core-principle of the Alliance but also insisted on future tasking associated with keeping the peace and stability of the Euro-Atlantic area through the instruments of crises management and preventive diplomacy,[3] implicitly understood as a complement for deterrence forces.[4] When Partnership for Peace was launched, Romania immediately understood its importance and was the first state to sign the Framework Document on 24 January 1994, considering it as a preparative step for full NATO membership and not a substitute for those friendly countries to be maintained outside the Alliance. Because the Western security communities had manifested its will to accept as closer partners their former ideological enemies and to set up a real security community extending from Vancouver to Vladivostok, Bucharest could not ignore such a salient reality which influenced Romania's behavior on the international stage after the Cold War.[5]

Within NATO, the United States of America had been the greatest security provider during the Cold War, through deterrence, and, after 1990, they remained firmly committed to the protection of the Euro-Atlantic security. In Romania it was remembered that the US was the active force which defeated, during the 20th century, the two main evils – Nazi Germany and Soviet Russia, not to speak of the hyper-militarist Wilhelmina Germany and Imperial Japan.

The Romanians, recently delivered from the Soviet hegemonic umbrella, still feared traditional Russian aggressions. Russia's location on the Eastern side of Romania has been perceived by the political elite as a real danger to Romanian territorial integrity and population for almost two hundred years;[6] the most prominent threat being the Soviet communist takeover by force and fraud. Even Boris Yeltsin's Russia was still considered by many Romanians as a potential danger, in spite of its current weakness, and this could explain indirectly the highly popular decision to try to obtain security guarantees from the US and NATO. Entering a collective defense organization, especially that one perceived as the winner of the Cold War, was generally considered the best option for Romanian foreign and security policy.

In order to achieve the fundamental objective of aligning Romania with the West – that is joining NATO and the European Union – a strong consensus of political forces of the entire national political spectrum was developed. On 18 September 1993, Romania's president, Ion Iliescu, addressed a letter of application to the NATO Secretary General, explaining the national decision to look for NATO membership. He stated that

> having in mind Romania's location, political and military potential, as well as its firm commitment to the cooperation with the North Atlantic Alliance, I consider that my country is able to contribute to the furthering of NATO's basic goals – freedom, democracy, rule of law, maintenance of peace and security. It can also contribute substantially to maintaining security in the Euro-Atlantic area. Consequently, Romania

has expressed its determination to participate effectively alongside with the NATO member states in their efforts aimed at strengthening European and regional security and stability.[7]

Since 1994, Romania has actively participated in Partnership for Peace activities, especially in exercises for crises management and enhancing regional stability and, since 1999 it has become part of the Membership Action Plan cycle to qualify for NATO membership. On 28 December 1994, the Statement of the National Advising Counsel for Euro-Atlantic Integration (*Consiliul National Consultativ pentru Integrare Euro-Atlantica* in Romanian), an organism including representatives of all the political parties, of the Presidency, the Government and civil society, was adopted expressing Romania's will to enter the Euro-Atlantic structures.

Gathered on 21 June 1995 in Snagov, the representatives of 13 main political parties, including those in power, signed a Statement supporting EU membership with a special chapter for military reform. It was a broad consensus for supporting the written 'Strategy for Preparing Romania's Integration in the EU.' They stated that

> the national strategic objective of Romania's adhesion to European Union constitutes a crucial point of solidarity and convergence of the country's political and social forces, representing a historical opportunity for promoting the ideals and fundamental interests of Romanian people, its identity and traditions in a wide international openness, giving the possibility of mitigating and eliminating the gaps to the advanced countries through our own efforts backed by a broad co-operation and of modernizing Romania, according to exigencies of transformational society and creation, on the basis, of the conditions for rising the Romania's citizens living standard and quality of life.[8]

On 22 June 1995, Romania officially announced its candidateship for EU membership, at the same time, Bucharest laid down the above mentioned Strategy which was the fruit of the work done by a national commission including representatives of the political parties. During the same year, Romania became an associate member of the European Union, participating at the Essen conference in this role.

There was also a declaration by the political parties represented in the Parliament concerning Romania's admission into NATO in March 2001. They assessed that "Romania's admission into NATO continues to be the cornerstone objective of its foreign and security policy" and the country "is prepared to promote and defend the democratic values which constitute the political foundation of the North Atlantic community."[9] "We will allocate resources to make the national defense system compatible with that of the NATO member states and to fulfill the commitments undertaken under the Annual National Program of Preparation for NATO Membership, while observing the social and economic balance." It is quite obvious that there is a consensus among the political parties of Romania concerning our country's future role and status as a NATO member, the key-words being 'security provider' and 'security anchor.' Until now, there were no great debates within the Parliament on the risks and opportunities brought by membership, all the political parties see this issue as a vital national interest and accept the idea that

Romania should assume all the tasks and responsibilities of a NATO member. Even the US proposal to set up military bases on Romanian territory was accepted and welcomed by the parliamentarian political parties, as they saw in it the expression of American interest for our country and surrounding region.

It is worth mentioning that not only the political establishment, but also public opinion, was aware of the importance of Romania's acceptance into the Euro-Atlantic security community. Between 18–25 March 1997, months before the Madrid NATO Summit, an opinion poll ordered by the Manfred Wörner Association to the Center for Regional and Urban Sociology ("Romania's admission into NATO") revealed that 77 percent of Romanian people supported Romania's NATO membership. The opinion polls realized in Romania each year always showed a huge popular support for becoming a NATO and EU member. Among the preoccupations of Romanian people, a poll realized in June–July 2002 by Metro Media Transylvania ("What is most important for Romania") situated the issue 'NATO integration' at fifth place (8.7 percent) after poverty (17 percent), corruption (15.6 percent), unemployment and quality of life.[10] When asked about Romania's chances for admission as a NATO member, 34 percent declared it was probable, 12 percent very probable, 25 percent less probable, 15 percent not probable, the rest did not answer.[11] These figures demonstrate that NATO membership certainly was, and still is an issue of public interest but less important than the current domestic concerns related to living standards.

We don't think there are significant divergences between the common people and political and military elites concerning the security threats and risks which could affect Romania. Everybody understands the importance of a collective security and defense umbrella as a final guarantee for the survival of our nation and state but the elites are more sensitive to the community of Euro-Atlantic values and principles (democracy, peace, solidarity . . .).

Regarding EU integration, Romania was an associate EU member since 1995. It was not until December 1999 that the European Council Summit in Helsinki agreed to start the process for full Romanian integration into the EU and to begin accession negotiations.

It was quite obvious for Romanian decision-makers and experts that the chances for joining the European Union in a first wave of enlargement were reduced because the implementation of the Copenhagen Criteria (1993) and of the *aquis communautaire* were in an incipient stage, compared with those of the more advanced countries. This explains why Romania's focus was on fulfilling the MAP requirements and on sustaining an efficient lobby activity in the Western capitals geared toward pushing Romanian membership in NATO. Bucharest has considered, in this context, that prospects for NATO membership seemed to be more realistic in the short run than European integration, having in sight the difficulties of the accession criteria in both organizations. The Study of NATO Enlargement from September 1995 first listed these expectations and showed the commitment for NATO enlargement.[12]

For Bucharest, the criteria listed in this document opened a window of opportunity for rapidly joining the west through NATO and it has acted to implement the criteria. The consequences were a very fast improvement of the bilateral relations with our neighboring states – the basic political treaties with

Hungary (1996) and Ukraine (1997), a precondition for becoming a NATO member. At the same time, the process of modernization and transformation of the Romanian armed forces became a top priority on the national agenda, with a view to have a military fully compatible (interoperable) with NATO member forces.

A highly relevant document from 1996, the "White Book Romania-NATO," exposes Romania's stand on the NATO evolution and the Alliance's enlargement process and their importance for our national interests. The document states that:

> Romania shares the view that at the core of the European order of the next century will stand an enlarged North Atlantic Alliance, whose all members, including Central-European countries, will participate at all the activities(...) The main feature of the NATO enlargement should be a gradual, voluntary and transparent process, based on commonly shared values, interests and solidarity and to offer all states having the will to join NATO a precise prospect for membership. Among the candidates to membership, Romania is the country the most advanced in adjusting its military doctrine, in transforming the domestic juridical framework and reforming the armed forces according to NATO standards.[13]

After the NATO summit in Madrid (July 1997), when membership was extended only to three countries (Czech Republic, Hungary, Poland), most Romanian politicians in power expressed their feelings of disappointment but also the hope that the North Atlantic Alliance's doors would remain open. The president, Emil Constantinescu, stated that the Madrid decision was below Romanian people expectations but the remarkable efforts made by the country nevertheless had been recognized by the Euro-Atlantic leaders, as they nominated Romania and Slovenia as the most advanced future candidates.[14]

After this summit which brought the first post-Cold War wave of enlargement for NATO, Romanian political and military decision-makers decided to make significant efforts especially concerning the process of the armed forces reform, as it was obvious that a strong and modernized army was a serious argument for future membership. Understanding that US support for NATO membership was irreplaceable, Romanian leaders in power took decisive steps in building a new kind of improved relations with Washington. To be backed by America was seen as a strong advantage within the Partnership for Peace framework and the support for domestic democratization a guarantee for being accepted within the Western community. On 11 July 1997 US president Bill Clinton visited Romania and met President Emil Constantinescu. He addressed people gathered in the University Square saying that domestic reforms must be carried out and NATO doors would remain open for other members. He added: "as long as you keep going on the long way of democracy, America will be with you."[15] A guarantee of these statements was symbolized by the launch of the US-Romania strategic partnership immediately after this visit. The strategic objectives dealt with by this co-operation formula are as follows: the development of the economic bilateral co-operation, US support for Romania's candidacy for NATO membership, American support for the economic reforms and consolidating democracy. There were four compartments of bilateral co-operation: the political and economic reform, the military partnership, the security field and dealing with the unconventional security risks. Both of the states began to co-ordinate their political strategies on the international stage, many bilateral conferences and conferences were held and the amount of American direct investments within the Romanian economy constantly increased.[16] In March 1998, US deputy secretary of state Strobe Talbott said that "generally speaking, NATO doors will stay open and for Romania in particular."[17] Not only did top politicians from allied states publicly supported Romania's candidature, but also military decision-makers like general Wesley Clark, chief SACEUR. When he visited Romania, in July 1998, he said that "regardless of decision to be taken, Romania will be seen as a key-state for NATO and a partner we will have closer and enhanced relations with."[18] When NATO secretary general, Javier Solana, visited Romania on 1–2 April 1998, he insisted on the 'open door' strategy and on the fact that Romania has to play an important role in regional stabilization, therefore suggesting that NATO membership is a tangible target for our country.[19]

Since the visit of US Undersecretary of State for Political Affairs, Thomas Pickering, in Romania, on February 2000, the 'intensified stage' began of the Strategic Partnership with the focus on the economic dimension, the American military assistance for Romania including the control of mass destruction weapons and support for combating security risks such as organized crime, corruption and, especially after 2001, terrorism.

Although the proving documents are scanty, it is obvious that, at the core of Bucharest national strategy for NATO and EU membership, a very important feature was the exigency of the admittance criteria set by these organizations. The European Union is a political and economic organization with clearly defined accession criteria and precise stages to pass through. The post-Cold War deteriorated economic situation of Romania certainly was a huge problem regarding EU membership.

A brief examination had demonstrated that the way to EU membership was longer in time and implying substantial changes within the national economy and administration, transformation of the legislation and so on. Therefore, getting into the EU was a much harder process. Even today, Romania has managed to adopt only parts of the *acquis communautaire* and not all the chapters. The negotiations for Romania's accession to the EU were officially launched on 15 February 2000, on the occasion of the Intergovernmental Conference on Accession. So, by the end of December 2003, Romania opened all 30 chapters of the *acquis communautaire* and provisionally closed 22 chapters of them.[20] Concerning the European Security and Defence Policy, Romania already committed itself, at the EU Capabilities Commitment Conference on 21 November 2000, to provide troops for the European Rapid Reaction Force[21] and even sent officers for the EU-led police mission in Bosnia-Herzegovina (9) and the peace-keeping mission in FYROM (3),[22] then welcomed the "Berlin plus" agreement between NATO and EU from December 2002, stipulating that European Rapid Reaction Force could use allied capabilities for "Petersberg tasks" (peace-keeping, support for refugees, humanitarian missions), but without harming the security interests of any NATO member or those of the Alliance as a whole. Generally speaking, Romania is likely to accept and to participate in any EU military mission that is not seen as a threat for the Euro-Atlantic security community, the ideal case being the complementarity and co-operation between these main international institutions.

Domestically, after 11 September Romania also took appropriate steps to cope with the new and overwhelming threat of terrorism alongside her allies and partners. On 19 September, Romanian Parliament adopted the decision regarding Romania's participation, alongside with NATO members, to the anti-terrorist campaign. Responding to NATO's request, Romania would provide the Alliance with all necessary facilities regarding its air, ground and maritime space as a means to support the operations. This is how overflights of Romanian national air space, including approval for the transit flight of US aircraft involved in support and medical missions, was authorized. At the same time, Romania adjusted its National Annual Program of Preparing the Integration into NATO (MAP, cycle 3) by introducing specific provisions in the field of combating terrorism. President Iliescu said, in April 2002, when he met secretary general George Robertson that, beyond the tragic events on 11 September, it was obvious that it was a major moment for the solidarity of the allies in the fight against international terrorism.[23]

One should mention the 2002 *National Strategy on Preventing and Combating Terrorism* which tackles the terrorism threat. Fourteen ministries are putting together their resources under the strategic coordination of the National Supreme Defense Council in order to achieve the goals of the strategy.[24] Romania also accepted the sharing of intelligence with the US and other NATO members' intelligence services as an effective tool for improving its anti-terrorist capabilities.

During the war in Afghanistan which began in October, 2001, Romania effectively joined the US side. Romania started its participation in the International Security Assistance Force (ISAF) in Afghanistan with a military police platoon and a C-130 Hercules transport aircraft. In July 2002, an infantry battalion was deployed as part of operation Enduring Freedom/Noble Eagle. One should not neglect the efforts made by our country for enhancing the European security within the institutional multilateral framework.

After 11 September 2001, being the Chairman-in-Office of the OSCE, Romania behaved as a de facto NATO member and took the appropriate measures to draft an international fighting plan against terrorism. "The Bucharest Action Plan for Combating Terrorism" within the OSCE framework was adopted on 4 December 2001 during the Ministerial Council meeting. Concomitantly, as Chairman in Office of the South East Europe Defense Ministerial (SEDM), Romania proposed a project geared toward WMD non-proliferation, secure borders and the fight against terrorism, one which was eventually endorsed by the Defense Ministers of the SEDM at their meeting in Turkey, on 18–20 December 2001.

The Romanian nation and its political elite prize very much the solidity of the transatlantic link which was strongly expressed when NATO invoked article V for the first time. There was strong confidence in Bucharest that in the war against terrorism there is a similar threat assessment and decision of action on both sides of the Atlantic which has to be of long duration; at least for the duration of the war against terrorism.

During the year 2002, Romania's strive toward westernization has been focused on NATO integration, a top national priority highlighted by the *National Security Strategy* adopted by the Romanian Parliament at the end of 2001. Officially published in December 2001 after being endorsed by the Romanian Parliament, this document expressed the preoccupation for the clear definition of the national interests in the context of a given international security environment, a fact that was made salient by the terrorist attacks on 11 September 2001. The international security environment at the beginning of the 21st century is described as being "ever more complex and interdependent", with the influence of the "irreversible process" of globalization. Special mention is made of the transformation in the structure and missions of NATO ("all these have proved the determination of the North Atlantic Alliance to shape the international security environment and cement peace and stability in the Euro-Atlantic area"[25]), the UNO, the OSCE and the EU ("has made major decisions and has given a fresh impetus to the efforts for building security and the defense component"). The document insists on the fact that the national interests of the states "can only be achieved through international cooperation," the recommended model being the so-called "co-operative security." A strong focus is directed toward the terrorism which "represents one of the most dangerous phenomena, being encouraged by the virulence of fundamentalist trends, based on frustration and extreme poverty in large areas of the planet" and which could be eradicated only through "open, multilateral, balanced and persistent co-operation."[26] Against this international background, Romania's national security interests are: the maintenance of independence, sovereignty, unity and territorial integrity "under specific conditions of NATO membership and EU integration," the rule of law and democracy as the core-functions of the state, the economic development, the emergence of a real market economy, developing a strong and active civil society and so on. Therefore, there is a persistence in the Westphalian pattern of international relations – but with the completion of some specific arrangements made indispensable by future NATO and EU membership (coordinated security strategies and military doctrines, 'pooled' sovereignty in some areas within the EU). The other interests are more liberal and institutional in nature (economic well-fare, civil society, rule of law, human rights), a sign of Romania's rapprochement to western ideas and principles.

The risk factors for the security of Romania are listed as follows:[27]

- *foreign risks and vulnerabilities* – The possible negative regional developments concerning democratization, respect for human rights, economic development, the proliferation of weapons of mass destruction, terrorist networks, transnational organized crime, clandestine migration and refugees, extremist/separatist actions, Romania's limited access to regional resources which are seen as vital for attaining national interests.
- *the new challenges* – transnational and international terrorism, attacks on the safety of domestic and international transportation networks, hacker attacks against strategic computer systems, strategies for affecting Romania's image abroad, economic and financial attacks, environmentally catastrophic accidents.
- *domestic risks* – economic and social problems enhanced by the difficult structural transition, the corruption and mismanagement of public goods, an expanding underground economy, economic crime, potential social conflicts, ecological disasters, excessive bureaucracy, some economic disparities among the country's regions, non-compliance with the commitments undertaken for NATO membership and so on.

Although the NATO Washington Summit in April 1999 did not contain a firm promise for integration, Romanian decision-makers decided to act as a *de facto* NATO member. This fundamental strategic orientation of Romania on the international scene coincided in 2002 with a growing consensus which had emerged among allies towards a robust and geographically balanced NATO enlargement, in order to build up an Alliance able to expand the zone of political stability and long-term democratic development from the Atlantic to the Urals.[28]

The Reykjavik NATO foreign ministers meeting on 14–15 May 2002 opened the way for a new and enhanced framework for a NATO-Russia partnership embodied in the NATO-Russia Council. The rapprochement between NATO and Russia eased the way for a robust enlargement of the Alliance towards the East. One should note that the US advocated a vigorous enlargement from the Baltic Sea to the Black Sea by accepting all '10 Vilnius Group' states (formally created in 2002) in the hope of projecting stabilization and peace towards the vast space between the Black Sea and the Baltic Sea and to further expand eastern security. As a consequence, it became an often-cited axiom that Russia was no longer considered an enemy or rival but a partner in the war against terrorism and WMD proliferation. The NATO-Russia Council became operational in late May 2003 during the Rome Summit with the media in Europe and the US insisting upon a real end to the Cold War competition and the transformation of Russia into an ally for the west.

But focusing on NATO did not mean that Romania neglected EU membership or that she had decided after 11 September to play vigorously the American card. Of course, Romania has a strategic partnership with the US (agreed in July 1997), but there was no competition between 'American' and 'European' lines in Bucharest's foreign policy. Rather, it was a conceptual and complementary approach towards both. A proof of this dual orientation resided within a statement of President Iliescu who told the MPs in December 2002 that "promoting its own interest, Romania is conducting a policy that is both pro-European and pro-American, as it considers that Europe's future depends essentially on the strength and continuity of the transatlantic connection."[29] As a matter of principle, Bucharest considers NATO and EU integration as a single process, both goals being targeted concomitantly. Tactical priorities have clearly been imposed by the political realities of events developing on the international arena and also by the rhythms of domestic reforms.

Romania and the Transatlantic Rift

Transatlantic tensions clearly mounted towards the end of 2002 and in the first months of 2003. Topics such as the Iraq war, the International Criminal Court (ICC), the Kyoto protocol, the George W. Bush's 'axis of evil,' the Middle East crisis, and the trade 'war' had their own weight in deepening the transatlantic rift. In the second half of 2002, the signs of the upcoming transatlantic rift were already present with the focused attention of many well known analysts.[30] According to them, there is an inherent moral tension between the aspirations of post-modern Europe and tradition-rooted America. This explains why the threat assessment of their national security is not similar: US fears terrorism, the proliferation of WMD, and rogue states, while EU leaders look at challenges like illegal migration, organized crime, ethnic conflict, poverty, and pollution.

At the Munich Security Conference (Wehrkunde) in February 2002, the first signs of a strong difference of opinions between Europe and the US were obvious with this cleavage already matured when the Iraq war became a question. US Defense Secretary Rumsfeld insisted on the need for US to act before the threats materialize, to adopt a pro-active strategy and build ad-hoc coalitions (coalition of the willing) in case the UN Security Council is not able to reach a consensus and deal with the threats of the 21st security environment. He spoke about the new relevance of NATO in this context. Concerning the already inexorable Iraq war, US defense secretary Donald Rumsfeld spoke on 23 January 2003, about 'new Europe' and 'old Europe.' This famous statement has to be put in the hot environment of the Iraq crisis when the rift between the countries opposing the war (France, Germany, Belgium a.s.o.) and those sustaining the US position (UK, Spain, Dutch, Italy plus the Central-Eastern European states, including Romania) was at its highest point. Some rumors referred to a US intention of moving military bases from Germany to Eastern European states like Poland, Romania, and Bulgaria because these states are friendlier and geographically closer to the Middle East region where most US security threats are.

Rumsfeld believed that 'old Europe' was no longer relevant for transatlantic security because its strategy of appeasement towards rogue states like Iraq would encourage them to become more aggressive and intensify WMD development.. The idea was that NATO's center of gravity center moving from 'old' Europe to a 'new' Europe (the former communist states which were grateful to US and saw Saddam's regime in the light of their common totalitarian experience).

When American President G.W. Bush unveiled his doctrine on the 'axis of evil' (that is Iraq, Iran, North Korea) in January 2002 and then claimed the right to intervene even militarily against terrorist networks and their state sponsors, many European states, as well as Russia and China, were worried of American unilateralism and asked for the respect of international law embodied by the U.N. Charter and of the multilateral framework of action. But the highest point in these debates concerning American conduct in its foreign policy was the publication of a new *National Security Strategy* (September 2002), a document which stated a US right to resort to pre-emptive attack against terrorist networks and rogue states if those states prepare anti-American actions and therefore are a vital threat to the American people and its legitimate interests.[31]

In Romania, the transatlantic rift was largely understood by some security analysts as due to the "systemic tension" between status-quo powers and revolutionary ones. The first side favors a multipolar world system and an adjusted balance of powers while the second side (US, primarily) want a readjustment in the world order.[32] A well-known political analyst spoke about a "Euro-Atlantic Cold War" between the US ("the New World") on one hand and France and Germany ("the Old Europe") on the other one, because the Iraq crisis seriously jeopardized the whole western world security. He remarked that not only the European Union but also the North Atlantic Organization, which guaranteed the survival of the free world during more than 40 years, were broken between two sides.[33] Concerning the public opinion on the coming war, a Gallup International Association poll realized in February 2003 showed that 49 percent of Romanians supported the war, 42 percent were against,[34] while 45 percent believed Romania should back the US in toppling Saddam's regime. It is worth mentioning that Romanians were among the main supporters of the US plan.

Some weeks before the military intervention in Iraq began, influential researchers insisted that the US would be resolute in its stance to attack Saddam's regime and forecasted that not only Iraq will be defeated but also the "harsh nucleus" of Europe – France and Germany, those countries which favor EU enlargement in order to counter-balance American power. If Europe will be defeated, the costs will be bigger than those necessary for eliminating Saddam; they will be supported by all Europeans, including Romania.[35]

On the other side, Romanian foreign policy decision-makers hardly recognized the reality of a trans-Atlantic rift and preferred to insist on the common values which bound together all the allied states since the beginning of the Cold War and continued to do the same after.[36] According to this approach, Romanian Foreign Minister, Mircea Geoana, declared in January 2003 that East-European states "should not let themselves be caught in the trap of a false loyalty dilemma, to differentiate hierarchically or to separate among the values of a world in which they were integrated or would soon be integrated" meaning that Romania should be loyal to both the EU and the US.[37] He considered that there is a debate among allied states that have been unified by common values for many decades adding that "we should not at all imagine that a (particular – m.s.) situation could endanger such a strong alliance, which was not the result of a haphazard, or a partnership based on common values between Europe and USA."[38] In an interview from March 2003, Geoana spoke about "a certain alignment within Europe and the Euro-Atlantic community" each following two separate camps – pro-intervention and anti-intervention. The former communist states are bound together by a common psychology, they had suffered 50 years of foreign domination and now they see the "US as an indispensable player for their long-term security."[39] He continues by saying that "if someone will count inside the European Union how many states support the US stance and how many don't, we will see a quite poised balance." Speaking about Romania's national interest, Geoana recognized the existence of a "massive wound (trauma), a rift which appeared inside Europe and within the transatlantic community" and this situation should represent for Romania, for the leadership, the strategic elite, for the civil society an opportunity for learning from and reflecting on." The European construction is a unique project and will face great risks, because "we are at the beginning of a new world order." Romania should avoid giving the impression that its foreign policy is still conjuncture-oriented and subject to frequent changes, as is the tradition of Romanian diplomacy, instead it must offer a profile of predictability and commit itself to sustain a solid and united Europe and a strong relation with the US.[40]

Concerning the transatlantic rift, Romania's official point of view was constant – there is not a real cleavage within NATO between the pro-American and the pro-European states but only unfortunate and occasional disputes related to specific interests. NATO is seen as the embodiment of a set of common values and principles, namely the Euro-Atlantic ones on behalf of which the Cold War was won by the west.

For some Romanian and foreign security analysts, there is a tension between NATO and the EU. Europe's rift linked to the recent Iraq war and US Defense

Secretary Rumsfeld's distinction between 'old/new' Europe could signify a real change of NATO's center of gravity towards the east. For example, in an interview given by the Romanian prime minister to the Chicago Sun Times, Mr. Nastate said that "we are on the verge of joining NATO, ready and willing to become a 'frontline' country with the US and other European allies, who like us, have tossed off the communist shackles. Romania, along with other new Eastern European members, will boost NATO troops by 200,000 and create a crucial pro-US force in Europe."[41]

Henry Kissinger wrote that "the aftermath of the terrorist attacks on the US on 11 September brought latent resentments to the surface under the banner of unilateralism versus multilateralism" and that "irritations over American tactics could not produce such a diplomatic revolution had not the traditional under-pinnings of alliance been eroded by the disappearance of a common threat." His verdict is tough: "if the existing trend in transatlantic relations continues, the international system will be fundamentally altered. Europe will split into two groups defined by their attitude towards co-operation with America." Therefore "a revitalization of the Atlantic relationship is imperative if global institutions are to function effectively and if the world is to avoid sliding into a return to 19th century power politics."[42]

However, there are signs of a healing of the division inside NATO, as the Alliance decided to take military command of the peace-keeping operation in Afghanistan and to support Poland and Spain in Iraq at the logistic level.[43]

Romania and the ICC

Romania was among the states which endorsed the proposal to build up an ICC and it accepted the status of this future legal body. The idea of a new legal order to account for pursuing and condemning genocide, war crimes and massive violations of human rights worldwide was attractive for Romania but there was no intention to support Europe against other western powers. On peculiar grounds, the US manifested its strong and immutable opposition to the emergence of the ICC, asking an exemption for its citizens and soldiers. Washington vetoed the ICC resolution in the UN Security Council and declared it would not participate any more in peace-keeping operations and would even withdraw from the Bosnian and Kosovo missions because the ICC could be an instrument for political manipulation against American interests by judging US soldiers participating in peace operations worldwide.[44] The European Union was not a unitary actor on this issue even if some states exercised pressures on Eastern Europeans to conform to the common position. Some countries, like Spain and UK, had been ready to sign bilateral exemption agreements with the US invoking article 98 of the ICC founding treaty which allows such actions. Italy's prime minister Berlusconi stated that his country and the UK "are not bound by EU's stand" as each state individually signed the ICC treaty while UK's prime minister, Tony Blair, said there would be no official British stance until the EU reached a common stance.[45]

Bucharest, applying Article 98 of the treaty, decided to sign a separate agreement with Washington guaranteeing immunity for American citizens in the ICC (1 August 2002). The EU immediately criticized Romania for manifesting a lack of solidarity with Europe. On 30 September 2002, EU members' foreign ministers gathered and issued a common stand towards the ICC, accepting only a limited exemption for Americans. Romania's position contrasts with most other Central and South European states which supported the European stance.

The Romanian stand was largely interpreted as pro-American. Nevertheless, there are analysts who thought that Romania adopted a pragmatic position toward the ICC. The Romanian political 'guru' and journalist, Silviu Brucan, remarked at the end of 2002, that Romanian leaders had began to make more pro-American statements, an example being the anti-Saddam Hussein stance expressed by prime minister, foreign affairs and defense ministers. In Brucan's words "Romania adopted a clearly pro-American stand in a moment when many European states, including NATO members, express reluctance towards the US war-prone posture."[46] It is not a matter of 'love' between US and Romania but a rational calculation: Romania needs American support for NATO membership and the US needs Romanian (and Bulgarian) sea-coast military ports and bases. Romania put at risk its relations with 'old' Europe again when the International Criminal Court was in question but Brucan thinks it was a "calculated risk" because America was more likely to provide us with material gains than the EU with its distance promise of membership.

A foreign expert like Janusz Bugajsky (East European Project Center Strategic and International Studies) wrote in April 2003 that "Romania has made significant progress as America's 'strategic partner,' backing American immunity from the ICC process, a stand which was at odds with the EUs interests.[47]

It is fair to say that Bucharest has disconsidered the deep difference between the two sides of the Atlantic regarding the ICC. As mentioned, it was considered that this is a temporary divergence which will soon be solved by compromise, avoiding Romania's falling in the middle of the Atlantic storm.[48] In fact, when the unfortunate political disputes arose among the US and some EU member states, the main concern for Romanian officials was to avoid diminishing chances for European integration, especially after some EU top officials stated that Romania could not be politically with Washington and economically with Brussels. When the US threatened those states which did not sign bilateral agreements on the ICC issue with the suspension of all military aid, Romania was not mentioned. The EU suggested, during the summer of 2003, that it could economically help those states which will suffer American sanctions but Romanian leadership avoided any comment on this proposal.

As mentioned above, the EU, on the other hand, had advised aspirant members to apply protection only to American citizens on official duty (diplomats), not all US nationals, a situation that US under-secretary of state Bolton describes as the "EU imposing an unfair choice upon our friends and allies."[49] Because no consensus arose between the EU and the US, Romanian leaders chose to delay the ratification of the bilateral agreement with the US until Europeans and Americans find a *modus-vivendi*. If something is obvious in this respect, it is the fact that Romania identifies itself to the western values and principles – democracy, freedom, human rights – and finds them embodied both in the US and the EU member states, so, our national preferences go to the west as a unitary political, economic and cultural pole.

The Iraq Divide

When the Iraq war became an issue for both its supporters and opponents, on 30 January 2003, a letter signed by eight European states (including Poland, Czech Republic and Hungary) expresses their support for US policy. It was quite obvious that the Common Foreign and Security Policy of the EU was a mere dream.[50]

In an interview given to the daily paper *Le Figaro* on 29 January 2003, Romanian prime minister, Adrian Nastase said that "we are a part of the old Europe, our history is longer than two thousand years. Therefore I don't believe in this differentiation." Rejecting the manichean patterns (bad/good guys) he expresses his confidence that "Europe is on the way to build up a solidarity relationship which is absolutely necessary" because the old continent is already an economic force and it needs a political identity on the international stage.[51] In Mr. Nastase's opinion, the fundamental values of Europe and America are similar and the disputes are merely *accidents des parcours*. The worst thing would be letting Saddam Hussein to divide the west "precisely before starting a war" and therefore there is a strong need for a unity of action. When asked by the media about Romania's stance in case of a transatlantic divide, on 10 February, Romanian President Ion Iliescu said "we are not faced with an option that we should make – USA or Europe, Europe or France and Germany, because we see from both sides an attempt to diminish this state of irritation." Optimistically, he argued that "there is no crisis within NATO."[52]

Unfortunately, not all the western states saw reality in such a manner. In February 2003, French President Jacques Chirac addressed hard critics especially towards Poland, Romania and Bulgaria for being "ill-educated" and unaware of their risky behavior, after these countries expressed their solidarity with those states which had signed the letter of solidarity with the US. Chirac stated that "Romania and Bulgaria had an irresponsible and superficial behavior when they strongly supported US, keeping in mind their already delicate position for the European Union. If they wished to diminish their chances to EU membership, they could not have found a better way."[53]

If Central-Eastern states want to belong to the EU they should refrain from expressing opposite points of view – this was the core message of French President and of Romano Prodi, Chief of the European Commission. France's chief of state was disappointed of the Romanian, Polish and Bulgarian stance because he considered those states as traditionally linked to France's diplomacy and interests and he had hoped to influence their positions through the perspective of EU membership, by invoking the necessity for all EU member states to speak on one voice in world affairs.

In fact, not only was there no consensus within the EU concerning the Iraq crisis, but the three admonished states were not yet part of the EU, so no one could ever asked them to show more discipline than full members themselves! On the other side, German Chancellor Schröder said, in a parliamentary speech from 19 March 2003, that the support given by former communist states to the US was "understandable," having in mind the fact that these countries "don't have the same awareness of their sovereignty" as the western European states. In his opinion, Germany had to work hard to level these differences, firmly and patiently, during the Iraq war and after.[54]

Therefore, it is obvious that in this generally unfavorable context, Romanian foreign policy decision-makers adopted the strategy of minimizing the rift within the transatlantic framework, in the hope that finally a necessary compromise will prevail. It was considered the best strategy since Romania's national interests required both NATO and EU membership to reach the target of joining the west. Rejecting the 'either/or' strategy, they have chosen an 'A plus B' scenario, implying the avoidance of taking part in any quarrel between allies and waiting for inter-institutional accommodation and compromise.

The core-argument of Romanian political leaders was that there is not a basic cleavage between two power 'poles' developed during the Iraq crisis and war, because their values, norms and principles are common (democracy, freedom, peace) and the agendas of threats and risks are quite similar. Romanian Prime Minister, Adrian Nastase, stated that Romania should not opt either for EU or for NATO, suggesting a policy of non-implication in the developing Western transformation process.

The Romanian leaders reacted saying that the Chirac and Prodi statements about the unity of the Common Foreign and Security Policy are merely 'wishful thinking' rather than reality. Romanian President Ion Ilescu declared President Chirac should regret his statements because "we don't live in the XIX century and it's not normal that in a XXI century family some should have more the right to their own opinions than others" and denied any rift between dominant and dominated countries.[55]

As can be surmised, Romanian officials have refused to choose between Americans and Europeans. Against this background it should be mentioned that the chosen Romanian strategy is not the equivalent of not taking reality into consideration, or worse, retreating from it and waiting for history to happen, from the position of an outside observer. On the contrary, Romania asked actively for transatlantic unity, stressing the fact that any rift is potentially damaging the efficiency of the west's stance on the anti-terrorism war and benefits the enemy.

In April 2003, Romanian chief of diplomacy, M. Geoana, in an interview for French channel TV 5 said tensions in Franco-Romanian relations are history because France supports Romania for EU integration and the European and Euro-Atlantic families share the same core-values. "We think our relations with a strong Europe and also with our American and Canadian friends, said minister Geoana, are not contradictory facts, on the contrary." Along these lines, Geoana mentioned Romania as a supporter of a military strong Europe, asking for more efficient money expenditures in the realm of European common defense.[56] Romania wants to be part of a powerful Europe, said Geoana when he met his French counterpart Dominique de Villepin.

It is fair to mention that not everybody understood the Romanian stance. There were statements which pushed some European officials to say that Romania had already opted for the US and acts accordingly, contrary to the EU interests.

Let's take another example. In October 2003, Vice-President of European Parliament Catherine Lalumiere spoke about Romania as a 'Trojan horse' for US interests if accepted as an EU member. Foreign Minister M. Geoana dismissed the remark as "residual elements of the very intense debate during this summer, concerning mainly the situation in Iraq." Such an expression was, in fact, highly suggestive because implicitly it described the US-EU relations as a 'zero-sum' game in a balance of power world. Both America and Europe explicitly reject such patterns of the international state system and insist on multilateral co-operation with mutual benefits.

Conclusion

Was Romania's situation in the context of the future NATO and EU enlargement so desperate, as Chirac, Prodi and Lalumiere's statements seemed to suggest? We do not think so. The NATO Prague Summit in November 2002 has confirmed Romanian optimistic expectations and its various efforts in Afghanistan, Bosnia, Kosovo to prove its status as a security provider. Allied leaders accepted an enlargement with seven new members, including Romania, they also launched an anti-terrorism plan, a NATO Response Force and the Prague Capabilities Commitment in order to transform NATO and make it relevant for the twenty-first century security environment. Romania declared it would wait for membership (2004) in order to participate in the NRF but immediately made an offer of forces within the Prague Capabilities Commitment. It committed itself to continue the reform and restructuring of its armed forces and allocated 2.5–2.8 percent of its GDP for defense.

After that, the EU Copenhagen Summit declaration in December 2002 stated that Romania could also qualify for membership and the 2007 term was indicated as a possible accession date for Romania and Bulgaria. EU has the power to strongly influence the foreign and domestic policies of aspirant countries by leveraging the perspective of a faster membership. Alyson Bailes is not wrong when saying "as to the supposed old/new division, one should never underestimate the EU's capacity to alter the general security culture as well as specific policies of countries who join it." She adds that a more important aspect of the EU is "the divisions between EU members who are inward-looking and conservative, and outward-looking and interventionists," a line which "cuts right across the categories of small and big, Western and Eastern, Allied and non-Allied EU members."[57]

In the realm of foreign affairs, a further step towards the enhancement of the inter-regional security structure was the signing of a Romanian-Russian bilateral treaty for good neighborliness and friendship relations in July 2003. The main reason for Romania to accept the deal with its former geopolitical master was the need for closer relations with NATO's Eastern neighbor, and the hope of penetrating Russian markets and reducing the huge trade imbalance between the two states; perhaps also the secret hope of playing the interface role between the EU and the Russian Federation after joining the Union. But this would require an economically more powerful and politically more influential Romania as an EU member. The bilateral treaty allows the two states to freely choose or change their security arrangements including alliances, acknowledging the indivisibility of the security and the "indestructible link between each side's security and the security off all states which are OSCE members" (Article 3). There is a special reference made to a common fight against terrorism and organized crime (Article 13) and to the support of the two states towards the establishment and efficient work of "general European structures and of the enhancement of confidence-building measures" in order to favor prevention/peaceful settlement of conflicts.[58]

Much more ambiguous is the relationship between Romania and the Republic of Moldova, especially after Moldavian communist leaders accused, without reason, the Romanian government of behaving in an anti-Moldavian way and refused to conclude a bilateral treaty. One can suppose that a Romania as an EU and NATO member will become more attractive for Chisinev, at least in economic terms.

Combating corruption, continuing the administrative and justice transformation a.s.o. are conditions required by both NATO and EU for membership, so Romanian leaders have to continue to speed up reforms in these sectors. If 2002 was the year when NATO membership was the top priority, 2004 and 2005 will be consecrated to EU integration. Because economic and administrative issues are decisive for this purpose, national efforts should converge on it.

Romania sincerely hopes that any future transatlantic (and European) rifts will be avoided and wants to valorize its NATO 'acquis' to ensure its EU membership. In Romania's view, the west should remain unified and move beyond accidental differences. The main threats to international security – the asymmetric ones – are a matter of concern for both the US and Europe, so they have to have a common agenda. European-American efforts to carry out such an agenda are immediately needed. Romania does not see Europe and the US as alternative tracts to a western orientation, but instead Romania sees these two tracts as working concurrently to better guarantee its future security and welfare; pillars of world stability.

The Romanian political elite and a huge part of public opinion are fully aware that the transatlantic crisis is dangerous because it could provoke instability in South East Europe, delay the EU enlargement process, create resentment and block or slow down domestic reforms and even allow the transfer of instability from the Black Sea region or the Caucasus.

Therefore, Romania supports a new transatlantic agenda setting, one which could assert the same 'threat assessment' for both the EU and the US. If the transatlantic rift deepens following the Iraq crisis and the EU-NATO relations tend to become more competitive, "NATO will be fatally harmed and perhaps will disappear and European Union integration process will slow down dramatically, if it will continue at all."[59] Little and weak states would face increased intra and inter states tensions as great powers rivalry would foster different foreign affairs agendas and domestic political frictions in such a way that tendencies to increase regional cooperation could stop. If NATO and the EU will have a similar threat assessment and will assume a complementary role in extending international stability and security, then regional cooperation in the Balkans would be enhanced and the stabilization patterns will spread towards the Greater Middle East through cooperative security arrangements. A constructive compromise for a new transatlantic agenda would imply the extending of both NATO and the EU beyond the 2004 wave. Between the Balkans, which would be quasi-sure of their admittance into both organizations, and the Black Sea-Caucasus area there will be a level of interdependence. A new jointly developed common agenda is indispensable in my opinion.[60] So, EU strategy for expanding its influence in its neighborhood via extending the zone of security to the European periphery, supporting the emergence of a stable and multilateral, peaceful world system and take countermeasures to security threats[61] is welcomed in Bucharest on condition that it is compatible with NATO security frameworks and trends.[62]

Since both organizations share common values and principles and many common members, plus a historic heritage of solidarity during the Cold War, one could be optimistic and hope in the best destiny for the west as a power pole of civilization in the world. Many experts are optimistic considering that America and Europe share basic core-values (human rights, democracy, rule of law) even if they implement them differently, and this fact cannot be doubted even if the Westphalian world order should collapse.[63] They believe there is no coincidence that states sharing universal values are politically the most successful and the wealthiest. The world needs them unified and consensual in order to root out the security threats which endanger the peace of the world.

Notes

1 For more analyses, see books such as: John Arquilla and David Ronfeldt (2001), *Networks and Netwars: The Future of Terror, Crime and Militancy*, Santa Monica: RAND; Alan Dershowitz (2002), *Why Terrorism Works*, New Haven: Yale University Press.

2 Florin Constantiniu (1997), *O istorie sincera a poporului roman* (A True History of the Romanian People), Bucuresti: University Encyclopedic Publishing House, 517–518.

3 "Le concept stratégique de l'Alliance, Rome, 7 et 8 novembre 1991" (The Strategic Concept of the Alliance), in *La Revue Internationale et Stratégique*, 32 (Hiver 1998/ 1999),135–139.

4 NATO (2001), *NATO Handbook*, Brussels: NATO Office of Information and Press, 67–80. In 1997 was set the Euro-Atlantic Partnership Council (EAPC) which succeeded to the NACC, bringing together the 19 NATO member-states and 27 Partners (including Romania) in order to have a common security framework for regular consultation and cooperation. The Partnership for Peace was, maybe, the most important initiative launched by NATO at its January 1994 Brussels Summit of the North Atlantic Council, in order to enhance stability and security in all Europe. The main topic on the PfP agenda is the dialogue and consultation between allies and partners in case one of them perceives a direct threat to its territorial integrity, political independence or security. Military exercises were, since carried out in order to increase interoperability among the national armed forces in order to better deal with common risks and threats. The PfP Framework Document include specific aims like the transparency in national defense planning and budgeting processes, the democratic control of the armed forces, the readiness to contribute to peace operations, the development of co-operative military relations between allies and partners, the interoperability of their forces.

5 After the Dayton agreement, NATO launched its IFOR/SFOR operations in Bosnia-Herzegovina, in which Romania participated with more than 1,012 militaries between 1996–2000. On 12 June 1999, Romania alongside another 17 states, declared itself ready and willing to participate in the KFOR mission in Kosovo, a sign of Romania's willingness to share the burden and responsibility of building a stable security architecture in Europe. In June 14–28, 1999, Romania participated to the NATO/PfP "Cooperative Partner 99" exercise at Varna (Bulgaria); from 15–25 September, 1999, to the NATO/PfP exercise "Cooperative Nugget '99" at Suffolk, in March–April 2000, to the military exercise "Dynamic Response 2000" in Kosovo; to the NATO/PfP

exercise "strong Resolve 2002" in March 2002, in Poland and Romania also organized the common exercise NATO/WEU (CMX/CRISEX) in February 2000, and so on.

6   See Serban F. Cioculescu (2003), *"Relatiile romano-ruse contemporane din perspectiva intereselor nationale de securitate ale Romaniei* (Contemporary Relations between Romania and Russia through the National Security Interests of Romania)," in *Studii de Securitate*, January, online at www.studiidesecuritate.ro. For more information, see Florin Constantiniu.

7   Romania (1993), "Letter of Application on NATO Membership from the President of Romania to the Secretary General of NATO", 18 September, online at www.presidency.ro.

8   "Statement, June 21, 1995," in *Romania's Westernization and NATO membership*, IPSDMH, Occasional Papers, No.3(1)/2002,41–43. See also Teodor Melescanu (2003), *Renasterea diplomatiei romanesti (The Renaissance of Romanian Diplomacy) 1994–1996*, Cluj: Dacia Publishing House, 122.

9   "Declaration of the Political Parties Represented in the Parliament concerning Romania's Admission into NATO" (fragments in Romanian) in *Cotidianul*, 2 April 2001, p.1. See also "The Forum NATO 2002", *Rador Daily News*, 2 April 2001, online at www.ici.ro/romania/news/arheng2001/e_apr02.html.

10 "The National Political Barometer," *Metro Media Transilvania*, June–July 2002, Avaiable online at www.mmt.ro.

11 Ibid.

12 See NATO (1995), "Study on NATO Enlargement," September, online at http://www.nato.int/docu/basictxt/enl-9501.htm:
   • future members unite their efforts for collective defence and for the preservation of peace and security; settle any international disputes in which they may be involved by peaceful means in such a manner that international peace and security and justice are not endangered, and refrain in their international relations from the threat or use of force in any manner inconsistent with the purposes of the United Nations;
   • contribute to the development of peaceful and friendly international relations by strengthening their free institutions, by bringing about a better understanding of the principles upon which these institutions are founded, and by promoting conditions of stability and well-being;
   • maintain the effectiveness of the Alliance by sharing roles, risks, responsibilities, costs and benefits of assuring common security goals and objectives.

13 *Carte Alba Romania-NATO* (The White Book Romania-NATO), 1996, 13–19.

14 See *Observatorul Militar*, no. 28, 16–22 July 1997, 1–2.

15 Ion Calafeteanu (2003), *Istoria politicii externe romanesti* (History of Romanian Foreign Policy), Bucharest: Encyclopedia Publishing House, 742–743.

16 Cornel Paraniac (2002), *Parteneriatul Strategic dintre Romania si SUA* (The Strategic Partnership between Romania and USA), Bucharest: Pro Transilvania Publishing House, 128–132.

17 *Observatorul Militar*, 24–30 March, 1998, 2.

18 *Observatorul Militar*, 14–20 July, 1998, 1.

19 *Observatorul Militar*, 7–13 April, 1998, 1.

20 *The Evolution of Romania's Accession Negotiation with the EU*, online at www.mie.ro/english/mie.htm.

21 Romanian offer included an infantry company, a group of divers, a military police platoon, an engineer battalion, a rescue ship. See the statement of Ioan M. Plangu, State secretary and chief of the Department for Defence Policy, Relations with the Parliament and other Public Authorities on this occasion in *Monitor Strategic*, 1st year, no.2/2000.

22 See Antonio Missiroli (2003), "The EU, Just a Regional Peace-keeper?", *European Foreign Affairs Review*, 8, 493–503.
23 *NATO Secretary General in Romania*, Rompres Agency, News, 26 April 2002, online at www.rompres.ro.
24 Romania (2002), *The National Strategy on Preventing and Combating Terrorism*, Bucharest.
25 Romania (2001), *The National Security Strategy of Romania*, The President of Romania, Bucharest, 11–17.
26 Ibid, 13.
27 Ibid, 17–21.
28 Charles Gati (2002), "All That NATO Can Be", *The National Interest* (Summer), 79–88.
29 Ion Iliescu (2002), *Sa consolidam speranta inascuta* (Let us Consolidate the Reborn Hope), address to the reunited Chambers of Romania's Parliament, 19 December.
30 Among them Robert Kagan who wrote an article named "Power and Weakness" (2002), lately transformed in a book, "On Paradise and Power" (2003). He explains the transatlantic cleavage by a lot of reasons: the power and the broad ideological-cultural gaps, collective psychology, the different historical experience and says that "American military strength has produced a propensity to use strength. Europe's military weakness has produced a perfectly understandable aversion to the exercise of military power." See Robert Kagan (2002), "Power and Weakness," *Policy Review* (June/July).
31 US, White House (2002), "The National Security Strategy of the United States of America," Washington: Government Printing Office, September, online at www.whitehouse.gov/nsc/nss1.html.
32 See Mihail E. Ionescu (2003), "Tensiunea sistemica" (The Systemic Tension), in *Monitor Strategic*, IV (1), 1–3.
33 Bogdan Chirieac (2003), "Razboiul rece eurotlantic" (The Euro-Atlantic Cold War), in *Adevarul*, 10 February, 1.
34 CSOP opinion poll, 1 February 2003, online at http://news.itbox.ro/wmview.php (CSOP is the Romanian division of GALLUP).
35 Ibid; "Europa second-hand" (Second-Hand Europe), in *Adevarul*, 14 February 2003, 1.
36 Mircea Geoana (2003), "Statele din Estul Europei nu trebuie sa cada in capcana falselor dileme de securitate," in *Adevarul*, 25 January 25.
37 Ibid, "Statele din Estul Europei nu trebuie sa cada in capcana falselor dileme de loialitate" (East European States Not to Deal with False Loyalty Dilemmas), *Adevarul*, 25 January 2003, 9.
38 Ibid.
39 Intervention of the minister Mircea Geoana during the Prima TV Broadcast "Evenimentul saptamanii" (The Event of the Week), first part, 23 March 2003, online at http://domino.kappa.ro/mae/presa.nsf.
40 Ibid.
41 Adrian Nastase (2003), "Romania is a proud partner of the US in new Europe", *Chicago Sun Times*, 27 December.
42 Henry Kissinger (2003), "Old Allies Face New Dilemmas," 14 April, online at www.expandnato.org.
43 In November 2003, Polish former deputy minister for defense and foreign affairs Radek Sikorski explained the difference in perceptions between Western and Central-Eastern European states towards US by historical arguments and hope for political-economic gains. See Radek Sikorski (2003), "Losing the New Europe," *Washington Post*, 7 November.

44 Dace Akule (2003), "Brussels Could Intervene in ICC Row," 7 April, online at www.euobserver.com.
45 "Italia si Anglia dau dreptate Romaniei" (Italy and UK agreed with Romania), *Independent*, 2 September 2002.
46 Silviu Brucan (2002), "Jucam cartea americana" (We play the American Card), *Ziarul Financiar*, 23 September 2002, 9.
47 Janusz Bugajski (2003), "The Future of NATO: Do Bulgaria and Romania qualify?," 3 April, online at http://www.csis.org/hill/ts030403bugajski.pdf.
48 This perception has been strengthened by the unity shown by allies on the eve of the Prague Summit in November 2002. They have agreed on the command structures transformation, the launch of the NATO Response Force suggesting the readiness for out of area operations and especially on a second post-communist wave of enlargement.
49 Guy Dinmore (2003), "US Attacks European Union over Immunity Agreements," *Financial Times*, 4 November.
50 *BBC Romania*, news, 24 January 2003.
51 *Le Figaro* (2003), "Adrian Nastase: Nu trebuis sa i se permita lui Saddam sa divizeze Occidentul" (Adrian Nastase: We Should Not Allow Saddam to Divise the West), *Adevarul*, 1 February, 10.
52 Iulia Vaida (2003), "Romania a acceptat solicitarea SUA" (Romania agreed with US request), *Romania Libera*, 11 February, 3.
53 Andreea Enea (2003), "Jacques Chirac, la atac impotriva Romaniei" (Jacques Chirac attacks Romania), *Curentul*, 19 February, 3.
54 "Schröder: Estul nu are aceeasi constiinta a suveranitatii ca Vestul" (Schröder: The East doesn't have the same awareness of its sovereignty like the West), in *Ziua*, 20 March 2003, 3.
55 Ibid, *Curentul*, 19 February 2003, 3.
56 Mircea Geoana (2003), "Tensiunile franco-romane tin de domeniul trecutului" (Franco-Romanian Tensions are History), *Ziua*, 9 April, 5.
57 Alyson Bailes (2003), "The Iraq War: Impact on International Security", a *DCAF Policy Paper*, Geneva, August, 13.
58 "The Treaty of Friendship and Cooperation between Romania and Russian Federation," in *Studii de Securitate.Ro*, 1 (2003), online at www.studiidesecuritate.ro (Archive).
59 Mihail E. Ionescu (2003), "The Balkans After 2004 Enlargement of NATO and European Union: What Next?," paper delivered at the *Transatlantic Security Conference* in Krakow, October.
60 Ibid.
61 Javier Solana (2003), "A Secure Europe in a Better World," available online at http://ue.eu.int/pressdata/EN/discours/76423.pdf, 21 June.
62 Mihail E.Ionescu.
63 Istvan Gyarmati (2003), "Iraq: Symptom, Catalyst or Cause of Friction between Europe and America," a *DCAF Policy Paper*, Geneva (July), 11.

Chapter 14

Conclusion: Values and Interests: European Support for the Intervention in Afghanistan and Iraq

Michael Mihalka

Introduction

The coalitions that were formed after 9/11 to deal with transnational terrorism in general and to intervene successively in Afghanistan and in Iraq provide an opportunity to test some cherished notions about security cooperation. Are common values a motivating factor for cooperation? Or does self-interest better explain joining with US in Afghanistan and Iraq? The extent of a European state's participation depended on its specific interests in these conflicts and whether it belonged to or was seeking to join NATO. As this paper will show, the preponderance of US power provides significant "free-rider" benefits for its alliance partners in NATO. This paper will assess whether European states were motivated by a sense of common values or national interest in cooperating with the US in Afghanistan and Iraq. Finally it will show that common values and common interests do coincide when if Eastern Europe faces another Iraq-style Hobson's choice between the US and the EU.

Common Values as Motivating Cooperation

Common values are often cited as a major factor motivating international cooperation. The secretary general of NATO, Lord Robertson, has common or shared values as a continuing theme in his speeches. For example his speeches in March 2003 in several countries invited to be members of NATO included the same phrase: "And for NATO, the invitation of seven countries represented a major step towards a strategic objective: to create a Europe truly whole and free, united in peace, democracy and common values, from the Baltic Sea to the Black Sea." In looking at the new challenges facing NATO he argued: "There is no better way to face such threats and challenges than as part of community. And NATO is just that: a community of democracies that share values, and both the determination and the capabilities to uphold them."[1] At a meeting with the American president George W. Bush in April 2002, Lord Robertson said that NATO "remains strong because the ties that bind us together are enduring, and they lie in the common values of freedom and democracy and of liberty."[2] The EU High Representative for the

Common Foreign and Security Policy, Javier Solana, has also argued that common values promotes security cooperation and stability:

> John Hume once remarked that the European Union is itself the most successful example of conflict prevention. I believe that our most successful tool for conflict prevention has been the enlargement process which has created an ever wider area of stability and peace in Europe. It has enabled us to encourage and support the heroic and often painful efforts of our neighbors to transform their societies and economies following the cold war.[3]

The Finnish speaker of parliament, Paavo Lipponen, said that NATO is ultimately all about the common values the Finns share with the United States.[4] He argued that at the level of principle, Finns, like other Europeans, shared the right to freedom and justice, to democracy, and to the market economy with their American counterparts. But in practice, Finns and other Europeans disagree with the American application of those values from the intervention in Vietnam to the one of Iraq. Following this line of argument, the Finnish foreign minister, Erkki Tuomioja, concluded: "If NATO develops into a community for crisis management, Finnish membership could be justified. But if NATO is a 'reserve for US power politics,' from which the United States calls allies for 'coalitions of the willing,' it does not appeal to us. Right now, NATO appears to be a little of both."

Scholars also stress the role of shared and common values as factors motivating cooperation. For example, Stephen Walt notes that liberal theory says that there will be "increased cooperation as liberal values, free markets and international institutions spread."[5] In the same issue of Foreign Policy, Lawrence Freedman said that scholars in the international political economy subfield have argued that "as states come to share economic views and political values, it becomes easier for them to act on a multilateral basis through international institutions and to isolate the malevolent and the disruptive."[6] Robert Keohane, one of the leading theorists of institutional liberalism maintains, "Institutions whose members share social values and have similar political systems – such as NATO or the European Union – are likely to be stronger than those such as the Organization for Security and Cooperation in Europe or the Association of South East Asian Nations, whose more diverse membership does not necessarily have the same kind of deep common interests." Importantly he also goes on to say that "The distribution of power is also important."[7] In a section entitled the "Power of Values", Helen Milner stresses the importance of nonmaterialistic explanations such as ideas for security cooperation.[8] She also argues that construction of a common identity based on these ideas should lead to more cooperation.

Following Robert Kagan's infamous article in the summer of 2002, a veritable cottage industry has arisen regarding the similarity or dissimilarity of values between the United States and Europe.[9] He starts off his article with the claim, "It is time to stop pretending that Europeans and Americans share a common view of the world, or even that they occupy the same world." However a closer examination of his article reveals that he seems to be mostly talking about France and Germany and their unwillingness to use force. "Americans are from Mars and Europeans are from Venus." Most European countries are not mentioned at all and some only in passing. Kagan focuses on power as the value upon which the

"Europeans" (but really Germany and France) diverge from America: "On the all-important question of power – the efficacy of power, the morality of power, the desirability of power – American and European perspectives are diverging. Europe is turning away from power, or to put it a little differently, it is moving beyond power into a self-contained world of laws and rules and transnational negotiation and cooperation."

From this literature we can develop several hypotheses. The first we might call the general common values hypothesis: *The more countries share values in common the more likely they are to cooperate.* A corollary of this might be: *The more countries share values in common the greater the degree of cooperation.*

By this hypothesis countries that are similar in values are more likely to cooperate with each other. There is a belief among liberals that democracies will not go to war with each other but will find peaceful means of adjudicating their differences. But this democratic peace argument provides little guidance if democracies disagree with each other as to how to approach particular security challenges, such as intervening against a country that is brutalizing its population.

The corollary simply means that countries will cooperate more the closer in values they are to another country. Thus countries close in values may cooperate militarily, those farther apart may only cooperate politically and those sufficiently distant may not cooperate at all.

Of course in order to test this hypothesis we would need some widely accepted assessment of values by country. The World Values Survey housed at the Institute for Social Research provides such an assessment.[10] Building on the European Values Survey first conducted in 1981, the World Values Survey was carried out for the first time at a global level in 1990–1 and later in 1995–6 and 1999–2001. Representative samples of 1,000 respondents are drawn from a number of countries.

The first two dimensions that result from a statistical analysis of the data are one reflecting a continuum from traditional to secular-rational authority and another with concerns for scarcity versus post-modern values.[11] The most recent results in Figure 14.1 appeared in *The Economist*.[12] Those countries closest to the United States would thus be more likely to cooperate with the United States than those farther away. Thus Ireland would be more likely to cooperate with the United States than Bulgaria. Kagan however suggests that perhaps another factor ought to added, the willingness to use force in pursuit of a state's national interests. This gives us the Kagan corollary: *States are more likely to cooperate in the use of force the more willing their publics are to use force in general.*

In his article, Kagan contrasts Americans and so-called Europeans. He says that Europeans argue, "When confronting real or potential adversaries, Americans generally favor policies of coercion rather than persuasion, emphasizing punitive sanctions over inducements to better behavior, the stick over the carrot."[13] In contrast, these same Europeans argue, "They generally favor peaceful responses to problems, preferring negotiation, diplomacy, and persuasion to coercion." Although Kagan admits that these characterizations are a caricature, they also highlight important differences. The key here is the willingness to use force. Europeans do not cooperate with the Americans because they are reluctant to use force.

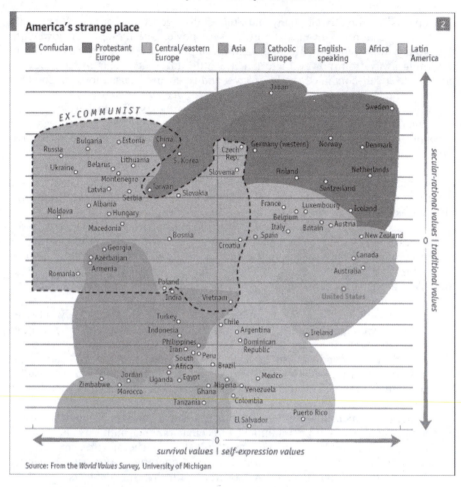

Figure 14.1 States and common values

The most comprehensive recent assessment of whether countries are willing to use force to further their national interests in the absence of an attack appears in the Pew Global Attitudes Project 2003.[14] Of 21 countries surveyed, only six had a majority who thought that force was often or sometimes justified if a country had not attacked them: the United States, Canada, Great Britain, Australia, Pakistan and Israel. Other countries such as Turkey and Nigeria had strong pluralities but the population was polarized with large minorities contending force was never justified. Given the hypothesis, then, we would expect countries such as Spain and Italy to be less likely to support the US than Canada.

Table 14.1 Global Attitudes: 21 Population Survey (2003)
Q.21 Do you think that using military force against countries that may seriously threaten our country, but have not attacked us, can often be justified, sometimes be justified, rarely be justified, or never be justified?

	Often Justified	Sometimes Justified	Rarely Justified	Never Justifed	Don't know/ Refused	
United States	22	44	13	17	3	=99
Great Britain	15	50	13	20	2	=100
France	7	35	26	30	2	=100
Germany	7	24	31	35	3	=100
Italy	8	30	19	40	3	=100
Spain	9	19	18	51	3	=100
Russia	11	16	21	42	11	=101
Turkey	27	19	11	37	6	=100

EU or NATO?

The common values hypothesis also provides us with a prediction if NATO and EU should advocate different policies. The countries in the upper right hand quadrant of Figure One form the core of the EU. Many of the countries in the upper left hand quadrant are both EU and NATO applicants. With the exception of Ireland, the members of the EU group are closer to each other than they are to the United States. The members of the (NATO/EU) applicant group are closer to the EU group than they are to the US. Therefore we would expect that, all other things being equal, the EU group to act together and the (NATO/EU) applicant group to follow the lead of the EU over the United States. By this hypothesis we might expect Ireland to break from the EU group and follow the US lead.

Self-interest and Free-riding

Rational choice theory provides a different basis for assessing whether countries will join in a coalition. Basically the argument is not common values but common interests, or more accurately compatible interests. There are three related hypotheses here, one having to do with the direct security interests served by cooperating, the second having to do with positive inducements to cooperate and the third having to do with sustaining an alliance such as NATO which provides substantial free-rider benefits.

The first hypothesis in this section is straightforward: *Countries will cooperate in a coalition if it is in their immediate security interest to do so.* Thus, countries immediately adjacent to another country that has proved a source of instability to them will cooperate with the coalition that has intervened in that country to remove the source of instability. For example, Central Asian countries were willing to provide access and support for the US-led coalition that intervened in Afghanistan.

The second hypothesis is also straightforward: *Countries will cooperate in a coalition if they expect tangible benefits for doing so.* Thus country A may provide political, military or economic support for an intervention if the leader of the coalition can provide some support in areas that do matter to country A. Such inducements would cover a wide range from preferential economic arrangements to support against local insurgents.

The third hypothesis is more complicated and will require more explanation: *A country A is more likely to cooperate with country B if country B underwrites an alliance from which country A can derive significant free-rider benefits.* The so-called free-rider problem commonly occurs in social choice settings where one actor is willing to foot the bill for the social good. Social goods have two important characteristics and a lighthouse provides a good example. First, once the good is provided, all consumers share equally. Thus all ships receive the same benefit from the lighthouse. This is called the non-exclusion principle. Second, the marginal cost of providing the good to an extra consumer is zero, the non-rivalry principle. Therefore there is no extra cost of providing the benefits of the lighthouse to additional ships. Perhaps the classic example of such a public or collective good in the literature is a national defense. All citizens share in the benefits of national defense equally and none can be excluded.

Because of their characteristics, entrepreneurs are often unwilling to provide public goods because consumers are unwilling to pay for them, the so-called free-rider problem. Why pay for a good, when you cannot be excluded from benefiting from it? The classic solution has been for a government to tax consumers to provide the good. However, in voluntary associations among states to assure security, taxation is generally not an option and other mechanisms need to be used to assure a continuing supply of the good. Among these mechanisms is the threat that the good will be withdrawn, an effective threat in an alliance such as NATO where one country provides most of the security. NATO has appeared in the literature over and over again as a special case of the free-rider problem.[15] Olson and Zechhauser noted that larger countries in an alliance will bear a disproportionate share of the common burden (for example, spend proportionately more on defense as a percentage of GDP, for example).

Olsen and Zechhauser were primarily concerned with defense burden and didn't take nuclear deterrence into account. However, it is quite clear that the steps that the United States took to deter nuclear attack against its homeland, also provided nuclear deterrence for all members of the NATO alliance, something for which they did not have to contribute. The other members of the alliance were in essence free-riders – the United States provided a public good for private reasons. Moreover, during the Cold War European countries were especially keen that the US do nothing to undermine nuclear deterrence, because otherwise they would have had to spend more on conventional forces.

After the Cold War, most countries significantly reduced their defense expenditures but NATO remained. Some realist authors, who should have known better, predicted the demise of NATO because they thought that NATO without a threat could not continue to exist.[16] But NATO persisted because it provided existential security against as yet unspecified threats. Moreover they continued to allow the smaller countries in the alliance to underspend significantly on defense and make correspondingly greater reductions because of the security advantages of being in an alliance with the United States.[17] Gompert and Kugler bemoaned the fact that NATO allies would not provide a power projection capability, even though it was clearly irrational for them to do so. If the NATO allies could benefit from US capabilities and willingness to project power abroad, why should they do it themselves?

This argument also has echoes in hegemonic stability theory. Doyle notes: "A Liberal hegemon can resolve the dilemma of cooperation by providing the collective good if its private good is larger than its private costs."[18] In essence US efforts to provide security on its own behalf provided security as well for its allies. Even though the other NATO members provide the US very little in the way of tangible military capability, the US gains through financial and political support at critical moments such as after the first Gulf War.

The Kosovo intervention confirms the importance of the having the United States within NATO. Although NATO ran the operation, the United States contributed the 60 percent of the aircraft and flew a corresponding percentage of the sorties. However, these percentages significantly understate the operational effectiveness of the US. The allies were lacking in precision strike, secure communications, mobility and command and control. Because NATO lacked adequate precision strike munitions, the United States was forced to conduct the preponderance of the missions early in the campaign.[19] Italian Admiral Guido Venturoni, the Chief of the NATO Military Committee, observed that Europeans "could never have mounted a successful air campaign" without the US.[20]

Despite their poor performance in the Kosovo campaign, the European allies did little to rectify the situation. NATO launched the Defense Capabilities Initiative to improve capabilities in critical areas, but this effort proved a failure. Despite entreaties to the contrary, both my the United States government and their own military, European governments behaved like good free-riders and refused to spend more on defense.

After 9/11 the United States demonstrated its willingness yet again to provide global security as a private good for itself and the same time provide security for other countries as a collective good. The US was concerned about its own security and acted accordingly in Afghanistan and Iraq. Unlike Kosovo, the US rather than NATO led the operation. The US acted against what it considered to be the major global threats of transnational terrorism and weapons of mass destruction. Such actions by the US substantially enhanced the value of belonging to NATO, especially to applicant countries. They could be assured of protection against transnational terrorism and weapons of mass destruction, but they would not have to pay much if anything for it. NATO members and applicants continue to have a limited ability to act decisively against transnational threats in places like Afghanistan and Iraq. So long as they belong to NATO they don't need such a capability because the US provides it as a public good for them. Thus NATO members are every bit as much free-rider beneficiaries post 9/11 of US global power projection capability as they were of US nuclear deterrence in the Cold War.

In contrast, the European Security and Defense Policy provides no such free-rider benefits. There is no liberal hegemon within the EU. EU members provide no security that is not already provided by the US within NATO. By themselves, EU members and applicants lack the capability to deal militarily with transnational terrorism. A report to the Western European Union parliamentary assembly in June 2002 said, "Europe has a formidable task if it is effectively to redress its deficiencies in military capabilities against terrorism."[21] Rather this report contended, "There has been a tendency among European governments to concentrate more on the EU's institutional priorities in the development of a European security and defense identity than on the creation of the military capabilities relevant to today's dramatically altered security environment." Nor, according to the free-rider argument, would it be rational for EU members to spend money to develop such capabilities so long as the US provides them for free through NATO.

Therefore, if given a choice between the US or the EU in matters of security, countries would choose the US because of the security it provides through NATO. So common values dictates that these countries would choose the EU over the US. Self-interest and the free-rider argument suggest that countries would choose the US over the EU.

Free-riding with the US and NATO in Afghanistan and Iraq

Without NATO, the US could not have secured the kind of military support it received for the Afghan conflict nor the political support it received for Iraq. After the terrorist attacks on the United States on 9/11, NATO was very quick to invoke Article 5. However, this support was conditional on evidence that the attacks came from abroad.[22] On 2 October 2001, Ambassador Frank Taylor briefed the NATO Council on the results of the investigation on who was behind the 9/11 attacks. The NATO Secretary-General Lord Robertson announced that the evidence was sufficient to make Article 5 operative. The North Atlantic Council agreed.[23]

Evoking Article 5 – Thanks, But No Thanks

The idea to evoke Article 5 came from a small group inside NATO working with the NATO Assistant Secretary General for Defense Planning and Operations Edgar Buckley. They thought that NATO needed to show solidarity with the United States and its continued relevance as an organization. Lord Robertson immediately accepted the idea and called the American Secretary of State Colin Powell, who agreed with this offer after first consulting with others in the US administration. Some at NATO recall that the support for declaring Article 5 was universal; others said they expressed doubts because it was unclear what NATO could do for the United States.[24]

On 8 October that question was probably answered when the North Atlantic Council agreed to eight measures: to enhance intelligence sharing and co-operation; to provide assistance to Allies and other states which are or may be subject to increased terrorist threats as a result of their support for the campaign against terrorism; to provide increased security for facilities of the United States and other Allies on their territory; to backfill selected Allied assets in NATO's area of responsibility that are required to directly support operations against terrorism; to provide blanket overflight clearances for the United States and other Allies' aircraft for military flights related to operations against terrorism; to provide access for the United States and other Allies to ports and airfields on the territory of NATO nations for operations against terrorism; to deploy elements of its Standing Naval Forces to the Eastern Mediterranean; and to deploy elements of its NATO Airborne Early Warning force to support operations against terrorism.[25] Elements of the NATO's standing naval forces began operating from 26 October 2001 in the eastern Mediterranean monitoring shipping and from 10 March 2003 escorting ships through the Strait of Gibraltar. NATO AWACS flew in the United States from mid-October 2001 to mid-May 2002.

In Afghanistan meanwhile, the United States and the UK launched air strikes against the Taliban in October 2001 because they were providing safe haven to al Qaeda. The war was quickly over. The Taliban abandoned Kandahar on 7 December 2001 and Hamid Karsai was sworn in as interim head of government on 22 December.

One of the first orders of business after the conflict ended was how to oversee the peace. NATO members led the International Security Assistance Force (ISAF) in Afghanistan from its inception in January 2002. Leadership rotated every six months, with the United Kingdom, Turkey and finally Germany and the Netherlands combined. From August 2003, NATO itself assumed the leading role taking over strategic coordination and commend and control of ISAF.[26]

But NATO's efforts to offer assistance were not warmly received throughout Washington. Reportedly Rumsfeld opposed accepting NATO's offer and was only convinced to agree because it would provide "political cover." "The allies were desperately trying to give us political cover and the Pentagon was resisting it," one senior administration official said. "It was insane. Eventually Rumsfeld understood it was a plus, not a minus, and was able to accept it."[27] Rumsfeld did not want NATO to gain control of military operations and thus have a repeat of operations in the Kosovo war, where all members of NATO had an effective veto on targets.

But the support that NATO allies offered was much less than the Americans were willing to accept. When the Deputy Secretary of State Paul Wolfowitz visited NATO headquarters in late September 2001, the impression was that he said: "Thanks. Don't call us. Don't expect us to call you."[28] Wolfowitz reportedly told NATO to continue with business as usual.[29] Collective action by NATO wasn't necessary.[30] In other words, NATO countries were willing to provide more support if they could have a greater control over the process – the US wasn't interested.

US Secretary of Defense Donald Rumsfeld reiterated shortly afterwards that there was no single coalition against terrorism: "From time to time, I see references in the press to 'the coalition' – singular. And let me reiterate that there is no single coalition in this effort. This campaign involves a number of flexible coalitions that will change and evolve as we proceed through the coming period. Let me reemphasize that the mission determines the coalition, and the coalition must not determine the mission."[31]

The Europeans became increasingly distressed by what they saw as greater unilateralism in the US approach to terrorism. George W. Bush's first State of the

Union address that called for action against the axis of evil, Iraq, Iran and North Korea, caused them particular anxiety. This anxiety was reinforced when Bush said: "Some governments will be timid in the face of terror. But make no mistake: even if they do not act, America will act."[32]

On the other hand, the Russian view on the "axis of evil" comments contrasted sharply with the other Europeans. When asked about the Bush's "axis of evil" comment, Putin suggested that this usage was very similar to Putin's "arc of instability" theme which underscored that terrorism was international in character.[33] The Russian defense minister made similar comments.[34] He objected to singling out individual states but applauded the removal of Afghanistan from those countries serving as sanctuaries for terrorism.

Enjoying the Benefits of Free-ridership – The Applicants and New Members Speak

Before 9/11 the prospects for a "big bang" enlargement of seven Central European and Baltic countries seemed small. There was considerable dissatisfaction with the progress of integration of the three new members that had joined in 1999 – Poland, Hungary, and the Czech Republic. For example, two days after he his government came into office in May 2002, the Hungarian defense minister Ferenc Juhász paid what he thought would be a routine courtesy call at NATO headquarters. Instead of offering the pleasantries customary on such an occasion, NATO Secretary-General Lord Robertson read Juhász the riot act: "You don't meet the requirements. You don't do what you are supposed to."[35] "You do not have any time," Juhász remembers Robertson saying. "If you don't [fulfill these requirements], you are in trouble." "It was two days after I took office," Juhász said. "Usually, the new government gets a hundred-day honeymoon."[36] The Hungarians had been simply enjoying the benefits of free-ridership. Once in NATO there was no way to coerce them to spend more on defense, so they spent less.

Moreover, many of the NATO applicant counties had little to offer militarily and were not easily defended. A 1999 congressional study said, "It is unlikely that NATO members would wish to ensure a country's protection through a nuclear guarantee alone." Thus some Pentagon and NATO military planners thought that the Baltic states would not be able to join "until alliance relations with Russia improve dramatically."[37] In essence, few thought that the applicants would be "security providers."

Shortly after the Washington NATO summit in 1999, Bruce Jackson put together a briefing that later became know as the "big bang." *The Financial Times* describes Jackson as a "former military intelligence officer and ex-Wall Street banker [who] is a sort of freelance US envoy to the former Soviet bloc" and who "for much of the past 10 years, ... has acted as a go-between for Washington and the would-be members of NATO in central Europe."[38] He proposed that seven countries form the next wave of NATO enlargement – Lithuania, Latvia, Estonia, Slovakia, Slovenia, Bulgaria, Romania. These seven and two others – Albania and Macedonia adopted the proposals contained in this briefing in Vilnius on 19 May 2000. Croatia later joined this group creating the "Vilnius 10."

Despite the efforts of the Vilnius group, much of the commentary in summer 2001 suggested a smallish enlargement. Until George W. Bush's speech in mid-June 2001, most commentators had assumed that any NATO enlargement would be limited to Slovenia and Slovakia in order not to alienate Russia over the possible membership of the Baltic States.[39] "As we plan to enlarge NATO, no nation should be used as a pawn in the agendas of others. We will not trade away the fate of free European peoples," he vowed. "Russia does not need a buffer zone of insecure states ... NATO as it grows is no enemy of Russia ... America is no enemy of Russia."[40] Indeed it wasn't until a NATO summit in Brussels in June 2001 that the zero option on no new members was taken off the table, according to Robertson.[41] Up to this point, only Slovenia and Slovakia were seen as having any chances of success.

But the events of 9/11 all changed that. Russian president Vladimir Putin was willing to trade acquiescence over Baltic membership for closer relations with NATO and a "freer hand in Chechnya, Ukraine, Moldova and Georgia."[42] In a visit to Romania and Bulgaria in March 2002, US Deputy Secretary of State Richard L. Armitage praised their contribution to the war on terrorism. He noted that Bulgaria had allowed access to its air bases while Romania had sent a contingent of forces to Afghanistan – "Sept. 11 had a riveting effect on NATO and applicant countries," Mr. Armitage said. "A lot stepped up to the plate."[43] These countries realized that by making a small, almost symbolic contribution, they could gain substantial free-rider benefits once they joined NATO.

On 22 January 2003, Germany, France and Belgium blocked a US request for NATO to provide assistance to Turkey. This crisis was only resolved on 16 February 2003 when the NATO secretary-general Lord Robertson avoided France by taking the issue from the North Atlantic Council, which includes France, to NATO's Defense Planning Committee, which does not. Germany, France and Belgium had felt that any move by NATO with reference to Iraq would undercut their objection to a possible war within the UN. Robertson accused the three countries of "vandalizing" the alliance, according to an internal memo.[44]

In April 2003, the US ambassador to NATO, Nicholas Burns commented on the efforts of the three in the following terms:

> During several weeks in January and February, France, Germany and Belgium blocked consensus in the North Atlantic Council for providing assistance to fellow member Turkey, which requested help under Article 4 of the North Atlantic Treaty because it feared an attack by Iraq in the event of a war. Commenting on that bit of theater just last week, the head of the important French think tank – an important French think tank made the following statement: Quote: 'That NATO was unable to meet the challenges of the age came as no great surprise to close observers of the organization. In the Kosovo war, its military structure was shown to be an American – to be too American-dominated to satisfy European needs; and while its political side could be used by the Europeans to constrain US power, that made NATO too multilateral for the Americans. Its future as an effective and viable body has been very much in doubt ever since,' end of quote.[45]

Then the Americans contributed the bulk of the air power, yet its use was subject to constant bickering among NATO members who demanded a say in the choice of targets and, on occasion, vetoes. The Americans could see no correlation between the weight of actual military contributions and the influence demanded in return. To the allies, the equation was different. By signing up to the war they could not avoid the political consequences of military mishaps, and they felt that this gave them the right to suggest how these might be avoided. So in military terms, coalitions can be more hindrance than help. Every extra capital city to be accommodated complicates and slows down the command arrangements. In political terms, by contrast, coalitions have much to commend them.

The Vilnius 10 furthered their cause for enlargement by coming out strongly in support of the United States after some of the European NATO colleagues had already done so with the so-called Letter of Eight. In an open letter of 30 January 2003, eight European countries and members of NATO, (the United Kingdom, Spain, Italy, Denmark, Portugal, Hungary, Poland and the Czech Republic) called for the West to support the United States and stressed that Saddam Hussein only had a limited time to comply.

Bruce Jackson had drafted a letter for the Vilnius 10 to show even more support for the US position on Iraq.[46] The intent of the letter was to nail down US Senate support for the seven countries that had been invited to join NATO from this group. The letter was timed to appear after Secretary of State Colin Powell would make an appearance at the UN citing the evidence of Iraqi non-compliance. Although the letter references that presentation it was written before the presentation was made.

Despite the differences that surfaced over Iraq, many NATO members supported efforts in Afghanistan. Many members believed that taking on the onerous task of leading ISAF in Afghanistan was a small price to pay in turn for the security provided by the US through NATO. Turkey followed the Unite Kingdom in leading this force. When the joint leadership of Germany and the Netherlands ended at the end of July 2003, NATO itself assumed command. By 8 April 2003 no country had volunteered to take over ISAF and its current commander had said that "there's a little bit of a panic" in the international community on this point.[47] Germany had proposed that NATO take over. NATO finally agreed to do so on 16 April 2003. This is the first NATO-led operation completely outside of Europe.

The United States had also made a request for NATO to participate with a stabilization force in Iraq. NATO was not interested but has supported a request by Poland for support in setting up the stabilization force in its assigned area but nothing specific had been worked out by the time of the announcement in early June 2003.[48]

NATO allies and those seeking to join NATO (Vilnius 10) provided substantial support for the US war in Afghanistan. Most NATO countries and those seeking to join NATO also supported the United States in its war in Iraq. Four NATO countries actively opposed the United States when it sought assistance for Turkey during the crisis – France, Germany, Belgium and Luxembourg. Eight NATO countries signed the letter of support in January – the United Kingdom, Spain, Italy, Denmark, Portugal, Hungary, Poland and the Czech Republic. Three NATO countries remained relatively quiet – the Netherlands, Greece and Iceland. Even though the US had pushed for Turkey's protection and supported the Turkish application for the EU, Turkey did not authorize the use of its territory to open a second front against Iraq.

Considering the uniformly negative reaction of their publics to the war in Iraq, the support of the NATO countries and those wishing to join NATO would seem to be truly remarkable. But self-interest motivated this support of the United States so that it would continue to underwrite NATO from which the members gained substantially and the applicants hoped to gain.

The persistent opposition of the four NATO countries to the US position can be explained largely by the unexpected opposition of Germany. France often opposes the US position but when it receives the support of no other major NATO ally it sometimes goes along with and then does not actively oppose the consensus position. Belgium and Luxembourg were supporting France and would not have on their own have opposed the US.

The explanation for the German opposition lies with the fragile nature of the SPD-Green coalition that runs the country. The Greens as well as the left wing of the SPD generally oppose foreign intervention and have strong pacifist leanings. This is even truer of their party members. Chancellor Schröder belongs to the centrist-pragmatic wing of the SPD. He suffered the misfortune of having to conduct an election campaign during the controversy over Iraq. His opponent sent out mixed messages but Schröder was clear – he would not support German participation in Iraq even if the US secured a UN mandate. Many commentators believe that Schröder's stance on Iraq was one of the major factors that won him the election.[49] The situation would have been different had the opposition CDU/CSU won the election. Indeed, right before the election in September 2002, the opposition party leaders both criticized Schröder for "playing with people's fears of war and terror."[50]

According to pollsters, the SPD/Green coalition overtook the CDU/CSU/FDP coalition because of Schröder's opposition to an intervention in Iraq. "Schröder is following a tactically skillful short-term strategy with his course against an attack on Iraq," said Klaus-Peter Schoeppner, managing director of the Emnid polling institute.[51] "In the present situation, about 80 percent of Germans do not want a military strike against Saddam Hussein," Schoeppner added. Since there is "no concrete threat scenario," people opt for peace.

Whatever the politics of the German election campaign, Europeans in general disagreed with US policy. Although Europeans agreed with the war on Afghanistan many took issue with the US rhetoric and the approach to Iraq. Although the West Europeans believed that Iraq was threat and Saddam Hussein should be removed, they did not agree that he should be removed by force. In December 2002, only the UK showed strong support for force with as many for 47 percent as against. Except for the UK most Europeans believed that the US was more interested in controlling Iraqi oil than getting rid of the Saddam Hussein as a threat.[52]

In a series of polls conducted for Gallup-International throughout January 2003, popular support for military action in Iraq within the Vilnius 10 was weak as can be seen in Table 14.2. Only in Romania did a plurality of the people support military action if it should occur.

NATO was key to the support the US received in Afghanistan and Iraq. NATO members and NATO applicants provided important military support both in the campaign against Afghanistan and in the reconstruction period. Most NATO members and all NATO applicants also provide key political support to the US intervention in Iraq. These countries did not consider Afghanistan or Iraq as a direct threat. Neither common values nor the long habits of NATO cooperation explain

Table 14.2　If military action goes ahead against Iraq, do you think <your country> should or should not support this action?

	Should support	Should not support	DK/No
Albania	31	45	24
Bosnia and Herzegovina	12	84	8
Bulgaria	21	62	17
Estonia	30	59	11
Georgia	24	59	17
FYR Macedonia	10	77	14
Romania	45	41	14
Russia	7	79	14

Source: http://www.gallup-international.com/surveys.htm (accessed May 30, 2003).

this support. NATO members and applicants supported the US because they wanted NATO to continue as a viable alliance through which the US provides security for which they need not pay.

Common Values and Identity-based Cooperation – the EU and Internalized Cooperation

Despite the substantial cooperation in combating transnational terrorism, the EU as an organization offered the US no military assistance over Afghanistan and Iraq. To a certain extent no help was forthcoming because EU members who were also members of NATO provided help through the latter organization. But it is also the case that the EU has no common national security identity, especially on the major security issue for EU – the relationship with the United States. The EU, however, did provide substantial assistance in those areas of national security policy that it has "domesticated," that is, made an internal matter of the organization itself. Thus, the EU and its members states have cooperated extensively against terrorism in the area of law enforcement and intelligence matters related to law enforcement.

Identity-based organizations tend to internalize their security cooperation, making domestic what once was interstate relations. The European Union has been doing this with respect to terrorism. The EU is handling terrorism primarily under pillar three – justice and home affairs. Interestingly, terrorism is not considered a sufficiently important EU-wide problem to warrant an entry on the website that contains the index for Justice and Home Affairs in the European Union.[53] Instead, the website lists terrorism as a subhead under "Criminal matters – judicial cooperation."[54] In the past, the EU has treated terrorism as a particular kind of transnational organized crime rather than a national security problem.[55] Prior to 9/11 only six EU countries had legislation specifically against terrorism.

In the week immediately following 9/11, Antonio Vitorino, the commissioner for justice and home affairs, proposed a European arrest warrant and a common definition of terrorism, but only because these projects had been underway for a year.[56] The EU definition of terrorism is quite broad and would seem to include efforts by organized crime to secure protection money.[57] The crisis after 9/11 also provoked the EU to move forward on efforts to deal with money laundering.

Romano Prodi, European Commission president, and Guy Verhofstadt, prime minister of Belgium, which held the rotating European Union presidency in the last six months of 2001 had asked the US how the EU could help. George W. Bush sent a letter in early October 2001 spelling out areas where the US and the EU could cooperate on counter-terrorism apparently annoyed the EU. Many the 47 proposals were seen as little more than a shopping list which ignored the cooperation already taking place and offered little in the way of reciprocity.[58]

The EU agreed to a common definition of terrorism and a European arrest warrant at the Laeken summit in December 2001. At the end of the month the EU listed terrorist groups for the first time and agreed to freeze certain of their assets. There were several differences between the US list announced earlier in the month and the EU's. In particular, the EU did not list Hizbollah which reportedly had appeared in earlier drafts.[59] Interestingly, the decision of the EU to deal with money laundering does not even mention terrorism.[60] Throughout 2002, the EU made several changes to the list denoting terrorist groups and individuals. The original list announced in December 2001 contained only 12 groups; the list prepared a year later included over 20 more groups.

Although there is some difference in the details over how to cooperate in police and intelligence-sharing and judicial matters (especially issues over extradition if the suspect would be subject to the death penalty in the US), the EU and the US take quite different approaches to how to deal with terrorism outside their borders. In particular the EU believes that the so-called "root causes" of terrorism need to be addressed and especially the Palestinian issue. This attitude was clearly reflected in the reaction of the EU to Bush's "axis of evil" speech discussed above.

The EU is unique among identity-based organizations in that it tries to promote and measure the sense of a European identity. The most recent poll (Table 14.3) showed that Luxembourg had the most "European" identity with only 18 percent identifying themselves with the nationality only. On the other hand the United Kingdom was the least European with around 65 percent identify themselves with the nationality only. The failure of the UK to identify with Europe can be seen as well in the willingness of the UK to ally itself more readily with the United States.

The EU also conducts an annual poll of those wishing to join. The public of these countries are often more European than those that already belong to the EU (see Table 14.4).

When the Vilnius 10 came out in support of the United States over Iraq, politicians in Germany and particularly in France were quite surprised. The French president Jacques Chirac said that these countries had lost an opportunity to keep quiet and intimated that Romania and Bulgaria may have difficulties joining the EU. *The Financial Times* of London said that Chirac had used the most undiplomatic language in his eight years as president.[61] "Quite apart from being childish behavior, this is also dangerous," he steamed. Bulgaria and Romania had

Table 14.3 European identity of EU members

	Nationality only	Nationality & European	European & Nationality	European only
Italy	22	65	8	3
Denmark	37	57	4	2
Spain	29	55	5	4
France	31	54	9	3
Luxembourg	18	51	15	14
Netherlands	40	49	7	2
Ireland	41	49	7	2
Portugal	46	47	3	1
Germany	37	47	10	3
Austria	40	46	9	3
Sweden	50	45	3	1
Belgium	38	44	11	6
Greece	52	42	4	2
Finland	56	40	3	1
United Kingdom	65	27	3	3

Source: http://europa.eu.int/comm/public_opinion/archives/eb/eb58/eb58_en.pdf, March 2003, fieldwork October–November 2002.

been "particularly thoughtless" and had done their best to "reduce their chances of entering Europe." Chirac reportedly thought strong words at this point would head off worse behavior later.

For their part, the Central and Eastern European countries reacted strongly to Chirac's words. The Polish Foreign Minister Wlodzimierz Cimoszewicz said that France could say what it wants but that Europe should be a "Europe of equals."[62] Slovakia's Foreign Minister Eduard Kukan was baffled. "I don't understand why Chirac didn't criticise Italy, Spain and Portugal who have the same opinion as us. I don't like that and I think that such grading of us is unjust." Bulgaria's European Integration Minister Meglena Kuneva dismissed Chirac's implied threats: "I am surprised to find a connection being made between positions on Iraq and membership talks with the EU. Entry talks are being held under strictly set rules announced in advance."

However, Chirac, in opposition to what he sees as the pro-American sentiments of this group and the American Secretary of Defense Rumsfeld when he sees this group as "the new Europe" may misread how they act in the future. In soft security areas such as economics, the new Europe may side with France and Germany. For one, the Letter of Eight endorsement of the American position might not have taken place if Spain and Italy had center-left rather than center-right governments. Spain, in particular, has a strongly anti-American public, but few countries in Europe actually believe that American actions were proper. Second as noted above the anti-

Table 14.4 European identity of EU applicants

	Nationality only	Nationality & European	European & Nationality	European only
Slovakia	27	50	10	6
Romamia	32	48	6	3
Cyprus	37	54	4	2
Poland	37	53	5	2
Czech Rep.	38	38	9	3
Latvia	38	40	6	4
Estonia	39	37	8	4
Malta	39	49	6	1
Lithuania	40	33	10	3
Slovenia	41	45	5	4
Bulgaria	41	38	5	1
Hungary	43	50	5	1
Turkey	49	38	3	4

Source: http://europa.eu.int/comm/public_opinion/archives/cceb/2002/cceb_2002_en.pdf
December 2002, fieldwork September–October 2002.

American "alliance" was also, as noted above, a bit of an historical accident. Had the center-right parties been in power the Germans would have found a way to support the Americans. As it was, Germany provided about the same support to the Americans in the second Iraq conflict as it did in the first. Third, it appears that the publics in Western Europe do not care overly much about what their governments do in the foreign policy sector. For example, despite the fact that only 15 percent of the Spanish public supported the war, the Popular Party of Eduard Aznar did much better than expected in local elections held at the end of May 2003. His party carried nine of 13 regions and 35 out of 52 cities, including retaining control of the capital Madrid. In contrast, the center right government in Italy lost badly in local elections but unlike Spain, the Iraq war was not considered a major issue.

The EU did not cooperate much with the US against Afghanistan and Iraq because it had virtually nothing to offer.[63] It did cooperate in the areas of law enforcement and intelligence. The disagreements within the EU and among its applicant countries reflect the failure of the EU to develop a national security identity. To the extent that the EU will develop such an identity in the future, it will do so by "domesticating" the area, such as the move to engage in peacekeeping operations in common. However, the development of a supranational EU defense will prove exceedingly difficult by no one country within the EU has a preponderance of power. EU members, especially those who are also members of NATO, will be extremely reluctant to pay for something they already have and for which they pay very little, the global security that the US provides through NATO.

The Split over Iraq, Eastern Europe and the Future of the Transatlantic Alliance

Central and East Europeans draw a sharp distinction between the actual security provided by the United States through the NATO alliance and the prospects for security provided by the European Union. The key here is contained in the words of the German foreign minister, Joschka Fischer, "The US *is* a world power. The EU, on the other hand, is still a power *in the making*."[64] The question in the minds of many of the political elite in Eastern Europe is whether France or Germany or the EU for that matter can provide the security that they believe they need.

The world looks considerably different in Eastern Europe than it does it the Western part of the continent. Although the Western media focused on the relationship between Germany and France, media and politicians in Eastern Europe were much more concerned that Russia joined the group in the opposition to the war in Iraq. Countries in the region still have bad memories of the Molotov-Ribbentrop Pact. The Latvian president remarked in an interview in March 2003, "Obviously, in the past the Berlin-Moscow axis had terrible consequences for our country. And we just hope that the axis that is now emerging will not be on those lines." Along these lines the Latvian defense minister believed that supporting the US over Iraq would encourage the US to remain engaged in European security: "For America, it is becoming less important to have presence in Europe, because many questions are being raised about this in the US Congress. Meanwhile, for Europe, it is vitally important that America participates in the handling of European security affairs."[65]

The future of transatlantic relations depends on a number of factors that have in the main little to do with the countries of Eastern Europe themselves – developments in Russia, in America and in the governance of EU. However, there is something about the East European countries which will be a major driver – their common values that dictate a continuing interest in "modern" concerns such as economic and physical security. As we can see from Figure One the upper left hand quadrant is occupied mostly by countries from Eastern Europe – they are largely secular and modern. Thus achieving security is a much more important value for them throughout the region whether it is assurances of security from Russia or from Serbia. Moreover, for somewhat different reasons, the countries of Eastern Europe do not trust Germany and France to come to their aid. In Eastern Europe, the memory of the Molotov-Ribbentrop pact and the failure of France to come to the aide of their allies still sears. In Southeast Europe, the bumbling politics of the EU through the UN cannot be forgotten. In both cases, it was the might of the US that eventually assured their security.

Mass Values and Elite Behavior – Ne'er the Twain Shall Meet?

Because the Iraq war did not have particularly high salience among the publics in Central and Eastern Europe, the governments could take an unpopular position without losing much support. According to Petr Drulak, a political scientist at the Prague-based Czech Institute of International Relations,

That's why governments and political elites can ignore the popular sentiment to a large extent, because they can be sure that even if the country supports possible American military action, that there will be no huge mass demonstrations in the street, because even if people are against the war, they don't feel about it that strongly to punish their government for participation in it. So the government, clearly, has to decide between public opinion, which is against war but doesn't feel too strongly about it, and its commitments to Americans and to its Atlantic orientation. And the governments tend to choose the Atlantic orientation.[66]

Publics in Eastern Europe do not much care about the details of foreign policy issues. They want to join the EU because in their view joining the EU will help resolve the bread and butter issues regarding unemployment and the economic situation. When asked to identify the two most important issues facing their country at the moment, the EU candidate countries from Eastern Europe – Bulgaria, Czech Republic, Estonia, Hungary, Latvia, Lithuania, Poland, Romania, Slovakia and Slovenia – answered in November 2003, unemployment – 48 percent, the economic situation – 33 percent and crime – 30 percent. Terrorism was mentioned by only 2 percent and defense and foreign affairs by 1 percent.[67]

The political elites in Eastern Europe realized that their publics were not particularly energized by issues of national security. They realized that after the letter of eight that Western Europe, and the EU, was divided on the Iraq issue. They knew full well that Germany would not join France in blocking their entry into the EU. German diplomats said repeatedly throughout the region that the stance of the Vilnius 10 would not affect their chances for joining the EU.[68] So by supporting the US over Iraq, the governments of Eastern Europe knew that they risked very little from the displeasure of France and their own publics and gained considerable good will with the United States.

Conclusions: Self-interest and Free-riders rather than Common Values

With perhaps one significant exception, common values are a poor predictor of coalition participation in Afghanistan and Iraq. Given a choice between an "EU" position expressed by France and Germany and a "NATO" position expressed by the United States, member states and applicants chose the US position, despite the fact that their publics had values closer to those held by France and Germany than they did to the US. Moreover the common values hypothesis predicted that Ireland would break with the EU and cooperate with the United States over Iraq.

The Kagan corollary does seem at least partially confirmed. Of the six countries that share with the US a willingness to use military force even if not attacked, five joined the Afghanistan coalition and four the one against Iraq. In this and in several other instances, the nature of the ruling parties in government seemed to make a difference. A Conservative government in Germany probably would have supported the US over Iraq. On the other hand, left wing governments in Spain and Italy probably would have opposed the Iraqi intervention. This observation suggests that governments do indeed make a difference and can act against the inclinations of their people. A more detailed discussion of this point will be dealt with in a subsequent paper.

The support that the US received from NATO members and applicants derived from their desire to see NATO continue to exist as an institution from which they received substantial benefits. After 9/11, the US provides global security to its fellow NATO members for free. Most NATO members understand that they need to provide political support to the US in critical moments for NATO to survive. France in contrast would rather support the ESDP in opposition to NATO and set up a multi-polar world. Therefore it opposed the Iraqi intervention.

The French position is rather short-sighted because the EU can never provide the kind security at virtually no cost as that provided by the US through NATO. The end of NATO would mean less security at greater cost for Europeans. Fortunately, most European countries understood this and supported the US tangibly in Afghanistan and politically in Iraq.

Common values, however, can correspond to common interests. The countries of Eastern Europe are "modern" states with publics who are still very much concerned with achieving physical and economic security (unlike their West European counterparts). Moreover they have a clear recent memory of direct threats to their well-being – in the northeast part of Europe from Russia and in the southeast part of Europe from Serbia. They also recall that Germany and France if anything made matters worse for their security not better and thus fully realize the need to continue to engage the United States. Thus, should it come to another Hobson's choice between the US and EU over security for the foreseeable future, they will pick the US.

Notes

1   Lord Robertson (2003), Speech at the Slovenian Parliament, 10 March, online at http://www.nato.int/docu/speech/2003/s030310a.htm. A similar speech was given in Romania, 3 March 2003; Latvia, 28 February 2003; Lithuania, 27 February 2003; Bulgaria, 17 February 2003, Slovakia, 10 March 2003; and Estonia, 24 March 203.
2   Remarks by NATO Secretary General, Lord Robertson and US President George W. Bush after their Bilateral Meeting, 9 April 2002, online at http://www.nato.int/docu/speech/2002/s020409a.htm.
3   Javier Solana (2002), Regional EU Conference for Conflict Prevention, Helsingborg Sweden, 29–30 August, online at http://www.utrikes.regeringen.se/inenglish/projects/partners_ip/news/solana.htm.
4   Bjorn Mansson (2004), "Finland Remains Nonaligned While Waiting for Future Developments in NATO," Hufvudstadsbladet, 27 February, FBIS EUP20040227000309.
5   Stephen M. Walt (1998), "International Relations: One World, Many Theories," *Foreign Policy*, 110 (Spring).
6   Lawrence Freedman (1998), "International Security: Changing Targets," *Foreign Policy*, 110 (Spring).
7   Robert O. Keohane (1998), "International Institutions: Can Interdependence Work?," *Foreign Policy*, 110 (Spring).

8 Helen Milner (1998), "International Political Economy: Beyond Hegemonic Stability," *Foreign Policy*, 110 (Spring).

9 Robert Kagan (2002), "Power and Weakness," *Policy Review*, 113 (June & July).

10 See, http://wvs.isr.umich.edu/index.shtml.

11 See particularly Figure 3.2 in Ronald Inglehart (1997), *Modernization and Postmodernization: Culture, Economic and Political Change in 43 Societies*, Princeton: Princeton University Press, 82.

12 *The Economist* (2003), *Living With a Superpower*, 2 January. For an earlier chart comparing the results of the first two surveys see, http://wvs.isr.umich.edu/fig.shtml.

13 Kagan.

14 The Pew Research Center for People and the Press (2003), *Views of a Changing World 2003*, 3 June, online at http://people-press.org/reports/display.php3?ReportID = 185.

15 For the classic treatment of this issue, see Mancur Olson and Richard Zechhauser (1966), "An Economic Theory of Alliances," *The Review of Economics and Statistics*, 48(3), (August), 266–79.

16 John Mershheimer was often associated with this view.

17 David Gompert and Richard Kugler (1995), "Free-rider Redux," *Foreign Affairs* (January/February), 74(1).

18 Michael W. Doyle (1997), *Ways of War and Peace*, New York: Norton, 224.

19 US, Department of Defense (2003), *Report to Congress: Kosovo/Operation Allied Force After Action Report*, 31 January, online at http://www.defenselink.mil/pubs/kaar02072000.pdf.

20 "After Kosovo: Closing the Capabilities Gap," *The Northrup Grumann Review Online*, Issue 2, November 1999, online at http://www.northgrum.com/news/rev_mag/splash09_12.html.

21 Assembly of the Western European Union (2002), "European Military Capabilities in the Context of the Fight against International Terrorism," Document A/1783, 3 June, online at http://www.assembly-weu.org/en/documents/sessions_ordinaires/rpt/2002/1783.html.

22 See statement of the North Atlantic Council, online at http://www.nato.int/docu/pr/2001/p01–124e.htm.

23 Interviews, NATO headquarters, May 2002.

24 Interviews, NATO headquarters, May 2002.

25 Lord Robertson (2001), "Statement to the Press by NATO Secretary General, Lord Robertson," 4 October, online at http://www.nato.int/docu/speech/2001/s011004b.htm.

26 NATO, NAC (2003), "Final Communiqué Ministerial Meeting of the North Atlantic Council Held in Madrid," 3 June, online at http://www.nato.int/docu/pr/2003/p03–059e.htm.

27 Elaine Sciolino and Steven Lee Myers (2001), "Bush Says 'Time is Running Out'; US Plans to Act Largely Alone," *The New York Times*, 7 October, B5.

28 Philip Stephens (2002), "Europe's Struggle to be Heard: Insensitivity in Washington and Disunity in Brussels Have Damaged Transatlantic Trust. A War With Iraq Would Harm it Further," *Financial Times*, 10 May.

29 Daniel Vernet (2001), "The Supermarket of War," *Le Monde* (Internet Version-WWW) 2 October, as translated in FBIS Document ID: EUP20011002000033.

30 Deputy Secretary Wolfowitz (2001), Press Conference in Brussels, 26 September, online at http://www.dod.mil/news/Sep2001/t09272001_t0926na.html.

31 US, Department of Defense (2001), News Briefing – Secretary Rumsfeld and General Myers, 18 October, online at http://www.dod.mil/news/Oct2001/t10182001_t018sdmy.html.

32   US, White House (2002), "President Delivers State of the Union Address," 29 January, online at http://www.whitehouse.gov/news/releases/2002/01/20020129–11.html.

33   "Russian President V.V. Putin Interview," *Wall Street Journal*, 11 February 2002, FBIS Document ID: CEP20020212000079.

34   "Defense minister critical of President Bush sticking labels on 'rogue' states," *Interfax*, 12 February 2002, as translated in FBIS Document ID: CEP20020212000013.

35   James Geary (2002), "Lacks Discipline, Must Try Harder: Hungary's experience in NATO isn't a pleasant one," *Time Europe*, 25 November, online at http://www.time.com/time/europe/magazine/printout/0,13155,901021125–391502,00.html.

36   Keith B. Richburg (2002), "NATO Tells Hungary to Modernize Its Military," *The Washington Post*, 3 November, A22.

37   Patrick E. Tyler (2001), "Baltic States Seek Bush's Help in Joining NATO as Political Insurance Against Russia," *The New York Times*, 15 June, A6.

38   Gerard Baker, Tony Barber, Judy Dempsey, James Harding, Joshua Levitt and Quentin Peel (2003), "The Rift Turns Nasty: The Plot That Split Old and New Europe Asunder," *The Financial Times*, 28 May.

39   Lawrence Freedman (2001), "The Transformation of NATO: The Prospect for an Expanding Alliance is Not That it Will Tear Itself Apart, But That it Will Become a Quite Different Institution," *Financial Times*, 6 August, 17.

40   Ian Traynor (2001), "Bush Projects NATO to Russian Border: US President Tells Poles He Wants the Alliance to Embrace Former Soviet States Whether Russia Likes That or Not," *The Guardian*, 16 June.

41   "Analysis: NATO Enlargement Prospects," *BBC News online*, 15 June 2001, online at http://news.bbc.co.uk/2/hi/europe/1390456.stm accessed 4 June 2003.

42   Steven Erlanger (2002), "Romania and Bulgaria Edge Nearer to NATO Membership," *The New York Times*, 26 March, A14.

43   Ibid.

44   Peter Fray (2003), "Belgian Aid Could End NATO Crisis," *Sydney Morning Herald*, 17 February, 10.

45   US, Congress (2003), "Panel One Of A Hearing Of The Senate Foreign Relations Committee," *Federal News Service*, 1 April.

46   Baker, Barber, Dempsey, et al, 19.

47   "No Volunteers Yet for Next Afghan Peacekeeping Mission: ISAF Commander," *Agence France Presse*, 8 April 2003.

48   NATO, NAC (2003), "Final Communiqué, Ministerial Meeting of the North Atlantic Council, Held in Madrid on 3 June 2003," online at http://www.nato.int/docu/pr/2003/p03–059e.htm.

49   Matthias Benirschke (2002), "Der Stimmungsumschwung hin zur SPD laesst die Demoskopen staunen," *Deutsche Presse-Agentur*, 15 September.

50   Hans-Juergen Leersch (2002), "Iraqi Conflict Brands Budget Debate," *Die Welt* (Internet Version-WWW), 14 September, as translated in FBIS Document ID: EUP20020913000521.

51   "Iraq Debate – Mood Turns in Schröder's Favor; Anti-American Course Mobilized and Surprisingly Strong. 'Without Me' Mood in East. Stoiber – 'Fraud Maneuver'", *Die Welt* (Internet Version-WWW), 13 September 2002 as translated in FBIS Document ID: EUP20020912000618.

52   Pew Research Center for the People and the Press (2002), "Americans and Europeans Differ Widely on Foreign Policy Issues," 17 April, online at http://people-press.org/reports/print.php3?ReportID = 153; Pew Research Center for the People & the Press (2002), "What the World Thinks in 2002: How Global Publics View: Their Lives, Their

Countries, The World, America," 4 December, online at http://people-press.org/reports/print.php3?ReportID = 165.

53 Online at http://europa.eu.int/comm/justice_home/atoz_en.htm.

54 Online at http://europa.eu.int/comm/justice_home/doc_centre/criminal/terrorism/wai/doc_criminal_terrorism_en.htm.

55 "Communication From The Commission To The Council And The European Parliament Biannual Update Of The Scoreboard To Review Progress On The Creation Of An Area Of "Freedom, Security And Justice" In The European Union (First Half Of 2003)" online at http://europa.eu.int/eur-lex/pri/en/dpi/cnc/doc/2003/com2003_0291en01.doc.

56 Peter Norman (2001), "EU Machine Feels Strain of Terrorism Battle," *Financial Times*, 22 October, 2.

57 Online at http://europa.eu.int/smartapi/cgi/sga_doc?smartapi!celexapi!prod!CELEX numdoc&lg=EN&numdoc=32001E0931&model=guichett.

58 Judy Dempsey (2001), "Doubts Over Second Phase of War on Terror," *Financial Times*, 30 November.

59 Stephen Castle (2001), "Campaign Against Terrorism: European Union Lists Terror Groups," *The Independent*, 29 December.

60 Online at http://europa.eu.int/smartapi/cgi/sga_doc?smartapi!celexapi!prod!CELEX numdoc&lg=EN&numdoc=32001L0097&model=guichett.

61 Robert Graham (2003), "Chirac Vents Ire Over Behavior of EU candidates," *Financial Times*, 19 February.

62 "EU/Iraq: Chirac Blasts Candidate Countries For Pro-US Stance," *European Report*, 19 February.

63 WEU Parliamentary Assembly (2002), "European Military Capabilities in the Context of the Fight Against International Terrorism," DOCUMENT A/1783, 3 June, online at http://www.assembly-weu.org/en/documents/sessions_ordinaires/rpt/2002/1783.html.

64 German Foreign Minister Joschka Fischer at Princeton University on 19 November 2003: "Europe and the Future of the Transatlantic Relations," italics in text FBIS EUP20031120000125.

65 Lithuanian Defence Minister Backs US Stance on Iraq in Dispute with Anti-NATO MP Vilnius Lithuanian TV1 in Lithuanian 1900 GMT, 24 February 03, FBIS CEP20030228000134.

66 Eugen Tomiuc (2003), "Eastern Europe: Do Citizens Of Vilnius 10 Support Action Against Iraq, Or Only Their Governments?," RFE/RL Online, 7 February, online at http://www.rferl.org/nca/features/2003/02/07022003192525.asp.

67 Candidate Countries – Eurobarometer 2003.4, DG Press and Communication, Annexes, page B-46 http://europa.eu.int/comm/public_opinion/archives/cceb/2003/cceb2003. 4_annexes.pdf.

68 "Latvia's Support To Iraq Disarming Will Not Hinder EU Enlargement: German Ambassador," Baltic News Service, 28 March 2003; "Differences Over Iraq Unlikely To Affect EU Accession Treaty – Polish Premier," BBC Monitoring International Reports, 18 March 2003.

Select Bibliography

Books

Almond, Gabriel (1960), *The American People and Foreign Policy*, New York: Praeger.

Art, Robert J., and Kenneth N. Waltz, eds. (2004), *The Use of Force: Military Power and International Politics*, 6th ed., New York: Rowman and Littlefield.

Banchoff, Thomas (1999), *The German Problem Transformed: Institutions, Politics, and Foreign Policy, 1945–1995*, Ann Arbor: The University of Michigan Press.

Barnet, Richard (1972), *The Roots of War*, New York: Atheneum.

Biermann, Rafael, ed. (2002), *Deutsche Konfliktbewältigung auf dem Balkan: Erfahrungen und Lehren aus dem Einsatz*, Baden Baden, Germany: Nomos Verlagsgesellschaft.

Callahan, Patrick (2004), *Logics of American Foreign Policy: Theories of America's World Role*, New York: Longman, 2004.

Campbell, Colin, and Bert A. Rockman (1991), *The Bush Presidency: First Appraisals*. Chatham, NJ: Chatham House.

Constantiniu, Florin (1997), *O istorie sincera a poporului roman*, Bucuresti: University Encyclopedic Publishing House.

Daalder, Ivo H., and Michael E. O'Hanlon (2000), *Winning Ugly: NATO's War to Save Kosovo*, Washington, D.C.: Brookings Institution Press.

Daalder, Ivo H., and James M. Lindsay (2003), *America Unbound: The Bush Revolution in Foreign Policy*, Washington, D.C.: The Brookings Institute.

Davies, Norman (1984), *Heart of Europe. A Short History of Poland*, Oxford: Oxford University Press.

De Graaff, Bob, Duco Hellema and Bert van der Zwan, eds. (2003), *De Nederlandse buitenlandse politiek in de twintigste eeuw*. Zoetermeer, Netherlands: Boom.

Doyle, Michael W. (1997), *Ways of War and Peace*, New York: Norton.

Duffield, John (1998), *World Power Forsaken: Political Culture, International Institutions, and German Security Policy after Unification*, Stanford: Stanford University Press.

Haass, Richard N. (1997), *The Reluctant Sheriff: The United States After the Cold War*, New York: Council on Foreign Relations.

Hastedt, Glenn and Kay Knickrehm, eds. (1994), *Toward the Twenty-First Century: A Reader in World Politics*, New York: Prentice-Hall.

Honig, Jan Willem, and Norbert Both (1997), *Srebrenica: Record of a War Crime*, New York: Penguin Books.

Howorth, Jolyon, and John T. S. Keeler, eds. (2003), *Defending Europe: The EU, NATO, and the Quest for European Autonomy*, New York: Palgrave Macmillan.

Hunt, Michael H. (1987), *Ideology and US Foreign Policy*, New Haven: Yale University Press.

Inglehart, Ronald (1997), *Modernization and Postmodernization: Culture, Economic and Political Change in 43 Societies*, Princeton: Princeton University Press.

Johnson, Chalmers (2004), *The Sorrows of Empire: Militarism, Secrecy and the End of the Republic*, New York: Metropolitan Books.

Kagan, Robert (2003), *Of Paradise and Power: America and Europe in the New World Order*, New York: Alfred A. Knopf.

Kaplan, Lawrence F., and William Kristol (2003), *The War Over Iraq: Saddam's Tyranny and America's Mission*, San Francisco: Encounter Books.

Kaysen, Karl, Steven E. Miller, Martin B. Malin, William D. Nordhaus, John D. Steinbrunner (2002), *War with Iraq – Costs, Consequences, and Alternatives*, Cambridge: American Academy of Arts and Sciences.

Kerry, Richard J. (1990), *The Star-Spangled Mirror: America's Image of Itself and the World*, Savage, Maryland: Rowman & Littlefield.

Kissinger, Henry (2001), *Does America Need a Foreign Policy? Toward a Diplomacy for the 21st Century*, New York: Simon & Schuster.

Kmec, Vladimir (2002), *Security of the Slovak Republic and Integration to NATO and European Union*, Bratislava: Institute of Public Affairs.

Kuhlmann, Jürgen, and Jean Callaghan, eds. (2000), *Military and Society in 21st Century Europe: A Comparative Analysis*, New Brunswick, NJ: Transaction Publishers.

Kuzniar, Roman, and Krzysztof Szczepanik, eds. (2002), *Polityka Zagraniczna RP 1989–2002*, Warszawa: ASKON.

Lansford, Tom (2002), *All for One: Terrorism, NATO and the United States*, Aldershot: Ashgate.

Melescanu, Teodor (2003), *Renasterea diplomatiei romanesti, 1994–1996*, Cluj: Dacia Publishing House.

Meseznikov, Grigorij, and Miroslav Kollar, eds. (2004), *Slovakia 2003: A Global Report on the State of Society*, Bratislava: Institute for Public Affairs.

Moens, Alexander, Leonard Cohen and Allen G. Sens, eds. (2003), *NATO and European Security: Alliance Politics from the End of the Cold War to the Age of Terrorism*, Westport, CT: Praeger.

Paraniac, Cornel (2002), *Parteneriatul Strategic dintre Romania si SUA*, Bucharest: Pro Transilvania Publishing House.

Pauly, Jr., Robert J. (2004), *Islam in Europe: Integration or Marginalization*, Aldershot: Ashgate.

Philippi, Nina (1997), *Bundeswehr-Auslandseinsätze als Außen- und Sicherheitspolitisches Problem des geeinten Deutschland*, Frankfurt am Main: Peter Lang Verlag.

Phillips, Ann L. (2000), *Power and Influence after the Cold War: Germany in East-Central Europe*, New York: Rowman & Littlefield.

Pietsch, Lajos (1998), *Magyarország és a NATO*, Euroatlanti Könyvtár, Budapest.

Pond, Elizabeth (1999), *The Rebirth of Europe*, Washington, D.C.: Brookings Institute.

Sarkesian, Sam C., John Allen Williams and Stephen J. Cimbala (2002), *US National Security: Policymakers, Processes, and Politics*, Boulder: Lynne Rienner.

Serfaty, Simon (1999), *Memories of Europe's Future: Farewell to Yesteryear*, Washington, D.C.: Center for Strategic and International Studies.

Shawcross, William (2004), *Allies: The US, Britain, Europe and the War in Iraq*, New York: Public Affairs.

Sloan, Stanley R. (2003), *Nato, the European Union and the Atlantic Community*, Lanham, MD: Rowman & Littlefield.

Smith, Geoffrey (1990), *Reagan and Thatcher*, London: Bodley Head LTD.

Stastny, Marek, ed. (2002), *Visegrad Countries in an Enlarged Trans-Atlantic Community*, Bratislava: Institute for Public Affairs.

Stein, George J. (1990), *Benelux Security Cooperation: A New European Defense Community*, Boulder, CO: Westview Press.

Stephens, Philip (2004), *Tony Blair, A Biography*, New York: Viking Press.

Volmer, Ludger (1998), *Die Grünen und die Außenpolitik–Ein schwieriges Verhältnis*, Münster: Verlag Westfälisches Dampfboot.

Westerman, Frank, and Bart Rijs (1997), *Srebrenica: Het Zwartste Scenario*, Antwerp: Uitgeverij Atlas.

Woodward, Bob (2002), *Bush at War*, New York: Simon and Schuster.

Journal Articles, Reports and Essays

Albright, Madeleine (2003), "Bridges, Bombs, or Bluster?" *Foreign Affairs* 82 (5), September/October, 2–18.

Croci, Osvaldo (2002), "The Second Berlusconi Government and Italian Foreign Policy," *The International Spectator* 37 (2), April-June.

Forsyth, Douglas J. (1998), "The Peculiarities of Italo-American Relations in Historical Perspective," *Journal of Modern Italian Studies* 3 (1), Spring, online at http://www.brown.edu/Research/Journal_Modern_Italian_Studies/3.1/.

Freedman, Lawrence (1998), "International Security: Changing Targets," *Foreign Policy*, 110 (Spring).

Gompert, David, and Richard Kugler (1995), "Free-rider Redux," *Foreign Affairs* (January/February), 74 (1).

Huntington, Samuel P. (1997), "The Erosion of American National Interests," *Foreign Affairs*, 76 (5), September/October, 28–49.

Huntington, Samuel P. (1999), "The Lonely Superpower," *Foreign Affairs*, 78 (2), March/April, 35–49.

Kagan, Robert (2002), "Power and Weakness," *Policy Review*, 113 (June & July).

Keohane, Robert O. (1998), "International Institutions: Can Interdependence Work?" *Foreign Policy*, 110 (Spring).

Lieber, Robert J. (2000), "No Transatlantic Divorce in the Offing," *Orbis* 44 (4), Fall, 571–85.

Milner, Helen (1998), "International Political Economy: Beyond Hegemonic Stability," *Foreign Policy*, 110 (Spring).

Nuti, Leopoldi (2003), "The Role of the US in Italy's Foreign Policy," *The International Spectator* 38 (1), January-March.

Rotberg, Robert I. (2002), "Failed States in a World of Terror," *Foreign Affairs* July/August, 127–40.

Rubin, James P. (2003), "Stumbling Into War," *Foreign Affairs* 82 (5), September/ October, 46–66.

Skillet, Wayne A. (1993), "Alliance and Coalition Warfare," *Parameters* 23, Summer, 74–85.

Treacher, Adrian (2001), "Europe as a Power Multiplier for French Security Policy: Strategic Consistency, Tactical Adaptation," *European Security* 10 (1), Spring: 22–44.

Tripodi, Paolo (2002), "Operation Alba: A Necessary and Successful Preventive Deployment," *International Peacekeeping* **9** (4), 89–104.

Walt, Stephen M. (1998), "International Relations: One World, Many Theories," *Foreign Policy*, 110 (Spring).

Zborowski, Marcin, and Kerry Longhurst (2003), "America's Protege in the East? The Emergence of Poland as a Regional Leader," *International Affairs*, 79 (5).

Index

Note: Numbers in brackets preceded by *n* are note numbers.